Sources Of
American Spirituality

Orestes A. Brownson

SELECTED WRITINGS

Edited by Patrick W. Carey

PAULIST PRESS
New York ◊ Mahwah

Library of Congress Cataloging-in-Publication Data

Brownson, Orestes Augustus, 1803–1876.
   [Selections. 1990]
   Selected writings/Orestes A. Brownson: edited by Patrick W. Carey.
      p. cm.—(Sources of American spirituality)
   Includes bibliographical references.
   ISBN 0-8091-0433-4
   1. Spiritual life—Catholic authors. 2. Brownson, Orestes Augustus, 1803–1876. I. Carey, Patrick W., 1940– . II. Title. III. Series.
   BX2350.B742   1990
   282′.092—dc20
                                          89-48600
                                          CIP

Published by Paulist Press
997 Macarthur Boulevard
Mahwah, N.J. 07430

Printed and bound in the United States of America

CONTENTS

V. UNITARIAN MINISTRY: 1832–36

VI. SOCIAL REFORMER: 1836–41

VII. LIFE BY COMMUNION: 1842–44

VIII. A CATHOLIC: 1845–76

In Memory of My Father
George L. Carey (1908–88)
Sirach 3:1–16

GENERAL INTRODUCTION

Though he has become better known in recent years, Orestes Brownson (1803–76) certainly is not exactly a household name, even in the Catholic family. Yet if one were to measure his influence on his own time, his reputation and the effect that his ideas had on his contemporaries, one would find that he had a far greater impact than those like a Henry David Thoreau or Emily Dickinson, who in our century have enjoyed far greater popularity than did Brownson. Certainly one reason for Brownson's relative obscurity is the genre he most frequently employed. The vast majority of his voluminous writings were done as journalistic pieces, mostly for his own magazines, *The Boston Quarterly Review* and the later *Brownson Quarterly Review*. Those volumes today may be found only in badly deteriorated editions in our nation's research libraries. The collected edition of his works, done early in this century by his son Henry F. Brownson, is likewise unearthed only with considerable digging among dusty shelves. His books, like *The Convert* or *The American Republic,* though far from insignificant efforts, never received a great deal of attention, even in their own day.

Another reason Brownson's voice has not been widely heard was the belief, now hopefully out of fashion, that nineteenth-century Catholic Americans had nothing significant to say about religious questions—at least nothing that would be of value to anyone but a small group of antiquarians. Certainly there have been and still are many who find the self-educated Brownson no match for the felicitous Newman, the exhaustive Moehler, or the brilliant Rosmini. Yet, I would argue that Brownson deserves a place among those eminent

1

Catholic thinkers of the last century, not for his refinement, but for his passion and originality.

Anyone familiar with the Brownson corpus cannot doubt his passion. For years he was the sole editor of his *Reviews*. Every three months he would turn out 133 closely set pages on topics ranging from developments on the U.S. political scene to French philosophy. He reviewed fiction, secular works on politics and history, and of course works on philosophy and theology. In addition to his book reviews he wrote long feature articles, often running serially for two or more issues, on the pressing questions of the day, often tackling questions that few dared to address, especially in a review. As a Catholic he was a tireless defender of the faith, always quick to break the lance, never willing to accept the status of member of a persecuted minority. Relentlessly he argued for an exalted place for Catholicism in American life.

The contention that Brownson should be remembered for his originality is more difficult to sustain. There are some who would see in his most serious achievements little more than the pale imitation of European voices. His social critique and remedy in his church of the future, they would rightly see as a copy of St. Simonian positions. Even his theory of life by communion, they would contend, was nothing more than an adaptation of Pierre Leroux for the American scene.

One of the important things that Patrick Carey has shown with this volume is that such allegations are less than accurate. Carey has traced how Brownson first formulated his theory of Life by Communion based, to be sure, on Leroux's ideas in *L'Humanité*. That much has been commonly acknowledged in the literature on Brownson. But Carey takes this analysis a step further. By carefully studying Brownson's later writings on the philosophy of Vincenzo Gioberti, Carey suggests that there was an intimate relationship between Brownson's early theory and his mature attempts to discover the ontological basis for religion. That linkage is important, for it shows that the picture of Brownson as a constantly changing entity is false, and that there was a greater continuity to his thought than many realize. Also it points to the originality of his efforts to form an apologetic that would blend his concern for the unique role of the faith community in the process of revelation—which he derived from Leroux—with an effort to ground religion in the universal experience of consciousness à la Gioberti.

That effort, as original as it was, nevertheless was advanced in a form that has shaped its essence. It was a journalistic form. Relatively short, quickly written pieces make up the bulk of the Brownson corpus. They can be criticized for their superficiality, their redundancy, their lack of care—all of which was a reflection of a developing culture, a civilization of frontiersmen and merchants, of farmers and recent emigrants, all of whom were very much on the move with little of the patience of the Old World. Brownson's, then, was an effort that often stopped short of final achievement. Like so many of the steeples of the Catholic churches of the new land it rose from a solid and impressive base just high enough to suggest grandeur, without ever finally achieving it. A suggestion, then, a challenge, perhaps, to imagine the pleasing proportions of the whole.

John Farina

PREFACE

Arthur M. Schlesinger, Jr., noted some time ago that Orestes A. Brownson belongs to all Americans. His published sermons, essays and reviews, spanning much of the nineteenth century (1826–76), reflect significant aspects of the American religious heritage. This volume gathers a number of published and unpublished essays and sermons that reveal the spiritual journey of a man who experienced and reflected upon the religious revolutions of his times. His works deserve attention today not only because they reveal the dynamics of nineteenth-century religious life in the United States, but because some of the issues they raise are still vital for American spiritual life.

I have incurred a variety of debts in preparing this volume. I am grateful to Arie Griffioen and David Schimpf, who prepared a comprehensive bibliography of Brownson's published works from which the selections for this volume were made. I want to thank Patricia Bohach and Susanna Toumanoff of the Interlibrary Loan Department at Marquette University's Memorial Library for locating and obtaining materials for this project. Dr. Wendy Schlereth and her staff at the Archives of the University of Notre Dame were also helpful in preparing materials for this project. I especially want to thank Dr. Schlereth for her time and patience in restoring to its original condition the second volume of Brownson's spiritual notebook. Joseph Lienhard, S.J., of Marquette University's Theology Department, read the introduction and gave me valuable suggestions for improving the text. Throughout the project, Dr. John Farina has offered me encouragement and wise guidance. Marquette University granted me a sabbatical leave to complete the volume.

INTRODUCTION:

ORESTES A. BROWNSON'S SPIRITUALITY

After spending an evening in conversation with Orestes Augustus Brownson (1803–76) and James Walker (1794–1874) in 1836, Bronson Alcott (1799–1888) claimed that "the high works of poetic genius, the marvels of holiness, are beyond their grasp." Others, like Theodore Parker (1810–60), had a similar reaction to Brownson, especially if they had been burned by the "logic chopper's" singeing criticisms. Parker wrote that Brownson was "intellectual always, but spiritual never; . . . not a Christian, but only a verbal index of Christianity—a commonplace book of theology."[1]

Much in Brownson the man and in his writings was distasteful to some of his contemporaries. He could be and was at times overbearing, pugnacious, polemical, defensive and morose. To his friend Isaac Hecker, though, the source of all Brownson's difficulties with his contemporaries was not his contentious nature but his passion for truth and devotion to principle. "This was all his glory and all his trouble; all his quarrels, friendships, aversions, perplexities, triumphs, labors—all to be traced to the love of truth."[2]

Brownson was indeed all of this, but much more too. Like many of the leading lights of the generation of the 1830s, he drank the milk of his Puritan New England culture. For him, as for his contemporaries, religion was foundational for the human experience, and the religious question of man's origin and ultimate destiny was at the heart of every human issue whether ecclesiastical, philosophical, political, cultural or educational. Repeatedly during his life, Brownson asserted that religion was his one love. Beneath the sometimes rough and crusty New England exterior was a man in earnest about the religious life—his own and his culture's.

Brownson lived in a culture that experienced the First Great Awakening, the American Revolution, the Second Great Awakening, the Unitarian and transcendentalist reactions to Calvinism, and the massive immigration of the 1830s and 1840s. These revolutions greatly affected the religious life of the people. It has been said that these events drove the American soul in two quite distinct directions: toward a religion of the head or one of the heart. One was a rational approach to religion, manifested either in dogmatism or rational theism; the other was the emotional or intuitive approach, exhibited either in a broad evangelicalism or transcendentalism. Like many dichotomies, this is an oversimplification. The two approaches were never completely separated from one another. In fact, the boundaries between the rational and emotional approaches were flexible and not always clearly distinguished.

The American religious culture of the antebellum period experienced the attraction of rationalism and revivalism simultaneously. Nonetheless, there was a dialectic in the religious culture that evoked various American styles of spirituality—that is, ways of thinking about and living out religious beliefs, experiences and commitments. In the course of his life, Brownson emphasized one side of the dialectic or another and thereby revealed some of the forms of spirituality that were available to early nineteenth-century Americans.

In the upper Connecticut River Valley of Vermont where Brownson was cradled the "standing order" churches certainly held a prominent position, but they were no longer the sole arbiters of religious culture. Methodists, Baptists, Disciples of Christ, Universalists and Unitarians, among others, competed with each other for the region's religious soul.

Brownson was born into a Vermont household in which his father, who died when he was three, was Presbyterian and his mother a Restorationist Universalist. His parental guardians, who raised him from his sixth to his fourteenth birthdays, were Congregationalists. At the age of thirteen, a Methodist revival in Royalton, Vermont, provided him with a warm conversion experience. Shortly thereafter the pluralism and fluidity of his religious culture was intensified as he moved from his Vermont homeland and joined the westward movement into upstate New York. In Balston Spa, New York, during his late teens and early adulthood he identified himself first with his mother's Universalism, later with the Presbyterians, and then returned to Universalism where he remained until he was twenty-six. His personal religious experiences reflected in many ways the tensions and plasticity of the religious culture.

In his later life he experienced first the rationalist reaction to both dogmatism and revivalism, then the romantic and transcendentalist concern to recover the subject and to discover the religious mystery inherent in the human experience, and finally the realist need to find an objective ground for religious truth and experience. Underlying these various experiences, which reflect the smorgasbord of philosophical and religious options of the time, was Brownson's passion, particularly after 1842, to discover a way to synthesize the variety of these American experiences into a coherent and intelligible whole. He believed he uncovered this synthesis in his doctrine of life by communion, which is the key concept for understanding his thought after 1842 and his conversion to Catholicism in 1844. Even in his Catholic years, though, his restless search for the meaningful Christian life continued as he simultaneously appropriated and criticized a variety of Catholic religious practices. Throughout this religious wandering Brownson sought answers to questions that many others of his generation had raised: Where was true Christianity or the true religious experience to be found? What was the unconditional and absolute ground of spiritual religion? Was it to be identified with the inner experience or with external evidence and rational demonstration? Or was it to be found in one's moral duty to God and service to one's neighbor? Or was it a synthesis of the heart and the head, a harmonizing of external and internal experiences?

In many ways Brownson was a barometer of the religious restlessness in the American soul during the nineteenth century. He was a unique barometer, though. Not many followed his road to Catholicism or perceived the religious crisis the way he did. But, even in this particularity he represents the rugged independence and religious commitment of his Yankee roots. Like Jacob, he was more a wandering Aramean in search of his God than Bunyan's pilgrim, who knew where he was going.

Brownson's was an American spirituality simply because it was carved out of the New England Puritan religious quarry. His own experience of religion, the questions he raised about that experience, and the alternatives that were available to him were historically conditioned by American culture. His life, like that of America, was filled with ferment, turmoil and repeated change. In fact, he experienced so many different religious and intellectual conversions that some of his contemporaries considered him a weathervane. Although he did indeed try to come to terms with the religious winds that blew across the country, he was not always blown in the direction the winds were taking. A critical dialectic, especially after the 1820s, informed the religious and intellectual choices he made.

EARLY RELIGIOUS LIFE: 1803–23

Little is known about Brownson's early religious experiences in Stockbridge and Royalton, Vermont, where he lived until he was fourteen.[3] Reflecting upon these early years in 1834, Brownson noted that he was raised by "an old-fashioned Congregationalist who said his prayers for himself, and left me to stay at home or to go to meeting, and to any meeting I chose. I went to the Methodist and the *Christian* oftener than any others. I liked them the best because they were the wisest."[4]

During his early childhood, as his autobiographical accounts of the 1830s and 1850s reveal, religion was a vital concern. In his fifties he admitted with some sadness that "properly speaking I had no childhood."[5] Undoubtedly he lived in the adult world most of his life, but like most New England children of his day, he was introduced into Christianity through personal and family prayer, community worship, catechisms and his own reading of religious literature. At an early age, he read the Bible, Isaac Watts' (1674–1748) *Divine Songs* and *The Psalms of David, The Franklin Primer, The Shorter Catechism,* Samuel Davies' (1723–61) *Sermons on Important Subjects* and Jonathan Edwards' (1703–58) *A History of the Work of Redemption.*[6] The Bible in particular was religious pabulum for most New Englanders. Brownson had committed much of it to memory, as is evident in his published works, and throughout his life was fond of the King James version of the Bible, a translation he considered superior to anything Catholicism had produced in English.[7]

Brownson's childhood religion, like that of most New England children, was a preparation for conversion. He accurately records in *The Convert,* written when he was fifty, that his childhood religion was oriented toward the "change of heart" experience that would eventually make a person a full member of the Christian community.[8] What he fails to reveal in that confession is that in 1816, at the age of thirteen, he actually had his first conversion experience while attending a Methodist or Christian revival in Royalton.

In July of 1831, when he was twenty-eight, Brownson recalled, in what appears to be a quasi-fictionalized account of his early religious life, his first religious conversion. During the Royalton revival he experienced "what was then termed *concern of mind,*" the first phase of the Methodist conversion cycle. He then entered the second stage, called conviction, that is, a state of anxiety about one's alienated condition. The revivalist told him, he writes, "to give myself up to God. I strove

to do it . . . wishing the assistance of his holy spirit. . . . But all in vain."
He tried to "get religion," was "covered with cold sweat," but nothing
seemed to work. The experience, he noted later, made him anxious,
"lone and friendless." For him it was a "horrid state of mind. It makes
me pale, and feeble, and sick, to recall it. I would roll on the ground,
beat my sides and gnaw my tongue. . . . I would turn and turn, pray
and pray, plead and plead, for mercy, but it seemed their [sic]
was none."

Brownson reached the stage of conversion only after months of
anguish. One night during this state of anxiety he was home alone in
his room, and he felt the spirit come upon him. He experienced an
inner silence and calmness that he had not known before. He lay on
his bed "entranced," while "a soft, an inexpressibly sweet sensation
pervaded my whole frame." The anguish disappeared, and he entered
into a "new world," which was bright and lovely. Suddenly he called
out, "I have tasted heaven today, what more can I contain? Thus was I
born again."[9] Brownson never seems to have forgotten that he owed
his "born again" experience and "the principal part of our early education to the Methodists."[10] But, he did not become a Methodist.

In 1818, two years after his conversion experience, Brownson
moved to Balston Spa, New York, to rejoin his mother and family. At
Balston he joined a Universalist society, enrolled in the Balston Acad-
emy, whose teacher was a Universalist, and was employed at a printing
press that published Universalist literature, which he began to read.[11]

He claimed in 1834 that the Universalist emphasis upon reason
eventually made him a deist and "before I was seventeen an Atheist."
But he found his so-called atheism unsatisfactory. "I wanted to believe, to adore. I wanted rest of mind and repose of soul. I did not find
it in speculation. I doubted my reason, became sick of myself, loathed
myself and in this state of mind was found by a presbyterian clergyman who made a presbyterian of me."[12]

A month or so before his nineteenth birthday he began to have
serious doubts about reason's capacity to guide his religious life. He
experienced a "barrenness of soul." "Cold and lifeless," he was "as the
ocean when the tide is stilled—When the long and fatal calm rests
upon its stagnant bosom."[13] In this state of mind he entered a Presbyterian Church in Malta, New York, one Sunday during a revival meeting and the service "affected me even to tears." After leaving the
service he felt that he had "missed my way."[14] He related this experience to the Reverend Reuben Smith, pastor of the conservative Presbyterian church at Balston, and then gave an account of his conversion

to the elders of the church. The church accepted his account, and he was baptized (on November 10, 1822) and received into full membership.[15]

His spiritual diary for the years 1822 to 1823 records the state of his soul at the time, his acceptance of the Calvinist theological education he was receiving from Pastor Smith, and a gradual return to his earlier Universalism.[16] The diary, like many within the Puritan tradition, was his attempt to discern the evidences of regeneration in his soul and is a more accurate reflection of his mentality at the time than *The Convert*, written thirty years later. *The Convert* indicated that he joined the Presbyterian Church because he decided to "surrender *Reason*" and to be "guided by *Authority*."[17] The diary reveals no such decision. It records his struggle to come to terms with the experiences of evil and salvation in his own life.

Brownson's affiliation with the Presbyterians came to an abrupt end after nine months. In June 1823 he expressed doubts about his Presbyterianism to Pastor Smith and ceased attending the Presbyterian church. His spiritual diary for June of 1823 expresses some disdain for the religious divisions caused by the discordant principles disseminated by Calvinists and Arminians, but it discloses no personal religious trauma or change of heart and gives no particular reason for separation from Presbyterianism—revealing the fluid nature of his religious commitments at the time. Though the experience with Presbyterianism was short-lived, it had a significant impact upon his religious development. The doctrines of God's Providence, human sinfulness, and grace through Christ's mediation, though diminished in importance in his religious reflections during the next eight years of his life, were never totally eradicated from his vision of Christianity, as his later life reveals.

UNIVERSALIST PERIOD: 1823–29

Brownson's published and unpublished writings of the 1820s indicate that the Universalist advocacy of free inquiry attracted him to that denomination. Universalism, "the rural equivalent of Unitarianism," as Anne C. Rose called it,[18] asserted among other things reason's power to interpret the scriptures in the interest of human and social progress. In his twenties, Brownson was already caught up in the idea of individual and social perfectibility. The idea of progress would remain a controlling interest throughout much of his life.

Toward the end of 1823 Brownson went to the Detroit area to

teach, and in 1824 he began to copy into a notebook selections of what he was reading and thinking. Periodically he composed personal reflections on priestcraft, the meaning and interpretation of revelation, the transitoriness of life, the importance of knowledge for virtue, and began gathering biblical passages that he thought supported Universalism. The notebook reveals that he was becoming a rationalist in his approach to religion. Religious divisions caused by opposing interpretations of the Bible troubled his youthful mind, but he asserted: "For me who am but an illiterate youth to attempt to decide a question where Doctors cannot agree may seem the height of folly; but freedom of thought and opinion is our natural right and he who exercises the common [sense] which he finds allotted him will never be censured by any who have sufficient [sense] to comprehend it. For my own part I cannot see anything more wanting to decide this question than nature has given to every rational man."[19] In another place he railed against priestcraft because it prevented the rational mind from interpreting the Bible for itself. "The time is past when we must close our eyes and fold our hands & receive without a murmur whatever clerical machination and priestcraft were pleased to set before us. A light long obscured by the crafty, the ambitious, and the designing is begining [sic] to shine forth with additional lustre and ere long may its beams illumine the whole benighted earth."[20] Reason and free inquiry have been given fair play in "our favoured country," and they must be exercised in religion as in all other areas of human life or the mind would be enslaved.

After more than a year in Michigan, Brownson returned to upstate New York. He taught for a brief period at Elbridge, New York, and then decided to become a Universalist minister. What motivated him to become a minister is not entirely evident from the extant sources, but his spiritual diary periodically reveals his desire to "serve the Lord." On September 22, 1825, he received the "right hand of fellowship" at the Hartland, Vermont, Universalist convention of that year and was installed as an apprentice minister, an *evangelist* in Universalist terminology.[21]

Under Samuel Loveland's (1787–58) ministerial guidance, Brownson studied theology, learned the art of pastoral care and served as an evangelist in Vermont from September 22, 1825, until June 13, 1826, when he was ordained a Universalist minister at Jaffrey, New Hampshire.[22] In August of 1826, shortly after ordination, Brownson published a sermon in *The Christian Repository* (Woodstock, Vermont), the first significant Universalist magazine published outside of Boston.[23] The sermon revealed Brownson's identification of religion with morality and morality with the cultivation of a harmonious relationship among all human desires, thoughts and needs. Religion produced peace in the virtuous soul.

After his brief apprenticeship in Vermont, Brownson returned to teach at Elbridge, New York, where he married Sally Healy on June 19, 1827. From 1828 to 1845 the Brownsons gave birth to seven sons and one daughter, five of whom preceded the parents in death. Shortly after their marriage the Brownsons went to Ithaca and Auburn, New York, where Orestes began to preach in Universalist congregations and to write for and edit some Universalist magazines (*Utica Magazine, Cayuga Patriot* and *Gospel Advocate and Impartial Investigator*). During his years as a young Universalist minister (1825 to 1829), he battled with the "blind devotion" of the revivalists and the "dogmatic bigotry" of the Presbyterians in upstate New York.

In the midst of his battles in upstate New York, Brownson hammered out his view of the Christian life. True religion enabled human beings to reach happiness in this world, not just in the next. Humans were created with a natural desire to be happy, and God would not frustrate this desire that he himself had implanted. Human unhappiness, clearly evident in experiences of misery and suffering, was the result of ignorance, not some inherent depravity. The way to happiness was through knowledge. Intelligence was the only basis of true virtue. The human mind was created with imperfect knowledge, but it was unbounded and open to universal progress. That religion was best, therefore, that elevated the human character and influenced the morals of society by advancing the cause of truth, which was itself progressive.

One's movement toward human happiness was secured by knowing God and by following Jesus' way of life. Human beings came to know, love and trust God and his design for happiness in three ways: through a primitive revelation given to the human race before its dispersion, through rational reflection on nature, and through the testimony of the Bible. Human understanding of God's existence was first of all a matter of belief, not knowledge. Reason could not give human beings a knowledge of God's existence because it was limited to what was sensible. The belief in or intuition of God's existence arose from a primitive revelation or inspiration. This intuitive perception, which is the strongest kind of evidence we possess, is then confirmed by evidence supplied by our natural senses and the Bible.

Primitive revelation shows us clearly not only that God is, but that he is benevolent. This revelation produces a feeling in the heart that grounds our human confidence in his Providence and goodness. The Bible, then, confirms these intuitions and serves us like a spiritual telescope. It heightens our awareness of what is available to us through reason, expands the human sentiments and our intellectual capacities, and enables us to understand and obey the laws of nature, which secure human happiness.

Brownson's eudemonistic view of the Christian life made Jesus' life and work a confirmation of a natural religion as old as Adam. Jesus' mission was to destroy crude notions of religion and provide humans with a religion of reason and common sense. He came as a reformer to relieve human beings from suffering. He made humans righteous not by any supernatural means but simply by teaching the truth, pointing out that true religion was located in exercising love of God, worship, prayer, forgiveness, universal benevolence and the golden rule. In this he revealed the true character of God and the spirit of true religion. The "new birth" of which scripture speaks is the knowledge that we must cease to do evil and learn to do good. Christian piety is essentially morality.

Christian moral life, too, was more than a concern for one's spiritual security after death. It made one responsible for the physical and economic well-being of the human race. The Christian's mission, like that of Christ, was to eradicate all forms of social evil and to work for justice within this world. Such a view of the Christian life made Brownson sympathetic to the social reform works of Francis Wright, who had been much maligned in upstate New York Presbyterian and Universalist journals.

Brownson's views on inspiration and the knowledge of God's existence, and his support of Francis Wright got him in trouble with his fellow Universalists. Some of them charged that his opinions and premises led him toward atheism. He had, in their view, reduced all inspiration to natural inspiration and was unable to supply any rational evidence for human knowledge of God's existence. He had underminded the authority of reason, the only reliable access to knowledge of the divine. His sympathy for and association with the acknowledged atheist Francis Wright, moreover, confirmed the suspicion that Brownson was indeed leaning toward atheism.

In November of 1829, after some months of intense quarreling with fellow Universalists, Brownson left the Universalist ministry. His Universalism had functioned as a road to other forms of rational theism and because of this he, like other Universalists of his generation, has been called a "way-station Universalist."[24]

FREE THINKER: 1829–31

Brownson asserted in *The Convert* and other places that when he left the Universalists he became for a brief period (November 1829 to February 1831) a free thinker whose only religion was the religion of humanity. Such a statement must be treated with much caution because he has also indicated in other places that although he had had difficulties and doubts with some interpretations of the principal points of religious faith, he had never doubted the existence of God or the truth of Christianity.[25] His abandonment of Universalism was not a denial, even momentarily, of the truth of Christianity.

He dissociated himself from the Universalists in 1829, he claimed, because of the vexatious sectarian quarrels that arose over matters of narrow orthodoxy and religious exclusivism. Universalism, like other religious bodies, promoted denominational self-centeredness and did not give reason unbridled reign.[26] It, too, required a creed, even though a more benevolent creed than that of the rigorous Calvinists.

Brownson also claimed that he left the Universalists because his support of Fanny Wright (1795–1852) and other social reformers had created a great deal of opposition among the Universalists. They lacked a commitment to social justice, and social justice was an integral part of the Christian life. In 1838 he told William Lloyd Garrison (1805–79) that his doubts about Christianity arose not from Christianity itself but from the clergy's and the churches' indifference or even opposition to the great aims of social justice. Jesus, he declared, had come "to build up his Kingdom *on the Earth,*" and he taught his followers to "sympathize with the poor, the neglected, the oppressed, the enslaved."[27] Those who supported these great aims, like Fanny Wright, should not be considered infidels, as some Universalists and other dogmatists were wont to do.

When he left the Universalists, Brownson also left his preaching career. He continued to develop his interests in social justice, however. For a year and two months he edited a paper that encouraged political and economic reforms for the workingman's social and economic happiness. It is difficult to determine his state of mind during this period because most of his writings in favor of the workingman have apparently not been preserved.[28] What we do know is that after a brief association with the *Free Enquirer,* Fanny Wright, Robert Dale Owen and other radical socialists, he returned to the Christian ministry, dissatisfied with attempts to reform without the aid of religion.

INDEPENDENT PREACHER: 1831–32

In February of 1831, Brownson returned to preaching in Ithaca, New York, but this time as an independent minister. His first sermon as an independent minister indicates, however, that he was moving in the theological direction of Unitarianism.[29] During the early 1830s his reading of some of William Ellery Channing's works helped eradicate his so-called skepticism and moved him to a joyful belief in the fatherhood of God.[30] The testimony of God's fatherhood was found primarily in an internal intuition that was confirmed by the external witness of nature. "My own faith," he asserted, "rests on this internal revelation from God to the inner man. I have thus a witness within; and, having this witness, I can find its testimony corroborated by the whole of external nature."[31] Reason alone was insufficient to guide the religious soul.

Brownson's 1832 reading of Channing's "Likeness to God" (1828) provided him with a new spirituality. He now perceived the religious life as a gradual process of unfolding the divine within the human person. Like Channing he had come to a new understanding of the coherence or synthesis of the divine and the human in human nature. The presence of the divine attributes, rather than the indwelling of the being of God,[32] provided the foundation for the human likeness to God. This likeness had to be uncovered and cultivated in the soul. The discovery and development of one's human-divine potential involved a gradual process of conversion. The human soul had an unbounded spiritual capacity that demanded constant struggle with internal and external disorders that worked against the soul's growth. The development of the spiritual life, therefore, was not inevitable. The soul had to battle its lower drives in order to release its spiritual potential.

The God within humanity was not the only source of spiritual progress for Channing and Brownson. God, being above nature, could advance the human mind and spirit by miraculously intervening in the natural order. By such an intervention he could give supernatural aid to the human spirit and confirm the divine within the human. This "supernatural rationalism" provided grounds for the acceptance of revealed as well as natural religion. Revealed religion was the fulfillment and completion, therefore, of natural religion. The emphasis, though, was generally upon the unfolding of the divine within.

Reading Channing gave Brownson new life. It provided him with motives higher than inductive reason for accepting his childhood faith. The disposition to return to his early faith, a new disposition to believe and worship, was created, Brownson recalled later in his fictionalized autobiography *Charles Elwood,* by his feeling more than his reason.

> There may be intellectual beings, who are moved by thought alone,—beings who never feel, but live always in mere abstractions. Such persons are dependent never on the state of the affections, and are influenced not at all by the circumstances around them. Of these beings I know not much. I am not one of them. I have believed myself to have a heart as well as a head, and that in me, what the authors of a new science I have just heard of, call the affective nature, is stronger, by several degrees, than the intellectual. The fact is my feelings have generally controlled my belief, not my belief my feelings. This is no uncommon case. As a general rule would you gain the reason you must first win the heart. This is the secret of most conversions. There is no logic like love. And by-the-by, I believe that the heart is not only often stronger than the head but in general a safer guide to truth. At any rate, I have never found it difficult to assign plenty of good reasons for doing what my heart has prompted me to do.[33]

This account reflects Brownson's later, more-developed romantic mind, but it also indicates that his conversions were never purely intellectual affairs. His return to his earlier faith was an attempt to fill a void in his affective nature. For him, Christianity was not a creed to be intellectually affirmed, "but a life" to be lived and felt.[34]

UNITARIAN MINISTRY: 1832–36

Brownson's move toward Unitarianism was complete by July of 1832 when he joined the American Unitarian Association and accepted a Unitarian pastorate at Walpole, New Hampshire. During this pastorate he began a systematic study of philosophy and theology, learned French and German, and read a number of French Romantics on the nature of religion. While at Walpole he also wrote for *The Christian Register, The Unitarian* and the *Christian Examiner,* Unitarian magazines. He had not lost his interest in economic and social reforms, but now his interest reflected the "liberal pietism" of William Ellery Channing.[35] Liberal piety was a combination of reason, religious affection, and moral tastes—an attempt to unite head and heart.

The devotional and intellectual drives were natural to the human person, but they had to be united for a full realization of human potential. One could not leave the religious dimension out of any moral question. It was absolutely indispensable for all efforts to reform society. In fact, "the spirit of reform is the very spirit of the gospel."[36] Real reform meant that the individual had to be gradually improved. Institutional reforms would follow individual reform.

In May of 1834 Brownson accepted another Unitarian pastorate at Canton, Massachusetts, and remained there until May of 1836. During this period he continued publishing articles on the relation of the religious spirit to social justice. His most significant article during this period, though, was on Benjamin Constant (1767–1830).[37] His reading of Constant reinforced his romantic leanings and gradually moved him into an incipient transcendentalism.[38] With Constant's assistance Brownson demonstrated that man was by nature religious and religion was

> a sentiment, an inspiration. It is the poetry of the soul. It enables the soul to call up and solve by a sort of intuition, all the great problems relating to God and to human destiny, and to solve them, not by reasoning, not by reflection, but by faith, sincere, and so firm that it is to the soul like knowledge, only a knowledge of which it can give no account.[39]

The natural religious sentiment itself is eternal and universal, the very spirit of progress, though its forms are indeed transitory.

Brownson found support for the distinction he made between religion and its forms in the philosophy of Victor Cousin (1792–1867), who became a formative influence upon Brownson's thought. He began reading Cousin in 1833 and continued to follow that philosophy until the early 1840s. Although he criticized Cousin's philosophical positions after 1841, Brownson continued throughout his life to revise and develop his understanding of the subject-object dialectic that he first learned from Cousin. In the 1830s he provided Brownson with a philosophical foundation for his understanding of religion and the religious life.

Following Cousin, Brownson located religion, or the "idea of the holy," in reason, and the forms of religion in the understanding.[40] Forms—dogmas, doctrines, symbols, language, the Bible—are expressions of the idea of the holy and as such are variable, changeable sensations that are subject to the understanding. The idea of the holy, revealed intuitively by an objective impersonal reason, could not be expressed fully in any form. The ideal could not be realized adequately in the concrete. Brownson's distinctions here predated similiar ones made in Theodore Parker's "The Transient and the Permanent in Christianity" (1841).

According to Brownson, God spoke directly to reason. Job understood this phenomenon when he wrote: "There is a spirit in man and the inspiration of the Almighty *giveth* him understanding" (Jb 32:8). The Johannine gospel affirmed the same when it announced "the true light which enlighteneth every one that cometh into the world" (Jn 1:9). Humans could confide in the inspirations of God: "We *assent* to the truth of the written word, that is an act of the understanding, one in which the heart has nothing to do." The Bible was a mere form of religion and therefore not a revelation. It was only "a record of the views taken of a revelation made to others."[41] The universal religious sentiment had to be distinguished from the variable forms of religion. "This form [of religion] is constructed by the understanding, and constitutes religion for the understanding, as the idea of the holy constitutes religion for the reason."[42] By relying upon the senses, understanding perceived only the surface of things, only that which changed. Only through reason or intuition could one encounter the universal and permanent and discover the meaning of the forms themselves.

Although Brownson began reading Cousin in 1833, he did not write his first major exposition of Cousin's philosophy until 1836.[43] By that time Brownson was convinced that though religion had its seat in the human heart or sentiments, it needed to be sustained by the understanding. He believed, too, that the rationalist philosophies of the Age of Reason, although they were never able to unseat religion, had seriously damaged its intellectual foundations. Religion had lost its hold upon the intellect because there was no sound philosophy to sustain it. In Cousin's philosophy, which is summarized in the following paragraphs, Brownson thought he found intellectual support for the religious experience.

Cousin tried to harmonize the sensism and empiricism of the Scottish Common Sense Realist school with the idealism of Friedrich Schelling (1775–1854) and Georg W. F. Hegel (1770–1831). Brownson understood Cousin's philosophy as an attempt to provide a scientific or objective foundation for all knowledge and experience, thus transcending the limits of the Kantian and Hegelian methods. By making ideas of the Absolute and supersensible independent of the senses and human activity, moreover, Cousin also hoped to escape the limits of the empirical method, which made those ideas the result of finite causes or human activity, or reduced all understanding to the sensible. Cousin believed he had achieved this synthesis of the idealist and empirical schools by discovering in the fact of consciousness three classes of phenomena that accounted not only for the phenomenal but also for the noumenal world.

Psychology was the point of departure and ontology was the end of Cousin's philosophy, although, he claimed, the one did not of necessity lead to the other. He hoped to begin with observation and to end with reasoning. His method was experimental. Philosophy began by observing the phenomena of the world within, and there followed a classification of the internal operations of the human soul. Cousin saw in consciousness three classes of phenomena: sensibility, activity (or will) and reason. Though distinct operations of the human soul, they were never isolated from one another. Sensibility referred to all internal phenomena derived from sensation; activity to all internal phenomena humans are conscious of producing; and reason to all ideas of the Absolute, the supersensibile, and all the internal facts that are purely intellectual—that humans know they do not produce and that cannot be derived through sensation.

Reason, although never isolated from the other activities, had an independent existence. It was objective and independent of the self. It was impersonal. It was not confined, moreover, to the phenomenal world of appearances, but extended to being. In the fact of consciousness, that is, the *a priori* ideas that are necessarily valid, reason revealed spontaneously the existence of the subject, the object and their causal relation. Consciousness, too, contained primitive data of the finite, the infinite and their causal relation. The idea we have of God, therefore, is prior to sensation and independent of our personal activity. "It must be a primitive, spontaneous belief, the result of the spontaneity of the reason." This voice of spontaneous reason is indeed the "voice of God."[44]

Cousin also distinguished spontaneous reason, which was independent of the soul, from reflective reason, which was personal and in which the soul acted voluntarily. He made this distinction to give spontaneous reason an objective authority and validity outside of the self. Reflective reason was that activity in the individual that acted upon sensations, will and the *a priori* ideas supplied intuitively by spontaneous reason. Because it was personal, it was always subject to the limits of the finite human condition.

Brownson maintained that Cousin had not demonstrated the credibility of spontaneous reason, but this was not necessary because Cousin's discovery here was true to human experience. Reason was that true Johannine light, which enlightened every person who came into the world. Every human soul had this objective witness of the spiritual world.

Although Brownson would eventually criticize Cousin's psychological approach to ontology, he used Cousin's basic philosophical framework until the early 1840s to evaluate many of the American works on religion and philosophy that he read during the period. Throughout the 1830s Brownson tended toward an objectivist-idealist view of Christianity, emphasizing the Christian "spirit" or the "idea of Christianity" in opposition to and repeatedly in separation, not just distinction, from concrete historical forms. For him, religion and religious sentiment had an objective, not a purely subjective, grounding in the primitive *a priori* data of consciousness. Cousin established for Brownson the ontological, not merely psychological, truth of God and the external world—against both the empiricists and the subjective idealists.

SOCIAL REFORMER: 1836–41

From 1836 to 1841 Brownson's twin interests in the social dimensions of Christianity and in the philosophical foundations for religion occupied his attention. His attempts to apply Christianity to the problems of working-class poverty made him known to some liberal Boston Unitarians. In 1836 George Ripley (1802–80), one of Brownson's close Unitarian friends, invited him to Boston to be a Unitarian minister-at-large to the working classes. A few Unitarian ministers, notably Joseph Tuckerman (1778–1840), had been working among Boston's poor for a decade before Brownson's July 1836 arrival. Tuckerman ceased his pioneering urban social work in 1836, and Brownson took over. He moved to Chelsea, Massachusetts, and formed in Boston a "Society for Christian Union and Progress" to meet the spiritual and economic needs of the working-class poor. He hoped that his society would be the new church that would uphold free inquiry and social progress, both of which, Brownson argued, were grounded in a Christianity that perceived Jesus as the true liberator of the poor.[45]

Repeatedly during this period Brownson equated the Christian life itself with social democracy, thereby revealing his enduring concern for social salvation and the social side of Christianity.[46] His emphasis upon social equality took a radical turn in his "Essay on the Laboring Classes" (July 1840), which criticized the generally accepted

Unitarian view that education was the primary means to individual improvement and thus to social reform. Social problems related to poverty, he insisted, were a result of the current system of wages. Reforms, therefore, had to be systemic rather than exclusively educational or moral. Christianity demanded, Brownson argued, that the Christian make a "war on the mischievous social arrangements from which his brethren suffer."[47] The Christian could never be separated from those who were suffering. He or she must advocate intelligent social and structural reforms for eradicating the problems that plague the poor or there would be no effective redemption for them. Brownson's understanding of the need for structural economic reforms predated and was much more radical than that of most of his liberal Unitarian associates.[48]

Brownson's study of the philosophical questions of the day also made him a participant in the transcendentalist discussions of 1836, the *annus mirabilis* in Boston. Ralph Waldo Emerson (1803–82) published his classic *Nature,* and Brownson hailed the work in *The Boston Reformer,* which he edited for the working classes, as "a harbinger of a new literature." He had some difficulties with Emerson's views, however. Although *Nature* was aesthetical rather than philosophical, it manifested the subjective idealism of the German school and had pantheistic tendencies, both of which Brownson opposed. At this point, though, the grounds of his opposition were not clearly articulated. He simply asserted that Emerson's views provided no objective grounds for knowledge or religious experience. Emerson's *Nature* had undercut his own position by making religious experience exclusively personal with no necessary or universal validity. He had failed to consider the subject-object dialectic that was an inherent part of all human consciousness.[49]

In September of the same year some of the leading lights of liberal Unitarianism formed the so-called Transcendentalist Club. Brownson was a member of this original group, although he was never quite at home with some of the transcendentalist perspectives. In November Brownson published a quasi-transcendentalist manifesto, *New Views of Christianity, Society, and the Church,*[50] calling, in eclectic fashion, for a new church of the future. He argued that Catholicism by stressing authority had produced a religious-social system that tended toward exclusive spiritualism, denying the rights of the temporal and the rights of man. Protestantism, on the other hand, by emphasizing the rights of man had created a religious-social system that was virtual materialism, denying the spiritual that grounded the material. The present generation needed a new church that would realize a synthesis, a recurring theme in Brownson's works henceforth, of spirit and matter. A true harmony of the divinity in humanity with the humanity in divinity would ultimately achieve true union and progress for humanity and society. In this, the atonement Jesus intended would be realized.

Brownson considered himself a liberal Unitarian who had critically accepted some transcendentalist perspectives. For him, Christianity was not a doctrine or a species of knowledge; it was a life that appeared historically in a variety of changeable forms.[51] He preached this message before his society from 1836 to 1838. In 1838 he ceased working as a Unitarian minister when he accepted a stewardship position at the United States Marine Hospital in Chelsea, Massachusetts, and began his journal, the *Boston Quarterly Review,* as a new forum for the liberal phalanx among the Unitarians.

Through the new journal Brownson began to articulate a view of the Christian life that was critical of both the empiricist and idealist approaches and was consistent with Cousin's philosophical system. Increasingly he separated his own position from that of those supernatural rationalists who argued for historical evidence in the "miracles question." Some, like Andrews Norton, maintained that Christianity's supernatural foundation could be established and verified by the historical evidence of the miracles. Miracles alone, Brownson countered, do not demonstrate the authority of Christianity.

Miracles provided Christian evidence only on the condition that persons know enough of God beforehand to be able to recognize him when he appeared in them. Human beings had within them, Brownson argued, a supernatural light that gave them the capacity to receive and interpret external revelations and the presence of God in the miraculous. The light itself was the *a priori* condition for the possibility of perceiving something to be a miraculous intervention of God.

Those who rejected all but historical evidence in the confirmation of Christianity should read, Brownson asserted, Jonathan Edwards' *Divine and Supernatural Light,* which described that light accurately as a "sense of the divine excellency of things revealed in the word of God, and a *conviction* of the truth and reality of them thence arising."[52] The argument from historical evidence was a relatively "recent innovation" that obfuscated the true mystery of supernatural Christianity.

Brownson had troubles with the transcendentalists as well as with the supernatural rationalists during this period. He acknowledged, though, that he had rightly been called a transcendentalist. "Transcendentalists recognize a world lying beyond or above the world of the senses, and in man the power of seeing or knowing this transcendental world immediately, by direct cognition, or intuituion."[53] The term *transcendentalism,* vague though it was, was generally associated with the "movement party" and its common opposition to the old-school-Lockean approach to knowledge and religion. Brownson was a transcendentalist because he emphasized the presence of the divine light within and because he accepted an intuitive approach to knowledge.[54]

But Brownson's transcendentalism was distinctive. His philosophical method and his understanding of intuitive knowledge separated him from those who were usually designated transcendentalists in the United States. Like Cousin, he employed the experimental, not the speculative method as the starting point of philosophy. As used in the United States, he argued, transcendentalism appeared to mean that in philosophizing one "disregards experience and builds on principles obtained not by experience, but by reasoning *a priori.*" Even Kant could not be called a transcendentalist under such a definition because for him all knowledge begins with experience and the *a priori* conditions of experience.[55] Both experience and its conditions had to be considered simultaneously.

Brownson was not an exclusive intuitionist. His transcendentalism allowed for a sensible as well as an intuitive approach to knowledge. He disagreed with those transcendentalists who argued that the ideal world was presented only by intuition, instinct or inspiration. Their position tended toward an "exclusive mysticism" or idealism.[56] Those who opposed Transcendentalism saw it as an attempt to place feeling above reason, "dreaming above reflection, and instinctive intimation above scientific exposition." Brownson was not a transcendentalist in this sense. He could never accept "the substitution of a lawless fancy for an enlightened understanding."[57] The divine light within, as a true transcendentalist like Edwards had argued, affected the whole person, in his understanding as well as in his reason.

For Brownson intuition, the source of human knowledge of the spiritual world, had to correspond to something real in the external world. The religious experience needed an objective referent to ground its validity. His developing philosophical realism is clearly reflected in his reviews of Emerson's "Divinity School Address"[58] and Theodore Parker's "The Transient and the Permanent in Christianity."[59]

Brownson criticized Emerson because he had identified subject and object in his view that the soul's perfection consisted in obedience to its own laws or instincts. Such a position was for Brownson psychologically false. The moral sentiment demanded an obedience to a law independent of the self. Emerson, moreover, had laid no philosophical grounds for the obligation to obey one's instinct. Feelings themselves cannot be a solid ground for obligation. Brownson did not deny the fact of instincts or a primitive intuition, but he asked Emerson to legitimate them. What objective grounds make them universally binding? Here Brownson is calling for some valid correspondence between the noumenal and the phenomenal, between the ideal and the empirical world.

Although he did not explicitly attack Parker, he laid down his law of correspondence, which was implicitly critical of Parker's subjectivism. The Bible as well as the human soul, Brownson maintained, was inspired.

> By the interior inspiration, we detect that of the written word, and by that of the written word, we in part, determine and limit the interior inspiration. In the correspondence of the two, in their united testimony, which is the testimony of two independent witnesses, we have our highest degree of certainty.[60]

Both Emerson and Parker were, in their philosophical tendencies, not in their explicit professions, asocial, ahistorical and pantheistic. Although Brownson perceived the philosophical weaknesses in these transcendentalist works, he had not yet developed a perspective that could respond to them systematically.

Since his early days as a Universalist, Brownson had supported free inquiry and an unhampered search for religious meaning. He continued to do so, but he was becoming increasingly uncomfortable with the direction some of the free inquiry was taking. To a certain extent Emerson's and Parker's works mirrored some tendencies in his own thought, and he saw in their works not only wrong-headed philosophical presuppositions, but also radical departures from historical Christianity. In January of 1840, at the age of thirty-seven, he acknowledged:

> As we grow older, as we inquire more earnestly, and with a broader experience, into religious matters, we have a natural tendency to return to the simple faith of our childhood, and we become less and less inclined to depart from commonly received opinions.[61]

Brownson's inclination to return to his childhood faith was not nostalgia but a developing traditionalist conviction that asserted that faith is passed on through a community.[62]

Even in his Universalist period Brownson rarely spoke of the solitary individual. For him the individual was always a part of humanity. Consequently the testimony of universal assent generally held precedence in his mind over individual experience. As early as 1829 he argued that the common assent of humanity to certain universal ideas had origins in a common tradition. The universal assent to the idea of God, for example, was the result of a primitive revelation that was passed on from generation to generation. "We consider revelation a communication from God to man, and made in the early ages of the world. Being made before the dispersion of mankind, it was easily carried with them as they wandered from each other, and thus became spread over the earth."[63] This primitive revelation, transmitted by teaching and example, was appropriated in a variety of ways—some true and others false. Divine providence, however, intervened through the New Testament and other special interventions in history to help humanity distinguish between the true and false applications of this revelation.[64]

As he grew older Brownson placed even more emphasis upon the precedence of the community over the individual than he had in his Universalist days. He periodically asserted that the commonly received opinions, especially those that had been universally proclaimed by the church, could be safely accepted if one discovered their confirmation in the supernatural light. That light, the spontaneous activity of reason, was known by its "character of uniformity, fixedness, and universality, making it the same at all times, in all places, and with all individuals."[65] An interior supernatural light that corresponded to the received opinions of tradition provided humanity with the greatest degree of certainty. By the late 1830s Brownson was becoming more and more disposed to accept tradition as well as intuition as criteria of truth and sources of religious life.

LIFE BY COMMUNION: 1842–44

In 1842, another major turning point in his life, Brownson discovered the French Saint Simonian Pierre Leroux's (1797–1871) doctrine of life by communion. It changed his intellectual life and gave him a philosophical foundation not only for a systematic assault upon Cousin's and the transcendentalists' subjectivism and pantheistic tendencies but also for a new theological understanding of some traditional Christian doctrines.

Brownson read Leroux's *Réfutation de l'Eclecticisme* in 1841 and his *De l'Humanité* in 1842. During 1842 he also wrote six significant articles delineating Leroux's philosophy and demonstrating its implications for theology.[66] The doctrine of life by communion was central to Leroux's and Brownson's philosophical systems. It was their attempt to overcome the subject-object dualism of empiricism and the subject-object monism of subjective idealism.

Communion was *the* ontological principle that combined an immediate relationship with God through intuition and a mediated relation through history and tradition. The human was fundamentally open to God through intuition and yet was in need of external revelation to bring that immediacy to full awareness and realization. In the late 1850s and thereafter Brownson would ground his understanding of this mediated immediacy in the divine creative act.

Communion was the ultimate ground of truth and the bond of human love and unity. It provided an ontological basis for Brownson's theory of knowledge by making thought the joint product or synthesis of the activities of a subject and an independent object. All life, moreover, not just thought, was the result of communion. God, humanity and nature were organically interrelated in every concrete manifestation of being. The idea of communion gave Brownson an organic view of all reality, uniting and simultaneously distinguishing the created universe and God. It explained the origin of the human race, made community and human solidarity ontologically prior to the individual, provided for historical continuity and tradition, was the source of all human progress and growth, and even established grounds for revelation from the divine. Leroux's philosophical system, which is outlined in the following paragraphs, gave Brownson a new insight, which he developed and transformed throughout the rest of his life. The doctrine of communion became consciously or unconsciously the central governing idea in his view of Christian life.

Leroux followed Cousin in perceiving in the fact, not the act, of thought three classes of phenomena: subject, object and their relation. Unlike Cousin, however, he made the object independent of the subject's activity. Cousin's distinction between the spontaneous and reflective reason was invalid for establishing the objectivity of the object because both the object and the subject were located in the soul, the starting place of Cousin's philosophy. Ultimately Cousin made the object passive in the production of thought and consciousness. The subject alone was responsible for the creation of thought and for supplying the causal relation between the subject and the object. The error of a psychologist like Cousin was in thinking that all thought was in the act of the soul or subject alone—that is, that thought is a purely psychological fact.

Leroux discovered in the fact of consciousness an independent subject and an independent object in an indissoluble unity or communion. The reality of the subject, the object and their relation was simultaneously affirmed in the fact of thought. The subject cannot think without the concurrence of the object, and the object cannot be thought without the concurrence of the subject, or thinker. The subject affirms itself as subject, independent of the object, and the object affirms itself as object, independent of the subject. Both subject and object are independently active, therefore, in the production of thought.

The relation between the subject and the object is the notion, or what the subject notes, in the act of thinking, of both the subject and the object. The relation between the two, therefore, is supplied by the subject acting in conjunction with the object. This relation, the subject taking note of itself and its object, is called the fact of consciousness. Both the self and the non-self are in the fact of consciousness and therefore all reality (nature, man, God) lies under every notion or thought as its *a priori* condition.

This fundamental synthesis evident in thought was also evident in all life. Life, for Leroux, was not being, but the manifestation of being in the concrete world. To live is to manifest. All that an individual knows, loves, feels and does is life. It is a synthesis of the activities that have produced it. Life, therefore, is an ontological communion or simultaneous interaction of subject and object. It is simultaneously objective and subjective because it is the synthesis of the activity of the object upon the subject and of the subject upon the object. The law of life "resides jointly and inseparably in the subject and the object, and therefore that in life the subject and the object are not only placed in juxtaposition, mutually acting and reacting one upon the other, but are in fact unified, if we may so speak, *soldered* together."[67]

Humans cannot live without communion with an object outside themselves. This is the natural law of life, which provides the ontological basis or *a priori* condition for all experience and knowledge. The objects upon which an individual is dependent and with which he or she communes are nature, other humans and God. The individual communes with nature through property, with other humans through family and the state, and with God through humanity. His or her life, therefore, is organic, lived in solidarity with the entire human race in space and time, with nature and with God—in a word, with all reality. Community, therefore, was not an association or collectivity of individuals; it was an organic communion in the same life.

An individual is dependent upon all three not only for existence but also for growth and progress. Growth in humans as in nature takes place by accretion and assimilation of an object outside, not by some kind of inner power of development. The plant has life and grows only by assimilating life from the soil, sun and water. That which is not the plant's life becomes its life by assimilation. So too with human beings. They are not progressive by themselves. They grow only by assimilating what is outside themselves. The object of their life becomes a part of their life. Real progress and growth, therefore, can take place in human beings only when they assimilate from their objects what is higher and more advanced than they are. What is true of the individual's progress is equally true for the history of the human race.

How is the higher life communicated to the individual and the race? Leroux maintained that progress and true growth took place by the aid of "providential men" who had been endowed by their creator with special gifts that were higher than those possessed by the human race at a particular period in history. These persons (for example, Plato, Aristotle, Moses, Jesus, Confucius) exercised a strong influence upon other individuals who came into communion with them. Their higher endowments were infused into the life of other humans by communion and eventually became a part of the life of the entire human race. Thus, by communion with these providential men, individuals and the entire human race, which was soldered together in one common life, was raised to a higher plain of existence.

Leroux's philosophy of life by communion was not entirely acceptable to Brownson even in 1842. He believed, for example, that Leroux's understanding of religion was pantheistic. That individuals communed with God through humanity did not differ at all from their communion with other humans through family and state. Leroux's view ultimately led to pantheism because he did not provide for a real distinction between God and humanity. It was the old doctrine of the divinity of humanity in a new form.

Leroux was correct to maintain that the past history and progress of the human race could not be explained by having recourse only to a theory of natural development or even to a supernatural inspiration that was common to all humans. These theories could explain what was fixed, permanent and uniform in history, but they could not explain what was exceptional, variable, individual and diverse. These facts of history could only be explained by having recourse to a special intervention of God in history. There was a special providence as well as a general one that accounted for all the facts of history, the exceptional as well as the common. Leroux, however, was incorrect in identifying the divine with humanity, thereby making God's special intervention in history nothing more than a natural law of humanity.

Although Brownson saw the limits of Leroux's attempts to explain life, human solidarity and progress on purely natural grounds, he believed that Leroux's views provided insights that could effect "a complete revolution, not in religious belief, but in theological science."[68] He was awakened to the theological implications of Leroux's doctrine one Sunday in 1842 when he was trying to show his congregation the social implications of Leroux's philosophy. Suddenly he perceived "the theological application, of the principle in question [life by communion], and the flood of light it throws on long-controverted dogmas."[69]

He began almost immediately to construct an original theological application of Leroux's views. By extrapolating Leroux's philosophy theologically, he tried to make intelligible traditional Christian doctrines (such as human depravity, supernatural revelation, soteriology, Christology, the mediatorship of Christ, apostolic succession, communion of saints, purgatory) in a way that would not violate reason or nature.

Many contemporaries, Brownson argued, declared the traditional Christian doctrines null and void because they could not see their inherent intelligibility and interdependence. Brownson hoped to resurrect the old doctrines and explain their lucidity with the assistance of life by communion. His first attempt to do so was *The Mediatorial Life of Jesus* (1842), an open letter to William Ellery Channing.

This small pamphlet demonstrated the inadequacy of explaining human progress by having recourse only to the natural laws of human development. Brownson had formerly resorted to Channing's doctrine of the divinity of humanity to explain human development. Channing, of course, had allowed for supernatural intervention in nature, but this intervention was perceived as an interruption of the laws of nature. According to Brownson, Channing's supernatural rationalism was an inadequate explanation of divine intervention because he tended to limit it and almost to exclude divine intervention in Jesus. Rationalists like Channing had the tendency to conceive of the world as fixed, ruled by necessary laws. Their view actually made God subject to his own laws, limited his historical intervention and, in fact, made nature itself irresistible. In this world neither God nor humans were free.

Brownson maintained that the law of life made it possible, although Leroux did not himself see the implications, to escape from this dreary closed world of inexorable destiny. The law of life could not demonstrate that God actually did intervene supernaturally in history, but it could make reasonable the Christian tradition that asserted the fact of his full and free intervention in Christ and his elevation of humanity to union with himself. That law also made it possible to conceive of God as sovereign, free and responsive to human petitions and prayers.

The *Mediatorial Life* tried to elucidate the Christian doctrine of Christ's mediatorship. The scriptures represented Christ as the one sent by God to reconcile humanity to God. This Christian doctrine of redemption and atonement in Christ assumed that human nature was corrupted and unable to progress or grow by itself. Many, including Brownson, had challenged the traditional theology of the depravity of human nature. Brownson now tried to demonstrate by the doctrine of communion how the traditional Christian view could be sustained.

The first man, Adam, did not fall from a morally perfect state. He was born in an imperfect condition. He did sin, however, and that sin affected the entire human race. But how? Through the law of life Adam's corrupted life became the objective portion of his children's life. By communion with Adam, the children's life (a synthesis of their entire interaction with Adam) became corrupted, and this corrupted life, again by the law of life, was transmitted by moral generation (not by natural generation or imputation, as some Christians had believed) to every succeeding generation.

Individuals, being dependent and corrupt, could not progress beyond their state by communion with nature or other humans because by the law of solidarity both were equally corrupted. Only God could elevate humanity to a higher life. But human beings could not commune directly with God because they needed some visible, tangible object as a medium of that communion. To elevate human life a mediator was needed who partook of both divine and human life. Jesus, as Christians have always held, was that effective mediator or redeemer because he possessed both human life to enable him to commune with other men and divine life to enable him to elevate human life. The union of the divine and the human in Jesus became the objective source of the new life that he was able to impart to his disciples. By the law of life, Jesus was the objective dimension of his disciples' life. And by communion with him, the disciples' subjective life was raised to union with God; that is, by communion, Jesus' supernatural life became their life. Those, in turn, who came into contact with the disciples also communed with Jesus' divine life and had their own life transformed. This life, then, was communicated from generation to generation by the same law of communion, so that today Christians possess the identical life, although not the same being, that Jesus had.

Brownson's acceptance and transformation of Leroux's doctrine clearly separated him from Cousin's eclecticism, Channing's Unitarianism and Bostonian transcendentalism. One could no longer, Brownson argued, discover truth and the foundations of human progress simply by looking within the individual soul. Truth and progress were the result of assimilating what was exterior to the individual and superior to the individual's life. Individual and communal growth was never achieved by spontaneous effort or natural development; it came from the tradition of the race, from a more advanced nation, a providential person and divine intervention.

Brownson's theological discovery transformed his religious and intellectual life and caused him to resume his Unitarian ministry in April of 1842. In 1857 he recalled that his discovery was a religious experience. The revelation "filled me with an inexpressible joy"[70] and made him aware that neither nature nor history was frozen by some law of inevitability. God was free to intervene. Toward the end of his life (1871) he reiterated the sense of religious exaltation he felt when he reached this intellectual insight.

> I shall never forget the singular emotion, I may say rapture, I felt one day, while wandering in the mazes of error, when suddenly burst upon my mind, for the first time, this great truth that God is free, and that what most needs asserting of all liberties is the liberty of God. It struck me as a flash of light in the midst of my darkness, opened to me a new world, and changed almost instantaneously not only the tone and temper of my mind, but the direction of my whole order of thought. Though years elapsed before I found myself knocking at the door of the church for admission, my conversion began from that moment. I had seized the principle which authorizes faith in the supernatural. God is free, I said, then I can love him, trust him, hope in him, and commune with him, and he can hear me, love me, and raise me to communion with himself, and blessed be his name.[71]

Throughout 1842 and during 1843 Brownson continued to develop his doctrine of life by communion. After publication of the *Mediatorial Life,* William E. Channing told Brownson, "some passages of your letter would lead an incautious reader to think you a thorough-going Universalist and as asserting the actual appropriation of the life of Christ to the whole human race, past and present, will they or nill they."[72] As was his normal pattern in response to criticism, Brownson immediately rejected Channing's observation, but in 1843 he implicitly responded to it by placing more emphasis than he had in the *Mediatorial Life* on the application of salvation to individual life.

In a series of ten articles on "The Mission of Jesus and the Church" for the *Christian World,*[73] Brownson developed his doctrine of communion in response to Channing's criticism. He now stated that communion with Jesus was virtually but not actually universal. Belonging to a redeemed humanity was not sufficient to obtain personally the blessings of salvation. The individual could be brought into communion with Jesus only through the personal activity of repentance. But what induced the sinner to repent as a condition for entering the communion of salvation? Because of sin, humans were unable to live the higher life. What Jesus freely imparted to the sinner was the power or ability to repent and to live the life God demanded. How did Jesus impart this ability or power? What was the medium of this power that would lead the individual sinner to repentance? Brownson answered that that medium was the church, the visible living body of Christ. Outside of the church there was no salvation because outside of the church there was no Christ. The church, therefore, was the condition and the means for inducing the sinner to repent and for incorporating him into communion with Jesus. Even the Puritans, Brownson asserted, believed in the necessity of the church for the salvation of the sinner. The church was the ontological condition for the possibility of subjective repentance and personal appropriation of the supernatural life.

Within the church, Brownson continued, were seven sacraments, which were the church's visible means for communicating grace and incorporating the sinner into the supernatural communion. The church and the sacraments served as the active objective means for transforming the sinner's subjective life and incorporating him or her into the new life of Christ. Brownson's understanding of communion gave him a sacramental understanding of the Christian life. That life was always the result of a synthesis of individual repentance in response of Christ's grace mediated through a visible ecclesial community and the sacraments. The Christian community was not only a saved but also a saving community in which the life of Christ was actively present. The dialectic of subject and object inherent in his understanding of communion made his understanding of the Christian life communal and sacramental.

By 1844 Brownson had made a complete transition from what he called the naturalism of his twenties and thirties to the supernaturalism of his forties. In January of 1844 he resumed his editing career, establishing *Brownson's Quarterly Review,* a successor to the *Boston Quarterly Review* which he ceased publishing in 1842. His introductory article outlined the aims of the new journal and delineated his present creed.[74]

Throughout 1844 the church question, an issue that was widely discussed in European and American theological circles at the time,[75] emerged in Brownson's writings as the central preoccupation of his thinking. In January he raised a question he had promised to address in his last article for the *Christian World:* "Which is the true Catholic Apostolic Church?" He answered that "no one" of the current churches represented the true church; it existed now in a fragmentary state.[76] He thought that the more important questions, though, were those relating to the necessity of the church and the means for bringing these fragments together.

His interest in social reform continued, too, but now he asserted that before a practical reform of society could ever be considered, the visible unity and catholicity of the church had to be decided because there could be no true reform without it. The foundational principle of the church's unity was love. But love was impossible without the church's unity because that unity was the ontological precondition for the possibility of love.[77] The church was the community of mediated grace, and grace provided the power to love. The church's unity was the supernatural means for social reform and "social salvation."[78]

Brownson announced in January of 1844 that he could identify with neither the Protestant nor the Catholic churches. He was, in his own estimate, without a home. In May, though, he started taking instructions in the Catholic church, and by July he had moved so clearly in the direction of Catholicism that he finally announced

> that our ecclesiastical, theological, and philosophical studies have brought us to the full conviction, that, either the church in communion with the See of Rome is the one holy catholic apostolic church, or the one holy catholic church does not exist. We have tried every possible way to escape this conclusion, but escape it we cannot. We must accept it, or go back to the no-church doctrine.[79]

He also announced his formal withdrawal from Unitarianism, an announcement that was really unnecessary. His former Unitarian associates had for some time seen his movement toward Rome. In October of 1844 he entered the Catholic church.

A CATHOLIC: 1845–76

Historians have generally divided Brownson's Catholic life into three periods. They argue that from 1845 to 1855 he abandoned his doctrine of life by communion and assumed a militant, aggressive apologetic similar to that of post-Tridentine Catholic Scholasticism.[80] He developed a more conciliatory and optimistic apologetic from 1856 to 1864, and from 1865 to 1876 he returned to a more conservative apologetic, becoming in his last years an unquestioning champion of Catholic orthodoxy as defined by Pope Pius IX's *Quanta Cura* and the *Syllabus Errorum* (1864). Although this division of Brownson's Catholic life has some merits relative to his apologetics and his approach to accommodation, it is not particularly helpful in understanding his approach to the spiritual life. The dialectic that he developed in his understanding of life by communion continued to inform his thought throughout his Catholic period, even though he emphasized at one time the objective and at another the subjective side of the spiritual life.

During his early Catholic period, from 1845 to 1855, Brownson emphasized the objective side of the dialectic in continuity with his emphases throughout the year 1844. He presented the church as the exclusive and objective bearer of salvation, but his doctrine of communion was notably absent from his ecclesiology. That doctrine was replaced with a scholastic apologetic that demonstrated rational grounds for accepting the Catholic church's infallibility. The issue for him now was almost completely that of visible office and authority.

> When we contend for the church as a visible, authoritative, infallible and indefectible Body or corporation, we take the word *church* in a restricted sense, to mean simply the body of pastors and teachers, or, in other words, the bishops in communion with their chief. We mean what Protestants would, perhaps, better understand by the word *ministry* than by the word *church*.[81]

Even prior to his conversion to Catholicism he was moving in this direction, but it was not until some time after his conversion that he began to speak of ecclesiastical authority divorced from his doctrine of Christian life—even though the church continued to be the precondition for the development of that life.

Brownson's April 1845 essay, "The Church Against No-Church," indicates the change his thought had taken early in his Catholic career. The essay was his attempt to explain his response to the question, "How in the world have you become a Catholic?" Brownson recalled here that the issue which drove him into the church was one of salvation: "We were a sinner, and we wished to be reconciled to God."[82] That reconciliation could not come about except through some objective mediation. The Catholic church was the only church whose claims to be the objective mediation between God and humanity proved themselves true to Brownson. This essay demonstrates what Brownson considered to be the reasonableness of the scholastic defense of Catholicism.

Throughout this period, Brownson continued to defend external ecclesiastical authority—emphasizing more and more the indirect temporal powers of the papacy. From the vantage point of his newly acquired scholastic apologetic, he also continued his attacks not only upon the "paragons of Protestantism" (the Unitarians and transcendentalists) but also upon the developmentalism of John Henry Newman (1801–90), John Williamson Nevin (1803–86) and Horace Bushnell (1802–76).[83] Brownson associated the term *development* with a self-induced progress that had no reference to an active objective agent outside the self. He criticized most developmental views because he believed that they failed to distinguish clearly between object and subject and because they repeatedly made the subject alone the agent of progress. Bushnell, according to Brownson's understanding, made the subject alone active in the pursuit of truth and life; the object or forms were passive. This was contrary to Brownson's notion of growth.

Brownson, like Bushnell, perceived Christianity as life in process. But unlike Bushnell, he never divorced this life from objective forms. Bushnell, it is true, maintained that the Christian could obtain divine life and truth in and through the forms of language, nature, ritual, doctrines and persons. But, as Conrad Cherry noted, "his restless spirit drove him to feel that the human spirit can meet God in this life without the mediation of those forms."[84] Brownson never spoke of the Christian life separated from objective forms. The Christian life was both objective and subjective; outward forms were essential bearers of truth, grace and life. Brownson criticized Bushnell's understanding of the relationship between the form and its content as "Socinianism" because Bushnell saw forms as accidents having no essential relationship to the life and truth they express. Their only value was in what they evoked from the subject. This was ultimately pure subjectivism. The forms became mere occasions for self-development and growth.[85]

Brownson's emphases upon ecclesiastical authority, exclusive salvation, the superiority of the spiritual over the temporal, and the distinction between nature and supernature are all reflected in his own spirituality of withdrawal from a world of transitory pleasures. His review of Bishop Richard Challoner's (1691–1781) *The Lives of the Fathers of the Eastern Desert* (1852)[86] reveals his understanding of the pilgrim nature of the religious life and the difficulties of living that life in a world that seemed to appreciate only productive activity, economic success and self-affirmation. The emphasis in his thought immediately after his conversion to Catholicism was clearly upon the objective supernatural means of salvation. What remained undeveloped and relatively absent in his thought during this period was any corresponding stress upon the subjective side of the individual's dialectical life.

In 1855 Isaac Hecker's *Questions of the Soul* awakened Brownson to the fact that he had lost the dialectical nature of his own earlier thought and that he may have overemphasized the objective side of the Christian life to the detriment of its subjective side. That overemphasis, too, was in the end untrue to the positive Catholic experience because it had nothing to say to the heart. What was needed, and what Hecker had accomplished, was the articulation of a view of the Christian life that spoke to "the intellect through the heart." What Hecker had achieved Brownson had not even tried since becoming a Catholic, that is, presenting Catholicism

> in its purely affirmative or positive character, as the adequate object of the heart, which Tertullian says is naturally Christian, frankly recognizing its natural wants and activities, and showing it that Catholicism is that unknown good that it craves, the ideal to which it aspires, the true life it would live, and that superhuman help which it feels that it needs and which it has hitherto sought in vain, and must in vain seek elsewhere than in the Church.[87]

Even before 1855 Brownson had been slowly returning to his former philosophical interests in the subject-object dialectic and in intuition as the source of the knowledge of God. His study of the

Italian ontologist Vincenzo Gioberti (1801–52) in 1849 sparked this return and moved him away from the scholastic rationalism of his early Catholic period. Throughout the early 1850s he wrote a series of philosophical essays that demonstrated this gradual shift in his thinking and that provided intellectual grounds for a reformulation of his doctrine of life by communion.[88]

Brownson returned to an explicit articulation of his doctrine of communion in *The Convert* (1857). He wrote this intellectual autobiography not only to render a public account of his conversion but also to show how his doctrine of communion enabled him to eliminate his objections to Catholicism. The book called for a new apologetic in American Catholicism. He wanted the reader to discover "the connecting link between nature and grace, the natural and the supernatural, and to perceive that, in becoming a Catholic, a man has no occasion to divest himself of his nature, or to forego the exercise of his reason."[89]

In *The Convert* and a few other publications during this period[90] Brownson made two significant changes in his doctrine of communion. He strengthened the ontological basis of his doctrine by using Gioberti's ideal formula, *ens creat existentias,* to show that the relation between subject and object was to be found in the divine creative act; he also demonstrated how the divine creative act established two cycles of human existence that made Christian life doubly dependent: upon the creative act for existence and upon the Incarnation for its return to God.

Gioberti, like Cousin and Leroux, began his philosophical system with the synthetic dialectic of subject, object and their relation. As Leroux separated his system from Cousin's, so Gioberti separated his from Leroux's. Both Cousin and Leroux, Gioberti maintained, tried to avoid subjectivism by establishing objective grounds for knowledge and experience, but they were unable to do so because both made the subject the creator of the relation between the subject and the object. The subject, Gioberti asserted, can no more create the relation than it can create the object or itself. Cousin and Leroux failed to see this because they failed to analyze sufficiently the object of thought. A careful examination of the object would reveal three elements: the ideal (real and necessary being), the empirical (the fact of experience), and their relation (the divine creative act). A further analysis of the ideal revealed that the ideal creates the connection between the ideal and the empirical and between the subject and the object. In this examination Gioberti uncovered what he called the ideal formula; that is, Being creates existences. That formula made the object, not the subject, the creator of the relation.

The ideal formula was for Gioberti and Brownson a synthetic judgment *a priori,* an intuitive fact or a philosophical axiom that was beyond demonstration.[91] The divine creative act was the ontological condition for the possibility of experience and knowledge. The synthetic judgment, the necessary condition for all empirical judgments, became an object of reflection only through language that originated from a divine revelation passed on from generation to generation through tradition. By rational reflection and tradition persons became aware that it was God, not merely real and necessary being, that creates creatures.

All humans have this synthetic judgment, the primitive elements of which (Being, creation, existences) are given together in a real synthesis and are not separated in the ideal intuition. These primitive elements form one indissoluble whole. The creative act is the dialectic principle that at once distinguishes and unites creature and creator. The creative act, the copula of the synthetic judgement, is

> the real *nexus* between contraries, and hence a dialectic union means a real union of contraries made one by means of the middle term. A dialectic whole is a real living whole, an organism, and not a mere aggregation. By the creative act, the real *medius terminus* of the universe, all the parts of the universe are made one dialectic whole, in which all the parts are really connected with the whole and with one another.[92]

For Brownson the ideal intuition was a given ontological fact, not an act of the human mind. Knowledge of the foundational ontological reality, the creative act at the center of consciousness, was immediate and intuitive, available through the illumination of the divine light present in the creative act itself. "Divine reason, indistinguishable from the divine essence or being, at once creates the human reason, and presents itself as its light and its immediately object."[93] This did not mean that all humans had a reflective awareness of God, but it did mean that God was objectively present as creator in the act of knowing.

After 1864, and particularly in the early 1870s, Brownson asserted that the religious problem in the United States and in the Western world was no longer to demonstrate the necessity of the church, important as that was, but the very existence of God—and not merely his existence, but more fundamentally his existence as creator. The question was not so much does God exist as it was does God exist as first and final cause? The issue now was not so much between Protestantism and Catholicism as it was between Christian theism and atheism, Christianity and unbelief.[94] Christian theism perceived God as creator and those within Christianity who tried to demonstrate his existence alone had failed to perceive the real problem. Unbelief, arising from scientific naturalism, could not be overturned by arguing that God existed. Atheism could be overcome only by demonstrating that God was creative.

Gioberti's philosophy provided one way of explaining this fundamental article of the Christian creed. His ideal formula, combined with a quasi-Augustinian illuminationism, also furnished an objective, intuitive and ontological basis for a doctrine of life by communion that Leroux had failed to supply. The medium for communion with God was the divine creative act. In that act Brownson discovered by reflection and revelation[95] that all things are created by God and for him—that God was simultaneously first cause and final cause.

The creative act established two orders of human existence that were part of one dialectical whole: the initial order of creation, and the teleological order of return to God. The first movement is a procession from God as first cause; the second a movement of return to God, without absorption in him, as final cause. Both movements were facts, not necessities, revealed in analysis of the creative act.

Some critics objected that the teleological order, belonging to the Incarnation, cannot be a part of the creative act without destroying the gratuity of grace. Brownson responded that both creation and the Incarnation, although distinguished, could not be separated in dualistic fashion as if they were not a part of God's original plan of creation. Both were free and gratuitous interventions and equally supernatural because they were the result of God's immediate activity.

For Brownson the natural and the supernatural formed together one dialectical whole. "The supernatural is God and his immediate act. The natural is what is done, produced, or effected by second causes, operating according to their own laws."[96] God, *mediante* the creative act, is always present in the natural as the *causa causarum*. The natural is the realm of secondary causality. The secondary causes are themselves true efficient causes of their own acts. God does not act in the human acts, he only sustains and conserves human existence through his continuous creative act.

The Christian lived in the two cycles of existence simultaneously and therefore the Christian life was always a synthesis of the natural and the supernatural. From the beginning the Creator intended that the natural should be perfected, completed or fulfilled in the supernatural. Human life has always been under this gracious supernatural providence and was originally destined to a supernatural end, "attainable only through a supernatural medium."[97] That humans lived under a supernatural providence was at least partially evident in a primitive revelation given to Adam and communicated through tradition to the entire human community. Following some moderate European Catholic traditionalists, Brownson wrote:

> Every man bears about with him, whether he knows it or not, the evidence that God has revealed to the world an order of life above our natural life. The revelation has been made, and man is nowhere, left to the simple lights of natural reason. The sound of the Gospel has gone out into all the earth, and reverberates in all hearts from first to last, as a prophecy or a tradition. The intimation of a God-Man, of the fact of the Incarnation, as a fact that is to take place, or that has taken place, has in some form reached all the sons and daughters of Adam, and man is nowhere what he else would have been.[98]

The Incarnation is the supernatural medium through which the return to God is accomplished. The hypostatic union or Incarnation simultaneously completes the initial cycle of existence by fully realizing the creative act and initiates the teleological cycle by providing the means for entry into that cycle.[99] For Brownson, creation is the extrinsication of the Eternal Word and, given the fact of creation, the "full or complete extrinsecation [sic] requires the full and complete creative act; and the full and complete creative act requires the Incarnation, or hypostatic union of man with God, the finite with the infinite."[100] Given the fact of creation, Brownson argued, the Incarnation was a logical necessity. For him, though, the factual Incarnation was always the result of God's providentially free intervention into history, as was the creative act itself.

The Incarnation of the Word, as the fullest expression of God's creative act and the fullest manifestation of his providential intervention into human history, is the medium for bringing the teleological cycle to completion. For Brownson, the Incarnation

> is teleological, not cosmic, but it is no after-thought designed to meet some unforeseen difficulty, or repair some unexpected damage. It is integral in the original plan of creation, and was as necessary to complete the cosmos, before as after man had sinned. It redeems man from sin, provides the atonement, and thus manifests the infinite mercy of God. It

is, as redemption, an act of free, sovereign grace, for God is not obliged to pardon the sinner, and the sinner, who has knowingly abused his free will can do nothing to merit pardon, but it is always necessary to the fulfilment [sic] of creation, for never could man attain to the end of his existence, or to his complete beatitude, possible only in the supernatural, without being regenerated in Christ, united to him, and made one with him as he is one with God the Father.[101]

The Incarnation, as redemption, was for Brownson always ontologically and logically free. The Incarnation, as medium of the teleological order, however, was a logical, though not an ontological, necessity by the fact of a free creation. Brownson repeatedly agreed with those in the Christian tradition who speculated that God would have become incarnate to provide the supernatural means for humanity's glorification even if Adam had not sinned.

The Christian's life of communion with God through the divine creative act and the Incarnation was at once natural and supernatural. The two divine activities formed one dialectical whole in which the Christian freely participated. Through the creative act humans are brought from nothing and vitally joined to God—in him we live, and move and have our being. "We cannot live, think, hope, love or perform any operation without his act, his concurrence."[102] The supernatural, however, never destroys or violates the natural freedom and activity of the created order; it only enhances, perfects and completes that order, and gives it the means to attain its ultimate end.

The Christian's life by communion with God was dialectical. The Christian was absolutely dependent upon God for the establishment of that communion, and yet he or she remained free within that communion. Communion in the divine life established the dependence and the freedom simultaneously. In the teleological order of return to God as last end, the individual's natural freedom was not destroyed or superceded because he or she could always reject and break that communion. The individual's freedom was preserved in that communion because to destroy it would be to destroy the effects of the divine creative act, an integral part of that communion. In communion the individual's free and humble acceptance and assimilation of the divine life was guaranteed by the divine creative and redemptive activities. The Christian's life was always the result of a free interaction with the creative and incarnate life that came to the individual through the church and sacraments, which initiated, sustained and repaired that life.

Brownson's reformulation of the doctrine of life by communion within the two orders of existence provided the philosophical and theological context for his Catholic writings on the Christian life. Whether he spoke of the affective nature of the Christian life, the piety of Catholic devotional practices, veneration of Mary and the saints, prayer and personal meditation, or retreat from a corrupted and broken world, he did so from the perspective of this doctrine. The subject-object dialectic was not always evident in every article because he usually emphasized only one side of the dialectic at a time. Taken together, however, his Catholic writings on the spiritual life manifest the dialectic at the heart of his doctrine.

By the mid-nineteenth century American as well as European Catholics were in the midst of what has been called a devotional revolution, and Brownson encouraged and at times criticized some of the pious practices that characterized the revival. This growth of piety, which had its origins in European Catholic Romanticism at the end of the eighteenth century, has been characterized as "more sentimental and less rigoristic" than the piety that characterized Jansenism and the moralistic piety of those Catholics who had been influenced by the Enlightenment. The revival enphasized frequent reception of the sacraments and encouraged Catholics to participate in various paraliturgical pious practices: Sacred Heart devotions, Marian devotions, veneration of the saints, and other public displays of faith.[103]

At times during these years of the Catholic revival, and especially after 1855, Brownson stressed the affective nature of the Christian life. Christianity must influence the whole person, heart as well as head. He supported, for example, retreats and parish missions, agents of what Jay Dolan has called "Catholic Revivalism," because they appealed to the senses and helped to awaken the Christian life through "sensible devotions."[104]

If Christians were to assimilate the Christian life, they had to become active not only through "sensible devotions," but also through consistent reading and study of the scriptures, personal prayer and meditation.[105] Though Protestants had overemphasized the private interpretation of the scriptures, at least they read them. Catholics could do well to imitate their Protestant brethren in prayerfully examining the scriptures as a true source of Christian piety—without, of course, accepting their views on interpretation. Brownson also encouraged Catholics to personal prayer and meditation, using the *Spiritual Exercises of St. Ignatius* as one model for structuring this practice.[106] Although he had some personal difficulties with the Ignatian method, and in fact all methods of prayer, he saw the value in some individualized method to sustain and deepen the Christian spirit of humility and constant openness to the divine.[107]

The Christian life, Brownson maintained, could also be nourished by an intelligent participation in the cult of the saints, which had become popular for various reasons, not the least of which were a number of alleged Marian apparitions and the proclamation of the dogma of the Immaculate Conception (1854). Brownson rejected the bathetic and quasi-superstitious character of some practices associated with devotions to the saints because they tended to obfuscate the central Christian mysteries.[108] He also disliked works like Alphonse Liguori's *The Glories of Mary,* translated and republished in the United States in 1853, because they were too sentimental for most American or at least for most Anglo-Saxon American tastes.[109]

Although he had difficulties with some Catholic devotional practices and attitudes, he supported the veneration of Mary and the saints as a means of personal piety and as a reminder of fundamental Christian doctrines.[110] The cult of the saints was also consistent with Brownson's doctrine of communion. It was not only a praise of God in his works of creation and redemption, but also a reminder of the doctrine of the communion of saints, that is, of the organic unity of all who lived Christ's life. Communion with the saints, like communion with providential men, elevated the individual Christian's life of faith, hope and love. The saints' lives, moreover, were objective examples of pious Christian living.

Devotions to the saints helped to focus Catholic attention on a kingdom not of this world—a kingdom where Christ alone was king. They reminded Catholics not only that this world was passing but also that it was in this transitory world that the effects of the Incarnation were daily realized in the faithful lives of those called to be saints. The Christian should be separated from the world of the flesh, but never from the created order where the life of the spirit was incarnated.

As Brownson became increasingly alienated from the world of the late 1860s and 1870s—because of some opposition to his theological positions, the deaths of two sons in the Civil War, and the publication of the *Syllabus of Errors*[111]—a world-denying spirituality returned to the center of his interests.[112] He focused his thought upon the antagonism between the church and the world. The church was "always and everywhere in the midst of powerful, subtle, bitter and sleepless enemies who incessantly assail her, and seek her destruction." The enemies were the traditional ones: the world, the flesh and the devil. Some, liberal Catholics included, Brownson noted, believed that the warfare between the church and the world ought to be discontinued and that the church ought to form an allegiance with the spirit of the age because that spirit was the spirit of Christ. Brownson confessed in 1871 that he had himself held such a view for four or five years previous to 1864. His own experience and the *Syllabus of Errors,* "that great act of our century," convinced him that the church could make no compromise with the world.[113]

Brownson's understanding of *world* in the late 1860s and 1870s corresponded to the Johannine "world" and the Pauline "flesh," that is, whatever was perishable, weak, alienated from life in the spirit, and hostile to God and his plan of salvation. The antagonism between the church and the world and Brownson's spirituality of retreat from the world was not based upon an inherent dichotomy or fundamental opposition between grace and nature. For him,

> all the works of the Creator [creation and redemption] are dialectic, and considered physically, as the works of the Creator, there is no antagonism between earth and heaven. Both are parts of one stupendous and harmonious whole. But it does not follow from this that there is no moral antagonism between a life lived for the world and a life lived for God. The antagonism is moral, not physical, and is removable only by the renunciation of the world, detachment from it, and placing our affections on the unseen and the eternal.[114]

Brownson's article on "Nature and Grace"[115] clearly pointed out that his spirituality was grounded in his understanding of creation and the Incarnation. Creation placed persons in the initial historical order and the Incarnation supplied the means for reaching the teleological order of human existence. Thus, for Brownson, grace and nature were not two things, the one uncreated and the other created, but two divine moments or divine acts that create history and that orient human beings toward their ultimate destiny of union with God.

If one's spirituality is focused upon two orders of existence, the one initial and the other teleological, one must simultaneously affirm the good of nature and reject the natural as the ultimate goal of human existence. Thus Brownson's creation-Incarnation-oriented spirituality could either affirm the world as long as the teleological order was perserved or deny the world in order to perserve the final destiny of the initial order of creation. Brownson had done both. Many Brownsonian scholars have acknowledged that it is impossible to understand Brownson's shifting positions unless one perceives this dialectic at the heart of his thought. Changes of emphasis in his own spirituality must also be interpreted from this same dialectical perspective.

The world-denying spirituality asserted itself more forcefully during his last years for the reasons already mentioned, but also because he believed that the dialectic between the initial order of creation and the teleological order of redemption had been lost in American consciousness in favor of an almost exclusive emphasis upon the initial order. Such an emphasis could ultimately lead to naturalism and pantheism—positions Brownson had been battling throughout his career as an American religious thinker.

It is difficult to assess the impact of Brownson's thought upon the development of American spirituality. He founded no school of thought, as had Channing or Emerson. He wrote no major book that was widely read and subsequently reprinted. His major writings were periodical pieces that lie buried in journals that are no longer read. His conversion to Catholicism, too, as Perry Miller pointed out some time ago,[116] made him a forgotten man in American letters. Nonetheless, he did have an impact on his contemporaries and had some influence particularly upon the American Catholic community after his death.

One of Brownson's primary roles in mid-nineteenth-century America was that of critic. He found in Channing's supernatural rationalism and in Emerson's idealism and quasi-pantheism an excessive individualism and subjectivism that diminished the bonds of community life in church and in society. The advocates of self-culture and self-reliance had emphasized freedom at the expense of order and authority. Their preoccupation with self-development, he thought, was ahistorical and ultimately a denial of historical continuity and tradition. Their understanding of divine Providence, moreover, limited divine as well as human freedom. Brownson may not have fully understood his opponents because he generally tried to push their positions to what he perceived to be their ultimate logical and philosophical trajectories; but he did understand the necessity of community and tradition and therefore constructed a clear alternative to the liberal tradition in his doctrine of life by communion. That view tried to mediate between the excesses of the empirical and the idealist approaches to Christian life.

Brownson's emphasis upon communion put him in what R.W.B. Lewis has called the party of irony and distinguished him from the party of hope and the party of memory in American intellectual history.[117] Brownson's tragic optimism was based simultaneously upon his sense of the human solidarity in and capacity for evil and upon his belief that human progress was possible only through communion with the divine.

Brownson offered his contemporaries an alternative to Channing's and Emerson's individualism and subjectivism. He viewed the Christian life as a process of growth from creation through redemption to eschatological union with God. Like many of those influenced by the age of Romantic Idealism, Brownson asserted that the infinite, though clearly distinguished from the finite by the doctrine of creation, was historically and objectively present in the finite. Access to the divine, therefore, was available only in and through concrete communion—a synthesis of intuition and tradition. The individual's historical movement toward union with God was always the result of the divine life mediated objectively through Christ, the church and the sacraments. The Christian's mediated life was communal, ecclesial and organic. It was life in community and life that had a providentially guided tradition. That life was also sacramental; that is, the invisible divine life was made present in creation, in visible symbols, in human language, in tangible forms. It was a life, moreover, that was synthetic —it affected the whole person in the unity and interdependence of all individual human activities and relations. It was a life, too, that was simultaneously objective and subjective. The individual's subjective activity was not destroyed by the objective presence of imparted divine grace. The Christian's supernatural life brought to fulfillment and eschatological realization the natural life; it did not violate or suspend that life.

Brownson's mature emphases upon the doctrine of creation, divine enlightenment and intuition put him in the Augustinian Christian tradition rather than the Thomistic. His Augustinian tendencies also provided the nineteenth-century American Catholic community with a creative presentation of the internal dynamics of its own tradition. Brownson's incarnational theology, too, was akin to the theology that was emerging in the nineteenth-century Catholic community in parts of Germany, France and Italy. That it did not survive intact either in European or American Catholicism is due more to the rise and resistance of neo-scholasticism and neo-Thomism than to its own inherent weaknesses.

Something of Brownson's life by communion, however, did have a legacy in American Catholicism. His providential understanding of history and of the providential men who were responsible for its progress found its way into the thought of Isaac Hecker, and a late-nineteenth-century Catholic Americanist like Archbishop John Ireland of

St. Paul. His incarnational and communal ecclesiology, and his understanding of the social dimensions and responsibilities of Christianity, moreover, eventually reappeared in the American Catholic liturgical movement in the 1920s and 1930s. Virgil Michel, O.S.B., one of the leaders of that movement, was the author of the first dissertation on Brownson's thought ever written and was significantly influenced by his views.

From a contemporary perspective, Brownson's almost exclusively incarnational theology has its difficulties. Christ's death and resurrection, to say nothing of his earthly ministry, play almost no role in his theology, except to unfold what is already present in the Christmas event. The role of the Holy Spirit in the Christian's life, moreover, receives little attention in his theology. His incarnational view of the church and tradition, intended to emphasize the supernatural dimension of both, makes his theology subject to a host of critical questions about the church's historical appropriation of tradition and the role of the church in history. In spite of these weaknesses some contemporary Catholic theologians are beginning to see in Brownson's thought insights that need to be resurrected in American Christian communities, which are still facing the challenges of capitalism, industrialization, bureaucratization and individualism.[118]

Texts and Principles of Selection

Brownson was a prolific writer. From 1826 to 1875 he published enough to fill at least thirty-five large volumes of collected works.[119] Making appropriate selections from this voluminous production has been my major difficulty in preparing this anthology. From the beginning of the project I decided to arranged the texts chronologically to reveal the major shifts in Brownson's spiritual wanderings and to represent the different forms of American spirituality that he appropriated. I chose texts from each period of his life but concentrated upon the years 1822 to 1844 because most of the changes in his spiritual vision occurred during these years. The texts chosen (from his private unpublished diaries, published sermons, essays and pamphlets) reflect his personal religious experience and intellectual conversions, his views of the social as well as personal dimensions of the Christian life, and his evaluations of pious practices within American Christianity. His lengthy theological-philosophical and political writings, which represent some of his most thought-provoking work, were excluded simply because they were too long for inclusion.

Notes: Introduction

1. Quoted in Theodore Maynard, *Orestes Brownson: Yankee, Radical, Catholic* (New York: The Macmillan Company, 1943), p. 176.

2. Isaac Hecker, "Dr. Brownson and Catholicity," *Catholic World* 46 (November 1887), p. 234.

3. In much of what follows on Brownson's early life, I am indebted to William J. Gilmore, "Orestes Brownson and New England Religious Culture, 1803–1827," Ph.D. diss., University of Virginia, 1971.

4. Orestes A. Brownson to Edward Turner, 17 July 1834, in Universalist-Unitarian Archives at Andover-Harvard Divinity School.

5. Henry F. Brownson, ed., *The Works of Orestes A. Brownson* 5, 20 vols. (Detroit: Thorndike Nourse, 1882–87), p. 4. [Hereafter *Works.*]

6. *The Franklin Primer,* edited by Samuel Willard (1775–1859) was a catechism of the American Calvinist mind. The Westminster Assembly (1648) established *The Shorter Catechism.* It filled an important role in the catechesis of Presbyterian, Congregationalist and Baptist children. Samuel Davies was a New Side Presbyterian minister who believed that personal religious experience was essential to Christian affirmation. Jonathan Edwards was a Puritan pastor whose Calvinist theological works have influenced generations of American Protestants. Brownson returned in the 1830s and 1840s to Edwards' works, concentrating in particular upon *A Treatise on the Religious Affections* (1744) and the sermon *A Divine and Supernatural Light.* These two works seem to have had a significant influence upon Brownson's notions of religious intuition in the 1830s and 1840s.

7. *Works* 5, p. 5. See also "Reading and Study of the Scriptures," *Brownson's Quarterly Review* 18 (October 1861): 504. [Hereafter *BQR.*]

8. *Works* 5, p. 7.

9. "Patrick O'Hara, Chapter VI" *The Philanthropist* 1 (July 23, 1831): 141–43. This text is reprinted here. See also *Works* 4, p. 190, and Brownson to Turner, July 17, 1834.

10. *BQR* 4 (October 1841): 520.

11. Brownson read Elhanan Winchester (1751–97), *The Process and Empire of Christ, A Course of Lectures on the Prophecies That Remain to Be Fulfilled, The Universal Restoration;* Joseph

Huntington, *Calvinism Improved;* and particularly Hosea Ballou, *A Treatise on Atonement.* On these sources, see Gilmore, pp. 370–91.

12. Brownson to Turner, July 17, 1834.
13. "Priest and Infidel," *The Philanthropist* 2 (May 29, 1832), p. 211.
14. *Works* 5, pp. 9–10.
15. Reuben Smith to Orestes Brownson, August 22, 1841, quoted in Henry Brownson, *Orestes A. Brownson's Early Life (1803–1844)* (Detroit: H. F. Brownson, 1898), p. 419.
16. "A Notebook of Reflections, 1822–1825," unpublished manuscript in the Archives of the University of Notre Dame. Orestes Brownson Papers, Box I-4J. Microfilm copy, R10-0685/0760, in the Brownson Papers. See Thomas T. McAvoy, C. S. C., and Lawrence J. Bradley, *A Guide to the Microfilm Edition of the Orestes Brownson Papers* (Notre Dame, IN: University of Notre Dame Press, 1966). Parts of the notebook are reprinted here as "Spiritual Diary."
17. *Works* 5, pp. 9–10; see also Brownson to Turner, July 17, 1834.
18. Anne C. Rose, *Transcendentalism as a Social Movement 1830–1850* (New Haven: Yale University Press, 1981), p. 45.
19. Orestes Brownson, Notebook for 1824, *circa* p. 19, in Archives of the University of Notre Dame, Orestes Brownson Papers, Box I-4J. This notebook was originally entitled "A Notebook of Clippings From the *Boston Reformer*," but in 1986–87 Dr. Wendy Schlereth, director of the Notre Dame Archives, removed the clippings, uncovering this notebook.
20. Ibid. *circa* p. 93.
21. Even before this time, though, as his spiritual diary indicates, he had been preparing sermons or notes for sermons while he was in Balston Spa, New York.
22. On Brownson's ministerial training, see Gilmore, pp. 292–332.
23. Orestes Brownson, "The Influence of Religion on Prosperity," *Christian Repository* 7 (August 1826): 49–58, reprinted here.
24. Gilmore, pp. 249, 257.
25. Orestes Brownson, "To The Editor," *The Liberator* (May 1838), reprinted in Daniel Barnes, "An Edition of the Early Letters of Orestes Brownson," Ph.D. diss., University of Kentucky, 1970, p. 206.
26. Orestes Brownson, "To the Editors of the Free Enquirer," *Free Enquirer* (January 2, 1830): 95–96, reprinted here.
27. Barnes, pp. 206–8.

28. From 1830 to 1831 Brownson edited *The Republican and Herald of Reform* from Batavia, New York. I have been unable to locate this journal.
29. Orestes Brownson, "A Sermon on Righteousness," *The Philanthropist* 2 (January 14, 1832): 85–94, reprinted here.
30. On his use and reading of Channing, see *The Philanthropist* 2 (April 10, 1832): 209ff. and *Works* 5, p. 69; *Works* 4, p. 46.
31. "Essay on Reform," *The Philanthropist* 2 (February 14, 1832): 115. Earlier, in "An Essay on Christianity," *Gospel Advocate and Impartial Investigator* 7 (February 7, 1829), pp. 37–38 [hereafter *GAII*] he asserted, along Lockean lines, that intuition was indeed the strongest kind of evidence.
32. David Robinson, ed., *William Ellery Channing: Selected Writings* (New York: Paulist Press, 1985), p. 32.
33. *Works* 4, pp. 240–41. In 1834 Brownson began writing "Letters to an Unbeliever" to convert skeptics by retracing his own journey from orthodoxy to liberal Christianity. In 1840 he published this story as *Charles Elwood,* which Anne Rose calls "the earliest major statement of Brownson's Transcendentalism." See Rose, p. 46.
34. *Works* 4, p. 241. See also "Essay on Reform," *The Philanthropist* 2, p. 133.
35. "Christianity and Reform," *Unitarian* 1 (January 1834): 30–39, and (February 1834), pp. 51–58, reprinted here. On liberal pietism, see Daniel Walker Howe, *The Unitarian Conscience: Harvard Moral Philosophy, 1805–1861* (Cambridge, MA: Harvard University Press, 1970), pp. 152, 153, 155, 156.
36. "Christianity and Reform," p. 31.
37. "Benjamin Constant on Religion," *The Christian Examiner and Gospel Review* 17 (September 1834): 63–77, reprinted here.
38. On Brownson as a transcendentalist, see Rose, pp. 38, 42, 212.
39. "Spirituality of Religion," *Unitarian* 1 (September 1834): 410.
40. Samuel Coleridge is generally considered the source of the distinction between reason and understanding. No doubt Brownson borrowed the distinction from Coleridge or one of his American sympathizers, but I have not been able to discover in Brownson's works any evidence that he read Coleridge's *Aids to Reflection,* where the distinction is presented. As will be evident in what follows, Brownson does not always perserve Coleridge's distinction. During this period of his life Brownson periodically uses reason as a synonym for understanding.
41. "Spirituality of Religion," p. 410.

42. "Remarks on G.E.E.," *The Boston Observer and Religious Intelligencer* 1 (May 7, 1835): 146-7.
43. "Cousin's Philosophy," *The Christian Examiner and Gospel Review* 21 (September 1836): 33-64.
44. Ibid. pp. 51, 56.
45. *A Discourse on the Wants of the Times, Delivered in Lyceum Hall, Hanover Street, Boston, Sunday, May 29, 1836* (Boston: James Munroe and Company, 1836), pp. 17-18. See pp. 21-22 for Brownson's simple creed for the new church.
46. "Democracy of Christianity," *BQR* 1 (October 1838): 444-73 and "The Kingdom of God," *BQR* 1 (July 1839): 326-50.
47. *BQR* 3 (July 1840): 376.
48. Rose, p. 72.
49. "Nature," *Boston Reformer,* September 6, 1836. This article is pasted into the second volume of Brownson's "Notebook" located in the Archives of the University of Notre Dame. On Cousin's influence and philosophy, see Walter L. Leighton, *French Philosophers and New England Transcendentalism* (Charlottesville, VA: University of Virginia Press, 1908); Georges J. Joyaux, "Victor Cousin and American Transcendentalism," *French Review* 29 (1955): 117-30; Irving Bartlett, "Bushnell, Cousin, and Comprehensive Christianity," *Journal of Religion* 37 (1957): 99-104; Lucien Levy Bruhl, *History of Modern Philosophy in France* (Chicago: Open Court, 1899), pp. 983-94.
50. *New Views of Christianity Society, and the Church* (Boston: C. C. Little and J. Brown, 1836), parts are reprinted here.
51. "Christ Before Adam," *BQR* 1 (January 1838): 8-21.
52. "Norton on the Evidences of Christianity," *BQR* 2 (January 1839): 103-4.
53. "Emerson's Essays," *BQR* 4 (July 1841): 300.
54. On Brownson's analysis of and partial identification with transcendentalism see, "Two Articles From the Princeton Review, etc.," *BQR* 3 (July 1840): 270-83.
55. "The Eclectic Philosophy," *BQR* 2 (January 1839): 29-30.
56. "Introductory Statement," *BQR* 3 (January 1840): 11.
57. "Two Articles From the Princeton Review," pp. 322-23.
58. "Mr. Emerson's Address," *BQR* 1 (October 1838): 500-14, reprinted here.
59. "The Transcient and the Permanent in Christianity," *BQR* 4 (October 1841): 436-74.
60. Ibid. p. 458.

61. "Introductory Statement," 4.
62. On Brownson's traditionalism, see "Progress of Society," *The Christian Examiner and Gospel Review* 18 (July 1835): 345–68; "Jouffroy's Contributions to Philosophy," *ibid.* 22 (May 1837): 181–217; "Palfrey on the Pentateuch," *BQR* 1 (July 1838): 261–310; and "Democracy of Christianity." For a more extensive description of traditionalism, see Gerald A. McCool, *Catholic Theology in the Nineteenth Century: The Quest for a Unitary Method* (New York: The Seabury Press, 1977), pp. 37–58, 67–81.
63. "Mr. Reese's Letter," *GAII* 7 (July 25, 1829): 239.
64. Ibid. p. 239; "Progress of Society," p. 348.
65. "The Transcient and the Permanent in Christianity," p. 460.
66. "Reform and Conservatism," *BQR* 5 (January 1842): 60–84; "Charles Elwood Reviewed," *BQR* 5 (April 1842): 129–83; "Leroux on Humanity," *BQR* 5 (July 1842): 257–322; *The Mediatorial Life of Jesus;* "Parker's Discourse," *BQR* 5 (October 1842): 385–512; "Synthetic Philosophy," *United States Magazine and Democratic Review* 11-12 (December 1842): 567–78, (January 1843): 38–55, (March 1843): 241–54. On Leroux, see Jacques Viard, "Pierre Leroux, Michelet Péguy et l'Imitation de Jésus-Christ," *Etudes* 343 (1975): 235–58.
67. "Leroux on Humanity," *BQR* 5 (July 1842): 296.
68. *Works* 4, p. 138.
69. Ibid. p. 144.
70. *Works* 5, p. 132.
71. *Works* 8, p. 262.
72. Quoted in Henry F. Brownson, *The Early Life,* p. 444.
73. Brownson inaccurately recalls that he published seven articles in the *Christian World.* See *Works* 5, p. 156. On the articles, see "The Mission of Jesus," *Christian World* 1 (January 7, 14 and 21, 1843); "What Shall I Do to Be Saved?" (January 28, 1843); "The Church and Its Mission" (February 4, 11 and 18, 1843); "The Mediation of the Church" (February 25, 1843); "The Sacrifice of Our Lord Mediatorial" (April 8, 1843); "Discipline of the Church" (April 15, 1843).
74. "Introduction," *Brownson's Quarterly Review* 1 (January 1844): 1–28. [Hereafter *BrQR*.]
75. See Sydney E. Ahlstrom, *A Religious History of the American People* (New Haven: Yale University Press, 1972), pp. 615–32.
76. "The Church Question," *BrQR* 1 (January 1844): 74–77.
77. Brownson to Isaac Hecker, November 8, 1843, in Joseph F.

Gower and Richard M. Leliaert, eds., *The Brownson-Hecker Correspondence* (Notre Dame, IN: University of Notre Dame Press, 1979), p. 76.

78. "No Church, No Reform," *BrQR* 1 (April 1844): 175–94; "The Nature and Office of the Church," *BrQR* (April 1844): 243–56.

79. *Works* 4, p. 559.

80. *Post-Tridentine Catholic Scholasticism* is a term subject to tremendous ambiguity because it can refer to so many different kinds of scholastic thought between 1564 and 1830, before the rise of nineteenth-century neo-scholasticism. As used here the term refers to those scholastic theologians like Charles René Billuart (1685–1757), whom Brownson read as an early Catholic convert, (see *Works* 5, p. 166) and whose theological and apologetical works had been influenced by René Descartes' *Discours de la méthode.* Billuart's scholastic method was to proceed from the recognition of first principles and deduce necessary conclusions. For more on post-Tridentine scholastic apologetics, see *Works* 12, pp. 466–67, and Avery Dulles, S. J., *A History of Apologetics* (New York: Corpus Books, 1971), pp. 152–55.

81. "The Church Against No-Church," *BrQR* 2 (April 1845): 142.

82. Ibid. p. 194.

83. On Brownson's understanding of and reaction to developmentalism, see Daniel Barnes, "Brownson and Newman: The Controversy Re-examined," *Emerson Society Quarterly Supplement* 50 (1968): 9–20; Richard M. Leliaert, "Orestes Brownson (1803–1876): Theological Perspectives on His Search for the Meaning of God, Christology, and the Development of Doctrine," Ph.D. diss. University of California, Berkeley, 1974; *Works* 14, pp. 1–140; 183–96; *Works* 7, pp. 1–116.

84. Conrad Cherry, ed., *Horace Bushnell: Sermons* (New York: Paulist Press, 1985), p. 6.

85. *Works* 7, p. 92.

86. "The Fathers of the Desert," *BrQR* 10 (July 1853): 379–97, reprinted here.

87. "Questions of the Soul," *BrQR* 12 (April 1855): 214. For another dramatic shift in his thought this year, see "Liberalism and Socialism," *BrQR* 12 (April 1855): 183–209, and Leonard Gilhooley's commentary on it in *Contradiction and Dilemma. Orestes Brownson and the American Idea* (New York: Fordham University Press, 1972), p. 181.

88. See, for example, "An a priori Autobiography," *BrQR* 7 (January 1850): 1–38; "Vincenzo Gioberti," *BrQR* 7 (October 1850):

409–48; "The Existence of God," *BrQR* 9 (April 1852): 141–64. On Gioberti, see McCool, pp. 113–28; and Bernard M.G. Reardon, *Religion in the Age of Romanticism* (Cambridge: Cambridge University Press, 1985), pp. 146–56.

89. *Works*, V, 2. Maynard, p. 257, was the first author to acknowledge that *The Convert* was written to justify the doctrine. I have reprinted here a section from *The Convert* that reveals his 1857 understanding of communion.

90. "Primitive Elements of Thought," *Works* 1, pp. 408–37; "Vincenzo Gioberti," *Works* 2, pp. 140–270; "The Reunion of All Christians," *Works* 12, pp. 464–95; "Synthetic Theology," *Works* 3, pp. 536–64; *The American Republic*, *Works* 18, pp. 1–222; "Essay in Refutation of Atheism," *Works* 2, pp. 1–100; "Philosophy of the Supernatural," *Works* 1, pp. 271–83.

91. *Works* 2, p. 126. For a more extensive examination of Brownson's position, see Richard M. Leliaert, "Brownson's Approach to God: The Catholic Period," *Thomist* 40 (1976): 574–607.

92. *Works* 8, p. 33, n.

93. *Works* 5, p. 129.

94. *Works* 2, pp. 1–3. On the origins of unbelief in late-nineteenth-century America, see the excellent study by James Turner, *Without God, Without Creed: The Origins of Unbelief in America* (Baltimore: Johns Hopkins University Press, 1985).

95. On the inherent relationship between reason and revelation, nature and supernature, see *Works* 2, pp. 239, 241.

96. Ibid. p. 241.

97. Ibid. p. 276.

98. *Works* 12, p. 101.

99. *Works* 2, p. 281.

100. *Works* 12, p. 483.

101. *Works* 2, p. 240.

102. *Works* 1, p. 436.

103. On the nineteenth-century transformations in Catholic piety, see Roger Aubert "The Growth of Piety," in *History of the Church*, 10 vols., ed. Hubert Jedin (New York: Crossroad Publishing Co., 1981), vol. 8, pp. 218–28.

104. "Revivals and Retreats," *BrQR* 15 (July 1858): 289–322, sections of which are reprinted here. On the American Catholic devotional revolution see, Jay P. Dolan, *The American Catholic Experience: A History From Colonial Times to the Present* (New York: Doubleday & Company, 1985), pp. 195–220; and Ann

Taves, *The Household of Faith: Roman Catholic Devotions in Mid-Nineteenth-Century America* (Notre Dame, IN: University of Notre Dame Press, 1986).

105. See Brownson's "Reading and Study of the Scriptures," *BrQR* 18 (October 1861): 492–509.

106. "Meditations of St. Ignatius," *BrQR* 19 (July 1862): 360–73.

107. Maynard, pp. 310, 311.

108. On Brownson's warnings against excessive reliance upon sentimental and external forms of piety, see "Rights of the Temporal," *BrQR* 18 (October 1860): 464–67, and Maynard, pp. 306–7, 404.

109. *Works* 8, p. 316.

110. See, for example, "The Worship of Mary," *BrQR* 10 (January 1853): 1–25; "Saint Worship," *Works* 8, pp. 117–85; "Moral and Social Influence of Devotion to Mary," *Ave Maria* 2 (June 16, 1866): 377–80; (June 23, 1866): 385–88; "Mary Mother of God," *Ave Maria* 3 (February 8, 1867): 81–83; "Devotion to Mary," *Ave Maria* 3 (September 7, 1867): 564–66. "Our Lady of Lourdes," *BrQR* 24 (July 1875): 381–401, is reprinted here.

111. Brownson's early 1860s views on the dispensability of the pope's temporal principality and on the "natural blessedness" those in hell might experience during their eternal punishment got him in trouble with some Catholics who delated his views to Rome. On this episode, see Thomas R. Ryan, C.PP.S., *Orestes A. Brownson. A Definitive Bibliography* (Huntington, IN: Our Sunday Visitor Press, 1975), pp. 585–96. The Brownsons buried William I. and Edward P. in 1864, and three other sons before 1864: George, 1849; Charles, 1851; and John, 1858.

112. See, for example, *Conversations on Liberalism and the Church* (New York: D. & J. Sadlier, 1869).

113. On this confession, see "Religious Orders," *Ave Maria* 7 (January 28, 1871): 65–67.

114. "Religious Orders," *Ave Maria* 7 (February 4, 1871): 81–83.

115. "Nature and Grace," *Catholic World* 6 (January 1868): 509–27, reprinted here.

116. Perry Miller, ed., *The Transcendentalists: An Anthology* (Cambridge, MA: Harvard University Press, 1950), pp. 180–81.

117. R.W.B. Lewis, *The American Adam: Innocence, Tragedy, and Tradition in the Nineteenth Century* (Chicago: University of Chicago Press, 1955), p. 192. On Brownson, see also pp. 183–91.

118. John A. Coleman, "Vision and Praxis in American Theology:

Orestes Brownson, John A. Ryan, and John Courtney Murray,"
Theological Studies 37 (March 1976): 3–40.

119. Henry F. Brownson, Orestes' son, edited a selected representation of his works in twenty volumes, but he excluded from the
collected works most of what Brownson wrote before his conversion to Catholicism and much of what he wrote between 1865
and 1873.

I.

EARLY RELIGIOUS LIFE:
1803–23

1. PATRICK O'HARA

SOURCE: *The Philanthropist* 1 (July 23, 1831): 141–43.

The following story, written when Brownson was twenty-eight, gives a Unitarian perspective on Brownson's earliest Calvinist religious training and an account of his conversion at age thirteen. Although the story of his conversion may be romanticized here, it is confirmed by other sources.*

> Religion, strange mysterious word! I have asked the living, I have called upon the dead, I have pored over books, sought through all nature, by day, by night, in sickness, in health, in my hopes and in my fears, in my love, in my hatred, in my forgiveness and my revenge—all, all, have I implored with tears and in every accent of entreaty to unfold to me what thou art. *New School*

I must now be allowed to advert to my religious history, for the views I entertained of religion and the zeal with which I devoted myself to sacred subjects gave the bias to my mind and determined my future character.

I was born in the land of the Puritans; about the time when

---

* Orestes Brownson to Edward Turner, July 17, 1834. Letter in Universalist-Unitarian Archives at Andover-Harvard Divinity School.

modern revivals, as they are termed, were becoming frequent. The staid and drab-colored religion of the Puritans, which consisted in suppressing all emotions and resigning up all intellectual sovereignty, was giving way to a religion of impulse, fanaticism, and mere boisterous rant. My temperament, my situation, my education, all induced seriousness, disposed me to religious reflections, to silent and sombre meditation.

The thought of death was awful. When I first learned that I too must die, it seemed as if the springs of my life were broken. The buoyancy of my feelings left me, and for days I did little else than weep at the intelligence. To die, to be laid in the cold ground, to be left alone, to never see any one again, to never speak—O it was a terrible thought. I asked why I must die? why I could not live always? They told me God would take my life, I was in his hands, and whenever he chose he would take me away. "Why does God do this?" I asked. They answered not.

"What is God, that he should do this?"

"A spirit, your sovereign."

"But what is a spirit? and why is he my sovereign?"

No reply was given.

Surely, thought I to myself, God cannot be a very good being to take my life. It can do him no good, and I do not see why he cannot let me live. I was not more than five years old when this occurred. The impression was lasting. I have never escaped its influence. All my studies and nearly all my thoughts were henceforth to be of a religious cast.

I was soon informed that I was totally depraved, that I was born with a nature wholly corrupt; that I was infinitely hateful in the sight of my God; that I was not only born to die, but I was in danger of going to hell where I should be endlessly miserable. This was the unkindest of all their instructions. I could see much that was lovely in nature; I delighted to pluck the opening flower, to inhale its sweets; I delighted to gaze on the everlasting mountains and felt to adore when surrounded by the wild, rugged and romantic scenery amidst which I was reared; but to be told all this delight, all this pleasure, all this awe and devotion, proceeded from a corrupt heart, and could be only abomination to God, struck me dumb. My spirit fell, and inwardly I cursed my fate, cursed my maker for the wretched, the thankless existence he had given me.

I was soon instructed in all the mysteries of the "fall of man," the "incarnation of God," his "death for the elect," his "resurrection from the dead," etc. all of which I understood as well at eight years old as I do now at fifty. These doctrines are perhaps full as well suited to the comprehension of children as of grown people, and the infantile intellect will, perhaps, be full as ready to believe them as any. They however puzzled me a little at first. I could not understand how the eating of an apple by Adam, could make me guilty, but I saw it all plain, soon as I learned that Adam stood *proxy* for all his posterity, and by a very pleasing fiction, like many sanctioned by our laws, God counted him as the whole of the human race that was or ever should be. This had a remarkable beauty in it. It superseded all enquiry into our personal characters. To determine what we were, whether we deserved to be saved or damned, God had only to enquire whether Adam stood or fell. It thus saved a vast deal of labor on the part of God, and made it a matter of perfect indifference to us, whether we did good or evil; for in either case the answer "you deserve endless damnation for what Adam did," was enough. If we did well, "original sin" would damn us, if we did bad, it could do no more.

The incarnation of God was a holy mystery, I did not explain it to myself and as I was too young to appreciate the beauties of the "Miraculous Conception," that passed by without much thought. The death of God was quite another thing, but as Watts had said, in one of his hymns,

> Well might the sun in darkness hide
>   And shut his glories in,
> When God the Mighty Maker died
>   For man's the creature's sin.

I concluded it must all be right.

The doctrine of election and reprobation, I objected to in toto; and though they gave me Edwards, and Boston, and I know not how many books of the same stamp, I could not believe.[1] It seemed too much even for a child, eight years old as I then was, to embrace. The Bible had given me to understand God was good to all, better than an earthly parent, and I could not believe that earthly parent very good, who would give all his good things to a small part of his children and starve all the rest to death.

The doctrine of endless misery—I hardly knew what to think of it. My feelings revolted at the thought; all my notions of justice, love and mercy seemed to forbid it.—But as the idea of power was most prominent in my notions of God, as I was taught to view him rather as a sovereign, than as a Father, I assented, and reluctantly admitted it might be.

Thus stood my mind at eight years old. Thus far I had good calvinistic training, and in the main was considerably orthodox. The good pious sisters said I should be a great man yet, should be an ornament to the church, etc. I continued to read such religious books as I could find, to think, to reflect more and more upon my condition. At thirteen I became really under, what was then termed, *concern of mind.*

It is worthy of remark that in those days, the art of making saints was by no means brought to the perfection it can boast now. It then took many months, sometimes years, to bring one out. Now it is no trouble at all. The same labor-saving machinery seems introduced into this spiritual factory, that there has been in spining and weaving cotton, and a thousand other things not necessary to mention. It is not singular, for a man (or rather a boy) to get up in the morning totally depraved, lying under the curse of God's wrath, and exposed to all the torments of hell for his exceeding sinfulness; at nine o'clock, to attend a prayer meeting, polluted with sin, infinitely hateful to God; at half past nine to be convicted, at ten converted, examined and propounded; in the afternoon to sit with the saints a good christian. This is rapid work; but what else could we expect from this age of steam and rail roads?

We had no such easy times when I was a boy. Full three months I lay on the brink of hell, groaning in spirit, and praying to be born again. It was a long and a weary time I had. Long, long, did I weep over my sins, without being able to recall one thing I had done for which conscience condemned me. I prayed and prayed, but all to no purpose. They told me to give myself up to God. I strove to do it; I felt anxious to do it; I wished the assistance of his holy spirit; sought it with tears, but all in vain. They told me it was all my own stubbornness of will, and that I deserved to be damned for my obstinacy. They told me to go to Jesus. I looked for him; I prayed to him; besought him to come and reign in, and over, me. It availed nothing. There I stood, in my mind's eye, upon the very edge of a mighty precipice, down which it made my brain reel to look. Down there I could see the Devil with his imps, grining [sic] and shaking his grizzly sides, and tossing with his trident poor miserable souls from one pit to another; now fanning the sulphurous flame, and spreading its horrid glare over the pale and sepulchral countenances of the damned. Then he would turn towards me. The waves of fire would seem to rise; he would brandish his trident, as if to take my life. I would recoil, with horror, with my frame trembling and covered with a cold sweat.

Then I would look up to God. There I would see him in heaven, seated upon his great white throne, laughing, *tete a tete* with his Son and the Holy Ghost. The moment his eye caught me, all would change; frowns would settle upon his countenance; flames dart from his eyes; his hand grasp firmer the awful sword; his voice, as with myraids of thunders, would roar out "Begone!" Thus it was. Hell burned before me; heaven frowned above; all seemed rage, hatred, revenge and torture. Around among my fellow beings, all seemed cold and hateful and I felt lone and friendless in the universe.

It was then I felt the full curse of existence. I loathed all food; I could not sleep; I wasted to a skeleton; but I could not die. I felt I must live—must live eternally; waste and waste away, yet remain; burn and burn forever, yet never die! Must eternally feel the fire in my soul, spreading through all my limbs, my body, swell, and writhe, and burst with the intense heat, yet ever endure. O how I prayed to the mountains to crush me. O worlds would I have given to have been annihilated. All was vain. Life was given, and must remain. No remission, no mitigation. O mockery! I exclaimed, why speak of a God of mercy! I could curse, with all my soul, a being that would confer existence but to increase the sum of misery.

O it was a horrid state of mind. It makes me pale, and feeble, and sick, to recall it. I would roll on the ground, beat my sides and gnaw my tongue for very anguish. I would turn and turn, pray and pray, plead and plead, for mercy, but it seemed their was none. "Thou shalt be damned," rung in my ears, and I gave way to despair; my brain reeled, my eyes swam round—days and weeks passed—I know not how.

It was a dark and stormy night. I had been to a meeting, to hear one of the "New Lights," as they were called, several of my own age were *brought out,* and told their experience. I could say nothing. I could not weep. I scorned to beg for mercy after having been so often denied. I went home. I threw myself upon the bed, with an anguish of soul that only few ever feel, and fewer still survive. The night was dark, except when illumined by the fitful streams of lightning. The thunder rolled as if to announce the day of doom. I always loved to hear it thunder. There is something so majestic, so much of lofty grandeur and sublimity in that heavy roll, that I believe to hear it would give me a thrill of delight even in hell.

My case had approached its crisis. The time had come, when nature must sink or triumph. The darkness disappeared; the storm subsided; the thunder hushed his voice; all was silent, calm and bright. I lay entranced. A soft, an inexpressibly sweet sensation pervaded my whole frame. There was a light around to which the day would have seemed as night; yet it was midnight. I could see every part of my room clearly and distinctly, yet I was not startled. All my guilt, all my grief, all my anguish, were gone, and I felt as if ushered into a new world, where all was bright and lovely, where the air was perfumed with sweet spices, where soft and thrilling music breathed from every dwelling and warbled from every grove. I could bear no more. The contrast of feeling may be imagined. I broke out so loud that I was heard all over the house:

> I have tasted heaven to-day,
> What more can I contain?

Thus was I born again.

Note: Patrick O'Hara

1. Reference may be to Thomas Boston (1677–1732), the elder, who was a Scottish minister and author of *Human Nature in its Fourfold Estate* (Edinburgh, 1720). See *DNB*.

2. SPIRITUAL DIARY: 1822–25

SOURCE: "A Notebook of Reflections, 1822–1825," pp. 4–10; 12–21; 27–44; 55–56; 61–67; 75–76; 80; 84; 89–90; 93–98; 109–23; 143–49. The Notebook is in the University of Notre Dame's archives. See also microfilm roll 10 of the Orestes Brownson Papers. Thomas T. McAvoy, C.S.C., and Lawrence J. Bradley, eds., *A Guide to the Microfilm Edition of Orestes Augustus Brownson Papers* (Notre Dame, IN: University of Notre Dame Press, 1966).

Brownson wrote this diary when he was between the ages of nineteen and twenty-two. He examines the religious state of his soul at the time and shows how much he had accepted some of the major themes of Christian spirituality that were significantly influenced by Calvinism: the corruption of human nature; the deceitfulness of the human heart; the helplessness and misery of the human condition; the transitoriness and folly of all fame, wealth, security and happiness; the majesty, sovereignty and caring providence of God; the mercy of Christ for the sinner; the power of divine love; and the joy of Christian love. The diary contains, moreover, entries that reflect Brownson's gradual movement away from Presbyterianism toward Universalism.

*In these entries he discusses in particular "the culture of the mind,"
free will and the universal benevolence of God. The diary, furthermore, has what appears to be first drafts of articles and sermons
Brownson was preparing as a young Universalist. The sermons were
commentaries on 1 John 4, Job 3:15 and Ecclesiastes 12:1, biblical
texts that appealed to Brownson throughout his life. Entries from
December 31, 1822, to June 3, 1823, are from his Presbyterian period.
Entries after July 30, 1823, are from his Universalist period.*

*The diary is a loosely composed personal record of Brownson's
youthful thoughts and feelings that was never intended for publication. It is poorly written and reflects his lack of formal education. I left
the diary in its original form, revealing in many places a stream of
incomplete sentences.*

SPIRITUAL DIARY: 1822–25

. . . .

December 31st.[1]

Now ends another year—a few hours more and another year will
be reckoned with those beyond the flood. Reflect, O, my soul on what
has employed thee during this year,—on what characters thou hast
established and what thy general course of conduct, canst thou look
with pleasure on the scenes that have occupied thy attention? hast
thou done nothing which causes shame and regret? nothing which
makes thee mourn and condemn thyself, as vile in the sight of God—
nothing which makes thee abhor thyself "in dust and ashes" and cry
"unclean unclean"? Yes, I have sinned every day, every hour, year and
every breath has been drawn in inequity every thought and every
imagination of my heart has been evil only evil and that continually.
And yet thou dost exist? What a mercy, sinned every breath and yet
among the living? art thou not lost in the contemplation of that Power
which has preserved thee? Canst thou but exclaim "thou are all mercy
O Love Divine who did not cast me off and appoint me my portion
with them that go down into the pit?" doest thou not feel thy heart to
glow with gratitude to this great Preserver? Yes, for he hath not only
preserved my life and loaded me with unnumbered[2] temporal blessings but has taken my feet from a horrible pit and placed them upon a
sure foundation. Yea sought me dashing my speculative brains against
the rocks of infidelity bound up my wounds and gave me a new song
even of praises to the Most High God.

But ah! how little do I feel to praise my God! how cold! . . . for such unparalleled goodness! My heart how deceptious yet! What vileness remains how opposed to all good!

How long shall I love vanity and follow after empty wind? Shall I never apply myself to wisdom nor seek after instruction? Just Heaven since thou has condescended to open my eyes—still in thy wisdom purge them.

January 1st, 1823.

Another year by the annual round of time is ushered in—another year is numbered with them which are beyond the flood—another year of our short lives is gone—gone forever. Thus Time with his rapid motion rolls on stealing day after day, year after year till life's poor transient date is spent!

While thus the fleeting years pass away do we reflect that we are travelling to the grave—that every year counts the number less? Do I ever consider the privileges we have enjoyed—the opportunities of becoming virtuous I have neglected? How many warnings from Heaven? How many calls to repentance?—how much Divine instruction I have received? and what use have I made of it? Have I sowed that I wish to reap? O God help me, so to improve this year that I may have an inheritance unchangeable eternal in the heavens! O grant that I may apply myself wholly to the acquisition of knowledge! for O how ignorant!

Friday, 10th.[3]

Much agitated with the follies of men. Believe most [of] the misfortunes of the human family are chargeable on themselves. Look abroad into the world there appears every thing requisite to their happiness. Earth yields them a rich supply of food and clothing. Nature offers to their view every thing beautiful and pleasing to the sight with all things delicious to the taste. Propitious Heaven smiles with bounties,[4] its munificence to all. But ungrateful man turns all to his own destruction. Pleasure he converts to pain—he banishes hopes and reveals in despair! he rises—shades the morning in gloom by his unrestrained passions—at noon he gropes for the wall, perpetually walking in darkness he knows no light. See and feel the effects of the full,[5] the awful consequences of parental[6] with a blind partiality and indiscriminate fondness they train their children to dwell *in tents of* wickedness.

Saturday, 11th.[7]

Attended meeting last evening. Serious reflections on employing uneducated ministers as preachers of the gospel. Believe it is subject to substitute a superstitious enthusiasm for gospel piety and heartfelt religion. Thought of the privileges we enjoy, the advantages we possess over the heathen[8] or benighted Asia and Africa with the South Sea Isles and large portions of our beloved Continent. Desire that God may prosper the missionary cause and crown all efforts for the melioration of the human family. Mourn the deadness of my own feelings. Wish to be more engaged in religion.[9] reflect on the miseries of the human race their folly and wickedness—such the obstinacy of sinners. Think of the end of the finally impenitent—dread the torments of Hell—advert to the joys of Heaven—thirst for them. Hope I may participate in[10] them. Man satisfied with the world by considering that God is its Governour.

To day have various reflections on the different occupations of individuals—the apparent difference of their happiness—conclude that it exists more in appearance than in reality. Believe the true source of happiness is, the legacy of an Ancient Sage "Govern yourselves."

Sunday, 12th.[11]

Much depressions of spirits occasioned by a review of the fates of Authors with some slight bodily indisposition—Attend church. Much affected by the preacher's adverting to the death of an amiable woman lately deceased who in the bloom of youth left the world without sigh—who bade farewell to all the busy scenes of life nor cast one lingering look behind. View anew the death of my Saviour "See him in Gethsamane's garden stone. While bloody sweat down from his temple ran." See him dying and his body broken for our salvation.[12] Think of the victory he gained over death.

Monday, 13th.[13]

Retrospect my past conduct. Struck with its folly and inconsistency.[14] sentiments on Novel reading. Believe them calculated to vitiate the mind and to corrupt the morals. Instead of fortifying the mind against the attacks of vice, they lay it open for the reception of every romantick scene. Believe Ambition the greatest destroyer of happiness. . . .

Thursday 16th.[15]

The delight of Earth insufficient bliss. O vain and inconstant world what hast thou to offer to the never dying soul?[16]—what hast thou for me—thy pleasure is but pain, thy prosperity is perplexing adversity. I loath all your scenes.[17] there is nought in you that can afford me any thing but the most complicated misery. Thou art more accursed because thou offerest every thing with the alluring glare of happiness but no sooner tasted than they pall every sense.

My soul forsakes the vain delight of earth. No longer will I[18] ask its love, or seek its pleasure more. There is nothing round this spacious earth that can suit my large desire. Tis heaven above that can true pleasure give. In Heaven my hopes dwell where sit my Saviour and Redeemer God.

Friday, 17th.[19]

Wish there was some stability in man. O—man emblem of the wind, what hast thou or what canst thou do? With a great resolution thou commencest some act but ere thou hast performed any part thy strength faileth and thou givest thy vain undertaking over. In the morning thou rises fresh and vigorous but ere the sun approaches his meridian strength thou reclinest in the shade of despair. Would to heaven that my heart was more insensible than steel or endowed with power adequate to the scenes which haunt it. I languish in[20] despair. what can alleviate a mind burdened with painful recollection? O thoughtless youth, fly while blooming in innocence, fly the alluring snares of vice that when retrospecting past conduct recollection may be sweet!

Saturday, 18th.[21]

Dead to every sense of pleasure. Feel no life in religion. Can apply no promise of Gods word. Hope only because I know he is faithful who has promised "Think on Christian perfection—Believe the carnal nature always remains; and that nature is prone to sin not only prone to sin but it is evil all it thoughts and imaginations are evil and that continually. Believe I have no righteousness but in the Lord. Believe Christ as the Great Shepherd laid down his life for the salvation of the Sheep that he as the great Sponsor bore our iniquities in his own body that he fulfilled that law which man never could do. Believe that as man by the fall became corrupt there was a necessity of something more than barely an atonement for Adam's sin. Because I live ye shall also the words of Christ my only hope.

Sunday Evening, 19th.[22]

The pleasure of piety. Sing to the Lord all ye children of men, Praise him all ye nations of earth, for his munificence extends to all his works. Day unto day showeth us his goodness. Night unto night teacheth his wisdom and Sovereignty. Feel my bosom glow with gratitude to this great Dispenser of every thing which adds happiness to man. By whose power shines yonder firmament "with living[23]?" Who exhales the vapour and scatters the snowy morsels and binds in frozen chains the rivers and lakes? Now methinks although nature lies dead and all tunefull voices are silent I shall yet see all arrayed in living green while sweet music fills every grove. A little better I look and think though this body should lie laid in the grave and moulder to dust a triumphant man shall arise when new life shall awake every stone adorned with immortality.

11 o'clock, Sunday Evening.
How changeable the mind of man; one hour he appears happy in future prospects the next buried in despair! When I view man in himself I am lost. I feel all the dire forbodings of hell. What an inconsistant piece is man! Made up of joy and grief hope and despair. O Contemplation! how sad[24] bosom when pensive I court thy humble shade! When thinking over all the miseries of life how thou raisest the swelling tears to sympathize for others woes! Now to rest—but O my God grant that these sad forbodings which hang over my soul may disappear and one ray of hope may beam afresh upon a melancholy heart.
How sad the above![25]

Monday, 20th.[26] The Power of Religion.
How beautiful is Religion! It calms the rough passions and spreads peace over all the soul! Amid all the storm and bustle of life it enables its possessor to pass quietly along with a calm and serene air with a dignity of spirit and gracefulness of manners unknown to the children of vice. It gives true wisdom and knowledge—it gives true and genuine feelings of humanity, it awakens true sympathy and it withholds no right that tends to ameliorate the condition of the unfortunate. It diffuses through all its votaries a sweet, gentle temper, a meek, patient temper that is not easily elated never puffed up never cast down—that evenness of temper the same in prosperity as in adversity which never repines at misfortunes—which always sees a God employed in all scenes that pass—which views "Disappointments and distress as blessings in disguise."
How pleasing to look through nature to contemplate all transpiring events as the will of a Great and Wise Governour! What sublime felicity arises from the contemplation of God's Sovereignty.

Thursday[27]
How important the study of man! I am at a loss what to call the world! I am ignorant of its materials! so ignorant that I am every day

deceived with its appearances. To day it promises pleasure—but I receive nothing but pain! To day it seems to smile with prosperity but before tomorrow's sun shall have reached his evening declination all may wear a gloomy aspect shrouded in a mantle of black despair. Sometimes when wrapt in Melancholy, all nature seems a settled gloom a sudden ray of light beams upon the soul, the clouds disappear the horizon blazes with uncommon brightness but alas! it is but a prelude to a dark and dismal night—yea a baleful night of grief and wretchedness.

I scarcely know when to rejoice in prosperity or when to repine in[28] adversity. If I mourn in adversity it is useless for soon some unseen power will dispell the clouds and I may rejoice.[29] not rejoice—for the sun may go down at noon. To day I have found a friend but to morrow may prove him an enemy! My own heart deceives me it is deceptious above all things. My reason is but false balance[30]; my very sight is deceitful and all that belongs to me is double tongued! Alas! what can man do without the assistance of religion? The philosopher may say because the life of man alternately changes from pleasure to pain and pain to pleasure "that to be happy is only not to repine in adversity nor be elated in prosperity but to preserve a careful medium between the two extremes and to be contented with our situation. But what power has he to form such a state of mind? surely man must become more insensible than a stone with no other assistance than the feeble energies of nature before he can endure pain and know[31] repine or pleasure and not be pleased. Thrust thy hand into the fire thou dignified Philosopher and see if with all thy boasted insensibility the sensations do not reach the heart and rent themselves in shrieking agony. Apply to thy naked flesh hot plates of iron and see if no excuse can be framed to justify the man that repines at misfortune's touch? Inquire of yourself if it be not nature. If it is be silent for thy business is only with nature. To become happy is not to[32] extinguish the tender sensibilities of our nature but to refine them. The more tender a man's feelings are the more happiness he enjoys. And here is the difference between religion and philosophy, the former softens and refines the feelings while the latter tends to burden and render them more insensible. The philosopher thinks himself happy when he has extinguished all the fires of nature. The votary of religion when he has refined all the rougher passions of his soul when he has awakened each latent power of sympathy and enlightened himself by the pure blaze of never dying charity. Yea never more happy than when the pearly tear rolls down his cheek for others' woes and he can impart something, if but word, to[33] misery! Can it be imagined that a stone is happy? As well as the men void of feeling. Forbear O man to the happiness in aught but Heaven! No I have long listened to the voice of philosophy but it is vain, it can only tell us that we are poor blind and naked while its nothing to offer for our alleviation. What advantage can it be to be[34] told that we are miserable when we are told at the same time that it is the unavoidable lot of[35] our nature? Pray let us sport with vanity let us build on the[36] joys we can but be miserable and there may be some pleasure in thinking we know and enjoy something. What the use to discover the nature of a disease when we must be told that it is incurable? to deprive us of that blindness which hides the scenes of futurity and our real state when our present happiness consists in that blindness?

"O Star-eyed Science! travel not there
To waft us home the message of despair! . . . ."[37]

Monday, February 3.[38]

There has not been a day this three years that has given me an equal share of pleasure with this. There is a certain melancholy heaviness which sometimes hangs over my mind and clouds all my prospects—it is not occasioned by any trouble or any event that passes but it is a principle in my nature. Nothing when it approaches can avert it. It comes and goes of its own accord. . . .

Friday evening Feb. 7th.[39]

Believe if all my thoughts were written they would form a curious mass. I have to day perhaps thought[40] of a thousand things and not one of them is now present to my mind. I only know that I have been employed about something. For those powers which generate thought are ever active. Hence the reason of dreams. But one thing I have discovered that in the human mind there are two kinds of thoughts. There is the voluntary or those which are generated by known circumstances and involuntary or those that obtrude themselves into the mind. Believe it best to treat these uninvited visitors well for from them arises a great portion of our knowledge. . . .

Sunday, 9th.[41] On slander

O slander where canst thou hide so many poisoned darts? Deadly hate cruel envyings bitter falsehoods with all the Death distilling fruit of hell are the shafts of thy quiver! Thou destroyest peace from the habitations of men. Thou plantest destruction in their bosoms and reignest triumphant over truth and virtue.

Of all the vices which infest society there is none so pernicious as slander. There is none which so much destroy the happiness of community. Order peace and harmony fall before it as a tender plant beneath the scorching rays of the sun. No age, no age, no[42] escapes its[43] malicious tongue.

Are two men at variance and slander hath not made it? Is one mourning the loss of a character and slander has been not the cause? Is society involved in broils and shameful quarrels—each viewing his neighbours as his enemy and slander has not done it? Is one striving to rise from a state sunk to by the misfortunes of parents and slander does not vent all the spite of the infernal spirits against him. Pass along the world's wide stage—view, there a young woman where shortly since rosy pleasure bloomed, view her with a heart sickened with grief from those frightened[44] eyes, which once shot forth a thousand peculiar graces, now rolls the pearly tears, inquire the cause, "tis slander." See that child too bathed in tears lamenting the loss of parental affection trembling beneath the frowns of an enraged parent. See that pistol aimed at a friend's breast—yea, farther see raised aloft the ensigns of war, see that plain sound or that wood filled will combatants armed with death. See rank opposed to rank while now the thunder of cannons and volley of muskets roar. See the war horse stamping with footlocks bathed in human blood, see chariot wheels clogged with the dead and dying while their growns pierce the sky. . . . For what? For slander!

Monday, 10th.[45]

Read my Closet Companion.[46] My mind is particularly attentive to the resolutions, believe I am wholly unable to keep one. Feel all-dependent, on God for everything. Resolutions are vain except God smile upon them. No state is free from Trouble.

Evening.

I have often cast my eyes over the world and reflected on the situations of others. I often make it a practise to compare their condition with my own and thus learn my real happiness or misery.

When in adversity I take this survey every state seems better than my own, but when in prosperity I would exchange with none. I sometimes look for a situation that would please myself where I might enjoy uninterrupted happiness but I can discover none. . . .

Wednesday, 12th.[47]

Almost despair of Heaven—should quite were I to judge of my graces by their quantity. I see nothing in me that looks like religion. I am base I am corrupt "The good that I would do I do not. O wretched man that I am who shall deliver me from the body of this death. I thank God that giveth me the victory thro the Lord Jesus Christ".[48]

Various are the internal feelings of man. This state of mind changes almost every second. One moment he flatters himself that he is nearly happy the next black despair reigns triumphant over all his pleasings prospects. This moment his bosom begins to breathe with joy, the next a sullen gloom may pervade the whole frame! Man is all change known only in the moment we see him. Discontent. . . .

Saturday, 22.[49]

How toils vain man for this world's goods! how excessively he labours while his head is silvered over with age! Though wealth rises in vast heaps around him still his insatiable avarice impels him forward as at first.

While he dost more than he can tell still "are breathed endless sighs for more."

Wealth properly used is highly beneficial. And as this life without some portion of it would scarcely be worth possessing—it is important that every person should endeavour to accumulate some, but let himself some bounds to his desires.

O Man does thou think of long life, thy next breath may be thy last. youth beauty nor condition can avert the shaft of death nor prolong the lamp of life.

Sunday evening, 23.[50]

What a feeble piece is man! emblem of all that is weak and mutable. O how unlike his Maker "his full reverse in all." O when shall I be delivered from this vile nature! When shall I be freed from[51] corruption, when shall I see Jesus and be like him free from sin!

How shocking the ravages of death! At church to day how large a proportion of the assembly was dressed in mourning how many souls say "death is no stranger here! Yet how thoughtless for themselves, how few tears flowed for sin. O my soul art thou not led to inquire the cause of death and to weep for its baleful effects on thy happiness? Art thou prepared to meet it? hast thou learned that sin is the origin of death? and that unless thou art been washed in the regeneration thou will feel its sting forever? does thou still feel the sting of death? hast thou no peace with God? if not, where art thou Man—Believe self examination an all-important thing. O how deceptious is my heart! Try me O God search me and show me my iniquity. . . .

Wednesday, 26th.[52]

How weak and impotent is man!

He talks of strength but what can he perform? He tells too of the sufficiency of[53] nature's light to procure eternal salvation. He argues he can do works acceptable to God. How it is "O my soul? Canst thou? Art thou not" possessed of principles opposed to God? Art thou not vile corrupt and desperately wicked? How then does thou hope to please him? With thy corruption? will he accept thy vileness? . . . Canst thou be happy and live in rebellion against Him? Is there no distinction as to the consequence between virtue and vice? Or do you not consider it a virtue to please *him* who is the centre of all virtue?

Many traits are discernable in the greater part of mankind which seem to be good and in a great measure promote the peace of society, such as general sympathies and the kind affections and feeling of humanity. Man is not that monster in wickedness that misanthropick railers represent. Where one so hardened that is not moved when he sees his brother suffer some excruciating pain? some few examples indeed, there has been a few Neros who could sport with death, some void of feeling, but the greater part has in all ages been susceptable of sensibilities. Yet "there is no flesh in man's obdurate heart. it does not[54] for man!" "He invents with indefatigable care refinements in destruction and directs the murderous engine against his brother!"

27th.[55]

How heedless am I as thoughtless as though I had nothing to learn! What is there more desirable than knowledge? It should be the soul's highest aim. Say my soul are thou contented to yawn out thy life here in sordid ignorance? Shall others toil and win the prize and you sit inactive? The mingled ravages of death on either hand admonish thee of thy frailty. A voice is heard flouting aloud swelling breeze it comes through the cypress grove from departed shades, it thunders in thy ears, be ready, be ready for thou too must die!!!

28th.[56]

Just returned from church. though excellent discourse I[57] feel no life am cold and stupid; lost to every sense of religion. Feel an awful and desperately wicked heart. Just Heaven "and shall I always lie at this poor dying rate"? descend Great Comforter and take thy seat in this cold heart of mine. O illumine it by thy rays and warm it by thy spirit. O thou all wise Supreme self-existent Eternal and transcendently glorious Lord, my God, Thou who hast made Heaven and earth, thou who hast created[58] all worlds by thy strength and upholdest them by thy might, graciously condescend. O heavenly Father look down from thy lofty throne upon me an unworthy worm who am altogether unworthy to take thy great and holy name in my sin polluted lips. O Grant me humility of heart and strike, O strike me with the profoundest reverence as I approach thy presence. Tell me with just conceptions of thy great majesty, and forbid, O forbid that I would[59] thoughtlessly and without just fear of thy awful greatness rush into thy fearful presence. O God from whom all blessings come realize to me that thou art the fountain and the giver of all that I enjoy. Fill me with love and arouse my heart to glow with gratitude to thee for all the comforts of life but infinitely more than all for that unparalleled display of they power that unequalled manifestation[60] of thy infinite goodness that amazing condescension of thy great mercy in giving thy only begotten son a ransom for me. O Heavenly Parent grant that I may ever keep my thoughts fixed on this great point this first principle of salvation. may the great doctrine it inculcates be unalterably fixed in my mind and be the spring of every act. May it teach me my own vileness and the deceitfulness of my own heart. May it[61] realize to the worth of my own soul by showing the price of its ransom!!

Is there any thing more desirable than knowledge? Man, poor and ignorant by nature, is the dupe of his own passions—harrassed on every side by obdurate elements, he lives in constant misery. But knowledge, Heavenly power, breaks the stubborn earth and accomodates the unyielding element to his use.

Whenever we cast our eyes over society and discover the different sentiments and systems of people we are astonished that truth which is one and uniform should offer itself in such a variety of forms, and is it truth? Truth is simple, it is always clear from doubt and mystery unless it be enveloped in them by its antagonist—wherever then we see people diametrically opposed to each other in any particular subject each producing about the same strength of argument in support of their favourite dogmas Is it not a pretty good proof that neither are right? We complain of the miseries of life and are continually railling at the world because it yields us not more complete enjoyment; But may we not with much more propriety complain of our own depravity and rail at our own follies. . . .

April 6th.[62]

. . . .

Afternoon.

Occasioned by a sermon by Mr. R. S.[63] It is curious to observe the connection between causes and effects. Every thing appears to be so constituted that when the cause is known we need be under no apprehension as to the result. Whenever we see a man pursuing the direct course of vice we may as surely predict his misery as if we actually see his vice. Mark that man who but lately was respected by society—beloved by all. The good who filled many important offices in his country discharged the several domestick functions with alacrity, whose children were educated and trained to paths of usefulness, he smiled with prosperity. Pass by his house it is shattered, the windows are broken, his children are clothed in rags, his wife half furnished is bathed in tears, his fields are grown up with weeds, all is utter desolation. Pass by the tavern, there[64] sits the wretch carousing with the vilest. His conduct changed, the whole scene is reversed. An ornament of society is changed to its vagabond and perhaps his career in a state prison!

End of the first part. . . .

On the Pursuit of Fame.

What is this fame for which all the world are toiling with ceaseless care? Is it substantial bliss? Is it that which will ensure lasting peace of mind? Is it that which will buoy up the soul amid all the trying vicissitudes of life? When friends are taken away when life itself draws near to the tomb, can it give a soothing healing balm to the broken heart? . . .

How vain the course in which the evil runs! Wealth and fame are the grand objects of man's desires; for these he toils, for these he foregoes the pleasure of life; for these he endures the extremes of hunger and thirst and of heat and cold no object is too[65] great to be surmounted, no means too hazzardous to be undertaken! no secret of knowledge is left unexplored to gain what? a fleeting nothing, an empty name! Wealth! what is it?—the pride of fools and scorn of the wise! a some thing that entails on its possessor endless cares—a nothing, an illusive glare sent to employ the rabble—a bubble presenting a thousand pretty colours touched and its gone! And what is fame? an empty name, a shadow without a substance, an ignis fatuus[66] forever eluding the grasp of the most vigilent pursuer. Forbear then to labour for that which is not meant nor spend money for that which satisfieth not. Mirabile dictu. . . .[67]

Monday, 12th.[68]

How wonderous are thy ways O King of Kings! On every side are seen the wonderful works of the Deity. A few days ago the vegetable kingdom lay dead, the tuneful buried in silence, all was sad—all presented one scene of desolation. all filled the mind in the deepest emotions of Melancholy, the soul hung only upon Hope and anticipated the spring—it is realized. The fields are arayed in living green, sweet musick fills every grove, and smiling joy pervades every heart. So with the body tho dead it shall live again and every[69] immortal lustre wear.

Amidst all the vicissitudes of fortune a virtuous man may lead a life of happiness. Virtue has an universal charm. Bad as the world is, respect is always paid to genuine Virtue.

May 13th.[70] "How ungrateful is man!"

I once found a *friend* he professed the most exalted esteem for my person and character. he would frequently tell me of many virtues that he said I possessed and always seemed studious to invent some palliation or concealment for my most flagrant crimes. He listened with pleasure to the recital of past conduct. I told him all I had ever done. I made him acquainted with every secret of my life and revealed to him every hidden thought and imagination of my heart overjoyed to see with what pleasing colours he painted the whole! But he betrayed me—he published my conduct thro all the country, he repeated them with an evil exaggeration, it acquired strength by being related and increased to monstrous size. I found an enemy—he reproved my wickedness—diminished my virtues—I despised him. I turned from him with cold disdain—I would answer him never a word the oft he called—but closed my mouth and ears in willful silence. One day pensive with the trouble and the misfortunes of life, he came and showed me "all that ever I did"—he told me the deceitfullness of my Friend—he showed me the many good offices he himself had done for me—but it was on his benefice that I lived—that my father's having sold himself entailed perpetual slavery on me, that he paid the ransom and had given me my liberty and that too by performing the labour that was exacted of me. how often he had warned me of dangers and protected me from the secret snares of my enemies. Struck with the baseness of ingratitude I fell at his feet before the half was told and implored forgiveness but how could I hope for it—but he gently raising me by the hand said I was forgiven. I looked he was all comely. I loved him. He told me never to want for I should always live with him and his riches are inexhaustable. With him I feast on the most delicious food and soon he assures me I shall eat with him in his Father's house—forever!

The following sentiments are extracted from "The almost Christian discovered or falsed Professor detected" By Matthew Mead.[71]

Almost thou persuadest me to be a christian. Doctrine. There are very many in the world that are almost and yet but almost christians: Many that are near heaven and yet never the nearer; many that are within a little of salvation and yet shall never enjoy the last salvation; they are within sight of heaven and yet they shall never have a sight of God.

1st.

Reasons. A man may have much knowledge, much light, he may know much of God and his will, much of Christ and his ways and yet be but almost a christian—he may have great and eminent gifts yea spiritual gifts as the gift of prayer, which is different from the grace of prayer—he may have a high profession of religion—be much in the external duties of godliness, he may go far in opposing his sin—he may mourn for sin—he may make a large confession of his sin to God and others—he may forsake sin—he may hate sin and yet be but almost a christian. He may make great vows and promises to God—he may have strong purposes and resolutions; he may strive against sin and combat sin in himself; he may desire grace; he may tremble at the word of God, delight in the ordinances of God, be a member of the church of Christ, share all church privileges—have great hopes, be under great visible changes and these be wrought by the ministry of the word and yet be but almost a Christian. A man may[72] be zealous in matters of religion, be much in prayer—suffer for Christ—have faith —love the people of God, obey many of the commands of God—be sanctified—do all as to external duties that a true Christian can and having done all be but almost a christian.

2nd.

Why are they but almost christians when they have gone thus far? Because, if natural conscience puts a man on duty he rests on the duty because he seeks to[73] stop the mouth of conscience rather than satisfy it—the natural man in most exalted state retains his bosom lusts—he prides himself in his duties—he does not their glory to God—natural conscience never can be holy, it being the spring of duties all are earthy and of the earth.

3rd.

What is the reason men go no farther in their profession of religion than to be but almost christian? Because they deceive themselves as to the truth of their condition—from the wiles of satan—from worldly and carnal policy—from some beloved lust which bars Christ from the heart. The above sentiments are admirably demonstrated from scripture by the Author Matthew Mead.

Nothing is more deceptious than the heart of man! we all at once acknowledge our incapacity to discern the hearts of others but are not equally unable to discover the wickedness of our own. We often think we are pretty good when vice with all its indignant qualities lies run concealed in our bosom ready at the first opportunity to raise its[74] hideous head. Hazeal[75] thought himself incapable to commit the crimes in which he afterwards exulted. When the prophet foretold him what he would do he seemed[76] enraged and vehemently exclaims "what is thy servant, a dog."[77] But mark the sequel. This same Hazeal who knew so little of himself as to imagine that he should never deviate from the path of virtue, fearful lest his master might recover from an illness with which he was afflicted becomes a tyrannicide a usurper and thus paves the way for those bloody scenes which the prophet foretold he would act. "And Hazeal smote the children of Israel in all their earth."[78] And is none but Hazeal deceived? who among us does not, when temptation offers, find himself possessed of principles at which humanity shudders and which he himself would not have believed to have been in the breath of any individual not even in the most abandoned malefactor. And however good, we may flatter ourselves we are, there lies concealed in each heart those principles which if not cleaned by the blood of Christ will damn every one of us forever. How important then that we examine ourselves and by our righteousness whether it be of God or man? If of man beseech the Lord that he will clothe us with his. . . .

25th.[79]

Attended church a most precious day. There was exhibited that love, that self moved love that gave a saviour to a lost and perishing world—there was shewn the death and sacrifice of the spotless lamb the son of God, the Mighty Maker of all we behold. O what heart will not weep when all exposed to view the glorious sufferer stoned? who can repress the tear, when up Calvery's rugged way we see him fainting[80] beneath the ponderous wood—or extended between the heavens and the earth. O sin what hast thou done? Was it not enough that you hurl from heaven legions of angels? must thou rage till the son only begotten Son of the Father descends and dies an ignominious death upon the cross? Tremble O my soul as thou does contemplate all other deeds but this the sun permitted to pass—but ashamed to see his[81] dying—hid his face and shrouded the earth in darkness! O hide thy face in shame and confusion for thou hast murdered the King of

Heaven and he forgives thee, grants thee pardon and bids thee live! O adore his goodness love his mercy and praise him forever. . . .

Tuesday, June 3rd. 1823 On Death
    Death! T'is a terrific word! it fills the stoutest heart with[82] horror! How shrinks the atheist soul at the pale monster, with what vehemence do infidels implore mercy of that power they affected to deny!
    How little attention do we pay to matters of the highest importance. We hear a sermon the preacher[83] has not captivated the senses in his address to the understanding—we go home although appealed to by the soundest reason and most profound arguments—we sit down careless and forget all that has been said. . . .

Wednesday, July 30th.[84]

    Tis Education forms the common mind
    Just as thee twig is bent thee tree's inclined.

    When I turn my thoughts to the culture of the mind I am presented with an object at once grand and inviting. It is there I discover those latent principles which when drawn out and properly cultivated produce those towering geniuses which astonish the world. And considering that the greatest genius that ever lived was once but an[85] "blossom" in no point superior[86] to the common class of mankind I am surprised that parents take no more pains to draw out the hidden virtues of the mind. . . .

August.[87]
    There is something in society or the social circle that is congenial to the human mind and truly pleasing! but my mind has so many peculiarities that unless it finds another formed in the same mould it chooses to remain in contemplative solitude. Perhaps it is because I have not learned the true springs of reciprocal pleasure, but how can the mind that rouses the flowery fields of imagination content itself to walk the insipid circle that real life often presents? Can the mind that would accustomed itself to learn the intrinsick value of things be pleased with this man's caprice that man's scorn—with this man's jest and that man's laugh? No, let me spend my time alone or with one confidential friend or some kindred soul with whom I can think and think without restraint. . . .

July 3rd. 1825.[88]   O.A.B.

There is not a more noble principle in human nature than Sympathy. It is the surest proof we have of our Divine extraction. There is something great and heavenlike in the heart that bleeds for other's woe that prompts the rising sigh that administers the balm of comfort—pours the oil and wine and binds up the wounds of a fellow brother bowed down by the pressure of adversity. Notwithstanding what Stoic souls have urged to the contrary the happiest moment a mortal feels is in relieving suffering humanity. What sublime Satisfaction elevated the soul when engaged in the benevolent calls which the many vicissitudes of life daily present! My brother! have you seen humanity bleeding—have you seen your fellow suffering from the injustice of others or his own misguided choice, have you sympathized [with] his lot—have you with the balm of kindness endeavoured to dissipate his grief, have you[89] administered to his wants, have you done all in your power to counteract the rigours of his condition and not found a sufficient reward?

Look at the babe of Bethelem. Mark as he grew in stature to the measure of a man. See him tho he had not where to lay his head constantly going about doing good. O may we imitate our pattern in all things and be always ready to listen to the calls of benevolence—always alive to others' woes[90]—prompt to relieve suffering sons of affliction.

August, 1825

. . . . He who expects to meet with happiness from external causes must be greatly disappointed. Happiness dwells within or no where. That man must be ever miserable who has no source of pleasure within him who is entirely dependent on the capricious circumstance without. The smiles of fortune cannot impart. Happiness the embroidered garment may often cover an aching heart. . . .

Man often complains of misery of the unhappiness inevitable to our condition but would he look a little more impartially around him, he would find little reason to accuse fate or to arraign the Providence of God. Let him look into himself, let him scan the several springs of action that hurry him on in the midst of confusion, let him see if no excuse can be found to clear the Deity of our own misguided choice. Man is the arbiter of his own fortune a certain consequence will attend every act. Though God governs all things he does not infringe upon the power he has delegated to man.

It has long been a question whether man is a subject of free will or necessity. This may be a difficult question to decide but we will suggest a few thoughts which have occurred. If man is a free agent capable of pursuing a will that is free and uncontrolled he must possess in himself the power of action & no circumstance from without can in the least affect him. To act or not to act will be his, to be or not to will likewise be dependent on his will. It would therefore be absured to say one man kills another, he only dies because he wills to die! But should it be said this is carrying free agency too far—nothing more being meant than liberty to follow good or evil. I answer this controuls will! If A be not free in every instance what is the criterion of freedom? If it be contra in some instances have we not reason to infer that it is in all cases under an overruling power?

Tuesday, Aug. 19th.[91]

What end *should regulate* all our conduct? All sentiments of religion whether natural or revealed declare the glory of God to be the end that should regulate all our conduct. For he has created all things by the word of his power and for his glory they are and were created, but another thing meets the inquirer what is the glory of God? What course must I pursue to gain the character of glorifying God. To these I answer God's glory is his own attributes. We can add nothing to his glory because all his attributes are infinite. His own exalted nature, then his glorious essence, is glory. How then can we glorify God? By exhibiting his attributes by displaying the perfections in all our conduct. We glorify God when we declare him lovely and glorious to all with whom we have any connection. God is love. Can I do more to the glory of love than to be governed by it and to exhibit it in all my conduct in all my relation to the productions of love? God is good. Can I add more to the glory of goodness? God is Power but it is exercised in mercy, should I not therefore be merciful? God is truth can I honour it more than by avoiding with the utmost care a lie? God is knowledge, can it be glorified than by the acquisition of wisdom and understanding? God is a sin pardoning God, how can he receive greater glory than by our forgiving offenses?[92] To glorify we must imitate his character. He is good unto all and his tender mercies are over all his works. To be like him we must possess the same benevolent spirit. God seeks the good of his creatures. The glory of God is therefore the good of his creatures, to glorify him we must seek their good.

July 12, 1825[93]   O.A.B.

Who ever is conversant[94] with the institutions of the present day must readily[95] perceive that whoever would claim a share in their administration must consider a religious profession as his chief qualification. This doubtless is all very good. Religion should never detract from a man's honour, he should always obey its mandates be prompt to every call and must scrupulously follow all its dictates in all his transactions with his fellow; but as long as there is no infallible standard to all with one consent agree to follow how shall we know what is the correct profession we should make?

Amor est the Universalists Credo est Deus. Veritas filius Dei.[96]

1. I believe in *one* God, *infinite in power* and *wisdom* and of *unbounded goodness,* Creator of all things and absolute *Governour* of the *universe.*

2. I believe *man* is subject to *vanity* actuated by principles which are constantly involving him in *unhappiness.* All are alike subject to *errour. All alike* suffer the bitter consequence of their *aberration.*[97] All have *common wants*—equal *rights* and are equally *regarded* by *Heaven.*

I believe Jesus Christ is the Son of God. That the *doctrines* he taught are *eternal truth.* That he has exhibited the true character of God. That this *character* if exhibited to *all men* will *reconcile* all to their creator. That it will cause *discord* to cease sorrow and sighing to flee away.[98]

3. I believe this character *must be exhibited* to *all people, be preached* for a witness to every creature and then *every creature* in heaven and on the earth and under the earth and such as be in the sea and all that in them is shall sing the songs of joy and peace forever and ever. Amen. Orestes A. Brownson.

Ballston August 12th, 1825[99]
. . . .

"*GOD IS LOVE*" 1 JOHN 4

God is love, said the inspired penman. God is love, and creation confirms the glorious truth. God is love is imprinted on every page in the great volume of nature in characters which the fool can not mistake. The winged light shines the truth conspicuous. The moon reflects the same. The revolutions of the planetary world the regular return of the seasons confirm the grateful truth that "God is love." The beauty with which we are surrounded. The admirable faculties with which we are endowed. The magnificent supply prepared for our wants infix the heaven born truth. The burden of revelation is, God is love. Was man lost, had he strayed from the fate of the good shepherd. Were we in darkness, did we grope for the wall at noonday, did we forget the God that made us, make unto ourselves a God after our own imagination. Travelling through the mazes of sin did we sink in the cells of misery. Did despair seize our hearts, did the whole head become sick and the whole heart faint? God is love. Gabriel descended Glory to God, goodwill to man. "fear not for behold I bring you glad tidings"[100]—a saviour is born. Christ is anointed. The Lord hath sent him "to bind up the broken hearted to proclaim liberty to the captives and the opening of the prison to them that are bound."[101] "He shall not fail, not be discouraged till he have set judgement in the earth and the isles shall wait for his law!"[102]

It is an important truth that God is love. Are we sinners, do we hate God? Herein is love not that we loved him but he loved us and sent his son to be the propitiation for our sins. Brethern, How great is that love wherewith he hath loved and doth appear what we shall be, but this we know when he shall appear for we shall be like him for we shall see him as he is. How we sinned the Lord hath laid on him the iniquities of us all! Have we destroyed ourselves in God is our help "for God is love and in this was the love of God manifested because God sent his only begotten son into the world that we might live thro' him."[103]

I pass by the great argument in favor[104] of the salvation of all men drawn from the consideration that love always seeks the good of its object and joined with infinite wisdom to determine what is good and infinite power to execute, the greatest good will be accomplished. But the endless misery of all or part of the objects of Gods love is inconsistent with their greatest good. Therefore at some period short of eternal duration all must be happy. This must be obvious to every rational man. the apostle sums up the whole character of God in these words God is love, we can not suppose there is any imperfection in this love. all the perfection of the Deity centre in this one attribute. We love some times an object which if we were wise perhaps we should not, but "God is wise and knoweth all things. We sometimes wish good to an object which we have not power to communicate, but God is Omnipotent, he can do all things "and none can stay his law." Therefore none need fear if they are the object of God's love. He is unchangeable and no one in his sober sense will deny that God is Good unto all and his tender mercies are over all his works.

But I wish from the consideration that God is love and has manifested his love to us in that he sent his son to be the propitiation for our sin, That we should also love one another. Love is the fulfilling of the law. If we love one another God dwelleth in us and his love is perfected in us. "This is the first principle of all religions. What is the use of my professions of Godliness unless I love God and how can I love God whom I have not seen if I hate my brother whom I have seen? We are commanded to love God but what is the use if I remain equally inexorable to my brother. If I loved God should I not endeavour to imitate his character? Do we consider God the fountain of all excellence? are we desirous of partaking at that fountain? God is love, and if we love him we must love the children of God for every one that loveth him that begat loveth him also that is begotten."

"My brother! do you see one in transgression, blinded by error destroying himself. God beholds him too. Do feel hard against him because he does not do right. How does God feel? O Israel thou has destroyed thyself but in me is thy help." Do you see an enemy striving to injure you. God has enemies. Do you wish to exert a vindictive rage? how does God deal with his? God commendeth his love toward us in that while we[105] were yet sinners Christ died for us. Are you overtaken by the rage of cruel persecutors? How Prayed heavenly love when nailed to the cross? Father forgive them for they know not what they do.

God is love. he sendeth rain upon the just and upon the unjust. He is compassionate upon[106] the works of his hands. He considers our frame, he knows we are but dust, he will not contend forever but will return and have compassion according to the multitude of his tender mercies. Should we not then exercise the spirit of charity and forgiveness. Who has commanded us to pursue with unrelenting vindictiveness him we judge our foe? Ferocious cruelty may be the characteristick feature of those malignant spirits that people the regions of darkness but all that is great or good in the universe is on the side of clemency and mercy. I know the world is full of[107] offences but brother! who has given thee right to remain inexorable? have you[108] done no wrongs? have you no reason that mutual offensiveness[109] should be a pledge to mutual forbearance? Would you be godlike? He is the perfection of holiness yet he is a sin pardoning God. Do you look to him for forgiveness? hast thou ought against thy brother, "go thy way first be reconciled to thy brother and then come and offer thy gift upon—the altar."[110]

There is not a more noble principle in our nature than sympathy. Every day calls for its exercise. How often do we see suffering humanity lie bleeding before us! How often do we see the man fallen among thieves—stript and left to perish! Shall we pass by "on the other side" without offering relief? God is love if we would be like him we must keep his commandments! How did the Samaritan? Though an enemy, he poured in the oil & wine and bound up his wounds and set him upon his own beast carried him to an inn and paid his fare. What was the injunction of the saviour? Go and do likewise.

Though I may have said enough, yet I cannot dismiss my subject without particularly calling upon my readers to exercise compassion[111] and mercy to compassionate the failings of our brethern. God is love. Fury is not in him he loves all things which he has made for surely he never would have made any thing if he hated it. He is our Father we are all the workmanship of his hands. Do I believe God my God, my father that he loves me? He has made my neighbours also why Shall I be more beloved. Do you think your neighbour a great sinner? who has made thee[112] thy neighbours jury? What was God's answer to Elijah when complaining of the licentiousness of his people "I have reserved me seven thousand who have not bowed the knee to Baal."[113] Can you say God has reserved no Good principle in your neighbour? Has he become entirely reprobate? Do you know his heart? Man not God who is love nourishes[114] much good in his heart though unseen by us? And again can you pronounce[115] definitively of any man's character[116] that it is certainly bad and flows from a depraved heart—known to you are all the arcana of futurity, can you fully determine the result of every act, know you all the consequences that will follow so that you can unhesitatingly say this man is a reprobate, he is possessed of no good principle he[117] can do no commendable act? Admitting all this I would address you in the words of our Lord. "Let him that is without sin cast the first stone."[118] We will know the misery that arises from the inveteracy of our conduct and the implacability of our desposition. When the apostles would have called down fire from heaven upon some they judged their foes what was Christ's reproof? "Ye know not what spirit ye are of."[119] In receiving the cruelties that the Jews were about to[120] inflict on his person what were the feelings he exhibited? he looked upon the city and O Jerusalem & may we go and do likewise.

There the wicked cease from troubling and the weary are at rest.[121]

Many are the sorrows of the human family. Man seems born unto trouble, his days appear vanity and full of evil. For a moment let us take a view of the character that uttered the saying we have chosen for the subject of our remarks. Tho apparently prosperous during the first part of his life. Though introduced to our notices as excelling all the east in the vastness of his possessions. How soon do we find him suffering under the sorest affliction. Stript of everything, reduced to indigence, vexed by the foolish counsel of his wife and tormented with the wretched arguments and consolations of his unfeeling friends. Conscious of the rectitude of his mind, he endeavoured to maintain his integrity nor suffered himself to charge God foolishly! He knew he had paid his vows daily that the widow and orphan had no claim unsatisfied. He knew he feared God and refrained from evil. Why then were his days swifter than a weaver's shuttle and spent without hope? My soul is weary of life. "Oh that thou wouldst hide me in the grave that thou wouldst keep me in secret. Well might he inquire. Why died I not from the womb? Why did I not give up the ghost. Poor man he had known prosperity it now was gone. Once had known friends but now they cannot console him; his children are gone! his health is turned into painful disease, his days are consumed in grief his nights are wasted in anxious dreams, he[122] drew near the grave, he felt anxious to lie down with kings and counsellors of the earth, where the wicked cease from troubling and the weary are at rest. There the prisoners rest together; they hear not the voice of the oppressor. The small and great are there and the servant is free from his master. Whatever were the views of Job in uttering our text, we shall draw from it consolation for all the miseries of life. My Brother, or my sister! Do you see the wicked prosper, does he flourish like a green bay tree? do you feel the pressure of misfortune? the grave is the grand leveler of distinctions, there the wicked cease from troubling and the weary are at[123] rest. Has prosperity flown by the injustice of others? Have your friends forsaken you or sleep they in the dust, have you surrounded the death-bed of your parents or your children? Is your life burdensome through incessant care, does your soul draw near to the grave, remember there the wicked cease from troubling & the weary are at rest. Suffer you now the lofty frowns of the ignobly great. Does your heart bleed beneath the cruelty of tyrants—feel you the scourging lash of madening despots. The great and the small are there and the servant is free from his master. There the wicked cease from troubling and the weary are at rest. The grave knows no distinction all rest alike within her silent walls, the rich and the poor lie down together. The king and his subject, the prince and the peasant are there. There prisoner rests, there the inhabitants of ever clime meet in peaceful slumbers. There they lie forgotten by the living, but they complain not, no discordant sound disturbs their tranquil sleep. no vain wrangling no envyings, no bitter rage no one fears lest his right should lie trampled upon, no one bids his fellow not come near him lest his mouldering dust should be polluted. None appear anxious who shall wear the ensign of superiority. They are mute yet how they mock our vain strivings our[124] about superiority, our pride of self distinction, our anxious care about the insignia of empty titles, our incessant toil to heap up stores of shining dust.

There are the "princes that had gold who filled their houses with silver."[125]

But there is another view I would take of this subject. There the wicked cease from troubling and the weary are at rest. Raise your thoughts my brother! Do you consider earth a tiresome place, are you sickened with misfortune and bowed down with grief, does your heart bleed at the calamities of others. See you "the lone widow pine in starving solitude" the helpless orphan fall in the street, does the heart of man grow obdurate with no feeling for his fellow man. Remember Christ has gone to prepare a place for us where wicked ceased from troubling and the weary are at rest. There will be joys for evermore. There will be no sorrow, no sin, no pain, no sickness, no death. The Lord God will be there. The light of his countenance will be our sun and the song of Moses and the Lamb our divine[126]. There will be no night, there no Eclipse of Divine light, no eye hath seen, ear hath not heard, nor hath it entered into the heart of man to conceive what is laid up for us where the wicked cease from troubling and the weary are at rest. Complain no more my brother! of the miseries of life! Tho we suffer a momentary affliction let reason's hand brush away the intervening clouds & disclose the unsullied light that will soon arise to shine thro endless day. Tremble not when you convey the bodies of friends to the silent tomb. Suppress the rising tears as the clods of the valley hide from your sight, what was once so beautiful what once shot forth so many peculiar graces, for there the wicked cease from troubling and the weary are at rest. Yet do not indulge as tho' there they unconscious lie but fled are they to the right hand of God where are joys forevermore. . . .

ECCL. 12.1[127]

"Remember now thy Creator in the days of thy youth, while the evil days come not, nor the years draw not nigh, when thou shalt say I have no pleasure in them."

Among the many admonitions of the Wise King of Jerusalem I know of none which evinces his wisdom than the passage we have just quoted.[128] How much soever the proud son of earth may scoff at the idea of regarding God experience has fully demonstrated the insufficiency of all terrestrial bliss to afford real satisfaction to the soul of one individual. All below the sun is fleeting scarcely tasted ere they are gone. Today we see man surrounded by prosperity, he basks in the smiles of fortune, adversity appears far from his dwelling, but even in this calm here the storm may be fomenting, the bolt may be riven that shall lay all prospects in the dust! Had he no hope beyond the reach of misfortune's blast? had he no treasure beyond the reach of thieves? and corruption? If not where is his consolation? Where shall he find support in this trying hour? Lover and friend may be put far from him and his acquaintance into darkness! In his youth worldly prosperity was all he sought. He neglected the culture of the mind, the cultivation[129] of moral & virtuous feelings. He must now sink under the weight of his calamity. This the wise man had seen but all in his was "vanity of vanities." Aware of the many vicissitudes of life the many calamities incident to vain mortals he admonishes youth of their approach and by considerations the most tender & affecting exhorts them to "Remember their creator while the evil days are far away." While they enjoy the light of heaven, they should remember its authour.

There is no sentiment so important, none I wish to impress more indelibly upon the minds of my youthful friends than the one under consideration. I would call upon them to survey the magnificent scenery around, observe the beauty which decks the field, the rich yield for your gratification, mark the sun that rolls over your heads—an image of your creator. Life, beauty & vigour he dispenses to creation. The grateful showers descend to cheer the thirsty land. All round behold a scene of gaiety delight. God your Creator does this! Are you happy in the arms of your parents, in the softening embrace of friends. God is the Author of every parental feeling of every sentiment of friendship. But another view I wish you to take. The wise in the sunshine prepares for a storm, he does not wait till some unforeseen calamity overwhelms him. But knowing that being prepared for an evil that comes he is in no fear but can look with calm and unruffled countenance upon all transpiring events. What my young friends can yield you confidence in the hour of adversity? It is said thou will keep him in perfect peace, O God! whose mind is staid on thee! Remember then O beloved youth thy creator while years draw not nigh when thou shalt say I have no pleasure in them. He will cause light to shine in darkness and cheer all thy lonely paths.

Another reason why you should Remember your Creator in thy youth is the salutary influence it has upon the mind and sentiments it implants. Accustomed to reflect on the ways of your Creator while young, remembering all things transpire agreeable to his will, you have a salva for whatever may come. You are thus led to cultivate the mind, to acquire[130] correct ideas. you thus learn to weigh the intrinsick value of things. You become acquainted with yourself and never place dependence on what you are well aware will leave you in the time of your greatest need. God is a sure refuge, a munition of rock, a place of defence. the youth who has remembered his creator has a place to flee from the approaching storm when evil is in view, he can flee from danger to a strong hold where no evil shall befall him.

What a pleasing influence this remembrance must have upon every one who has the least degree of sensibility. Can you my young friends contemplate the amiable character of your Creator and feel no emotions of love and sensibility rise in your bossoms to the author of all good. Filled with[131] these pious emotions, will you not be led in the path of virtue, will you not pursue a course of benevolent action towards your fellow creatures, like God seek their good, like him be complacent and forgiving? and thus have a sure support when the transitory object of an hour shall have passed away and we no longer find any satisfaction in the vain glitter which now amuses the gay and thoughtless. Be assured my friends the day draws nigh when one[132] can no longer dress the most insignificant toys in fascinating colours. The time will come when we must depend entirely for pleasure on the fund already acquired. The time will come when you must sink into yourselves and draw all your happiness from the acquisitions of your own mind. If they are vacant or tortured with guilt, great indeed will be your misery. Wisdom would therefore dictate to lay up a fund of knowledge to "Remember Our Creator in youth while the evil days come not nor the years draw nigh when thou shalt say I have no pleasure in them. . . ."

Notes: Spiritual Diary

1. 1822
2. *unnumbered* for "unumbered" in original
3. January 10, 1823
4. word indecipherable
5. word indecipherable
6. word indecipherable
7. January 11, 1823
8. *heathen* for "heathe" in original
9. word indecipherable

10. "in" inserted
11. January 12, 1823
12. *salvation* for "salarvation" in original
13. January 13, 1823
14. word indecipherable
15. January 16, 1823
16. "thou" and question mark inserted
17. period inserted
18. "I" inserted
19. January 17, 1823
20. an additional "in" deleted from original
21. January 18, 1823
22. January 19, 1823
23. word indecipherable
24. word indecipherable
25. "How sad the above!" is written in a different hand, perhaps Henry Brownson's.
26. January 20, 1823
27. January 28, 1823
28. *in* for "or" in original
29. word indecipherable
30. *balance* for "ballance" in original
31. *know* for "no" in original
32. "to" inserted
33. word indecipherable
34. "to be" inserted
35. "of" inserted
36. word indecipherable
37. pages 23 to 26 in original missing
38. 1823
39. 1823
40. *thought* for "though" in original
41. February 9, 1823
42. word indecipherable
43. *its* for "it" in original
44. *frightened* for "fright" in original
45. February 10, 1823
46. George Burder (1752–1832), *Closet Companion, Or a Help to Serious Persons in the Important Duty of Self Examination* (Boston, 1808). Burder was a Congregationalist English minister who supported old side Calvinist theology. On Burder, see Wil-

liam Gilmore, "Orestes Brownson and New England Religious Culture, 1803–27," Ph.D. diss., University of Virginia, 1970, p. 351ff.

47. February 12, 1823
48. Rom 7:19, 24–25
49. February 22, 1823
50. February 23, 1823
51. "from" inserted
52. February 26, 1823
53. "of" inserted
54. word indecipherable
55. Thursday, February 27, 1823
56. Friday, February 28, 1823
57. *discourse* for "discours" in original; "I" inserted
58. *self-existent* for "selfexisten" in original; *created* for "creat" in original
59. "that I would" inserted
60. *manifestation* for "manifestans" in original
61. "it" inserted
62. 1823
63. Reuben Smith, Brownson's Presbyterian pastor
64. *there* for "the" in original
65. *too* for "to" in original
66. Latin idiom for something illusory or unreal. Reference seems to be to a light seen at night moving over swamps, believed to be caused by the combustion of gases arising from rotting organic matter.
67. Latin for "Wonderful to relate."
68. May 12, 1823
69. word indecipherable
70. 1823
71. Matthew Mead (1630?–99), *The Almost Christian Discovered; or the False Professor Tried and Cast* (London, 1661), was a dissenting English Congregationalist minister who was a strict Calvinist. On Mead see, *DNB* and Gilmore, pp. 185–86.
72. "may" inserted
73. *seeks* for "seek" in original; "to" inserted
74. "raise" inserted; *its* for "it" in original
75. Hazeal (c. 842–806 B.C.), King of Damascus
76. *seemed* for "seem" in original
77. 2 Kgs 8:13
78. 2 Kgs 10:32

79. May 25, 1823
80. *fainting* for "faiting" in original
81. word indecipherable
82. "with" inserted
83. "preacher" inserted
84. July 30, 1823. By this date Brownson had already left the Presbyterian church. On page 84 of the original manuscript he noted critically the "baneful effect" of Calvinist and Arminian religious quarrels.
85. word indecipherable
86. *superior* for "superious" in original
87. 1823
88. At this point in the diary, there appears to be a gap of a year or more when Brownson made no entries. The chronological order of his diary is also extremely confusing prior to this entry. Entries from August of 1825 are followed by one from April of 1823 and another from August 19, 1825.
89. "you" inserted
90. *woes* for "wo" in original
91. 1825
92. *offenses* for "offenceness" in original
93. The previous three entries were from July and August of 1825. This July 1825 entry appears in the same chronological order it has in the original.
94. *conversant* for "converant" in original
95. *readily* for "readly" in original
96. Bad Latin, to say the least. Roughly translated: "Love is the Universalists I believe God is. Truth is the son of God." I believe he is trying to articulate his Universalist creed here.
97. *aberration* for "aberation" in original
98. *away* for "awaway" in original
99. The following entries appear to be sermons and drafts of articles that Brownson was preparing while at Balston Spa, New York, in the summer of 1825. Some of them, however, may come from his latter Universalist period.
100. Lk 2:10
101. Is 61:1
102. Is 42:4
103. 1 Jn 4:9
104. *favor* for "faviou" in original
105. "we" inserted
106. "is" and "upon" inserted

107. "of" inserted
108. "you" inserted
109. *offensiveness* for "offenceness" in original
110. Mt 5:23–24
111. *compassion* for "compacency" in original
112. "thee" inserted
113. 1 Kgs 19:18
114. *nourishes* for "nourish" in original
115. "you" inserted; *pronounce* for "pronounced" in original
116. *character* for "charter" in original
117. "is" after "he" deleted from original
118. Jn 8:7
119. Lk 9:52
120. "to" inserted
121. This appears to be another sermon on Job 3:17.
122. *he* for "his" in original
123. "at" inserted
124. word indecipherable
125. Job 3:15
126. word indecipherable
127. This appears to be the beginning of a new sermon prepared for young people.
128. "quoted" inserted
129. "cultivation" inserted
130. *acquire* for "aquire" in original
131. "with" inserted
132. *draws* for "draw" in original; "one" inserted

II.

UNIVERSALIST PERIOD:
1823–29

3. THE INFLUENCE OF RELIGION ON PROSPERITY

SOURCE: *The Christian Repository* 7 (August 1826): 47–58.

The following is the first of Brownson's many publications. He was twenty-three when he preached this sermon. He argues that genuine religion is manifested in a harmonious inner life in times of prosperity as well as in times of adversity.

Psalms i.3.—*He shall be like a tree planted by the rivers of water, that bringeth forth his fruit in his season; his leaf also shall not wither; and whatsoever he doeth shall prosper.*

The kindly influence of religion on the heart and condition of man has, by most men, in all countries, and in all ages of the world, been received and generally acknowledged. But she has been chiefly confined to the *shades* of life. Mankind are willing to receive her as a *comforter*—to call in her assistance on any occasion of deep distress, or when suffering under some great and unexpected calamity. But it is not only in the dark and adverse parts of a man's life that religion is useful, she is no less salutary in the hour of prosperity, than in the day of adversity.

Those who would confine her influence to the gloom of disappointment or the melancholy of old age, greatly mistake her nature. She is indeed useful in such seasons, and without her assistance, we should find it extremely difficult to bear up against the many painful sensations, that then unite to overwhelm us. But to those who are acquainted with her character—to those, whose hearts have felt her warm invigorating touch, she will ever be a welcome companion. They will seek her when the sun is clouded—wish her to cheer the evening of life; but will wish her no less—will find her powers no weaker, in the morning of prosperity.

And then she puts on her lovelier charms and appears in her more engaging dress. Imagination cannot present a more pleasing object than the youth animated by the pure emotions of genuine religion—than the man smiling with prosperity, obedient to her calls and faithful in the discharge of her offices. "He is like a tree planted by the rivers of water, that bringeth forth his fruit in his season; his leaf also shall not wither, and whatsoever he doeth shall prosper."

A more lively and beautiful figure, to represent his prosperity, could not have been selected from the whole compass of nature, than the one chosen by the Psalmist in our text. A tree is an object of beauty. Few things in nature can awaken more pleasing emotions in the bosom. To see one stand on a barren heath with short and shrubbed branches and withered leaves is, I confess, calculated to depress our feelings, and overwhelm us with melancholy reflections. But to see one growing beside the running stream, that moistens its roots and replenishes the soil—to behold it bearing its "fruit in its season," giving fragrance, beauty and shade to the surrounding scenery, will fill with admiration every lover of nature. Add the evergreen leaf with the assurance it "shall not wither," and you have a picture on which you may gaze with emotions of delight and tranquility.

To point out the man that is likened unto *this tree,* and show the increase of his prosperity, is the design of what follows.

The Psalmist has assisted us in the first part of this inquiry. He begins by informing us he is blessed; "Blessed is the man that walketh not in the counsel of the ungodly, nor standeth in the way of sinners, nor sitteth in the seat of the scornful. But his delight is in the law of the Lord, and in his law doth he meditate day and night." Such a one, we are informed in our text, "shall be like a tree planted by the rivers of water," etc.—He is one then, we may say, who has withdrawn himself from ungodliness—has not mingled with the vicious multitude, nor joined with scoffers—one who studies the law of God, carefully inquires his duty, cultivates the warm and generous emotions of religion, feels them in his heart, and acknowledges them in his conduct; one we may suppose who has enlarged his mind, expanded his heart with benevolence, learned "to do justly, to love mercy, and to walk humbly with his God"; one whose hands are clean, whose intentions pure, whose conscience void of offence, who listens with interest to the calls of humanity, commiserates the calamities of his brethren, studies to remove the load of common misery, and to enable all to smile beneath the gracious bounty of our heavenly Father.

He is one who has subdued his desires for unlawful pleasures, weaned his affections from things of this world, and placed them on things above.[1] One who puts his trust in his God, rests all his hopes of happiness on the will of his Father, pays his early vows in the sanctuary, rejoices to come before the Lord, and bow himself before the high God. And, to sum up his character in a word, he is one who avoids vice and vicious companions, loves virtue, reverences religion, and is kind, generous and humane in all his intercourse with his brethren. Such is the man who is religious—such is the man that shall stand beside *the rivers of water,* yield his *fruit in his season,* whose *leaf also shall not wither, and whatsoever he doeth shall prosper.*

Let us then turn to consider the increase of his prosperity, and to show in what manner he is more prosperous than the *irreligious or bad man.*

1. *Prosperity is increased to him because religion has prepared his mind for enjoyment.* If we look into the heart of the bad man, we shall find it filled with a multitude of rough and discordant principles, which are continually raging and opposing each other. We shall see inordinate love of wealth, unreasonable ambition for greatness, a burning thirst for unlawful pleasures and sensual gratification. These are increased by appetite, strengthened by indulgence, and confirmed by habit. Their demands are loud and imperious. Their objects different, and often contradictory. The man is compelled to follow each, which must be done at the expense of its rival. Thus it happens, the satisfaction gained by the gratification of one favorite passion, is generally lost in the disappointment it occasions another. A thousand desires are constantly springing in his bosom, so equally balanced in their weight, so nearly powerful in their strength, that he no sooner decides to follow one, than his purpose is shaken, and he is drawn back by another. Hence he lives in constant turmoil and perplexity. Hence his mind in a state of perpetual fluctuation, hangs vacillating between these imperious masters; all which he wishes to obey, but their variety and discordance is such, that he seldom yields obedience to any. Or grant some one, more powerful than the rest, has gained the ascendency, and reduced the others to submission—a thousand obstacles intervene, which delay or embitter its gratification.

We grant the man wealth; we grant his external condition may appear flourishing; his houses and lands may increase; his fields yield the plenteous harvest. But something is wanting still to complete that plenitude of felicity he desires. His mind, yea his heart has become attached to his possessions. A mean, sordid, avaricious disposition, ever characteristic of wealth, renders him incapable of happiness, deadens all the finer feelings, cools all the warm emotions of the heart, closes all the small springs of pleasure, which excite and spread joy and delight through the bosom of the good man.

Or is he bent on worldly pleasure? Every lisp of censure carries dejection to his soul, and fills him with the most painful sensations. But the good man having subdued these vain desires, hears unmoved the praise or scorn of the world. Conscious of the rectitude of his own heart, and the purity of his intentions, all *within* is calm, and heaven will take care of that which is *without.*

Still further, the bad man has a never-failing source of uneasiness and deep regret in the improper means he has used to gratify his appetites and passions. The cries of the injured orphan, the complaints of the oppressed widow, haunt his sleeping and waking hours! Bleeding innocence torn from the bosom of her parents, from the society of her friends, rifled of her charms, ruined, left bleaching in the tempest of fortune, strikes daggers to his soul! Conscience tells him his guilt is great—his condemnation is sealed. Trembling at the account she reads, horror presents him before the bar of his God. His own heart condemns him—God is greater than his heart! Struck aghast at the picture, sleep becomes a stranger, "food insipid, society wearisome, pleasure disgusting, and life itself a cruel bitter."

But the good man having ever aimed well, trusts the mercy of his God for the pardon of those offences which through the weakness of his nature he may have committed. His past life brings to his mind no instance of cruelty or deception; no enormous crime or act of injustice. He delights to call up the hours that have gone by. He can view them with a placid serenity. He looks around on the present with pleasing tranquility, and forward with confidence and hope.

2. *Prosperity is increased to a good man because he is free from all the terrifying apprehensions of unseen calamities and impending ruin.* The bad man has no source of happiness but the world. All his dependence is placed on the good of fortune; his wealth, his pleasures, his family, or friends. Little experience is sufficient to convince those of the least discernment that these are not durable goods. "Riches take to themselves wings and fly away." The elements often burst their rage with resistless fury, in one movement hurl with them the labors of years, and leave him destitute.

Fame's shrill clarion may sound his achievements, proclaim the multitude of his friends and pleasures; competition may slink to the caverns of envy, and slander to the shades of night. Yet the sun of prosperity will grow weary of gilding the habitation of uninterrupted repose; the clouds of sorrow will arise, the tempest of adversity gather round, and the thunder of disappointment burst upon him. His friends will leave him, his name be enrolled on the black list of infamy, or crowded away with the thousands that are,—die and are forgotten!

These are ordinary occurrences. These fill his mind with dreadful apprehensions, and the most gloomy forebodings. In the absence of *real,* he adopts *imaginary* ills, and mourns over anticipated woe, as tho he actually felt its direful hand. But the good man having cultivated his mind, acquired habits of virtue, has a source of happiness independent of his external condition. He has a fund within himself—a permanent fund, whence he can continually draw fresh pleasures. He has learned all sublunary things are evanescent. He expects they will leave him. He guards against their flight; but prepares himself to meet, unmoved, the shock. But should they leave him, he is not destitute; his peace of mind remains. That rests on the rectitude of his heart, the purity of his intentions, the consciousness that he has ever discharged his duty, and been faithful over those things which were placed under his care.

This source of happiness no change of fortune can destroy. It remains the same whether she smiles or frowns, and this being the source of his greatest and chief happiness, he can dread no attack from without, fear no approaching calamity or impending ruin. He trusts in his God. "He shall hide him in his pavilion, in the secret of his tabernacle shall he hide him, he shall place him upon a rock." Hence, secure from all imaginary ills, from all forebodings of future woe, he can enjoy his prosperity with cheerfulness and tranquility.

3. *But prosperity is still farther increased to the good man by the generous manner in which he uses it.* Reason and religion both assert the fact that every thing is good and proper when properly used; that the only evil there is in any thing is the improper manner in which it may be used. Hence the bad man by the improper use he makes of his prosperity, converts it into adversity. He allows it to corrupt his temper, debase his mind, produce a feverish and sickly appetite, enervate the nobler faculties of his soul, harden his heart, blind his eyes and deafen his ears to the complaints, sufferings and wretched condition of those around him; to generate that frame of mind which becomes confident of its own importance and superiority; proud and haughty looks, with contempt on others, and secures their hatred and detestation. He hears no one proclaim his benedictions; sees no one happy through his munificence; has no consoling reflection that he has stud-

ied to lighten the load of common misery; receives the kind embrace of no worthy, virtuous and affectionate friend. The behavior of all with whom he associates is characterised by cold civility, or disgusting obsequiousness. Hence he languishes in the midst of his studied refinements and vast possessions, envied and envying, unloving and unbeloved.

But on the other hand, mark the good man. Religion has softened his heart, rendered him feelingly alive to the wants and distresses of others. He has not possessed wealth for himself alone, he has made it a common blessing. He has compassionated the sufferings of the wretched; his presence has gladdened the lonely cottage; his bounty rescued the hungry soul from death. He sees a happy land smiling with content, made so by his benefactions. The blessing has returned upon his own head; and the secret delight of benevolence and gratitude has fully demonstrated the fact, "it is more blessed to give than to receive!" He can adopt the language of the once prosperous Job: "When the ear heard me then it blessed me; and when the eye saw me it gave witness to me; because I delivered the poor that cried, and the fatherless and him that had none to help him. The blessing of him that was ready to perish came upon me, and I caused the widows' heart to sing for joy. I put on righteousness and it clothed me; my judgment was as a robe and a diamond. I was eyes to the blind, and feet was I to the lame. I was a father to the poor; and the cause which I knew not I searched out. My root was spread out by the waters, and the dew lay all night upon my branch. My glory was fresh within me, and my bow was renewed in my hand."

4. But lastly, *prosperity is increased to the good man from the happy prospect he has in his children.* The greatest and chief concern of a man's life is his children. To provide for them, to see them walk in the paths of usefulness, fill places of honor and respectability, constitutes a large proportion of the felicity allotted his pilgrimage journey of life. While the bad man has been engrossed in the cares of the world, neglecting the education of his children, vainly thinking to ensure their felicity by worldly splendor, the good man has been faithfully cultivating the minds of his children, suppressing their evil propensities, drawing out the latent virtues of their nature, and with "pious care," endeavored to form them to all that is truly great or good in man. While the bad man has the mortification to see his children grow up with all their natural propensities, unrestrained appetites and passions strengthened by his own indulgence and confirmed by his own practices; while he sees them plunge into excess, sink in the vortex of

dissipation, rove in the labyrinths of folly and inconsistency, or fall before the tribunals of justice, the good man sees his grow up in the ways of virtue, walk the paths of wisdom, sing in the bowers of understanding, or ramble over the flowery lawns of religion; sees them shine with lovely graces, endeared by a peculiar sweetness of temper to their parents, attracting the esteem of their acquaintance and the friendship of all who know them. Early impressed with filial piety, they remember him, and do not forsake him in his old age; but study to make his decline of life smooth and easy. Hence "his leaf also shall not wither." He sees his children green, they do not wither away with evil or vicious companions; dissipation does not blast their verdure; and even the storms of the winter of life cannot destroy their freshness. They bud in his bosom in this terrestrial soil, but they shall bloom with unfading glory in the bosom of his heavenly Father in the regions above. Hence the influence of religion on prosperity, hence the superiority of the good man over the bad; a mind free from perturbation, guilt, or remorse, firmly relying on his God, believing his pardon sufficient for the past, praising for the present, and trusting him for the future—a heart susceptible of the highest felicity rendered supremely happy in himself in the love and gratitude of others in the good conduct and bright and brightening prospects of his children. "His wife is a fruitful vine by the sides of his house, his children like olive plants round about his table."

Such is the influence of religion on the prosperous, and such I presume is the desire of each of my respected auditors. Cultivate then, suffer me to entreat you, the benevolent affections of the heart, acquire habits of virtue, place your dependence on God, keep his commandments, retreat from vice and the company of the ungodly, and this prosperity shall be yours; you "shall be like trees planted beside the rivers of water, that bear their fruit in their season, and whatsoever you do shall prosper."

Note: The Influence of Religion on Prosperity

1. When Brownson republished this essay in 1829, he made the following editorial comments on this passage: "The expression, this world should be restricted to the vain things of the Jewish age, or if applied at the day, to the pleasures of sense, in opposition to those above, or to the more noble things of the Gospel, which is righteousness." See *Gospel Advocate and Impartial Investigator* 7 (September 19, 1829): p. 292.

4. REMARKS ON UNIVERSALISM

SOURCE: *The Gospel Advocate and Impartial Investigator* 6 (January 5, 1828): 6–7.

Brownson supports the doctrine of universal salvation because it is easily reconciled with God's character and because it conforms to the Christian morality of forgiveness. Endless punishment is an absurd doctrine because it contradicts the nature of a merciful and loving God. The Universalist teaching upholds true piety and morality.

The sentiment named in the caption of this article is one that presents itself to the benevolent mind as truly desirable. Even the most depraved in principle and the most abandoned in morals must in every moment of sober reflection devoutly pray for its truth.

The believers in endless misery may endeavour to reconcile themselves to the awfulness of their creed, and the partiality of their God, but every time they mingle their sympathies with their friends around the bed of the dying and the dead, they must wish, anxiously wish, that their faith is ill founded and the horrid doom they had anticipated for their fellow creatures exists only in imagination.

While on the other hand the believer in a full salvation, in the like situation, clasps his faith the firmer, and prays the more fervently it may not prove false. His faith also reconciles him to the character of his God. Disappointments and distress do not cause him to murmur against his heavenly Father because he views them as necessary in the chain of Divine Providence to serve the purposes of salutary discipline—to prepare him for the reception of a purer and more permanent enjoyment.

Death to the universalist has lost half its terrour. To him it does not appear "an eternal sleep" nor the gate of endless woe, but the door through which he must pass to enter the mansion of his Father, the apartment of his felicity. He who believes that death opens to a scene of inconceivable pain for the greatest part of mankind, must have a very exalted opinion of his own goodness or he will have some doubts respecting his own security.

The direct tendency of universalism is to prompt an ardent piety to God and a benevolent course of conduct to mankind. This system is the only one ever published that does not limit the Almighty. Arminianism may allow God to have *goodness* for it says he desires the salvation of all men, but it must limit his wisdom or his power, or else it would admit this desire would be satisfied. Calvinism indeed allows

Jehovah infinite *power* and infinite *wisdom,* for it declares God can do whatever he wills, but represents the Deity deficient in goodness, or else it would say he willed the happiness of all his children. Universalism supplies the defects of both by allowing with the Arminian that Deity desires or wills the salvation of all men, and with the Calvinist that he has power and wisdom to perform whatever he desires or wills should take place.

The God of the universalist is just such a being as every rational man must love. Indeed all that is required to make every one love him is to teach him his true character. He is represented as the fountain of all excellence, as being good unto all, having a tender regard for the welfare of his children, and as taking efficient measures to produce the happiness of his sentient creation. In a word it represents him just such a being, as such poor weak erring creatures as we, all need for our Father, our Friend and our Benefactor.

Universalism lays the foundation for the most extensive usefulness from man to man. It represents all as members of one family bound to each other by the ties of fraternal affection. A partial doctrine or one that supposes only a few of this vast family are regarded by their heavenly Father might lead its admirers to suppose they were under no obligation to love or do good to any more than they imagined belonged to the favoured class. Universalism by rejecting this distinction, by teaching all men are beloved by God, says in very clear language to its followers, "ever follow that which is good with all men." The command to be godlike rests with due weight upon his heart and he finds it impossible to contract his charity to those of his own way of thinking or to confine his benefactions to those of his own particular sect.

God disregards all distinctions of this kind. His sun shines as gloriously, to light the *heretick* as the orthodox, and his showers distil their grateful influence alike over the fields of all parties and "I do not" says the universalist, "discover that God has shown any preference to the persons embracing one creed more than to those embracing another, and why should I? He has commanded me to be like him and to obey the command I must love all men alike, do good to all as I have opportunity."

Universalism is the only system that has ever been preached which properly enforces the duty of forgiving our enemies. The highest point of perfection in any system of religion is to be like the God that system admits. Now a doctrine which teaches that God does not forgive his enemies but will punish them eternally, must not pretend to command its disciples to forgive their enemies, for if they should they would become more forgiving than their God. But universalism

teaches God forgives his enemies, and therefore the command has a
binding tie upon the consciences of those who believe forgiveness is a
characteristick of their God.

These are some of the recommendations with which universalism
presents itself to mortals desirous of truth, and these alone, it is
thought, are sufficient to ensure it a cordial reception by all sober and
reflecting minds. Many objections are indeed raised against this
heaven-born system, but they are neither so many nor so weighty as
they were in the days of Christ and his apostles. Ignorance has so long
ruled in matters of religion, superstition so long reigned over the consciences of men, that multitudes are afraid to embrace the sentiment,
because they think it so good, and so desirable that it cannot be true.
But the sentiment spreads and through the good providence of God we
believe it will continue rapidly to increase.

Man is a rational being and when he recovers the exercise of his
intellectual powers he will bid adieu to those systems which originated
in ignorance and have been perpetuated by fraud or tradition; he will
then embrace enlarged and liberal views, he will consider Jehovah the
Father of mankind, and mankind as brethren, he will then love with
all his heart the Father, and love with all his faculties the children.

5. THE FAITH AND CHARACTER
OF THE TRUE CHRISTIAN

SOURCE: *Gospel Advocate and Impartial Investigator* 6 (April 12,
1828): 113–17.

*Brownson preached the following sermon before the First Univer-
salist Society in Ithaca, New York, on the first Sunday of February
1828. He argued that nothing in Christianity is contrary to natural
religion and presented Christianity as a system of morality. Moral
activity has a priority over mere belief and faith has value because it
leads to benevolent activity.*

And the disciples were first called Christians at Antioch: Acts
xi. 26.

In the earliest records of mankind, religion holds a prominent
rank. It was so early in its adoption, and so general in its extension,
that many have pronounced man naturally a religious being. Some,
rejecting this hypothesis, contend that religion owes its origin to reve-

lation from God, made to man during a state of innocency, which has been perpetuated through successive generations, and extended to different nations by the aid of tradition and the dispersion of mankind.

Others again, resort to reflection and experience, and conclude that man first obtained the idea of a God, and the utility of worshipping him, from reasoning upon his works, and duly considering the nature and variety of the circumstances of their condition. In support of this it is remarked, that in the infancy of our knowledge, our religious ideas were vague and unintelligible and our practices absurd and often pernicious; but as knowledge increased, as the laws of nature became better and more satisfactorily developed, our ideas of God and his worship became more rational and more salutary in their influence on the morals of society.

But whether mankind first imbibed the idea, that religion was necessary, from instinct, from revelation, or reflection, this much is certain—they have made but little proficiency in this most interesting science, without the extraordinary influences of the Spirit of the Most High.

Few, since the age of history, have denied the utility of some kind of religion; but alas! it cannot be concealed, that this offspring of love, designed to cheer our gloomy path and smooth the asperities of the road of life, has too often been degraded from the dignity of her station, and prevented from executing the benevolent office with which she was entrusted. She has too often been compelled to second the schemes of the amibitious, and cover with her sacred garb the insiduous designs of those who wished to aggrandize themselves or their party by the depression of the rest. And even amid the knowledge and refinements of the present age, this heavenly messenger has been obliged to lend her name to sanction the ravings of fanaticism, the effervescence of passion, the zeal and enthusiasm of sectarian ambition. But we are permitted to hope that the time has nearly arrived when she will assert her dignity, and extend to all that kind assistance which she is empowered to give.

A little short of two thousand years ago, there appeared a personage, who, by his example and precepts, and the subsequent preaching of his disciples, has made the most important revolution in the opinions and practices of mankind, ever before known, or ever hereafter to be expected.

Previous to his appearance, men had made many valuable discoveries, and many useful improvements. The Jews had taught the unity of the Deity in a clear and conspicuous manner. The attributes of Jehovah were, in a good degree, rationally explained; the immortality of the soul, or the resurrection from the dead, had been suggested and believed by some; a retributive providence, founded on man's accountability, had been defended; moral philosophy in the pagan school had been closely and successfully studied;—but the great mass of mankind were deeply sunk in ignorance and superstition. A fashionable atheism was in high repute in many places, riot and obscenity disgraced the temples of the Gods in almost every instance. While those who held a more rational religion, degraded it by their mean sophisms, by their superstitious attachment to the minor parts of religious worship, and unwarrantably passing over the more important and more benevolent duties.

Something was requisite to correct the abuses every where prevalent—to give additional light to the religious world, and to religion itself a more imperial sanction, that it might rest upon a more permanent basis, be more extended in its authority, and more benevolent in its influence. To effect this was the end the great Founder of our religion proposed to himself, and to this desirable object he adapted his preaching. Success attended his labours; but amid the convulsions of the church and government of the distracted and unhappy people of the Jews, where he made his first appearance, he found the most severe opposition—the most virulent persecution—was accused of blasphemy against God, and of conspiring against the Roman Government to which they were subject—was insulted with a mock trial, and finally perished upon the cross.

But his miracles, together with the purity of his life, the benevolence of his character, the excellency of his doctrinal and moral precepts, the dignity and sublimity of his preaching, had collected a number of disciples, who became confirmed in what he had taught them, by his now appearing to them risen from the grave. They joyfully embraced his doctrine; and animated by the cheering influence of the Holy Spirit which they received from heaven, they began to proclaim the resurrection of their so lately crucified master, and to enforce what he had directed them to teach. Churches or congregations of believers were collected in several places, as in Jerusalem, Samaria, Antioch, and others. As the religion they taught was different from all others, it became necessary that it should be distinguished by some name. While they were but few the term disciple, among themselves, answered every purpose of designation; but increased in numbers, and beginning to have an extensive intercourse with the rest of the world, a name more specifick in its import was required. Hence, at Antioch, they took the appellation of their Master Christ; "and the disciples were called Christians first at Antioch."

In after times they have been distinguished by other appellatives, such as Catholicks—believers in one universal church under one visible head; Episcopalians—or those who contend for the regular succession of bishops and the hierarchial government; Congregationalists or Independents—such as maintain the sovereignty of each separate congregation; Unitarians—those who strenuously contend for the unity of God, and the subordination of the Son; Universalists—those who maintain that all mankind will be raised to a state of progressive holiness and happiness; and various other names designed to express some peculiarity in faith or practice. But with these we have no concern at present; it being our object to point out the true Christian, and delineate his character.

It may be asserted without adducing any proof, because all will admit it, that the true Christian is a disciple of Christ. A disciple is a scholar, or one who learns. The disciple of Christ is one who learns of Christ—believes what Christ taught, and practices the duties he enjoined. What Christ taught and enjoined, is the religion of Christ or Christianity; an examination of this will enable us to ascertain the character of the true Christian.

All systems of religion resolve themselves into two parts, theoretical and practical.

With regard to the theory of the Christian religion, there is much difficulty, and perhaps some uncertainty; which unhappily have given rise to many painful contentious and aggravated controversies that have ended in the separation of brethren. The occasion of this difficulty is found chiefly in the fact that almost every man commences the study of the doctrine with preconceived ideas, which it becomes his main object to defend. We generally have determined in our minds what Christ *ought* to teach, before we come to him for instruction, and his words must be turned to speak our own sentiments, which indeed would be correct if we were masters, but since we profess to be his disciples, we ought to shape our opinions according to his directions.

There may be another cause: Christ did not deliver his doctrinal precepts in that connected, systematick form which we moderns are apt to imagine essential to a body of divinity. It may here be remarked, that our Master does not seem to have designed so much a regular system of divinity by his instructions, as he did to give wholesome rules for our practice. Hence the theory of his religion is to be learned from casual allusions, and perhaps must be collected from his practical observations.

Our great and ever blessed Master was not ignorant of human nature: he knew how extremely difficult, if not absolutely impossible, it is to bring all mankind to a uniform faith; he seems therefore to have anticipated a contrariety of sentiments, and to have adapted his instructions to the circumstances of each. He doubtless knew if he laid down a series of doctrinal propositions, time in its operations, might obliterate their meaning, and render them useless or pernicious. He knew also that language was continually fluctuating, and might easily be made to speak that which its authour never designed to teach. He knew how exceedingly fond men were of establishing a creed; how prone they were to raise faith over morality, and to substitute correctness of opinion for a life of benevolence and humanity. And indeed, notwithstanding his precautions, the consequence which he most disapproved has actually followed. What would have been the case, had he been as particular in teaching men what they should believe, as he was in directing them what they should do? As he knew what would be the consequences of his instructions, and as it was his great object to produce righteousness, he chose never to gratify idle curiosity with doctrinal ideas or theoretical speculations, at least no farther than it was necessary to lay a permanent foundation for his moral superstructure. He never expressed so much solicitude about what particular opinions we should imbibe as he did about what actions they should perform or what course of conduct they should adopt. Good works are always useful; faith is nothing only as it adds to a man's comfort and stimulates him to benevolent exertions; so far it is necessary and so far Christ regarded it, but no farther. This regard for faith the true christian ever cultivates, but always bears in mind, "faith without works is dead."

The unity of the Deity was an article already in the creed of Christ's countrymen but it certainly receives additional sanction from his authority. Hear O Israel the Lord thy God is One Lord. Mark xii. 29. The Apostles also bear witness to the same sentiment and seem to have maintained it in all their preaching. Hence they assert there is "One God the Father of our Lord Jesus Christ, etc."

The benevolence of the Deity together with his Universal Providence was clearly taught by our great Master.

That God is benevolent is what every reflecting man does and must admit. Infinite in wisdom, illimitable in power, there is no conceivable inducement for him to be evil. Whatever he desires his wisdom is at hand to devise the best possible means for its acquisition, and his power is ever ready to carry his plans into execution, and as we have been unable to find in the depths of wickedness a being sufficiently malignant to desire evil for the sake of evil the conclusion is evident, God must be benevolent. But this sentiment is put beyond the reach of doubt by the language of him who spake as never man spake. If ye then being evil know how to give good gifts unto your children, how much more shall your Father which is in heaven give good things unto them who ask him? Mark vii 11.

God's universal providence is taught by the operations of nature and to these operations Christ refers his disciples for proof of the same—to the sun which rises on the "evil" and the "good"—to the rain which falls upon the "just" and the "unjust." Observe the fowls of heaven. They neither sow nor reap. They have no storehouse; but your heavenly Father feedeth them. Are not ye more valuable than they? Mark the lilies of the field. They toil not; they spin not. Yet, I affirm, that Solomon, in all his glory was not adorned like one of these. If then God so array the herbage which to-day is in the field, and to-morrow will be cast into the oven; will he not much more array you O ye distrustful!—Therefore say not anxiously, as the heathen do, what shall we eat; or what shall we drink, or wherewith shall we be clothed? For your heavenly Father knoweth that ye have need of these things. Matt. vi 27–32.

The doctrine of rewards and punishments is very clearly stated and the principles on which they will be dispensed forcibly illustrated in many observations which may be collected.

The righteous will be rewarded because they have performed acts of benevolence and humanity, and the wicked punished because they have neglected them. Or in a word, the doctrine rests upon the fact that man is an accountable being, and that he must in the day of judgement give an account of every foolish or improper action and of every idle word. See Matt. xii, 38[36].

Where the day of judgement will be we are not particularly informed, neither is it a matter of much importance that our information should be more specifick; for since we are assured the servant that knoweth his Master's will and doeth it not, shall be beaten with many stripes and the one who knoweth it not, though he do things worthy of stripes shall be beaten with few, we are permitted to believe the decision will be according to our deserts, and as we know the punishment comes from a kind and compassionate Father, we need be under no apprehension that it will be greater than our best good requires.

Forgiveness of sin on condition of repentance is another doctrine taught and illustrated by our great Master.

It is taught in the prayer he has left us "forgive us our debts, as we forgive our debtors." It is illustrated in several of his parables, particularly in the parable of the prodigal son; by which we are taught the most abandoned sinner may return and find the affectionate embrace of his

Father and his God. The same truth is contained in the object of his mission, which was not to call the righteous but sinners to repentance. That is, he came to reform the world, to recal the guilty sons of our race from their wanderings and restore them to the bosom of their God— Found also in that ever to be remembered declaration,—"God so loved the world that he gave his only begotten son to die that whosoever believeth on him should not perish but have everlasting life."

That all will finally repent, return and come to Zion in such a manner as not to be cast out is pretty clearly taught by his asserting all things were delivered into his hands, that he had power over all flesh for that purpose and that all which were given to him should come once not to be cast out. See Matthew xi. 27, John vi. 37–40, xii. 33.

He taught the resurrection of mankind from the dead and exemplified it by rising himself.

The particular condition of those that shall rise is not revealed but we are assured that in the resurrection they will be spiritual, immortal, like the angels, and will also be the children of God because children of the resurrection. See Matt. xxii. 35, Luke xx. 35–37, 1 Cor. xv, 22, 42–55.

As it respects himself, Christ uniformly taught he received his authority from God, that he was commissioned by the Father who was greater than he, to whom he was subject and to whom he directed his prayers.

These seem to be the leading points in the theory of the christian religion. To these the true christian pays attention and from these he draws the conclusion God is one, even his Father, the Father of all, providing for all his children; forgiving all upon the condition of reformation, giving his Son to bring all to repentance, assuring them though they die they shall live again, and because their Saviour lives they shall live also.

My brethren will allow me to remark here that in all we can discover in the preaching of Christ we can find nothing that is contrary to natural religion. Natural religion indeed could never have soared so high but when the authour of these sublime sentiments discloses them or to continue the mataphor brings them within our reach. Natural religion embraces them with the warmest affection. When we find a revealed religion thus corroborated by natural, we have strong presumptive evidence of its truth and utility.

The practical part of the Christian religion is more plain because more important. This consists of two parts, our duty to God, and our duty to mankind.

Our duty to God is, that we love him with all the heart, mind, and strength. This may surely be ascertained to be our reasonable service. God is our Father, the Fountain of all excellence, the source whence we derive all our enjoyments. He is our friend, our benefactor, our Redeemer, and our everlasting Saviour. All that we are, all that we have, all that we can possess, is the gift of his love the effect of his munificence. However great the happiness we enjoy, however valuable our possessions, we received them from him, and it is no more than reasonable that they should endear the character of him who bestows them, and render us grateful to the Being that has shown us so tender a regard and such powerful proofs of his fatherly affection.

Worship to God in order to be acceptable must be in "spirit and in truth." It must be the spontaneous offspring of grateful affection, seated in the heart. The performance of his worship is not confined to any particular place nor to any prescribed form, because none are necessary. God is every where present, and wherever the creature is, there we may find the Creator, and in whatever manner the heart is grateful will its gratitude be accepted.

Christ established no rites or ceremonies because he would not countenance superstition. He however permitted his disciples to baptize and he himself instituted the sacrament of bread and wine. The first was only an initiatory performance which served as a witness or seal of one's profession, but made him, in itself considered neither more virtuous nor vicious. The last was a memorial of his own sufferings and death and might have a tendency to refresh the minds of his followers and perhaps bind them more closely to each other with the cords of brotherly love.

Worship to God is proper and is enjoined by our Saviour, but he has left us no prescriptions respecting it any more than that it must be the incense of the heart. From which it is inferred, every act which does not make the heart better or convey some good to some fellow being, will not be acceptable. The mode must be left to time and circumstance to dictate. Christ has left us a prayer, but it is to be considered rather as a specimen than as a form; designed to serve as a guide, to teach us the nature of the petitions we should prefer to our heavenly Father.

Christ's own example is the best instruction we can have relative to this department of our duty; by studying this and endeavouring to imitate it, we shall be preserved from falling into gross mistakes or irretrievable errours.

Remark then his deportment, always meek, always sober, always dignified. No violent emotions were discovered; no rapturous exclamations were heard. No bursts of zeal, or fiery enthusiasm were seen emitting their destructive flames. Mark his prayer—it breathes a calm, sober, and rational devotion. It speaks a good heart and an enlightened mind. See him in the garden, on the eve of his departure. His soul was exceedingly sorrowful, unto death; his prayer was affecting, it discovered feeling, it told deep devotion and pious resignation, but it was sober and rational. He possessed in this hour of trial, in this moment of severe affliction, that same fortitude and self-command which he always maintained. From the whole of his character, we may collect this truth, that to worship God acceptably, it requires the exercise of all the powers, and faculties, we possess. The heart must feel, but the head must direct, the affections must be engaged, but reason must guard their operations. We must pray fervently, but not enthusiastically, and in all our expressions, in all our modes of worship, in all our devotional zeal, in all our pious affections, we are to maintain, a calm and considerate manner;—a propriety of address an unostentations manner, yet that dignity of deportment which to enlightened minds, will ever be deemed most becoming rational beings, in the presence of their Creator.

I cannot avoid remarking, in this place, how different is this description, from the character of many of the professed followers of our great and ever to be revered Master. I say nothing of their doctrines, for of them, I have already spoken; but to what extravagance do some people run, in their ideas of the worship of God! From the loudness and boisterous manner in which they pray, one is led to conclude, that they suppose their God is deaf and cannot hear, or is asleep and must be waked. But, brethren, let us compassionate their mistakes, and watch diligently over ourselves, lest we run to the same or a worse excess.

2. The other department of practical religion, regulates our conduct to each other.—This belongs to ethicks, and can be only slightly touched in this place.

I confess myself highly pleased with the morals of Confucius. So far as I have learned them, they elicit an enlightened mind and a benevolent heart. I admire many things to be found in the writings of the pagan philosophers. Plato has sublime flights. Cicero has many maxims that should be engraven on the tablets of the heart, and I can never read Seneca without feeling my heart softened, my virtue confirmed, and my philanthropy increased. But to me these all fall far below the practical observations of Jesus of Nazareth. Notice forgiveness to enemies: What heathen philosopher ever taught this? Most of them represent that not to resent injuries is the result of meanness and pusillanimity. How much better the sentiment of him who knew what was befitting man! "Ye have heard that it hath been said, thou shalt love thy neighbour or friend, and hate thy enemy; but I say unto you, love your enemies." The reason assigned, is, that we may be the children of our Father who is in heaven: See Matt. v. 43, etc. This duty might also be inferred from the nature of our relations and the fitness of things; but he who has once forgiven an enemy will require no argument to induce to forgive again.

Forgiveness stands opposed to revenge; and we are taught that the true Christian should never indulge in resentful feeling, and by no means a vindictive disposition. He is commanded not to resist the injurious; but if a man strike him on the right cheek, to turn to him also the left; that is, he is to be always placable in his temper and forbearing in his manner.

Notice as the next trait in the Christian's character, universal benevolence. The national character of the Jews was illiberal and cruel; but very different is the case with the disciple of Christ. He is taught that all mankind are brethren—all are neighbours, and he must love them as he does himself. No peculiarity of nation, language or manners, is allowed to break the social tie, or dissolve the moral obligation; no sectarian interests must prevent reciprocal kindness and mutual good offices.

The Jews and Samaritans were bitter enemies, alienated by prejudices of religion and country; yet to the lawyer who asked, "who is my neighbour?" Christ proposed the example of a Samaritan assisting a Jew, for his imitation. "Go," he would say, "wherever you see a fellow mortal in distress, ask not to what country he belongs—ask not what religion he professes—ask not whether he be a friend or enemy; but bind his wounds, heal his broken heart, and take care that he suffers no more. Would to God the sectarians of this day had a little more of this philanthropick spirit.

3. But to conclude: As a general rule, the Christian does to others whatever he would wish them to do to him. No rule can be better adapted to popular practice than this. It is short. It is no burden to the memory, yet it is sufficiently comprehensive. It may always be at hand, and, if observed, it will solve any doubt that may arise. We have only in our minds to exclude circumstances, and self-love will generally give a correct decision.

We may sum up the character of the true Christian: He is one that loves God, and worships him in a sober and rational manner—one who, though he may contend for faith, does it only because he believes it will be subservient to good works—one who recognizes all mankind as brethren, bound on the same voyage, destined to the same haven, and beloved by the same Father—one who compassionates the follies of his brethren, weeps over their calamities, reproves their vices, but omits nothing of his kind offices or good wishes. He is the sober, devout worshipper, the universal friend and consistent moralist. May we all bear his character and receive his reward.

6. MY CREED

SOURCE: *Gospel Advocate and Impartial Investigator* 7 (June 27, 1829): 199–201.

Repeatedly Brownson tried to summarize his beliefs in creedal statements. He wrote his first creed in his spiritual diary on July 12, 1825. The following creed was written in response to those Universalists in upstate New York who accused him of infidelity, charging that he had denied the existence of God and the truth of divine revelation.* Here Brownson summarizes what he considers the essentials of true religion.

Almost every man has a creed. There are few who do not worship their creed with more devotion than they do their God, and labour a thousand times harder to support it than they do to support truth. Now I do not like to be singular, and I know not why I may not have a creed as well as other folks. But—if I publish my creed, consistency may require me to defend it and when I have once enlisted self-love in its defence, I may become blind to the truth and may choose rather to abide my first decision than to admit I have once decided wrong. But a creed I must and will have, and my readers shall know what it is.

My creed shall consist of FIVE points,[1] and shall embrace all the essentials of true religion; and furthermore I wish to premise, that my creed was not adopted merely to-day, but has been cordially embraced and of its correctness I have had no doubts, for at least nine months, though I may not have lived agreeably to its injunctions. But we are all frail creatures and it is very difficult to find no discrepancy between a man's faith, and his practice. Moreover I would alledge in behalf of my creed, that it is plain, easy to be understood, and withal involves no mystery. The pious may, however, from this circumstance be led to doubt its *divine* origin, and infidels may like it so well that I shall be

---

* See "Infidelity," *Gospel Advocate and Impartial Investigator* 7 (April 8, 1829): 121–23.

shut out of the church. But I will state it—though I must still further alledge, that I believe it to be based on eternal truth, and that it is calculated, if obeyed, to harmonize the world and enable the vast family of man to live forever beneath the smiles of fraternal affection. But for the creed.

Art. I. I BELIEVE every individual of the human family should be HONEST.

Art. II. I BELIEVE that every one should be BENEVOLENT and KIND to all.

Art. III. I BELIEVE that every one should use his best endeavours to procure FOOD, CLOTHING and SHELTER for himself, and labour to enable all others to procure the same to the extent of his ability.

Art. IV. I BELIEVE every one should cultivate his *mental powers,* that he may open to himself a new source of enjoyment, and also be enabled to aid his brethren in their attempts to improve the condition of the human race, and to increase the sum of human happiness.

Art. V. I BELIEVE, that if all mankind act on these principles they serve God all they can serve him that he who has this faith and conforms the nearest to what it enjoins, is the most acceptable unto God.

This O ye! who accuse me of infidelity is my creed—read it, obey it and never again tell me I am a disbeliever. Do you ask for evidences of its correctness? find them where you can—in the bible, in the Koran in the volume of the universe, in our individual capacities, in our social relations or wherever else you can. The best evidence I can offer is that if any one will believe, and obey, he will want no evidence. That is to say, if any one will do the works here required, he will find so much pleasure in the performance that he will ever after wish to continue to do the same. I would quote scripture, but people say I do not believe it,—how they should know I do not, is more than I can divine. They have never derived that knowledge from myself for I have never had it to give. But there is one passage so much in point I will quote; "The ways of wisdom are ways of pleasantness and all her paths are peace." But here is another still better; "Righteousness keepeth him that is upright in the way." "There shall no evil happen to the just." "The lips of truth shall be established forever," and, "The just man walketh in his integrity and his children are blessed after him." And again; "Thou shall love thy neighbour as thyself," and "whatsoever ye would that men should do unto you, do ye even the same unto them, for this is the law and the prophets." Moreover I must be permitted to quote still further, "But if any provide not for his own, and especially for those of his own house, he hath denied the faith and is worse than an infidel." "Do good unto all men as you have opportunity" "But whoso hath this world's goods and seeth his brother have need and shutteth up his bowels of compassion from him, how dwelleth the love of God in him?" "Prove all things hold fast that which is good." "Apply thy heart unto instruction and thine ears unto the words of knowledge." "To do justice and judgement is more acceptable unto the Lord than sacrifice." "To love God—and his neighbour as himself is more than all whole burnt offerings." "Pure religion and undefiled before God and the Father is this to visit the fatherless and the widows in their affliction and to keep ourself unspotted from the world." "And this commandment have we from him, that he who loveth God love his brother also."[2]

These among many other passages of the same import I might adduce to show my creed is scriptural, but presuming each one reads the bible for himself I leave it to him to find evidence in the book itself. I forbear to expatiate on the moral beauty of my creed or to dwell upon what I consider will be its salutary tendency; and, though not skilled in the language of cursing, I will yet say that to expect happiness without obedience to this creed is vain. I shall not tell people they shall go to hell if they do not believe it, but I will leave them, if they do not obey its injunctions, to say, whether they have not a hell in their own bosoms.

I have now stated my creed, yet I am not so vain as to suppose all will embrace it. The orthodox will reject it because it is not mysterious, and the priests generally, because it will require them to pay as much attention to the flock as they have hitherto paid to the fleece. The heterodox will dislike it, because it will require them to treat the orthodox as kindly as they do themselves, and what perhaps is still worse, it will not allow them to be illiberal against illiberality—And Infidels of all descriptions will reject it because I have proved it by scripture. All hypocrites will condemn it because it strips off their mask and compels them to be useful in order to be respected. The selfish will anathematize because it requires them to regard the welfare of others. And the indolent will be outrageous upon it because it requires them to be active. Hence I conclude there will be only *few* who will hear it with gladness. As it is likely to meet opposition from every quarter, I shall flatter myself that it is true.

If any one complains it is defective, I will tell him if he performs all it enjoins, I will engage St. Peter shall open the gates of heaven, to admit him to the mansions of the blest. But I will just whisper in the ear of my reader, I conceive this creed to be the END towards which all should labour, that I do *not say* it is unnecessary to believe any thing else, but that nothing else is useful any farther than it tends to this end.

Now my reader, if you by believing that Jonah [was] swallowed [by] the whale or the story about the witch of Endor, with various others of the same character, I say dear reader, that if believing these marvellous stories will make thee a better man, and a better man, whoever thou art, I knew thou dost need to be, then I have not the least objection even shouldst thou believe the moon is made of "green cheese." Now ye doctors of divinity hurl your anathemes. Let every one be HONEST.

Notes: My Creed

1. An illusion to the five points of Calvinism defined by the Synod of Dort (1618–19); that is, total depravity, unconditional election, limited atonement, irresistible grace and perseverance of the saints. Brownson's creed is an attack upon Dortian theology. See *Works* 5, p. 43.
2. The scripture passages are from: Prv 3:17; 13:6; 12:21; 12:19; 20:7; Mt 19:19; 7:12; 1 Tm 5:8; Gal 6:10; 1 Jn 3:17; 1 Thes 5:12; Prv 23:12; 21:3; Mk 12:33; Jas 1:27; 1 Jn 4:12.

7. A GOSPEL CREED

SOURCE: *Gospel Advocate and Impartial Investigator* 7 (October 3, 1829): 311–12.

"My Creed" got Brownson into trouble again with some Universalists because it seemed to deny historical revelation and to reduce all inspiration to natural inspiration and all religion to this-worldly preoccupations. "My Creed" was indeed reductionistic because Brownson was articulating what he thought all reasonable persons could accept. "A Gospel Creed" outlines Brownson's beliefs about this world and the world to come.

Sometimes since I published "my creed," and so far as I can learn, contrary to all my expectations, every body liked it, only some thought it did not go far enough. That creed, I considered necessary for every one to believe; the one I am now about to present my readers, is a matter of opinion; on which every one may exercise his own judgement, believe or reject, and still, for ought I know, be a good man. I do not consider myself any better, merely because I believe it, nor do I believe any one any the worse because he does not believe; though it is my opinion, that its tendency will be the production of good feeling and an increase of enjoyment. My reasons for writing it are to gratify a class of readers, who are anxious to know what a man believes, and also to remove a complaint made to me by a valuable brother in the ministry, viz. that I do not let what I aim at be known.

I. The Gospel, according to my view of it, recognizes the existence of ONE God and of only one, who is the prime mover of all things, whose will has established the laws of nature, whose moral character is impartial justice, based upon universal goodness and infinite mercy.

II. This God exhibits, in the government of the world, wisdom to admire and goodness to adore; that all which is necessary for us to know of his power and Godhead, is instampted on his works and may be read in his word.

III. A particular display of divine love and mercy is recorded in the writings of the New Testament—display made by Jesus of Nazareth, the greatest and best Reformer ever vouchsafed us by Heaven.

IV. The object of Jesus, (or of God in raising him up) was to reform the world. Not to appease the anger of God, not to make an expiatory sacrifice to render God propitious, but to lead men to repentance or reformation.

V. The means used to effect this reformation are the example, the precepts, the sufferings, the doctrine and the death, of Jesus Christ. These operate in a natural way, same as a good example to follow and a correct faith, tends to purify the heart and lead to the practice of virtue. They operate not irresistibly but persuasively, do not compel us to be good but entice us to virtue.

VI. That no man will be sentenced to endless misery and that no one shall be doomed to endure more misery than naturally grows out of his physical and moral condition is a doctrine of the Gospel. Yet this misery all must endure, and their only hope of relief is in the improvement of their condition, which improvement it is the duty and interest of all to effect.—Deity forgives us past offences, gives us motives to reformation and exhorts us to reform, but Deity does not reform for us, we must effect this ourselves. The means are given us and if we do not use them the fault is ours.

VII. That all will finally become holy seems highly probable. Though some consider this point positively settled, yet as one class of these consider a part will never become holy, and the other are positive that all will, I deem it a matter not positively decided, I should consider the salvation of all men as an inferential doctrine, rather than as one positively taught. I infer it from the goodness of God and the perfection towards which all his works tend, which makes it almost certain that in their progressive operations the period will come when man will cease his folly and learn to pursue virtue as his chief good. It is also inferred from the fact that the goodness of God has made happiness possible to all, giving all the means of procuring it, and it would be absurd to say God will ever take them away, if they always remain we shall some time or other learn to use them.

VIII. Endless misery is no Gospel doctrine, Annihilation is no part of philosophy, and to suppose a total unconsciousness of being to last through eternity is not reconciliable with the resurrection of all as taught by all the new testament writers. Hence my opinion is that all mankind will by some process or other, not known to me, pass from this state of being to another analagous to it. As man is a progressive being here, as his happiness is generally in proportion to his knowledge and active virtue, so I conclude it will be hereafter. And though my heaven has not so much immediate felicity as the Universalist supposes neither has it the misery of the orthodox hell.

I do not like the notion of teaching men they may sin all their lives and be equally happy at death with the most virtuous. I do not say this because I think it would be any loss to the virtuous, nor because I am unwilling the wicked should fare so well, God forbid that I should ever envy any one the small pittance of happiness he may obtain. But the order of the divine government seems to be on different principles, and moreover such a sentiment does not seem to place the reward of virtue in a light sufficiently clear to arrest the attention of the thoughtless and the careless. The rewards of virtue are permanent and lasting, and to have a good moral effect man ought to be taught the road to happiness lies only through the practice of moral goodness. As I am unable to perceive any thing in death which can work a moral change any farther than a change of some physical properties may change the directions of the passions, I conclude our happiness in another world will be proportioned to our moral goodness, and I know no better criterion by which to determine that moral goodness on entering that world than by measuring the degree of improvement with which we left this.

We call a vicious man miserable. It is so in this world and I conclude it will be, so long as he retains his vicious character, whether in this world or in the next. This makes the restraint of vice clear and powerful. It comes "home to men's bosoms and business," and deters us by every consideration which can influence the mind. Heaven and hell are not considered local dwellings but mere states of the mind, both are felt in a certain degree here, and both for ought I know may be felt hereafter.

These notions make the other world one with which we can have some sympathy. If you will tell me of another world, tell me something tangible to the mind, something which I can feel. The vague report of a song eternal sounding upon golden harps, may be very pleasing to those who love musick. But an idle song may loose its charms and it is a thousand times more pleasing to my mind to contemplate the future world as a scene of active virtue, where all the kind and benevolent feelings of the heart may be exercised, where we may do good to each other and employ our leisure and our new faculties in examining the works of our Creator. But enough for the present. This article contains matter for much future speculation. My readers will pardon me for troubling them with any notions about an invisible world. I do not often trouble them thus, and they must view this weakness, if such they will call it, with an indulgent eye.

I have now presented my speculative creed and I know enough of human nature to know it will be read with interest, and enough of sectarism to know it will be most grievously censured. It will suit neither orthodox nor heterodox, for by pursuing a middle coarse adopting the excellences of all, none will find their own peculiarities flattering, none of their dear propensities retained, I deprecate no censure. For the gratification of some I have given my opinion, all may make as much of it as they can, believe it or not is the same to me.

III.

FREE THINKER:
1829–31

8. TO THE EDITORS OF THE FREE ENQUIRER

SOURCE: *Free Enquirer* 2 (January 2, 1830): 79.

The following explains why Brownson left the Universalists and indicates his renewed commitment to social justice for workingmen.

Locke Nov. 27, 1829.

I have now commenced my labors in the good cause of human improvement. I now feel myself fairly rid of my sectarian prejudices and can say to myself "I am slave to no sect." Now this is a very simple expression, and, one would think, an indication of a very natural condition; but I will assure you it affords more pleasure to one who has all his life been engaged in a sectarian warfare, to be able to say it, in truth of himself, than you can easily imagine.

There is something in "mental independence" peculiarly fascinating. I do not pretend to explain why, but such is the fact. Common sense has more charms for the mind, then the most beautiful theories —or rather dreams, of religionists. If we could only persuade mankind to follow common sense, I mean, if we could only convince them it is no harm to follow its dictates, and remove the fears they have that God will hate them if they dare be as he made them, RATIONAL, they would soon become reasonable and happy.

My youth was spent in studying religious matters, but even then I disliked the restraints the clergy imposed upon the young mind. Yet I dared not encourage a thought to stray beyond the prescribed bounds.

121

Still it would often be a subject of wonder to me why a Deity who did all things and could make all things just to suit him, should allow to youth aspirations after knowledge which they were forbidden to indulge—should give them an invincible curiosity, and forbid them to gratify it. But the clergyman told me, all was for trial; and, though I thought it for vexation, I let it pass.

As I advanced towards manhood I labored incessantly to bring my mind to the standard of the church. This was no easy matter; for profane thoughts would continually obtrude themselves, unsanctified doubts would arise, and I would often find myself on the point of giving up my "hope" and bidding farewell to the church and its spiritual food forever. But I finally succeeded in settling down in the full conviction of the truth of universal salvation. Then I felt to rejoice, because I thought I should be at liberty to use my reason and indulge charitable feelings to the world.

But man seems fated to be disappointed. I still found I had my bounds beyond which I must not think, or if I did, I must not express my thoughts. And to allow it possible that other denominations might be as good as my own, or have as good members, was a stretch of charity which even my Universalist brethren were not always willing to allow. It took away the main argument by which they enforced the necessity of believing their creed.

It will never do for any religions sect to allow that people may be as good in other sects, as in their own. For if it be so, why such a change? why trouble the world about a change from which no practical benefit can result? But many pretended that Universalism made the believer a happier man than could be the believer in endless misery. All I can say is, I have believed them both; neither made me happy. The happiness that either promises seemed too remote to afford much satisfaction. If the believer in endless misery sometimes trembles to think it possible some of his friends may be damned as well as his enemies, the believer in Universalism is but little comforted by thinking that his enemies as well as his friends will be saved. So far as my observations extend, very little solid happiness is received from the belief of any creed, however rigorous or however lenient; and the chief difference of character which I have found among professors of different creeds is: that persons of mild and benevolent dispositions embraced mild and benevolent creeds, and the reverse with those of opposite dispositions. As a general remark. I have found Universalists more benevolent and more forbearing than any other denomination; but this I consider not the effect of their doctrine, but the reason why they embrace it.

But even a member of this sect will find, that, though he has a wider range, he still has his enclosures. Not so much because they fear the individual may be lost, as that his wanderings may give the orthodox or other sects occasion to cast some expressions upon the one to which he belongs. The Universalists, in many instances, censure me for leaving them, not because they believe me less honest nor because they believe my welfare or the welfare of mankind endangered; but because it may prove injurious to them as a denomination or sect. Were it not for this, they would receive me as a brother, and have as much good feeling toward me as ever. This is the case with all sects; and it is one reason why persecution has been practiced.

All these feelings are now with me no more. I look upon mankind as brethren and feel desirous of ascertaining the means by which their happiness can be promoted; and I care not which sect supplies me with the best information. I am willing to learn from them all. I perceive not the necessity of blinding my eyes to the merit of one sect for the sake of exalting the worth of another; nor indeed of being a persecutor, to appease the wrath of him who persecutes me. My sect is now the world, my party is every where, my creed truth wherever I can find it, and under whatever name it may come—prized equally high if among the orthodox of the day, or if with the reputed heterodox, or if with neither. And this liberty to embrace truth wherever found, is the mental independence I prize so highly.

IV.

INDEPENDENT PREACHER:
1831–32

9. A SERMON ON RIGHTEOUSNESS

SOURCE: *The Philanthropist* 2 (January 14, 1832): 85–94.

Brownson delivered this sermon for his "friends" in Ithaca, New York, on the first Sunday of February 1831. It was the first sermon he preached since abandoning the Universalist ministry at the end of 1829. The sermon describes righteousness as a moral activity of benevolence, not a matter of believing. Here Brownson is not concerned with divine grace but with the righteous person, who is attentive not only to the dictates of nature but also to the divine voice within the soul. Piety is here identified with moral virtue.

"I have preached righteousness in the great congregation."
Ps. xl. 9.

The duty of a preacher, is seldom understood, and, perhaps, less often performed. But it was not to be expected that in the midst of an ignorant and corrupt world, any one class of men should be perfect in wisdom and in goodness. That the clergy should, sometimes, have neglected to ascertain their duty, and at others have been seduced from its performance, need excite no surprise. The clergy are but men— subject to the same passions as are others, affected by the same causes, governed by the same motives and exposed to the same, if not even greater, temptations; it does not, then, become us, as lovers of impartial justice, to vent any peculiar spleen at them, or to treat them as

124

more depraved than the rest of mankind. You should give them credit for all the good they have done, lament all the evil they may have occasioned, and pass it by with the assurance,

"To err is human; to forgive, divine."

I make these remarks because I am well aware, while one portion of my fellow beings are worshipping, as it were, the clergy, ascribing to them undeserved excellence, giving them credit for virtues they do not possess, and for benefits they have never conferred; another part look up to them as monsters in wickedness, and deem the term clergyman, but another name for all that is base and detestable among mortals. Either is wrong; either has a wrong temper, and acting under the influence of that temper will be mischievous to the human race. I wish you, therefore, my hearers, to lay aside whatever prejudices you may have on this subject. If, in what I now, or at any future time may say, you may discover any thing which may redound to the honor of the clergy, I pray you receive, it if it be true; or if I shall offer any thing which seems to lessen their worth, I would that you receive it, if it be not false.

My object, at this time, is to call your attention to what I conceive it the duty of a preacher to labor to effect; and also to give you a criterion, by which you may, hereafter, judge of my consistency, or inconsistency, with myself.

The Psalmist declares, in our text, that he had "preached righteousness in the great congregation." I conceive the only legitimate object of any preacher, is the production of righteousness. This should be his polar star, towards which, as the magnet of the soul, he should point all his powers. To this he should shape his doctrines, his reproofs, and his exhortations. Nothing is of any use that does not tend towards it, and my usefulness, as your preacher, will depend on the success I may have in producing it.

Before, however, I attempt to point out what righteousness is, I will ask your indulgence, while I notice some few things which, sometimes, pass for it, but which are either opposed, or unnecessary, to it.

All, or nearly all, who have preached to you as well as to others, have attached themselves to some party, and devoted themselves to the defence of some creed; too often acting as if they identified the progress of goodness with the prosperity and aggrandizement of their own sect. I belong to no party. I disclaim all sectarian names. You have called me a Universalist. I disown the name, though I may not oppose what an enlightened Universalist would wish to effect. I do not wish to be called a Universalist. Should I assume the name of any party, it should be Unitarian, as that denomination approximates nearer, in my estimation, to the spirit of christianity than any other. Unitarian discourses are mostly practical; their lessons inculcate charity, a refined moral feeling, and universal benevolence. They teach us God is our Father, that all men are brethren, and that we should cultivate mutual good will, and imbibe a liberal and manly feeling towards all men. Unitarian preaching, in general, I approve; but I discover no necessity of assuming any name that can become the rallying point of a sect. You will therefore forbear to associate my name with any party, either orthodox or heterodox. I am an independent preacher, accountable to my God, to truth, to my country, to the people of my charge, but to no other tribunal.

In this respect I differ from most other preachers. But in this I discover no disadvantage. Truth is the property of no one sect, righteousness is the exclusive boast of no one denomination. All have some truth, all have some errors. To join any one, you must support its falsehoods as well as its truths, or they will cast you out of the synagogue. You must study to conceal the faults of your party, and often be compelled to suffer reproach from the misconduct of your associates.

If you have a party to which you attach yourselves, you will most likely, have certain sentiments which you will feel bound to support, and which, in most cases, your associates will induce you to maintain through fear of losing your reputation, if not your means of subsistence. The party may at first be good; it may be organized for the noblest purposes; the first adherents may be men of enlarged and liberal minds, of benevolent hearts; they may have an eye single to the support of the dearest interests of mankind; but, it can hardly happen that none of more selfish purposes will at length assume the lead, or that, in the progress of events, the majority may not become more intent on building themselves up as a mere party, than on discovering and promulgating truth.

No man, who has attended to the subject, can doubt that the first Christian churches were founded by the best feelings of the human heart, and for the noblest purposes of philanthropy. But, how soon were they perverted to other ends, made subservient to the aggrandizement of a few, and the consequent depression of the many. Each sect, in its origin, has aimed well, and has had some really good things; but each in its progress, deeming itself bound by the perfection it boasted in its commencement, binding its adherents back to the starting point, prohibiting them on pain of excommunication, and often of death, from any innovation, or departure from what its projector enjoined, has destroyed its utility and involved a long catalogue of evils, too numerous to be named, and too painful to be dwelt upon.

At present, soon as one thinks of being religious, soon as he feels serious and desires to understand religion and enjoy its consolations, he immediately unites with some sect. This, too often, proves an end to his progress. The church has its creed, its rules, and its usage, which it not unfrequently holds dearer than truth. These the young convert must embrace, and zealously support, not only while he has the belief and feelings he has on uniting, but through all after life, let his future convictions be what they may.

Now, who is there that does not perceive the ill consequences of these misplaced and mistimed demands? who so foolish as to pretend that a child twelve or fourteen years old has mastered the whole subject, and learned so much that nothing remains to be learned? The fact is, the child, or the youth, usually unites with the church, and declares what he will always believe, soon as he commences learning, while the whole field of religious science is before him, as yet untraversed. For him, at this moment, to assume to know all that can be known, or to know so much as to know he shall never see cause to change his opinion, is most egregious folly, and those, who encourage him to do thus, are doing him and the world incalculable injury. The opinions he now adopts he may soon discover to be erroneous; those he now condemns farther and closer investigation may discover to be true. Ought he not to be free to renounce the one set and to embrace the other without injury to his character? Can he do this, without disgrace, if he be a member of any of our churches? The laws of our churches are like those of the Medes and Persians, they change not; aye, they allow no change. If he, who has unfortunately acknowledged their sway, presume to reason beyond the limits they prescribe, he is called a heretic, his standing in the church is lost, and he is turned out into the world with the damning brand of heresy on his forehead, an object of scorn to all who deem it a virtue never to doubt.

I do not speak at random, my friends. I speak from experience. I was a universalist—a universalist preacher. I was so unfortunate in the prosecution of my studies as to have doubts; I withdrew myself from the denomination, to which I belonged, and ceased to preach. What was the consequence? approbation for my honesty? No, They excommunicated me and published me from one end of the country to the other as a rejector of christianity, as an unprincipled villain! This is the principle by which all sects are governed. What encouragement has one to enquire after truth, or to aspire to any growth in knowledge, after he has united with a sect? Will it not be his wisest course to sit down with the remark, "my church is right, at least I will not enquire, lest haply I find it in the wrong?"

The fact is, nearly all churches, as now organized, are unfriendly to the full developement of religious or mental excellence. They are like the Phillistine's chains which bound Sampson when shorn of his strength, and those, who come within their enclosures, can do little else than grind in their prison houses. I know of no real advantage they offer to the world. The only bond of union I approve, is that which spontaneously springs from similar sentiments, similar feelings and the pursuit of similar objects. The sympathy of a like faith, of common objects, and common feelings, will bind us sufficiently close to each other.

To preach righteousness, then, I do not conceive it necessary to urge you to join a church. I wish you to observe all the good there is in any, or all of our churches, to ascertain all they have of truth, and make it your own; but if you will be wise, you will beware how you receive their fetters, and place yourselves in a situation by which you must father their faults as well as their virtues.

I think it has not failed to strike you that much of what passes for righteousness, with those who assume the direction of our consciences, is, to say the least, of doubtful utility.

I have observed the mass of mankind are not afflicted with any very deep thought; nor do they discriminate very clearly between what is important and what is unimportant. That which is the most noisy, or which makes the most show, almost invariably attracts the most attention. Hence it is, the ceremonies of religion are much more scrupulously observed than religion itself; and men frequently seem more attached to the *form,* than to the *power* of godliness. Yet, of what consequence is the form without the power? He were a simpleton indeed, who should deem the shadow of more value than the substance. There is, however, great fear many are in pursuit of only the shadow, and that while in pursuit of that they lose the substance.

The christian world has, at times, been wholly bent on external worship. It now enjoins a variety of rites and ceremonies and vague duties, which at best are only the lumber of religion. Take joining the church. This just now is all the rage. Is there any thing in the mere act itself that makes the heart better? May not a man be equally as greatful to his God and as benevolent to his brother, out, as in, the church? If so, what is the utility of joining? And, do we not often see many of those who join puffed up with a spiritual pride, imagining themselves a great deal better because they have done this act? Do not our churches tend to introduce artificial distinctions? Is there not a perpetual hostility between church members and those denominated the world? Does not the church indulge in the severity of invective against those who do not belong to it? and do not those called the world delight to make the churches the butt of their ridicule? Surely no reasonable man will pronounce this state of things favorable to virtue; and every good man every genuinely religious man, will do all he can to correct it.

Take also Baptism and the Lord's Supper. It is well known Baptism cannot purge the conscience from dead works, to the life of virtue. A man may receive the rite, while murder is rankling in his heart and while his hands are red with crime. It cannot, therefore, be considered as a purifying ordinance, and to suppose our God will love us any the better for being put all over under water, is not very rational. God looks at the heart, requires justice and mercy rather than burnt offerings or any external rite whatever. The same may be said of the sacramental supper. In itself it is of no use. A man can be as good without it, as with it. All these things are—useless? May I not say, often worse—mischievous? They draw off our attention from things important; they substitute, in the minds of the unenlightened, the form for the power of goodness, and often flatter them they can secure heaven without any practical usefulness to their fellow beings.

They often, lay the axe at the root of the tree of morality, strangle our virtues in the cradle and spread a feverish and sickly superstition over the moral world. True, we are told, they are only symbolical, admirably calculated to refresh our minds and remind us of what we should be and of what Christ has done for us; but, alas! symbols may do very well for the enlightened, for the discerning, but, they are always mischievous to those who cannot, or will not, look at what they are designed to prefigure. I make no war upon them. Education, habit, may have endeared them, and communion seasons may often be peculiarly precious to the Christian. Still, I think it would be advantageous to the moral world to pay no great attention to them. I think it were better to inform the people, that rites and ceremonies are superanuated; that these counterfeits of goodness do not pass current with our heavenly Father; that he requires us to worship him in 'spirit and in truth;' that in the days of our ignorance he winked at this mystical worship, but now commands all men every where, to repent; that is, break off from their sins, 'cease to do evil and learn to do well.'*

[*My objections are to churches as they usually exist. I want no other church than the parish; then all may be considered members, and made to feel, soon as they come to years of discretion, that they are bound to perform all the duties that belong to christians. My objections to Baptism and the Lord's Supper, are against the popular views of those

These remarks bring me to consider what it is to preach righteousness.

In illustrating this, I must be allowed to draw the picture of a righteous man, and in pourtraying his character I hope to be able to exhibit clearly my views of righteousness. I may be entering upon a difficult task. The world is almost a stranger to what I would describe. I seem to myself to be on untrodden ground—compelled to draw from the imagination. But I hope there is more than one who might sit for the likeness.

The righteous man has a lively sense of gratitude to God. I place this first, because, in my opinion, he who has no mind to admire the wisdom and order of the universe, no heart to adore the love and goodness every where displayed in the Creator's works, can lay no claim to correctness of thought, much less to goodness of heart. He who notes of what he is made susceptible, who marks the rich provision made for his wants, the vast variety of objects contrived to awaken his pleasure and gladden his heart, must be a cold, unfeeling wretch, if no gratitude glow to the munificent Author of the whole.

He does not attempt to scan the Deity, for that is useless. He does not pry into his will nor attempt to ascertain the secret decrees of God, for these are not revealed, and he is not aware of any good purpose that could be answered by his knowing them. He is satisfied God is love, he knows he is good, for his goodness is manifest in fitting up this world as a splendid palace for us to dwell in, by spreading a luxurious banquet of which all are urged to partake with grateful hearts. The good man is content with this; confides in his Father's love, and studies to be thankful for what he enjoys.

Towards his fellow beings, the righteous man cultivates kindness and good will. He looks upon them all as his brothers and his sisters, with whom his heart should be entwined with fraternal love.

He is sincere. Whatever he says to them is in good faith. He will not praise them for virtues they cannot claim, nor will he censure them for faults of which they are not guilty. He speaks to them kindly, but candidly. He is cautious that he drop no word which may be to them an occasion of deception. He will never preach doctrines he does not

---

institutions. I am willing Baptism as a simple initiatory rite should be observed, though I consider it not particularly enjoined upon us in the scriptures. Whatever may be the meaning of Jesus to his disciples to baptize, one thing is certain, no intimation is any where given it was to be observed through all stages of the church. To the Eucharist, if viewed simply as a mere token of respect to the Great Founder of our religion, and as a mark of our fraternal love and mutual fidelity I have no objections. On any other view of it, my conscience would not allow me to approach the communion table.]

believe true, nor will he ask them to support that which he deems false or mischievous.

He is honest. He gives to every one his dues. This he does from principle, not through the compulsion of the law. Laws are not for the honest man—they are for rogueś. Honest men do not require laws to compel them to do right.—They do it from principle, and they may be trusted alone, in the dark as well as in the light surrounded by a multitude of witnesses. For such men laws are useless, and if all were such, laws might be dispensed with. He is, therefore, careful to take nothing which does not belong to him, and never to withhold what belongs to another.

He is charitable. He is well aware all are imperfect beings, and says to himself, "it is hardly possible that, in the progress of events, no one should injure me. Towards him who does, I must be kindly affectioned. He may have wronged me inadvertantly, through some misunderstanding; some unforseen and uncontrollable event may have compelled him to do it. It may have been through his misfortune, and should excite my compassion, rather than my anger.—Moreover, my kind affection towards him will be the most effectual means of convincing him of his mistake, and of converting him from his error and of making him my friend. I would also treat him thus because I may myself do wrong and need forgiveness in return; and it is but just I give to others what I wish them to give to me."

He is merciful. He is tender of the feelings of his brethren. He is ready to pour the oil and wine into the wounded heart, to bind up the broken spirit and to make the sufferer whole. It is his study to lessen the miseries, the misfortunes and wretchedness of his fellow beings, to "light up a smile in the aspect of woe," and to convert the mourner's tears into streams of consolation. In a word, it is his study to diffuse truth, and kind feeling, to endear the members of society, to bind them more closely to each other, to create peace and joy in every heart, and make all his fellow creatures happy.

In public life, he studies for public spirit that he may be interested in the duties of his station—for integrity that the confidence of his fellow citizens may not be misplaced—for knowledge that he may discharge promptly, and accurately, the duties which may devolve upon him. In private life, he is prudent—studies frugality; industry and sobriety. Each of these is necessary to him as a man, much more, if he stand in the relation of a husband, a father, a child or a brother. To all these he aims to add gentleness of manners and amiableness of disposition.

Thus far is the righteous man towards his God, and towards his fellow beings. Towards himself he is temperate and industrious, as both of these are requisite to preserve his health and to develope his moral and mental vigor. He is not puffed up with pride, nor is he ever self-debased. He endeavors to form a just estimate of himself—to learn his strength, to know his weakness, and to think neither more highly nor more lowly of himself than truth will warrant. In his morals he is unbending, never in a single instance departing from the line of duty. Yet, he is not rigid except where principle is at stake. He studies to store his mind with useful knowledge, fortifies his heart with the precepts of sound philosophy, that he may not sink in the hour of adversity, nor be elated above measure in the day of prosperity.

Such I deem the righteous man, such I have aimed to be; and should my preaching make each of you what I have represented the righteous man, I too, like the Psalmist, may hereafter say, "I have preached righteousness in the great congregation."

Righteousness is gratitude to God, a lively sense of our accountability and relationship to him. This is nothing more than will be felt by every one who will read attentively the volume of nature, and carefully listen to the voice of the Divinity within his own soul. It includes love to our fellow beings—not merely to our own family and friends, or to our own party; but, to the world, to all, for "God hath made of one blood all the nations of the earth." Our love to them will make us sincere, honest, forgiving, gentle and merciful, in our intercourse with them. It will teach us to rejoice with those who rejoice and to weep with those who weep.

It is no trifling task to be a righteous man. It is a character that cannot be acquired in a few minutes, amid the turbulence of the mob, the turmoil of the crowd and by the aid of excited and inflamed passions. It requires good sense, good feeling, and sound judgment. It sanctions no fiery zeal, no ignorant enthusiasm. Its zeal is kindled at the altar of wisdom, and its flame is guided by just knowledge. The head must be clear, the affections pure, and the hands must be active. This character is seldom met, but it is never passed by unnoticed. It is a valuable character. It is one that well repays the labor of procuring. That serenity of soul, that tranquility of the passions, that vigor of mind, and that health of body which ever attend it, amply reward us for all the exertions which may be exacted to obtain it.—There is something in the practice of virtue that endears it to the heart. I will not attempt to describe it but *be* virtuous and you shall know for yourselves what it is.

Such, my friends, are the outlines of righteousness—shall I say of christianity? I will, for christianity consists not in *believing* as the world has unfortunately supposed, but in *doing.* Its Founder was constantly employed in acts of benevolence. He went about doing good even when derided, despised, rejected; not having, even where to lay his head, he was engaged in relieving the miseries of his brethren, and gladdening their hearts with the gracious tidings he proclaimed, O let us imitate him. That will at least, give us practical christianity.

I wish to be a good man myself, and to persuade each of you, male or female, to be good. If I can do this, I shall accomplish my object. If I can persuade you, to set an example of a people determined to receive truth wherever they can find it, practice virtue at all times, in all places, and towards all persons, if I can wake the love of excellence in your hearts, and kindle a flame of benevolence in you all, my object will be attained, and humbly submitting to my God, I will say with the Psalmist "I have preached righteousness."

V.

UNITARIAN MINISTRY:
1832–36

10. CHRISTIANITY AND REFORM

SOURCE: *The Unitarian* 1 (January 1834): 30–39; (February 1834): 51–58.

Brownson argues that social reform requires, as its precondition, individual improvement. Religion is absolutely indispensable for the reform of the individual. Those who have attempted to reform society without the aid of religion are unsuccessful because they do not pay attention to the culture of the individual mind and make no appeal to the whole person—to the spiritual as well as the material wants. A true reform must provide free and full scope for all natural capacities, religious as well as others. This cannot take place without Christianity because Christianity itself is the very spirit of reform.

Christianity and Reform.

Thousands assure us that we live in a wonder-working age, and refer us for proof to man's conquests over the material world. We are told that man has attacked the elements and subdued them,—made the most hurtful comparatively harmless, and the most stubborn ministers to his wants or his pleasures.

But man's moral conquests are far more striking proofs of his power, and are infinitely more encouraging to the philanthropist. Moral events, which are to influence all coming generations, have succeeded, and are succeeding, each other with astonishing rapidity. It

134

would seem that, in these later days, a new spirit had been breathed into the moral world. Mind breaks its long slumber and begins to exert its energies. Men begin to feel the workings of a nobler nature, and to indulge, and labour to embody, visions of a higher and lovelier destiny for the human race.

A war rages—a war of opinion—between the past and the future, between the advocates of the old order of things, and those who demand new and better institutions for time to come. It extends to every thing. Nothing is too sacred to be attacked. Nothing in politics, in morals, or in religion, is too venerable for its age, too well established by experience, to escape the hand of the ruthless soldier of the *movement* party in this new and fearful war. Blows are struck at the very foundation of the existing social order, and the ruins of all once held sacred are exposed to the idle gaze of the multitude.

All over the world the war has commenced. All over the world the demand for reform is uttered; in some places, in sounds half suppressed and scarcely audible; but in others, in tones loud, determined, and startling. In all communities there is a deep feeling, there are full hearts, there are quickened spirits, that will dare improvements in man's moral and social condition, with the hero's courage, with the saint's singleness of purpose, and with the martyr's firmness. The millions awake. They begin to perceive, or imagine they perceive, that they have been trifled with, that they have tamely submitted to an order of things which a little well directed exertion on their part would have exchanged for one immeasurably better. Urged on by a sense of real or fancied wrongs, they are collecting their forces and nerving their souls to the battle.

Such is the rising spirit of the times. We may deny or seek to disguise it, but proofs meet the eye at every glance. We may denounce it, declaim or reason against it, call it dangerous, impious, blasphemous, or what we will; its course is onward, and no power on earth can stay its progress or scatter its gathering forces. It may pass over the earth with desolation and death, may sweep off everything well established in government, pure in morals, or venerable in religion, but it must and will have its course. Of this we may be assured, great and lasting changes will be effected. The day has gone by to prevent it. The work is too far advanced to be arrested. Will the changes to be introduced settle down into salutary reforms, or will they prove only mischievous innovations? This is no trifling question. The wise and the good ask it with solicitude, if not with alarm. What answer shall be returned?

It may be answered, that the results of the impending struggle will be good or bad, according to the alliances which may be formed. If the spirit at work ally itself to infidelity, nothing valuable will be gained; if to religion, the most satisfactory consequences may be predicted.

This article will therefore labour to prove that no salutary reform can be effected by infidelity, and that the spirit of reform is, in fact, the very spirit of the gospel.

Those who are acquainted with man's whole nature require no proof of the first position here assumed. But these are not many. Enough has been witnessed, for a few years past, in our own country as well as in other countries, to convince us that those are not wanting who think they must commence reformers by making war upon the church, declaiming against the clergy, and breaking men loose from the restraints of religion. When the French reformer undertook to remodel society and to base his government on "the rights of man," he judged it necessary to reject religion. In England, at the present moment, many of the publications addressed to the labouring classes, publications which are the boldest and most popular advocates of reform, are either avowedly infidel, or else, under the pretence of opposing the Church Establishment, use arguments which strike at the foundation of religion itself. In our own country, within a few years, we have seen start up a large number of publications professedly advocating a radical reform in the social institutions of all countries, and, without a single exception, all have openly or covertly, attacked religion. Almost every young man, who learns, for the first time, that all, which is, is not right, charges the wrong he thinks he has discovered to the clergy, and believes himself aiding a reform by opposing them, and, too often, the cause they were set apart to defend. It is true, that he is soon cured of this folly, but seldom without the loss of those generous feelings by which he was governed. These are facts not without meaning. They admonish us that it is no work of supererogation to prove that infidelity can effect no real reform.

To effect any real reform, the individual man must be improved. The mass of mankind is made up of individuals. There is no such thing as reforming the mass without reforming the individuals who compose it. The mass of mankind is often spoken of as if it were a real individual; but in itself it is nothing. It has no head, no heart, no soul, no character, but as these exist in its individual members. Each member of the great whole has a separate existence, will, powers, duties of his own, and which cannot be merged in the mass. The reformer's concern is with the individual. That which gives to the individual a free mind, a pure heart, and full scope for just and beneficial action, is that which will reform the many. When the majority of any community are fitted for better institutions, for a more advanced state of society, that state will be introduced and those institutions will be secured. What the reformer, then, wants is the power to elevate the individual, to quicken in his soul the love of the highest excellence, and to urge him forward towards perfection with new and stronger impulses.

Will infidelity supply this power? Does infidelity seek to reform individual character? It is folly to pretend that it does. It attacks institutions. It deals only with some of the forms under which the errors of individual character may have been manifested, while it leaves the errors themselves untouched. It pronounces religion false, and its action on man's social relations mischievous. It declaims against government, but it does not propose a remedy for those depravities of individual character which render government necessary. Viewed in the most favourable light, it is powerless. Separated from what it often borrows from religion, it can present no motive to action. It has no power to kindle up a moral energy in the soul, and to arm it for a long and vigorous struggle for lofty and abiding virtue. The highest standard of morality it can recognise is expediency, and expediency for this short and transitory life.

Till within a few years, the unbeliever dreamed of no social reform, advocated no moral progress, imagined nothing better for man than the long train of existing abuses, unless, indeed, it were, that he should go back to the condition of the "untutored savage." What visions of a higher and better social existence than that they found already sustained, ever flitted across the minds of such men as Hobbes, Mandeville, Hume and Gibbon? What inward thirst, what promptings of the soul, had they for a purer virtue, a greater amount of human happiness—they, who seem to have had not the least sympathy with their fellow-beings? Indeed, what inducement can he who believes merely that he is to-day, and to-morrow will not be,—what inducement can he have to struggle with "the powers that be," to risk ease, property, reputation, perhaps life, to benefit those of whom he knows nothing, for whom he cares nothing, and who, like him, are only for a day, destined to flourish in the morning, to wither at noon, and to die ere it is night? Indeed, after the novelty of his disbelief has worn off, the unbeliever seldom troubles himself much about anything except his own immediate interests. He wraps himself up in his selfishness, looks in scorn upon the world, and bids it take care of itself. You often find him the loudest and most inveterate opponent of all useful changes. Where religion is popular, you may not unfrequently see him in the garb of the church, consoling himself for his hypocrisy by saying, Every man is selfish, following only his own selfish purposes, and that he must take the same course in self-defence. Long would reform sleep undisturbed, were it entrusted to the care of such as he!

It is true that infidelity, in these days, pretends to be a reformer. It speaks much of the debasement of the human mind, of the degradation of human nature, and makes loud and frequent demands for improvement; but, usually, without any clear conceptions of what would be an improvement, without any knowledge of what lies at the bottom of existing abuses, of man's wants and capabilities, or of what would supply the one or fully develope the other. One attributes all the wrong which exists to a mischievous government, another to the malign influence of certain indefinable, constantly varying external circumstances, another to the prevalence of religious belief, another to the priesthood, even where no priesthood exists, and so on to the end of the chapter. But in all their speculations, the idea of improving the individual man, as the means of improving the body of which he is a member, seems never to have come across the minds of unbelievers. They demand radical changes, but seem to have no suspicion that there can be no radical changes in society, or if there can, that none are desirable, any farther than they may be rendered necessary by radical changes in individual character. In France, the unbeliever, for a time, had an open field and fair play. He began by overturning the whole fabric of society, and then reörganized it according to his own mind. As he had modelled his new institutions after the principles of his ideal perfection, he was surprised to find that they did not produce the results he had predicted. It did not, at first, occur to him, that his new institutions and the character of the individuals for whom he had provided them were not in harmony; and when he did learn this, he believed the shortest way to remove the discrepancy was to destroy nearly all the then existing generation. Hence, his reform became a reign of terror, and his efforts in behalf of free institutions have retarded the march of liberty for centuries. All this evil would have been avoided, had he perceived that his work should begin with the individual, that he should first raise the individual and develope the powers of the individual mind. Had he done this, he would have elevated the standard of morality, and produced a discrepancy between individual character and—not his new institutions—but the old, and this would have inevitably involved their destruction, and have necessarily introduced new ones, as perfect as the new standard of individual excellence would admit. The notion, that government and social institutions can produce and preserve any given description of individual character, would never have been entertained, and tyrants would not have been furnished with another plea for despotism, to save society from the horrors of anarchy.

In this country, we established a free government, not because we had reasoned ourselves into a belief of its superiority to all others, not because we believed it would produce and preserve the virtues of individual character, but because such were already the virtues and the intelligence of our citizens as individuals, that none other than a free government would have been in harmony with their character. That even a free government and comparatively perfect social institutions do not necessarily preserve a corresponding excellence in individual character, is obvious from what we are daily witnessing among ourselves. Our people, as individuals, in the high uncompromising moral virtues, are very little, if at all, in advance of what they were at the commencement of our glorious struggle for freedom and national independence. We have thus far depended too much upon a free government and enlightened institutions, and have vainly thought to legislate people into high-toned moral beings. The better informed among us are daily perceiving the necessity of paying more and more attention to the culture of the individual mind. They are daily becoming better and better convinced that the only way to set the mass of our citizens forward in the career of virtuous improvement, is, to develope the capabilities of the individual man; to induce him to employ all his faculties in the accomplishment of just ends, and to exert all his energies to the perfecting of his own mind and heart.

Nothing, it should be added, will reform the individual, that does not appeal to his whole nature, and give full employment to all, especially his higher faculties. This infidelity cannot do. It addresses us as animals, not as men. It has no concern with the soul. It recognises no spirit in man, and, consequently, can appeal only to the body, to bodily appetites and bodily powers. It can give us no high and stirring views of our nature, no inducement to pure and elevated virtue, by assuring us that we are related to a Being who is infinitely great and supremely good, that we are kindred spirits and may attain to a kindred excellence with the everlasting God. In one word, it can make no appeal to the religious sentiment, can furnish nothing on which the religious affections can lay hold, and from which they may derive purity, strength, and delight. In this it leaves out a part, and that the noblest part, of our nature.

It is not necessary to prove that the religious sentiment is a part of our nature. We see this, we feel and know it. All ages, all countries, and nearly all individuals have the sentiment, and manifest it in combination with some form of religion. True, some few of our race have not always felt the inward workings of the religious sentiment, but to infer from this, that it is not natural to man, would be as absurd as to pretend that hunger and thirst are not natural, because, in certain morbid states of the stomach, there is felt no appetite for food or drink. Take away God and religion from the soul, its moral life dies, as quickly as does the body when deprived of wholesome nutriment. The soul hungers and thirsts for religion. Religion is its meat and drink; its bread of life; and is as strongly craved, as much needed for its growth and healthy action, as is food or drink for the body. How, then, can we hope to find the individual man morally strong and healthy, when deprived of this nutriment of the soul? Without this he must inevitably pine away, wither into a mere animal, to vegetate, propagate its species, and die. Yet of this would infidelity deprive us, and to this wretched fate would it abandon us.

No change, which does not tend to give free and full scope for the just exercise of all our faculties, can be a real reform. The only error of the present state of things is, that it infringes right action, supplies motives to wrong, and prevents the full development of the individual mind. What we want, are such changes, such improvements, as will develope, employ, task to their fullest extent, and rightly direct, all the faculties of our common nature. But such, infidelity cannot effect. Denying the religious sentiment, it can assign no place for its developement; discarding all the pious affections, it can afford them no employment in its new-modelled society, and shape nothing to their wants; contemplating only the human animal, it can make provision only for animal wants; and having no use for the spiritual nature, it must do all it can to break and destroy its power. Let any man ascertain accurately how large a portion of his nature finds employment only in that which belongs to religion, or is in some way dependant on the religious sentiment, and he may easily satisfy himself, whether infidelity would be likely to reörganize society, so as to give full scope for the free, vigorous and healthy exercise of our whole nature.

Now as infidelity does not propose to do this, has never done it, and never can do it, it can produce no salutary reform. The institutions it would introduce would always be opposed to the developement of much of our nature, and to individual improvement; consequently, they would be mischievous. They would place the social and the individual man in a state of perpetual war; the spiritual and the animal nature in an eternal struggle. The bosom would be torn by contending factions; government would be one thing to-day, and another to-morrow, and nothing would be fixed but anarchy and confusion.

That infidelity and the spirit of reform have sometimes been found in alliance, is not denied; but this alliance is unnatural, and has never produced anything worth preserving. Reformers have sometimes erred. Animated by a strong desire for human improvement, feeling an undying love for man, they have freely devoted themselves to his emancipation, and to the promotion of his endless progress towards perfection; but they have not always had clear conceptions of what would be an improvement, of the good attainable, nor of the practicable means of attaining it. Their zeal may have flowed from pure hearts, but it has not always been guided by just knowledge. They have often excited needless alarm, waged needless war, declaimed when they should have reasoned, censured when they should have pitied and consoled, awakened resentment when they should have gained confidence and attracted love. The consequence is, that they have been opposed by their natural friends, and this has obliged them to league with their natural enemies.

In the contest, the reformer has excited the alarms of the religious and armed against himself the guardians of the faith. He has met the minister of the church commanding him in the name of God to desist, and assuring him, that if he take another step forward, he does it at the peril of his soul's salvation. When the French reformer rose against the mischievous remains of the feudal system and the severe exactions of a superannuated tyranny, he found the church leagued with the abuses he would correct. Those who lived upon her revenues bade him retire. The anathema met his advance and repelled his attacks; and he was induced to believe there was no place whereon to erect the palace of liberty and social order, but the ruins of the temple.

Yet his cause was most eminently a religious cause. It was not that the spirit of reform was an infidel spirit, that it was opposed by the professed friends of religion. All reforms come from the lower classes, who are always the sufferers; and they are usually opposed by the higher classes, who live by those very abuses, or who are the higher classes in consequence of those very abuses which the reformer would redress. These classes, whether hereditary, elective, or fortuitous,—whether composed of the same individuals or of different ones,—have always the same spirit, and the same interests. The old order of things is that which elevates them; and that order of things they, of course, must feel it their interest to maintain. Hence it is, that the upper classes of society, all who are under the direct influence of those classes, and all who hope one day to make a part of them, are almost always opposed to all radical changes, and consequently to all real reform. In most countries, the ministers of religion, especially the higher orders of the hierarchy, make up a part of the higher and privileged classes, and hence the reason why they oppose the reformer, and force him into the ranks of the unbeliever. They, from their position, feel no need of a reform in the moral and social institutions of the community, and hope nothing from a change; and, as they are supposed to be like other men, they can but oppose it; they always have done so, and they always will do so, till they are made sensible that they must lose all their influence, and their means of benefiting themselves or others by continuing their opposition.

It is because the ministers of religion have, in most countries and in most ages of the world, formed one of the higher classes, or constituted one of the privileged orders, that we have so uniformly found them, in past times at least, advocates of the stationary principle. Where a man's treasure is, there will be his heart; and they had their treasure, they always have their treasure, in the existing order of things. This were no subject of complaint, were the existing order always the best order; were not progress a law of our nature and an inevitable condition of human society; were we able at any given time to reach the perfect, instead of being destined to be eternally approaching it. But such is not the fact. Man's course is onward. No state of society is perfect. No form of religion has ever yet been extensively embraced but it had its imperfections. Christianity has been everywhere presented under forms which ever have been and ever will be opposed, as mind advances and there is felt the want of something more liberal and more refined. Admit that the spirit of Christianity is always the same, yet its forms may be changed to suit the changes of individuals and of societies, and were this done no difficulty would occur. But its ministers and its professed friends declare religion to be identified with forms which have become revolting, and thus the reformer is driven from their company to that of the infidel.

It is never religion itself that the reformer opposes. He finds the gospel adulterated; he finds a foul and unnatural mixture presented him in the place of pure religion, and it is always those parts which are foreign to religion, but which are presented with it, that excite his hostility. Yet, in opposing the mixture, he may sometimes, innocently, because unintentionally, oppose the pure; in attacking the abuse, he may sometimes inadvertently strike the thing abused; in warring against the wrong-headed advocate, he may war against religion itself. He may not always clearly discriminate in his own mind; and if he should not, he is not more guilty than thousands who pass for good Christians. And should he make the proper distinctions in his own mind, he may fail to make others perceive them; for the vast majority of mankind identify religion with the abuses he would correct; and we need not, perhaps, be either surprised or angry, if, in his zeal for reform, wearied with effort after effort, opposed on every hand, and persecuted by the servants of the temple, he come to the conclusion, that it is best to cut the knot, and reject religion entirely. Men have so done, they may continue to do so, but no genuine friend to man ever did or ever will come to this conclusion, till driven to it by the professed guardians of the faith, "who neither enter into the kingdom of heaven themselves, nor suffer those that would to enter."

This should induce no Christian to decry reform. It should rather lead him to inquire, if he be not supporting religion under a form which is opposed to the progress of mind. The "overflowing scourge," which will sweep off "every refuge of lies," is now passing over the earth, and well doth it import us to surrender voluntarily whatever we love that is not based on eternal truth, that is not absolutely essential to the existence and free and healthy action of the religious sentiment. Well doth it import us all to return to the simplicity of the gospel, and to refuse, henceforth, to defend religion under any form not consistent with the endless progress of human reason and the ever advancing state of human society. . . .

We now proceed to the consideration of our second point, namely, that the spirit of reform is in fact the very spirit of the gospel. This proposition may require some proof. Every body may not perceive, at first sight, the identity of the spirit of the gospel with that spirit which now agitates "the millions." There are those who look only on the surface of things, and never have any notion of what lies at the bottom; let such as these suspend their judgment, till they have examined and collected facts to make their judgment worthy of attention.

The spirit which lies at the bottom of the movements among the people is the spirit of reform, of progress. It may seem to the superficial observer only the spirit of insubordination, of restlessness, of unnecessary, if not criminal, agitation. But discontent, insubordination, destructive as either may be, should not be condemned. Man is a progressive being. His uneasiness at his present condition is the result of an internal consciousness,—vaguely defined, poorly understood, perhaps,—that he is susceptible of something better. He has an inward thirst for perfection. The millions now feel the workings of this desire, this craving for a more perfect moral and social condition. They are conscious of wants which the present state of things cannot satisfy.

They demand something better; they resolve and struggle to gain it. They may not clearly perceive what would be an improvement; they may even place perfection in that which would be a deterioration; but this alters not the character of the spirit which urges them forward. They wish something which will satisfy all the wants of the soul; and if they direct their exertions towards that which will not do this, the defect is not in the spirit that moves, but in the judgment which directs.

The spirit whose movements have encouraged some, alarmed and offended others, is, thus, the spirit of reform, of progress,—a spirit always aiming at perfection. Is not this, in fact, the very spirit of the gospel? To answer this question, one should clearly perceive and fully comprehend the character of that work which the Author of the gospel came into the world to perform.

That work has greatly suffered by not having been understood. He who reads the gospel carefully, bringing to his aid enlightened philosophy and just criticism, cannot fail to perceive that it was not, as too many have imagined, the primary object of Jesus to make us happy in the world to come. If the good he laboured to effect was to extend beyond this life, into that which is eternal, it was only because the acquisition of holiness here sets one so much the farther forward in holiness hereafter. It was this world that he came to bless—man, in his earthly mode of being, that he preached, suffered, and died to make happy. He indeed alluded to another world; he promised the rewards of heaven to the good; he startled the wicked with fears of punishment in hell; but it was, to reach the hearts and consciences of men, to reform the individual, and, through the individual, the mass. The world was wrong, was wretched; he came to meliorate it, to set it right. Hence, the first words which broke from his lips in public were, "Reform, for the reign of God approacheth."

Are there those who deny this? What, then, does the gospel demand? What is it that Jesus requires? Did he not, in his mission, contemplate the production of greater purity of heart, a deeper sense of duty and of individual responsibility? Was not the gospel given to breathe new life into the soul, to urge it on by new and stronger impulses to a higher, a more abiding, an ever enlarging virtue? Did it not, does it not, appeal directly to the individual heart, and seek to kindle up a strong, undying love for all that is pure, useful, generous, and noble in character; and was it not expressly designed to impart the inward power needed to gain it? Is not here the spirit of reform, of a radical reform?

But this reform is not the production of a moment. It must be gradual, a progress, a growth. The gospel commands us to improve in knowledge and virtue, to "grow in grace," "to press onward and upward towards the mark of our high calling," "to become perfect as our Father in heaven is perfect." It is not with one degree of holiness, not with one step forward in the eternal career of moral progress, that the gospel is satisfied. It is the highest degree, the step farthest in advance possible, that it demands. It has no smile for mediocrity, no indulgence for the indolent. Its look is forward, and if it sometimes permits one to survey the ground over which he has passed, it is not that he may applaud himself for the progress already made, but that he may gather fresh courage and hope for the journey which still lies before. Is not here the spirit of progress, the spirit urging on to perfection?

Nor is it to one individual alone that the gospel appeals, not one alone it would quicken and urge onward in a glorious career of improvement. It appeals to all. What it demands of one individual it demands of every individual. It acknowledges no man's right to be a sinner—declares that no man can be exempt from the law of duty— declares, in terms not to be misinterpreted, to the high and the low, to the rich and the poor, to the bond and the free, that no one has the consent of his Maker to do that which is wrong, or to neglect that which is right. The spirit of the gospel, then, requires a universal reform; it requires every individual to advance, to grow in grace, to press on towards perfection; and does not this identify it, in reality, with the stirring spirit of the times? with the spirit—not of the stationary—but of the movement party?

Does the gospel demand that which is impracticable? Does it demand this extensive, this radical reform, without permitting us to hope that it can be realized? So, indeed, it would seem, from the language of its professed friends. Even religious men brand him who proposes such a reform, a disturber of the peace, call him a disorganizer, and enough of other epithets of reproach. He who ventures to predict that it will be realized, is pronounced a visionary, and people propose a strait jacket, or physic and good regimen, as the only suitable arguments to be urged against him. "The evils of society," we are gravely told, "always have existed, and always must exist. Man has always preyed upon man, and always will do so. It is in human nature to do so, and he but betrays his ignorance who dreams of a change." Perhaps so. Those who say so are doubtless wise men, men who are well acquainted with human nature in its diseased, if not in its healthy, manifestations. And yet, there is a singular inconsistency in these very wise men. They deny that the mass of mankind can possibly become virtuous; but point them to any particular individual of that mass, and they will admit, that that individual may, if he will, become a high-toned moral being. They thus deny of the whole, what they admit to be true of all its parts, and of parts, too, which are very much alike. For all men have, substantially, the same nature; all have within themselves all the elements of thought, of reason, of virtue. The greatest and best have nothing of which the least and worst have not the germs. And there is not an individual in whom those germs cannot be warmed into life and expanded into a generous virtue. Every man is commanded to love God with all his heart, soul, and strength, and his neighbour as himself. Single out one that cannot do this. Cannot *you* thus love God and man? Cannot your neighbour? his neighbour? and his? Where is there one who cannot? Nowhere? Then all can comply with the requisitions of the gospel. Each individual can reform, can improve, can attain a high moral standing. If each individual can, all can; and, of course, the great mass of mankind can become virtuous.

Should every individual become virtuous, acquire that purity of heart, that firmness of purpose, that love to God and to man, which the gospel demands, that moral growth which Jesus laboured to produce, there could remain no institutions of an evil tendency. All that now bears man down to the dust and darkens his soul would be removed, all social as well as all private evils would disappear, and all governments would be so remodelled, as to have no longer a deteriorating influence. Bad governments, mischievous social institutions, are not to be attributed to the defects of rulers, to their ignorance, to their vices, nor to their crimes, but to the people. No people, worthy of freedom, was ever enslaved. When the majority of a community are really free in themselves, have pure and just principles, firm and manly characters, no tyrant can enslave that community, no mischievous government can possibly be established over it. Whatever political evils there may be in any community, they must disappear in the exact proportion that the growth of individual virtue demands. Make all men good Christians,—and all can and should be,—all governments would become free, all social institutions beneficial, and man's intercourse with man, harmonious, pleasing, endearing.

That Jesus came to introduce a new order of things, to change, to perfect, man's moral and social institutions has indeed been admitted by some, but so timidly, with such coldness of assent, that the admission has led to little vigorous and well sustained exertion. The great mass of the friends as well as the opponents of the gospel have had but a slight glimpse of this truth. They have said, and still say, that such could not have been his object, because he has not yet accomplished it. But we have seen too many things effected during the last hundred years, which former generations would have pronounced impossible, to regard with much attention the reasoning that would measure the future by the past, that would infer that because a thing has not been it therefore cannot be. The work which Jesus proposed is not, indeed, yet accomplished. That work was immense. The gospel found the human race with false ideas of morality and religion, with mischievous governments, and institutions almost universally opposed to the interests of society. The prevalent modes of feeling, thinking, and acting were wrong. Things were valued in an inverse ratio to their real worth. Fame was obtained, not by real virtue,—not by the preservation, but by the destruction, of human life. War was the business and the glory of governments and rulers. The useful arts were menial, and were assigned to those who had, and could have, no share in what were esteemed honourable pursuits. The worship of God was an outward service, an observance of impure or debasing rites and ceremonies, performed, not at the command of conscience, but of the state or the priesthood. Now all this was to be changed. For the pompous was to be substituted the simple,—for the external, the internal. The mere member of the state or of a sacerdotal corporation was to be converted into an individual, with rights, duties, responsibilities of his own. The useless was to give place to the useful, war to peace, the destruction of human life to its preservation, the false estimate of things to the true; and nothing was to be valued except in proportion to its power to add something to the well-being of man; nothing was to be accounted virtue which might not do something to develope the spiritual nature, to make man a more elevated moral being, a more pious worshipper of God, a warmer or steadier friend to his race. This was not the work of a day. Without converting man into a different order of being, it could be done only gradually; and because it is not yet completed, shall we rashly say it was never designed?

One great reason why Jesus has not effected more may be found in the contracted notions which have been entertained of his design. Of those who heard him most gladly, few comprehended his object. The ignorant multitude of that day did not and could not comprehend it. It far exceeded their stage of mental progress, to take in the idea of a reform so extensive and so radical as he proposed. They were incapable of understanding that it was an entire new order of things which he wished to effect. They degraded him in their minds, from the dignity of a moral regenerator of the world, to the littleness of a theological disputant. They supposed he had come to change a few items of religious belief, to alter or abolish a few of the forms of religious worship, —that he had come merely to mend with a piece of new cloth a few of the rents in the old worn-out garment of the social and moral system; but they never imagined, notwithstanding they were so informed, that the new would tear away from the old, and the rent thus be made worse, and that the only rational way of proceeding was to throw off the old, and to put on an entire new garment. Consequently, though Christ was nominally preached, for a long series of years his power was scarcely felt, and the great object of his mission was unperceived. People (to borrow, with a slight variation, another scriptural illustration,) people "called themselves by the name" of Christ "to take away their reproach"; but they were "content to eat their own bread and wear their own apparel"—they would fain be known by his name, but in regard to anything beyond this, to any change of life consequent thereupon, they cared not, they thought not. That he had power to touch the heart,—power to quicken the soul, to give it the very life of virtue,—power to change the whole face of the moral and political world, was not dreamed of in the philosophy which, for centuries, usurped the schools and the churches.

Still, the spirit of Christ was in the world. Though the darkness of men's minds and hearts prevented it from being perceived, it was silently, gradually, effecting its work. It touched a heart, here and there. It kindled up the ethereal fire, now in this mind, now in that. It formed, here and there, little nuclei, around which began to gravitate the immortal atoms of a new moral world, pure and lovely in the sight of God and man. If its power was suspended in this place, repressed in this community, it burst forth with additional energy and glory in that. Meanwhile the world is agitated. Revolutions are daily occurring. All is in commotion. All is in a transition state, although to the spectator all seems settled. Letters revive. Science begins to shed its light. Young thought begins to feel its strength, and to be ambitious of trying its wing. The past is recalled; the present is surveyed. Man sees himself in a new light. Views of his wrongs and sufferings, of his wants and capabilities, are taken from more favourable positions. Governments, religions, social institutions, in general, are summoned to the bar of infant reason. Speculation rushes in the future, and dares picture forth worlds of ideal beauty and felicity for the human race. Practical spirits appear, and resolve to embody what others behold in idea. Now the Son of God comes with power and glory. Now his Spirit, which has so long been trampled upon, which has so long been struggling in secret, looks forth upon the world, and rolls back the clouds of mental and moral darkness. And there is a swelling of men's hearts; and there is hope stretching forth her arms, eager to grasp that greater good which the soul has beheld in vision. Mind redoubles its strength. The individual man now feels, almost for the first time, that he is not a mere cipher, nothing worth only as he is annexed to the state or the crowd, —but that he is a man, with rights and prerogatives. The human race begins its upward and onward career in moral and social improvement.—We call this the epoch of THE REFORMATION. It is that epoch when the power of Rome was shaken, and the human mind was reconquered from her despotism. And the philosophical spectator might have then discerned at work all the causes which are to effect the mightiest revolutions, and to secure results inexpressibly grand and glorious for the whole human race. The gospel works silently, but effectually. At times it may seem suppressed, and fearful souls may imagine the world abandoned to wretchedness and despair. But all this time of darkness and doubt, it is collecting its power for new and more astonishing victories. The gospel was compared to "leaven concealed in three measures of meal;" though concealed its power was not destroyed. In what we now see, in these agitations, these new parties, these new demands throughout the world, we should recognise its slow but energetic workings to "leaven the whole lump." The gospel is the power of God unto salvation. The mass now feel it struggling within them, and bear witness to its reforming energy; and we may "thank God and take courage." The time draws nigh when it will not be alleged that Christ did not propose to reform the world, because he has not yet done it.

Indeed, if all the glowing and majestic descriptions of the Messiah's reign be not so many rhetorical flourishes, changes of almost inconceivable magnitude are yet to be effected in man's moral and social condition. It was a glorious morning that which dawned on the birth of Jesus. If all Scripture be not a deceptive dream, then commenced a new age, that happy order of things which had been so often predicted, so rapturously sung by inspired bards, and so long desired by all nations. Then the Angel of Improvement hovered with joy over the earth, and saw with rapture, as he looked down the stream of time, the all-comprehensive principles then introduced, gradually, but effectually, working their way through all opposition, subduing all enemies, surmounting every obstacle, and finally regenerating the whole moral world. He saw wrongs and outrages disappearing,—ignorance, vice, and crime yielding up their empire,—man rising from the oppressions of a hundred ages, and looking forth, the image of his Maker, upon a world of beauty. He heard the last note of discord die away in the distance, the tear which the mother shed for her son slain in battle was wiped from her eye,—the sigh which bespoke unrequited affection was suppressed,—man everywhere opened his heart and gave his hand to his brother. He beheld; and gave the shout of joy, which rung back from heaven's hosts: "Glory to God in the highest, on earth peace and good will towards men."—The vision of the Angel shall be realized. Man shall yet be worthy of his origin, and be able to rejoice in his destiny.

11. BENJAMIN CONSTANT ON RELIGION

SOURCE: *The Christian Examiner and Gospel Review* 17 (September 1834): 63–77.

In agreement with Benjamin Constant and other Romantics, Brownson argues that the religious sentiment is a natural human sentiment, arising from a permanent and universal law of human nature. Thus, by nature, human beings are determined to be religious. The forms this natural sentiment take, however, are not universal, but variable and transitory. Forms are gradually outgrown as individuals and cultures progress. The religious sentiment itself, being the very spirit of progress, ceaselessly seeks the purification of all the forms to which it has attached itself. The excellence of Christianity is that it is the religious sentiment itself detachable from all forms and impregnable in all forms.

Why is man affected by religious considerations? Why has he, wherever found, some kind of religious worship? Why does he, by turns, embrace and abandon that vast variety of religious forms, which range from the loathsome fetichism of the savage, to the simple and sublime monotheism of the Christian? Is it by accident, or in accordance with certain invariable and indestructible laws? If in accordance with certain laws, what are these laws? Such were the questions which passed through the mind of Benjamin Constant, and produced the works . . . which, if they are not so perfect as to leave us nothing to desire on the topics they treat, open a new route to the philosopher, and let in light upon many a dark passage in the history of religions. . . .

He begins his work with the position, that all beings, created or uncreated, animate or inanimate, rational or irrational, have their laws. These laws constitute the nature of each species, and are the general and permanent cause of each one's mode of existence. We do not know, we cannot know, the origin of these laws. All we know, or need know, is, that they exist, and in all our attempts to explain any partial phenomena, we must assume their existence, as our point of departure.

Man has his laws,—laws which constitute him what he is, that is to say, man. By one of these laws, he is led to seek some object to venerate, to adore, between whom, and himself, he may establish mutual relations. That this is by a law of his nature, is inferred from its being peculiar to man, and common to nearly all men, in all ages, and in all positions, being always reproduced with the new generation. It follows from this, that man is not religious by accident,—has not religion because he is weak or timid, or through the influence of wily statesmen, as some have asserted, nor because he has reasoned himself into the belief of its truth and utility; but because he is man, and must be religious or divest himself of a part of his nature. It is no longer a question, then, whether we ought to preserve or destroy religion. That matter is settled. Religion man has, and will have. He is determined to it by an interior sentiment, by a fundamental law of his being, a law invariable, eternal, indestructible.

But if man is determined to religion by a fundamental law of his being, how comes it that men, even wise and virtuous men, at various epochs, are either indifferent or opposed to it? To solve this problem, we must distinguish between the religious sentiment, and religious institutions. The sentiment results from that craving, which we have, to place ourselves in communication with invisible powers; the institutions, the form, from that craving which we also have, to render the means of that communication, we think to have discovered, regular and permanent. The consecration, regularity, and permanence, of these means, are things, with which we cannot well dispense. We would count upon our faith. We would find it to-day what it was yesterday, and not have it seem ready at each moment to vanish and escape from us like a vapor. We demand the suffrage of those, with whom we have relations of interest, of habit, or of affection; for we take pleasure in our own sentiments only when they are attached to the universal sentiment. We do not love to nourish an opinion which no one shares with us. We aspire, for our thoughts as well as for our conduct, to the approbation of others; and we ask an external sanction to complete our internal satisfaction. Hence the necessity of religious institutions, the reason why the sentiment is always clothed with some form.

But every positive form, however satisfactory it may be for the present, contains a germ of opposition to future progress. It contracts, by the very effect of its duration, a stationary character, that refuses to follow the intellect in its discoveries, and the soul in its emotions, which each day renders more pure and delicate. Forced to borrow images more and more material, in order to make the greater impression upon its adherents, the religious form soon comes to present man, wearied with this world, only another very little different. The ideas it suggests are daily narrowed down to the terrestrial ideas, of which they are only a copy, and the epoch arrives when it presents to the mind only assertions which it cannot admit, and to the soul only practices which can no longer satisfy it. The sentiment now breaks away from that form, which, if one may so speak, has become petrified; it asks another form, one which will not wound it, and it ceases not its exertions till it obtains it. Here is the history of religion; but without the distinction between the sentiment and the form, it would be for ever unintelligible. The sentiment is lodged in the bottom of the soul, always the same, unalterable, and eternal; the form is variable and transitory.

But if the form be variable and transitory, it is not by accident that the sentiment combines now with this form, and now breaks from it to combine with another. That which we worship is always the highest worth of which we can form any conception. We always embody in our religious institutions, all our ideas of the true, the beautiful, and the good. Consequently, the object of our worship, and the religious institutions we adopt, or the form with which we clothe the religious sentiment, will always be exactly proportioned to our mental development and moral progress. At every epoch, there is cherished and defended, as pure a form of religion, as the general civilization of that epoch will admit. The lowest, the grossest form of religion is fetichism. But, low and gross as this form of religion is, it is the purest and the most elevated, which the minds and the hearts of the tribes who adopt it can grasp, and nothing better, more spiritual, can be received, till there be an advance in civilization. Yet this form, miserable as it may seem at more advanced stages of mental and moral progress, is good and useful when adopted. It then responds to the wants of the soul, is in harmony with the lights of the understanding, and has a binding tie upon the conscience. It is at that epoch desirable,—has an important mission to accomplish.

But the correspondence between this form and the wants of the mind and the heart, is soon broken. Man is a progressive being. The institutions which he adopts to-day help him onward, but as they do not advance with him, he has soon outgrown them, and begun the work of exchanging them for others. The religious sentiment itself is the very spirit of progress. It labors unceasingly to purify the form with which it is combined. It is for ever struggling to enlarge the sphere of its activity. It demands a broader horizon; it shoots off into the unknown, rises to the infinite, and seizes upon the perfect. Left to the workings of this interior sentiment, man would march onward with an uninterrupted progress, and every day become able to conceive a nobler object of worship, and to embody more of excellence in his form of religion. The unyielding nature of every religious form, combined with the influence of the sacerdotal corporations, which always have an interest in perpetuating the existing order, whatever it may be, interrupts, however, this regular progress, and keeps him wedded to the low and the worthless form, from which he should long since have been divorced. But, if interrupted, suspended, progress cannot be wholly prevented. Fetichism ceases to be in harmony with civilization. Its mission ends, and a new religious form is demanded. Polytheism is elaborated, improved, perfected, but in its turn it must yield to theism, to the theism of Christianity.

Each religious form has three epochs. At first, man seizes upon a religion,—that is, following his instinct, directed by the lights of his understanding, he seeks to discover the relations which exist between him and invisible powers. When he believes he has discovered these relations, he gives them a regular and determinate form. Having provided for this first craving of his nature, he developes and perfects his other faculties. But his very successes render the form, which he had given to his religious ideas, disproportioned to his developed and perfected faculties. Now begins the second epoch. From this moment the destruction of that form is inevitable. The polytheism of the Iliad no longer comporting with the age of Pericles, Euripides, in his tragedies, becomes the organ of a nascent irreligion.

If the old creed be prolonged by institutions, sacerdotal corporations, or other means, the human race, during this factitious prolongation, is furnished only with an existence purely mechanical, in which there is nothing of life. Faith and enthusiasm desert religion, and there are left only formulas, observances, and priests. But this forced state has its limits. A conflict commences, not only between the established religion and the understanding which it insults, but between it and the religious sentiment, which it has ceased to satisfy. This conflict brings about the third epoch,—the annihilation of the form, which stirred up rebellion; and hence the crises of complete unbelief,—crises, disorderly, sometimes terrible, but inevitable, when man wants to be delivered from what has become, and hereafter can be, only a bar to improvement. These crises are always followed by a form of religious ideas better suited to the faculties of the human mind, and religion comes forth from its ashes, with a new youth, purer, and more beautiful.

This distinction between the religious sentiment, and the religious form, is very necessary to be made. It explains many of the phenomena, which occur in the history of religion. This explains wherefore it is, that men of virtuous lives, of ardent enthusiasm, of generous devotion to liberty, and to the welfare of their fellow beings, have, at times, opposed themselves to religion. They are men who have outgrown the established form. It no longer responds to the wants of their souls, no longer comports with their understanding, nor comes up to their ideas of the perfect. They rebel against it, and the religious sentiment itself in them is found combating a religious form, which galls it, and restrains its free and healthy action. This explains the existence, and the great influence of certain infidel writers. Writers are the organs of their age. They collect and bring out the ideas of their times. Had Lucian been placed in the age of Homer, or merely in that of Pindar,—had Voltaire been born under Louis IX, or Louis XI, Lucian and Voltaire had not even attempted to shake the belief of their contemporaries, or would have attempted it in vain. They were less indebted to their own merit for the applauses which they obtained from their own times, and for the eulogiums which encouraged them, than to the conformity of their doctrines, to those which began to be accredited. They said plainly and unreservedly what every body thought. Each, recognising himself in them, admired himself in his interpreter. Men must begin to doubt, before one can have much success in shaking their belief, and certainly before one can gain celebrity by attempting it. This explains why it is impossible at some epochs to disseminate doubt, and equally impossible, at others, to establish conviction. This is not accidental. It is not by mere caprice, that people are devout or irreligious. When the religious form is in harmony with the religious sentiment, and with the faculties of the mind, doubt is impossible; when that harmony no longer exists, belief is equally impossible. A believing epoch marks institutions which respond to the wants of the soul, and of the understanding; an unbelieving epoch marks a growth, an advance, which has left those institutions behind,—a search after new institutions, which will answer to the new wants that have been developed, and with which the faculties of the human mind may unite, and gather strength to take another step onward in its endless career of perfectibility.

From Benjamin Constant's theory, slightly and imperfectly as we have now presented even its most prominent traits, we may derive much to soften our indignation at the past, and to inspire us with hope for the future. All the great institutions of former times have been good in their day, and in their places, and have had missions essential to the progress of humanity to accomplish. The Catholic institution, Catholicism, which still excites the wrath and indignation of many a religionist, as well as of many an unbeliever, was a noble institution in its time. It was a mighty advance upon the paganism which preceded it. It was suited to the wants of the age in which it flourished, and we are indebted to it for the very light which has enabled us to discover its defects. Its vices,—and they need not be disguised,—appertain to the fact, that it has lingered beyond its hour. It has now, and long has had, only a factitious existence. Its work was long since done, its purpose accomplished, and it now only occupies the space, that should be filled with another institution,—one which will combine all our discoveries and improvements, and be in harmony with the present state of mental and moral progress.

Protestantism cannot be said to supply the place of Catholicism. Protestantism is not a religion, is not a religious institution, contains in itself no germ of organization. Its purpose was negative, one of destruction. It was born in the conflict raised up by the progress of mind against Catholicism, which had become superannuated. Its mission was legitimate, was necessary, was inevitable; but may we not ask, if it be not accomplished? Catholicism is destroyed, or at least, is ready to disappear entirely, as soon as a new principle of social and religious organization, capable of engaging all minds and hearts in its service, shall present itself. And this new principle will present itself. Men will not always live in a religious anarchy. The confusion of the transition-state in which we now are, must end, and a new religious form be disclosed, which all will love and obey.

But we need not go out of Christianity to find this new principle. Christianity contains the germs of many new principles, which wait only the proper hour to develope themselves. We have, as yet, seen but little of Christianity, suspected but little of what it is, and what it contains. Christianity is unalterable, eternal, indestructible as to its foundation; but it is exceedingly flexible, as to its forms. In one stage of spiritual improvement, it unites enthusiastically with Catholicism, and, in another, it unites no less enthusiastically with Protestantism, and urges it on in its career of destruction. A great excellence of Christianity, and one of the most striking proofs of its divine origin, is the fact, that it is wedded to no form, but can unite with all forms, and exist in all stages of civilization. Indeed, in the last analysis, it is little else than the religious sentiment itself, detached from all forms, exhibiting itself in its divine purity and simplicity.

We think the time has come for us to clothe the religious sentiment with a new form, and to fix upon some religious institution,
which will at once supply our craving for something positive in religion, and not offend the spirituality which Christianity loves, and
towards which the human race hastens with an increasing celerity. We
think, we see indications, that this presents itself to many hearts as
desirable. And we think we see this especially among our own friends.
Every religious denomination must run through two phases, the one
destructive, the other organic. Unitarianism could commence only by
being destructive. It must demolish the old temple, clear away the
rubbish, to have a place whereon to erect a new one. But that work is
done; that negative character which it was obliged to assume then, may
now be abandoned. The time has now come to rear the new temple,
—for a positive work, and if we are not mistaken, we already see the
workmen coming forth with joy to their task. We already see the germ
of re-organization, the nucleus, round which already gravitate the
atoms of a new moral and religious world. The work of elaboration is
well nigh ended, the positive institutions, so long sought, will soon be
obtained, and the soul, which has so long been tossed upon a sea of
dispute, or of skepticism, will soon find that repose, after which it so
deeply sighs and yearns.

Here, perhaps, we ought to close; but we cannot let the occasion
pass without offering some remarks upon . . . the point . . . that religion and morality rest not on the understanding, not on logical deductions, but on an interior sentiment. Here is an important recognition,—a recognition of two distinct orders of human faculties. This
recognition is not always made by metaphysicians, but it never escapes
popular language. It is found in the distinction between the head and
the heart, the mind and the soul, the understanding and the affections,
which obtains in all languages. And this is not strange. One cannot
have made the least progress in psychological observation, without
being struck with internal phenomena, which can by no means be
classed with the operations of the understanding. There belong to
human nature, passions, emotions, sentiments, affections, of which,
the understanding, properly so called, can take no account, which pay
no deference to its ratiocinations, and even bid defiance to its laws.
The feeling which we have, when contemplating a vast and tranquil
sea, distant mountains with harmonious outlines, or, when marking
an act of heroism, of disinterestedness, or of generous self-sacrifice for
others' welfare, rises without any dependence on the understanding.
We feel what we then feel, not because we have convinced ourselves by

logical deductions that we ought so to feel. Reasoning may come afterwards and justify the feeling; but it did not precede it, and, if it had, it could not have produced it. The understanding cannot feel; it cannot love, hate, be pleased, be angry, nor be exalted or depressed. It is void of emotion. It is calm, cold, calculating. Had we no faculty but those it includes, we should be strangers to pity, to sympathy, to benevolence, to love, and,—what is worse,—to enthusiasm. Bring the whole of man's nature within the laws of the understanding, and you reduce religion, morality, philosophy, to a mere system of logic; you would, in the end, pronounce every thing which does not square with dry and barren dialectics, chimerical, and every thing which interest cannot appropriate, mischievous.

But we not only contend for the distinction of the mental phenomena into two different orders, but we contend, that the sentiments are as worthy of reliance, as the understanding; that, to speak in popular language, the testimony of the heart is as legitimate, as that of the head. We are aware, that the philosophy of sensation will condemn this position. Be it so. The philosophy of sensation reigned during the last half of the last century, and it is, as far as we have any philosophy, still the philosophy of our own country; but it is no great favorite of ours. It undoubtedly has its truth; but, taken exclusively, freed from its inconsequences, and pushed to its last results, it would deprive man of all but a merely mechanical life, divest the heart of all emotion, wither the affections, dry up the sentiments, and sink the human race into a frigid skepticism. The testimony of the senses requires an internal sanction, and, in the last analysis, that of the understanding is not credited till it is corroborated by that of consciousness. Neither our senses, nor our understanding, can prove to us, that we exist, and yet it is impossible for us, in a healthy state of mind to doubt our existence; neither our senses nor our understanding can prove to us the existence of an external world, nor the objective reality of any thing, yet we should justly regard him as insane, who should not believe in the existence of an external world, and there is no one, who, listening to the sweet strains of music, will not believe they come to his heart from some objective reality. It is a law of our nature, of which reasoning cannot divest us, that in these, and in a vast variety of cases, we must believe on the simple testimony of consciousness, or, in other words, we believe so, because our nature,—the very laws of our being,— compel us to believe so. But the moment we recur to the testimony of consciousness, to the laws of our nature, we desert the understanding, we leave the power of ratiocination, and have recourse to an entirely different order of testimony.

We may be told, that to admit, that the feelings, the sentiments, are worthy of reliance, is to go off into the mysterious, to stop we know not where. We know many are very coy of mystery. We know there are many who say, "Where mystery begins, there religion ends"; and we know, also, that in saying it, if they mean what is inexplicable to the understanding, properly so called, they pronounce a general sentence of condemnation upon all that is elevated, generous, and touching in human nature. We can explain to the understanding, none of the workings of the sentiments of the heart; none of the emotions, the affections of the soul. Indeed, we do not wish to explain them. We are not afraid of the mysterious. It is one of the glories of our nature, and one of the strongest pledges of its immortal destiny, that it delights in the mysterious; that it has cravings which go beyond what is known; that it dares rush off into the darkness, trusting to its own instincts for guidance; and that it has powers, which can out-travel the under-standing, and which can seize and shadow forth to its own eye a perfection, which reason cannot comprehend, of which it does not even dream. To condemn the mysterious, were to bring the soul down from the beautiful and the holy, to the merely useful,—were to kill poetry, to wither the fine arts, to discard all the graces, for all these have something of the mysterious, are enveloped in mystic folds, of-fensive it may be to the understanding, but enchanting to the soul. We say, again, we are not afraid of the mysterious. We love it. We love those mysterious emotions, which we feel, when we survey the magnif-icent works of nature, or the creations of genius; when we hear the wind sigh over ruins; or when we walk among the dead, and think of those who were and are not, of the hearts which once beat, but which are now still, of the sweet voices which once spoke, but which are silent now. We love those emotions, which start within us when we think of God, of the human soul, of its immortality, of heaven, and of eternity. Reasoning is then still, and the soul, asserting her supremacy, half escaping from the body which imprisons her, catches some glorious visions of her native land, her everlasting home, and of those sublime occupations to which she feels herself equal. It is to us, then, no objection to say, our doctrine leads off into the mysterious. All to us, human beings, is mysterious, except the little that we know, and it is only that interior craving of our nature which keeps us for ever hover-ing beyond the horizon of what we know, that enables us, by conquests from the dominions of mystery, to enlarge the boundaries of our knowledge.

But we would not merely rely on this order of our faculties, which we call the sentiments. We would have them appealed to, as the most essential part of our nature. We do not mean to depreciate the understanding; we would not underrate the power of ratiocination, nor, in any case, dispense with sound logic. We value man's whole nature; man's whole nature is essential. We should think clearly, reason closely, powerfully; but we should also feel justly and energetically. We should retain and develope all our faculties, each in its place, so as to preserve unbroken harmony through the whole man. But if we do this, we shall find, that the sentiments, the feelings, are entitled to a much higher rank than it has been customary to assign them for the last century. To us the sentiments seem to be peculiarly the human faculties. They give to man his distinctive character. They supply him with energy to act, and prompt him to the performance of grand and noble deeds. We fear that their power is seldom suspected, that little attention is paid to the mission which is given them to accomplish. We have schools for the intellect. We take great pains to educate the reasoning faculty, but we almost, at least so far as our schools are concerned, entirely neglect the sentiments. We cannot but regret this; for knowledge when not coupled with just feelings, strong reasoning powers when not under the guidance of pure and holy sentiments, only so much the better fit one for a career destructive to the best interests of humanity. And, let it be understood, men are not reasoned into good feelings, for the feelings do not depend on the intellect. Just sentiments are not the result of just knowledge. A man may know the truth, be able to defend it in language and with arguments that fix attention, and flash instantaneous conviction, and yet have no just, honorable, or benevolent feelings. It is an old saying, that men know better than they do;

> "Video meliora, proboque;
> Deteriora sequor."[1]

It will be so, as long as we trust to merely intellectual education to give right feelings. We would, therefore, without in the least neglecting the intellect, turn attention to the sentiments, appeal to them on all occasions, and make it the leading object of all education to develope them, to fit them for strong and beneficent action.

We would appeal constantly to the sentiments, for all that we have of the disinterested and self-denying pertains to them. Destroy the sentiments and we should never support any cause, however just, dear, or essential to humanity, when the nicer calculations of interest assure us that we have nothing to gain for our individual selves. Destroy the sentiments, and we could never identify ourselves with humanity, and at times come forth in its behalf with the reformer's zeal, and with the martyr's firmness. There is nothing great or good ever won without sacrifice. No man will devote himself to the defence of liberty, of justice, of his country, of religion, or of the welfare of his fellow beings in any shape, unless he has within him the power of self-denial, and is prepared to make almost any sacrifice. Had the Apostles not had this power of self-denial and of self-sacrifice, they never would, they never could, have established Christianity. Had it not been for this, the Reformers of Germany would hardly have succeeded, the Puritans would not have withstood the Prelates, left their homes, and all the fond recollections of childhood and youth, to brave the dangers of the deep and of a new and hostile world, to maintain liberty of conscience; nor would our fathers have staked life, property, and honor, to gain a country for their children, and liberty for the world. But this power, or rather spirit of self-denial and self-sacrifice, which Christianity was sent into the world to cherish and clothe with omnipotence, pertains solely to the sentiments. The understanding knows nothing of it. That, at best, knows only the self-denial of calculation, of temporary pleasure to obtain a lasting good, which is nothing more than selfishness would every day command.

We are not willing to dismiss the topic of self-denial without a farther remark. We speak not now of its necessity. We have already shown that. But we would refer to man's love of self-denial, of sacrifice, and to the power of that principle on which it depends. It is,—perhaps always was,—extremely fashionable to speak of interest as man's strongest, man's governing principle of action. If there is a good thing to be done, a religious institution to be patronized, a moral or political reform to be accomplished, appeal is almost invariably made to interest, to selfishness. But in this we do not show our deep knowledge of human nature. Paradoxical as it may seem, men will do more from a disinterested, than from an interested motive. It has been asked, how could Christianity, a self-denying religion, as it was, be established without a continual miracle? Had it not been a self-denying religion, its establishment would have required a miracle indeed. Once awaken the sense of duty in a man, and it is infinitely stronger than his sense of interest. Men will see every thing dear to them die, see their children drop into the grave, have their own flesh torn off by inches, sooner than they will abandon duty,—we mean those in whom the sense of duty is not dormant. But has interest ever shown itself equally strong? And what is the sense of duty, but another name for the spirit of self-denial, of self-sacrifice?

There is a standing proof of the weakness of men's sense of interest, obvious to every eye, in the indifference shown to religion. Who is not convinced, that it is for his highest interest, even in this world, to be religious? And does every one follow this conviction? Far from it. You may go into the pulpit and speak with the tongue of an angel,— you may prove, beyond the possibility of a doubt, that it is for the highest good, the greatest possible interest of every one of your hearers, for time and for eternity, to be religious, and induce no one to forsake a single sin, no one to cleave to a single virtue. Your success would be immeasurably greater, would you insist on self-denial, and show clearly, that heaven is not to be won without a struggle, without a costly and painful sacrifice. The successes of different religious sects, clearly evince this. With all the drawback of a most irrational creed, those sects among us who insist most upon self-denial and sacrifice, spread much faster than those sects, albeit they have a much more rational creed, who attempt to show, that religion demands no sacrifice, no self-denial.

We do not, in this, shut our eyes upon the fact, that a large proportion of mankind are selfish, governed by a sense of their own interest. We admit the fact, and we can account for it. Our own good has its place. The faculties which lead us to seek it, are on the surface of our nature, and are almost the only ones to which appeal is ever made; consequently, the only ones much developed, and the only ones suspected by those who never penetrate beneath the surface. But let us go deeper into human nature, let us go down into the depths of the soul, and stir up, from its bottom, the sense of duty, of the good, the beautiful, the true, and the holy, the spirit of disinterestedness, of self-denial, and of sacrifice, and we shall find a power infinitely stronger than our sense of interest.

To be sure, it costs us an effort to awaken this sense, an effort to obey it. But so much the better. The sentiments all demand an effort, a self-denial, a sacrifice; it is their very nature to carry us away from ourselves, to seek a good which does not centre in ourselves. But this is their praise. It costs us an effort to obey them, we own, and we are glad that it is so. Men love to make an effort. There is that in man, which delights in the struggle, which disdains repose, and pants for strong, varied, and continued action. The sailor on land feels its workings, and longs to be on his loved ocean, to be again amid the fury and excitement of the storm. The old soldier proves it; though he have lost a leg, an eye, or an arm, in battle, still, as his ears catch the strains of martial music, he is ready to rush into the conflict. Why? Because there is excitement there, because there is danger there, because there is a struggle, an effort, there. Take away the excitement, the danger, the struggle, and men would lose their passion for war. This shows us there is something within us, that loves the conflict, that delights to war with danger, to grapple with the enemy, even to the death-struggle. This at bottom is a noble principle. It is one which belongs to all men. We were made for war, to brave danger, and to face the enemy with a dauntless courage. But it was for a spiritual war, a war of the spirit against the flesh, a conflict with sin and satan, not with our fellow beings. Now this principle which delights in the struggle, pants to put itself forth in strong and continued effort, is very nearly allied to the spirit of which we have been speaking, if indeed it be not the same. This, then, explains wherefore it is that self-denial is so powerful, and wherefore it is, that the cause which demands it will always have adherents.

Let us not, then, overlook the sentiments; let us rely on their testimony in their own sphere of action; let us appeal to them, educate them, and depend on them to support us in all that is elevated, generous, or good. Let us venture to trust them for the support of religion. We may rest its cause securely on the disinterested and self-sacrificing affections. We shall not be disappointed. They will avail us immeasurably more than appeals to interest, for all experience will prove, that it is infinitely safer to league with the good than with the bad in human nature.

Note: Benjamin Constant on Religion

1. Latin for "I see the better and I approve; but I follow the worst."

VI.

SOCIAL REFORMER:
1836–41

12. NEW VIEWS OF CHRISTIANITY,
SOCIETY, AND THE CHURCH

SOURCE: Boston: James Munroe & Company, 1836. See also *Works* 4, pp. 1, 3–17, 19–24, 27–33, 47–55.

New Views *was Brownson's transcendentalist manifesto, but it shared little with Emerson's* Nature. *In fact, it was explicitly opposed to the idealism and excessive spiritualism of Emerson's Nature. It reflected Brownson's reading of Constant, Cousin, Heinrich Heine (1797–1856) and the Saint Simonians and advocated the establishment of a new church that would reconcile matter and spirit in such a way that the values of each would be preserved. The grounds for this argument Brownson found in the Christian doctrine of the Atonement. Jesus himself illustrated the fact that no essential or original antithesis existed between God and man. The future church, if it would be true to Jesus and the Atonement, had to restore this original synthesis between the spiritual and material orders of existence. Only by reconciling these elements could the holy, present in matter as well as in spirit, be realized within the human community, thereby creating universal harmony, justice and love—the conditions of human progress.*

Preface

It must not be inferred from my calling this little work New Views, that I profess to bring forward a new religion, or to have discovered a new Christianity. The religion of the Bible I believe to be given by the inspiration of God, and the Christianity of Christ satisfies my understanding and my heart. However widely I may dissent from the Christianity of the church, with that of Christ I am content to stand or fall, and I ask no higher glory than to live and die in it and for it. . . .

Introduction

Religion is natural to man and he ceases to be man the moment he ceases to be religious.

This position is sustained by what we are conscious of in ourselves and by the universal history of mankind.

Man has a capacity for religion, faculties which are useless without it, and wants which God alone can satisfy. Accordingly wherever he is, in whatever age or country, he has—with a few individual exceptions easily accounted for—some sort of religious notions and some form of religious worship.

But it is only religion, as distinguished from religious institutions, that is natural to man. The religious sentiment is universal, permanent, and indestructible; religious institutions depend on transient causes, and vary in different countries and epochs.

As distinguished from religious institutions, religion is the conception, or sentiment, of the Holy, that which makes us think of something as reverend, and prompts us to revere it. It is that indefinable something within us which gives a meaning to the words venerable and awful, which makes us linger around the sacred and the time-hallowed, the graves of heroes or of nations,—which leads us to launch away upon the boundless expanse, or plunge into the mysterious depths of being, and which, from the very ground of our nature, like the Seraphim of the prophet, is forever crying out, "Holy, holy, holy, is the Lord of hosts; the whole earth is full of his glory."

Religious institutions are the forms with which man clothes his religious sentiment, the answer he gives to the question, What is the holy? Were he a stationary being, or could he take in the whole of truth at a single glance, the answer once given would be always satisfactory, the institution once adopted would be universal, unchangeable, and eternal. But neither is the fact. Man's starting-point is the low valley, but he is continually—with slow and toilsome effort it may be—ascending the sides of the mountain to more favorable positions, from which his eye may sweep a broader horizon of truth. He begins in ignorance, but he is ever growing in knowledge.

In our ignorance, when we have seen but little of truth, and seen that little but dimly, we identify the Holy with the merely terrible, the powerful, the inscrutable, the useful, or the beautiful; and we adopt as its symbols, the thunder and lightning, winds and rain, ocean and storm, majestic river or placid lake, shady grove or winding brook, the animal, the bow or spear by means of which we are fed, clothed, and protected; but as experience rolls back the darkness, which made all around us appear huge and spectral, purges and extends our vision, these become inadequate representatives of our religious ideas; they fail to shadow forth the holy to our understandings; and we leave them and rise to that which appears to be free from their limited and evanescent nature, to that which is unlimited, all-sufficient, and unfailing.

We are creatures of growth; it is, therefore, impossible that all our institutions should not be mutable and transitory. We are forever discovering new fields of truth, and every new discovery requires a new institution, or the modification of an old one. We might as well demand that the sciences of physiology, chemistry, and astronomy should wear eternally the same form, as that religious institutions should be unchangeable, and that those which satisfied our fathers should always satisfy us.

All things change their forms. Literature, art, science, governments, change under the very eye of the spectator. Religious institutions are subject to the same universal law. Like the individuals of our race, they pass away and leave us to deck their tombs, or in our despair, to exclaim that we will lie down in the grave with them. But as the race itself does not die, as new generations crowd upon the departing to supply their places, so does the reproductive energy of religion survive all mutations of forms, and so do new institutions arise to gladden us with their youth and freshness, to carry us further onward in our progress, and upward nearer to that which "is the same yesterday, to-day, and forever."

Chapter I.—Christianity

About two thousand years ago, mankind, having exhausted all their old religious institutions, received from their heavenly Father through the ministry of Jesus of Nazareth a new institution which was equal to their advanced position, and capable of aiding and directing their future progress.

But this institution must be spoken of as one which was, not as one which is. Notwithstanding the vast territories it acquired, the mighty influence it once exerted over the destinies of humanity, and its promises of immortality, it is now but the mere shadow of a sovereign, and its empire is falling in ruins. What remains of it is only the body after the spirit has left it. It is no longer animated by a living soul. The sentiment of the holy has deserted it, and it is a by-word and a mockery.

Either then Jesus did not embrace in his mind the whole of truth, or else the church has at best only partially realized his conception.

No institution, so long as it is in harmony with the progress of the understanding, can fail to command obedience or kindle enthusiasm. The church now does neither. There is a wide disparity between it and the present state of intellectual development. We have discovered truths which it cannot claim as its own; we are conscious of instincts which it disavows, and which we cannot, or will not, suppress. Whose is the fault? Is it the fault of humanity, of Jesus, or of the church?

Humanity cannot be blamed, for humanity's law is to grow; it has an inherent right to seek for truth, and it is under no obligation to shut its eyes to the facts which unfold themselves to its observation. It is not the fault of Jesus, unless it can be proved that all he contemplated has been realized, that mankind have risen to as pure, and as happy a state as he proposed; have indeed fully comprehended him, taken in his entire thought, and reduced it to practice. Nobody will pretend this. The fault then must be borne by the church.

The church even in its best days was far below the conception of Jesus. It never comprehended him, and was always a very inadequate symbol of the holy as he understood it.

Christianity, as it existed in the mind of Jesus, was the type of the most perfect religious institution to which the human race will, probably, ever attain. It was the point where the sentiment and the institution, the idea and the symbol, the conception and its realization appear to meet and become one. But the contemporaries of Jesus were not equal to this profound thought. They could not comprehend the God-Man, the deep meaning of his assertion, "I and my Father are one." He spake as never man spake—uttered truths for all nations, and for all times; but what he uttered was necessarily measured by the capacity of those who heard him—not by his own. The less never comprehends the greater. Their minds must have been equal to his in order to have been able to take in the full import of his words. They might—as they did—apprehend a great and glorious meaning in what he said; they might kindle at the truths he revealed to their understandings, and even glory in dying at the stake to defend them; but they would invariably and inevitably narrow them down to their own inferior intellects, and interpret them by their own previous modes of thinking and believing.

The disciples themselves, the familiar friends, the chosen apostles of Jesus, notwithstanding all the advantages of personal intercourse and personal explanations, never fully apprehended him. They mistook him for the Jewish Messiah, and even after his resurrection and ascension, they supposed it to have been his mission to "restore the kingdom to Israel." Though commanded to preach the Gospel to "every creature," they never once imagined that they were to preach it to any people but the Jewish, till the circumstances, which preceded and followed Peter's visit to Cornelius the Roman centurion, took place to correct their error. It was not till then that any one of them could say, "Of a truth, I perceive that God is no respecter of persons; but in every nation he that feareth him and worketh righteousness is accepted with him." If this was true of the disciples, how much more true must it have been of those who received the words of Jesus at second or third hand, and without any of the personal explanations or commentaries necessary to unfold their meaning?

Could the age, in which Jesus appeared, have comprehended him, it would have been superior to him, and consequently have had no need of him. We do not seek an instructor for our children in one who is not able to teach them. Moreover, if that age could have even rightly *apprehended* Jesus, we should be obliged to say his mission was intended to be confined to that age, or else to admit that the human race was never to go beyond the point then attained. Either Jesus did not regard the future of humanity, or he designed to interrupt its progress, and strike it with the curse of immobility; or else he was above his age and of course not to be understood by it. The world has not stood still since his coming; the church has always considered his kingdom as one of which there is to be no end; and we know that he was not comprehended, and that even we, with the advantage of nearly two thousand years of mental and moral progress, are far—very far—below him.

If the age in which Jesus appeared could not comprehend him, it is obvious that it could not fully embody him in its institutions. It could embody no more of him than it could receive, and as it could receive only a part of him, we must admit that the church has never been more than partially Christian. Never has it been the real body of Christ. Never has it reflected the God-Man perfectly. Never has it been a true mirror of the holy. Always has the holy in the sense of the church been a very inferior thing to what it was in the mind and heart and life of Jesus.

But we must use measured terms in our condemnation of the church. We must not ask the man in the child. The church did what it could. It did its best to "form Christ" within itself, "the hope of glory," and was up to the period of its downfall as truly Christian, as the progress made by the human race admitted. It aided the growth of the human mind; enabled us to take in more truth than it had itself received; furnished us the light by which we discovered its defects; and by no means should its memory be cursed. Nobly and perseveringly did it discharge its duty; useful was it in its day and generation; and now that it has given up the ghost, we should pay it the rites of honorable burial, plant flowers over its resting place, and sometimes repair thither to bedew them with our tears.

To comprehend Jesus, to seize the holy as it was in him, and consequently the true idea of Christianity, we must, from the heights to which we have risen by aid of the church, look back and down upon the age in which he came, ascertain what was the work which there was for him to perform, and from that obtain a key to what he proposed to accomplish.

Two systems then disputed the empire of the world; spiritualism* represented by the Eastern world, the old world of Asia, and materialism represented by Greece and Rome. Spiritualism regards purity or holiness as predicable of spirit alone, and matter as essentially impure, possessing and capable of receiving nothing of the holy,—the prison house of the soul, its only hindrance to a union with God, or absorption into his essence, the cause of all uncleanliness, sin, and evil, consequently to be contemned, degraded, and as far as possible annihilated. Materialism takes the other extreme, does not recognize the claims of spirit, disregards the soul, counts the body every thing, earth all, heaven nothing, and condenses itself into the advice, "Eat and drink; for to-morrow we die."

This opposition between spiritualism and materialism presupposes a necessary and original antithesis between spirit and matter. When spirit and matter are given as antagonist principles, we are obliged to admit antagonism between all the terms into which they are respectively convertible. From spirit is deduced by natural generation, God, the priesthood, faith, heaven, eternity; from matter, man, the state, reason, the earth, and time; consequently, to place spirit and matter in opposition, is to make an antithesis between God and man, the priesthood and the state, faith and reason, heaven and earth, and time and eternity.

This antithesis generates perpetual and universal war. It is neces-

---

* I use these terms, Spiritualism and Materialism, to designate two social, rather than two philosophical systems. They designate two orders, which, from time out of mind, have been called *spiritual* and *temporal* or *carnal, holy* and *profane, heavenly* and *worldly,* etc.

sary then to remove it and harmonize, or unite the two terms. Now, if we conceive Jesus as standing between spirit and matter, the representative of both—God-Man—the point where both meet and lose their antithesis, laying a hand on each and saying, "Be one, as I and my Father are one," thus sanctifying both and marrying them in a mystic and holy union, we shall have his secret thought and the true idea of Christianity.

The Scriptures uniformly present Jesus to us as a mediator, the middle term between two extremes, and they call his work a mediation, a reconciliation—an atonement. The church has ever considered Jesus as making an atonement. It has held on to the term at all times as with the grasp of death. The first charge it has labored to fix upon heretics has been that of rejecting the atonement, and the one all dissenters from the predominant doctrines of the day, have been most solicitous to repel is that of "denying the Lord who bought us." The whole Christian world, from the days of the apostles up to the moment in which I write, have identified Christianity with the atonement, and felt that in admitting the atonement they admitted Christ, and that in denying it they were rejecting him.

Jesus himself always spoke of his doctrine, the grand idea which lay at the bottom of all his teaching, under the term "Love." "A new commandment give I unto you, that ye love one another." "By this shall all men know that ye are my disciples, if ye have love one to another." John, who seems to have caught more of the peculiar spirit of Jesus than any of the disciples, sees nothing but love in the Gospel. Love penetrated his soul; it runs through all his writings, and tradition relates that it at length so completely absorbed him that all he could say in his public addresses was, "Little children, love one another." He uniformly dwells with unutterable delight on the love which the Father has for us and that which we may have for him, the intimate union of man with God, expressed by the strong language of dwelling in God and God dwelling in us. In his view there is no antagonism. All antithesis is destroyed. Love sheds its hallowed and hallowing light over both God and man, over spirit and matter, binding all beings and all being in one strict and everlasting union.

The nature of love is to destroy all antagonism. It brings together; it begetteth union, and from union cometh peace. And what word so accurately expresses to the consciousness of Christendom, the intended result of the mission of Jesus, as that word peace? Every man who has read the New Testament feels that it was peace that Jesus came to effect,—peace after which the soul has so often sighed and yearned in vain, and a peace not merely between two or three individuals for a day, but a universal and eternal peace between all conflicting elements, between God and man, between the soul and body, between this world and another, between the duties of time and the duties of eternity. How clearly is this expressed in that sublime chorus of the angels, sung over the manger-cradle—"Glory to God in the highest, on earth peace and good-will to men!"

Where there is but one term there is no union. There is no harmony with but one note. It is mockery to talk to us of peace where one of the two belligerent parties is annihilated. That were the peace of the grave. Jesus must then save both parties. The church has, therefore, with a truth it has never comprehended, called him *God-Man.* But if the two terms and their products be originally and essentially antagonist; if there be between them an innate hostility, their union, their reconciliation cannot be effected. Therefore in proposing the union, in attempting the atonement, Christianity declares as its great doctrine that there is no essential, no original antithesis between God and man; that neither spirit nor matter is unholy in its nature; that all things, spirit, matter, God, man, soul, body, heaven, earth, time, eternity, with all their duties and interests, are in themselves holy. All things proceed from the same holy Fountain, and no fountain sendeth forth both sweet waters and bitter. It therefore writes "HOLINESS TO THE LORD" upon every thing, and sums up its sublime teaching in that grand synthesis, "Thou shalt love the Lord thy God with all thy heart and mind and soul and strength, and thy neighbor as thyself."

Chapter II.—The Church

The aim of the church was to embody the holy as it existed in the mind of Jesus, and had it succeeded, it would have realized the atonement; that is, the reconciliation of spirit and matter and all their products.

But the time was not yet. The Paraclete was in expectation. The church could only give currency to the fact that it was the mission of Jesus to make an atonement. It from the first misapprehended the conditions on which it was to be effected. Instead of understanding Jesus to assert the holiness of both spirit and matter, it understood him to admit that matter was rightfully cursed, and to predicate holiness of spirit alone. In the sense of the church then he did not come to atone spirit and matter, but to redeem spirit from the consequences of its connection with matter. His name therefore was not the Atoner, the Reconciler, but the Redeemer, and his work not properly an atonement, but a redemption. This was the original sin of the church.

By this misapprehension the church rejected the mediator. The Christ ceases to be the middle term uniting spirit and matter, the *hilasterion,* the mercy-seat, or point where God and man meet and lose their antithesis, the Advocate with the Father for humanity, and becomes the Avenger of spirit, the manifestation of God's righteous indignation against man. He dies to save mankind, it is true, but he dies to pay a penalty. God demands man's everlasting destruction; Jesus admits that God's demand is just, and dies to discharge it. Hence the symbol of the cross, signifying to the church an original and necessary antithesis between God and man which can be removed only by the sacrifice of justice to mercy. In this the church took its stand with spiritualism, and from a mediator became a partisan.

By taking its stand with spiritualism the church condemned itself to all the evils of being exclusive. It obliged itself to reject an important element of truth, and it became subject to all the miseries and vexations of being intolerant. It become responsible for all the consequences which necessarily result from spiritualism. The first of these consequences was the denial that Jesus came in the flesh. If matter be essentially unholy, then Jesus, if he had a material body, must have been unholy; if unholy, sinful. Hence all the difficulties of the Gnostics—difficulties hardly adjusted by means of a Virgin Mother and the Immaculate Conception; for this mode of accommodation really denied the God-Man, the symbol of the great truth the church was to embody. It left the God indeed, but it destroyed the man, inasmuch as it separated the humanity of Jesus by its very origin from common humanity.

Man's inherent depravity, his corruption by nature followed as a matter of course. Man by his very nature partakes of matter, is material, then unholy, then sinful, corrupt, depraved. He is originally material, therefore originally a sinner. Hence original sin. Sometimes original sin is indeed traced to a primitive disobedience, to the fall; but then the doctrine of the fall itself is only one of the innumerable forms which is assumed by the doctrine of the essential impurity of matter.

From this original, inherent depravity of human nature necessarily results that antithesis between God and man which renders their union impossible and which imperiously demands the sacrifice of one or the other. "Die he or justice must." Man is sacrificed on the cross in the person of Jesus. Hence the vicarious atonement, the conversion of the atonement into an expiation. But, if man was sacrificed, if he died as he deserved in Jesus, his death was eternal. Symbolically then he cannot rise. The body of Jesus after his resurrection is not material in the opinion of the church. He does not rise God-Man, but God. Hence the absolute Deity of Christ, which under various disguises has always been the sense of the church.

From man's original and inherent depravity it results that he has no power to work out his own salvation. Hence the doctrine of human inability. By nature man is enslaved to matter; he is born in sin and shapen in iniquity. He is sold to sin, to the world, to the devil. He must be ransomed. Matter cannot ransom him; then spirit must—and "God the mighty Maker" dies to redeem his creature—to deliver the soul from the influence of matter.

But this can be only partially effected in this world. As long as we live, we must drag about with us this clog of earth—matter—and not till after death, when our vile bodies shall be changed into the likeness of Christ's glorious body, shall we really be saved. We are not then saved here; we only hope to be saved hereafter. Hence the doctrine which denies holiness to man in this world, which places the kingdom of God exclusively in the world to come, and which establishes a real antithesis between heaven and earth, and the means necessary to secure present well-being and those necessary to secure future blessedness.

God has indeed died to ransom sinners from the grave of the body, to redeem them from the flesh, to break the chains of the bound and to set the captive free; but the effects of the ransom must be secured; agents must be appointed to proclaim the glad tidings of salvation, to bid the prisoner hope, and the captive rejoice that the hour of release will come. Hence the church. Hence too the authority of the church to preach salvation—to save sinners. And the church is composed of all who have this authority and of none others, therefore the dogma, "Out of the church there is no salvation."

The church is commissioned; it is God's agent in saving sinners. It is then his representative. If the representative of God, then of spirit. In its representative character, that is, as a church, it is then spiritual, and if spiritual, holy; and if holy, infallible. Hence the infallibility of the church.

The holy should undoubtedly govern the unholy; spirit then should govern matter. Spirit then is supreme; and the church as the representative of spirit must also be supreme. Hence the supremacy of the church.

The church is a vast body composed of many members. It needs a head. It should also be modelled after the church above. The church above has a supreme head, Jesus Christ; the church below should then have a head, who may be its centre, its unity, the personification of its wisdom and its authority. Hence the pope, the supreme head of the church, vicar of Jesus, and representative of God.

The church is a spiritual body. Its supremacy then is a spiritual supremacy. A spiritual supremacy extends to thought and conscience. Hence on the one hand the confessional designed to solve cases of conscience, and on the other creeds, expurgatory indexes, inquisitions, pains and penalties against heretics.

The spiritual order in heaven is absolute; the church then as the representative of that order must also be absolute. As a representative it speaks not in its own name, but in the name of the power it represents. Since that power may command, the church may command; and as it may command in the name of an absolute sovereign, its commands must be implicitly obeyed. An absolute sovereign may command to any extent he pleases—what shall be believed as well as what shall be done. Hence implicit faith, the authority which the church has alleged for the basis of belief. Hence too prohibitions against reason and reasoning which have marked the church under all its forms, in all its phases and divisions and subdivisions.

Reason too is human; then it is material; to set it up against faith were to set up the material against the spiritual; the human against the divine; man against God: for the church being God by proxy, by representation, it has of course the right to consider whatever is set up against the faith it enjoins as set up against God.

The civil order, if it be any thing more than a function of the church, belongs to the category of matter. It is then inferior to the church. It is then bound to obey the church. Hence the claims of the church over civil institutions, its right to bestow the crowns of kings, to place kingdoms under ban, to absolve subjects from their allegiance, and all the wars and antagonism between church and state.

The spiritual order alone is holy. Its interests are then the only interests it is not sinful to labor to promote. In laboring to promote them, the church was under the necessity of laboring for itself. Hence its justification to itself of its selfishness, its rapacity, its untiring efforts to aggrandize itself at the expense of individuals and of states.

As the interests of the church alone were holy, it was of course sinful to be devoted to any others. All the interests of the material order, that is, all temporal interests, were sinful, and the church never ceased to call them so. Hence its perpetual denunciation of wealth, place, and renown, and the obstacles it always placed in the way of all direct efforts for the promotion of well-being on earth. This is the reason why it has discouraged, indeed unchurched, anathematized, all efforts to gain civil and political liberty, and always regarded with an evil eye all industry not directly or indirectly in its own interests.

This same exclusive spiritualism borrowed from Asia, striking matter with the curse of being unclean in its nature, was the reason for enjoining celibacy upon the clergy. An idea of sanctity was attached to the ministerial office, which it was supposed any contact with the flesh would sully. It also led devotees, those who desired to lead lives strictly holy, to renounce the flesh, as well as the world and the devil, to take vows of perpetual celibacy and to shut themselves up in monasteries and nunneries. It is the origin of all those self-inflicted tortures, mortifications of the body, penances, fastings, and that neglect of this world for another, which fill so large a space in the history of the church during what are commonly called the "dark ages." The church in its theory looked always with horror upon all sensual indulgences. Marriage was sinful, till purified by holy church. The song and the dance, innocent amusements, and wholesome recreations, though sometimes conceded to the incessant importunities of matter, were of the devil. Even the gay dress and blithesome song of nature were offensive. A dark, silent, friar's frock was the only befitting garb for nature or for man. The *beau ideal* of a good Christian was one who renounced all his connections with the world, became deaf to the voice of kindred and of friends, insensible to the sweetest and holiest emotions of humanity, immured himself in a cave or cell, and did nothing the livelong day but count his beads and kiss the crucifix.

Exceptions there were, but this was the idea, the dominant tendency of the church. Thanks, however, to the stubbornness of matter, and to the superintending care of Providence, its dominant tendency always found powerful resistance, and its idea was never able fully to realize itself.

Chapter III.—Protestantism

Every thing must have its time. The church abused, degraded, vilified matter, but could not annihilate it. It existed in spite of the church. It increased in power, and at length rose against spiritualism and demanded the restoration of its rights. This rebellion of materialism, of the material order against the spiritual, is Protestantism.

Matter always exerted a great influence over the practice of the church. In the first three centuries it was very powerful. It condemned the Gnostics and Manicheans as heretics, and was on the point of rising to empire under the form of Arianism. But the oriental influence predominated, and the Arians became acknowledged heretics.

After the defeat of Arianism, that noble protest in its day of rationalism against mysticism, of matter against spirit, of European against Asiatic ideas, the church departed more and more from the atonement, and became more and more arrogant, arbitrary, spiritualistic, papistical. Still matter occasionally made itself heard. It could not prevent the celibacy of the clergy, but it did maintain the unity of the race and prevented the reestablishment of a sacerdotal caste, claiming by birth a superior sanctity. It broke out too in the form of Pelagianism, that doctrine which denies that man is clean gone in iniquity, and which makes the material order count for something. Pelagius was the able defender of humanity when it seemed to be deserted by all its friends, and his efforts were by no means unavailing.

Matter asserted its rights and avenged itself in a less unexceptionable form in the convents, the monasteries and nunneries, among the clergy of all ranks, in that gross licentiousness which led to the reformation attempted by Hildebrand;[1] and finally it ascended—not avowedly, but in reality—the papal throne, in the person of Leo X.[2]

The accession of Leo X to the papal throne is a remarkable event in the history of the church. It marks the predominance of material interests in the very bosom of the church itself. It is a proof that whatever might be the theory of the church, however different it claimed to be from all other powers, it was at this epoch in practice the same as the kingdoms of men. Poverty ceased in its eyes to be a virtue. The poor mendicant, the bare-footed friar, could no longer hope to become one day the spiritual head of Christendom. Spiritual gifts and graces were not now enough. High birth and royal pretensions were required; and it was not as a priest, but as a member of the princely house of Medici that Leo become pope.

The object of the church had changed. It had ceased to regard the spiritual wants and welfare of mankind. It had become wealthy. It had acquired vast portions of this world's goods, and its great care was to preserve them. Its interests had become temporal interests, and therefore it needed, not a spiritual father, but a temporal prince. It is as a prince that Leo conducts himself. His legates to the imperial, English, and French courts, entered into negotiations altogether as ambassadors of a temporal prince, not as the simple representatives of the church.

Leo himself is a sensualist, sunk in his sensual pleasures, and perhaps a great sufferer in consequence of his excesses. It is said he was an atheist, a thing more than probable. All his tastes were worldly. Instead of the sacred books of the church, the pious legends of saints and martyrs, he amused himself with the elegant but *profane* literature of Greece and Rome. His principal secretaries were not holy monks but eminent classical scholars. He revived and enlarged the university at Rome, encouraged human learning and the arts of civilization, completed St. Peter's, and his reign was graced by Michael Angelo and Raphael. He engaged in wars and diplomacy and in them both had respect only to the goods of the church, or to the interests of himself and family as temporal princes.

Now all this was in direct opposition to the theory of the church. Materialism was in the papal chair, but it was there as a usurper, as an illegitimate. It reigned in fact, but not in right. The church was divided against itself. In theory it was spiritualist, but in practice it was materialist. It could not long survive this inconsistency, and it needed not the attacks of Luther to hasten the day of its complete destruction.

But materialism must have become quite powerful to have been able to usurp the papal throne itself. It was indeed too powerful to bear patiently the name of usurper; at least to be contented to reign only indirectly. It would be acknowledged as sovereign, and proclaimed legitimate. This the church could not do. The church could do nothing but cling to its old pretensions. To expel materialism and return to Hildebrand was out of the question. To give up its claims, and own itself materialist, would have been to abandon all title to even its material possessions, since it was by virtue of its spiritual character that it held them. Materialism—as it could reign in the church only as it were by stealth—resolved to leave the church and to reign in spite of it, against it, and even on its ruins. It protested, since it had all the power, against being called hard names, and armed itself in the person of Luther to vindicate its rights and to make its claims acknowledged.

The dominant character of Protestantism is then the insurrection of materialism, and what we call the reformation is really a revolution in favor of the material order. Spiritualism had exhausted its energies; it had done all it could for humanity; the time had come for the material element of our nature, which spiritualism had neglected and grossly abused, to rise from its depressed condition and contribute its share to the general progress of mankind. It rose, and in rising it brought up the whole series of terms the church had disregarded. It brought up the state, civil liberty, human reason, philosophy, industry, all temporal interests.

In Protestantism, Greece and Rome revived and again carried their victorious arms into the East. The reformation connects us with classical antiquity, with the beautiful and graceful forms of Grecian art and literature, and with Roman eloquence and jurisprudence, as the church had connected us with Judea, Egypt, and India.

Chapter IV.—Protestantism

That Protestantism is the insurrection of matter against spirit, of the material against the spiritual order, is susceptible of very satisfactory historical verification.

One of the most immediate and efficient causes of Protestantism was the revival of Greek and Roman literature. Constantinople was taken by the Turks, and its scholars and the remains of classical learning which it had preserved were dispersed over western Europe. The classics took possession of the universities and the learned, were studied, commented on, appealed to as an authority paramount to that of the church and—Protestantism was born. . . .

In classical antiquity religion is a function of the state. It is the same under Protestantism. Henry VIII of England declares himself supreme head of the church, not by virtue of his spiritual character, but by virtue of his character as a temporal prince. The Protestant princes of Germany are protectors of the church; and all over Europe, there is an implied contract between the state and the ecclesiastical authorities. The state pledges itself to support the church on condition that the church support the state. Ask the kings, nobility, or even church dignitaries, why they support religion, and they will answer with one voice, "Because the people cannot be preserved in order, cannot be made to submit to their rulers, and because civil society cannot exist without it." The same or a similar answer will be returned by almost every political man in this country; and truly may it be said that religion is valued by the Protestant world as a subsidiary to the state, as a mere matter of police.

Under the reign of spiritualism all questions are decided by authority. The church prohibited reasoning. It commanded, and men were to obey or be counted rebels against God. Materialism, by raising up man and the state, makes the reason of man, or the reason of the state, paramount to the commands of the church. Under Protestantism, the state in most cases, the individual reason in a few, imposes the creed upon the church. The king and parliament in England determine the faith which the clergy must profess and maintain; the Protestant princes in Germany have the supreme control of the symbols of the church, the right to enact what creed they please.

Indeed the authority of the church in matters of belief was regarded by the reformers as one of the greatest evils, against which they had to contend. It was particularly against this authority that Luther protested. What he and his coadjutors demanded, was the right to read and interpret the Bible for themselves. This was the right they wrested from the church. To have been consequent they should have retained it in their hands as individuals; it would then have been the right of private judgment and, if it meant any thing, the right of reason to sit in judgment on all propositions to be believed. To this extent, however, they were not prepared to go. Between the absolute authority of the church, and the absolute authority of the individual reason, intervened the authority of the state. But as the state was material, the substitution of its authority for the authority of the church was still to substitute the material for the spiritual.

But the tendency, however arrested by the state, has been steadily toward the most unlimited freedom of thought and conscience. Our fathers rebelled against the authority of the state in religious matters as well as against the authority of the pope. In political and industrial speculations, the English and Americans give the fullest freedom to the individual reason; Germany has done it to the greatest extent in historical, literary and philosophical, and to a very great extent, in theological matters, and France does it in every thing. All modern philosophy is built on the absolute freedom and independence of the individual reason; that is, the reason of humanity, in opposition to the reason of the church or the state. Descartes refused to believe in his own existence but upon the authority of his reason; Bacon allows no authority but observation and induction; Berkeley finds no ground for admitting an external world, and therefore denies it; and Hume finding no certain evidence of any thing outward or inward, doubted—philosophically—of all things.

Philosophy is a human creation; it is the product of man, as the universe is of God. Under spiritualism, then, which—in theory—demolishes man, there can be no philosophy; yet as man, though denied, exists, there is a philosophical tendency. But this philosophical tendency is always either to scepticism, mysticism, or idealism. Scepticism, that philosophy which denies all certainty, made its first appearance in modern times in the church. The church declared reason unworthy of confidence, and in doing that gave birth to the whole sceptical philosophy. When the authority of the church was questioned and she was compelled to defend it, she did it on the ground that reason could not be trusted as a criterion of truth, and that there could be no certainty for man, if he did not admit an authority independent of his reason,—not perceiving that if reason were struck with impotence there would be no means of substantiating the legitimacy of the authority.

On the other hand, the church having its point of view in spirit, consulted the soul before the body, became introspective, fixed on the inward to the exclusion of the outward. It overlooked the outward; and when that is overlooked it is hardly possible that it should not be denied. Hence idealism or mysticism.

Under the reign of materialism all this is changed. There is full confidence in reason. The method of philosophizing is the experimental. But as the point of view is the outward—matter—spirit is overlooked; matter alone admitted. Hence philosophical materialism. And philosophical materialism, in germ or developed, has been commensurate with Protestantism. When the mind becomes fixed on the external world, inasmuch as we become acquainted with that world only by means of our senses, we naturally conclude that our senses are our only source of knowledge. Hence sensism, the philosophy supported by Locke, Condillac, and even by Bacon, so far as it concerns his own application of his method. And from the hypothesis that our senses are our only inlets of knowledge, we are compelled to admit that nothing can be known which is not cognizable by some one or all of them. Our senses take cognizance only of matter; then we can know nothing but matter. We can know nothing of the spirit or soul. The body is all that we know of man. That dies, and there ends man—at least all we know of him. Hence no immortality, no future state. If nothing can be known but by means of our senses, God, then, inasmuch as we do not see him, hear him, taste him, smell him, touch him, cannot be known; then he does not exist for us. Hence atheism. Hence modern infidelity, in all its forms, so prevalent in the last century, and so far from being extinct even in this.

The same tendency to exalt the terms depressed by the church is to be observed in the religious aspect of Protestantism. Properly speaking, Protestantism has no religious character. As Protestants, people are not religious, but co-existing with their Protestantism, they may indeed retain something of religion. Men often act from mixed motives. They bear in their bosoms sometimes two antagonist principles, now obeying the one, and now the other, without being aware that both are not one and the same principle. With Protestants, religion has existed; but as a reminiscence, a tradition. Sometimes, indeed, the remembrance has been very lively, and seemed very much like reality. The old soldier warms up with the recollections of his early feats, and lives over his life as he relates its events to his grandchild,—

"Shoulders his crutch and shows how fields are won."

If the religion of the Protestant world be a reminiscence, it must be the religion of the church. It is, in fact, only Catholicism continued. The same principle lies at the bottom of all Protestant churches, in so far as they are churches, which was at the bottom of the church of the middle ages. But materialism modifies their rites and dogmas. In the practice of all, there is an effort to make them appear reasonable. Hence commentaries, expositions, and defences without number. Even where the authority of reason is denied, there is an instinctive sense of its authority and a desire to enlist it. In mere forms, pomp and splendor have gradually disappeared, and dry utility and even baldness have been consulted. In doctrines, those which exalt man and give him some share in the work of salvation have gained in credit and influence. Pelagianism, under some thin disguises or undisguised, has become almost universal. The doctrine of man's inherent total depravity, in the few cases in which it is asserted, is asserted more as a matter of duty than of conviction. Nobody, who can help it, preaches the old-fashioned doctrine of God's sovereignty, expressed in the dogma of unconditional election and reprobation. The vicarious Atonement has hardly a friend left. The Deity of Jesus is questioned, his simple humanity is asserted and is gaining credence. Orthodox is a term which implies as much reproach as commendation; people are beginning to laugh at the claims of councils and synods, and to be quite merry at the idea of excommunication.

In literature and art there is the same tendency. Poetry in the last century hardly existed, and was, so far as it did exist, mainly ethical or descriptive. It had no revelations of the Infinite. Prose writers under Protestantism have been historians, critics, essayists, or controversalists; they have aimed almost exclusively at the elevation or adornment of the material order, and in scarcely an instance has a widely popular writer exalted God at the expense of man, the church at the expense of the state, faith at the expense of reason, or eternity at the expense of time. Art is finite, and gives us busts and portraits, or copies of Greek and Roman models. The physical sciences take precedence of the metaphysical, and faith in rail-roads and steam-boats is much stronger than in ideas.

In governments, the tendency is the same. Nothing is more characteristic of Protestantism, than its influence in promoting civil and political liberty. Under its reign all forms of governments verge towards the democratic. "The king and the church" are exchanged for the "constitution and the people." Liberty, not order, is the word that wakes the dead, and electrifies the masses. A social science is created, and the physical well-being of the humblest laborer is cared for, and made a subject of deliberation in the councils of nations.

Industry has received in Protestant countries its grandest developments. Since the time of Luther, it has been performing one continued series of miracles. Every corner of the globe is explored; the most distant and perilous seas are navigated; the most miserly soil is laid under contribution; manufactures, villages and cities spring up and increase as by enchantment; canals and rail-roads are crossing the country in every direction; the means of production, the comforts, conveniences, and luxuries of life are multiplied to an extent hardly safe to relate.

Such, in its most general aspect, in its dominant tendency, is Protestantism. It is a new and much improved edition of the classics. Its civilization belongs to the same order as that of Greece and Rome. It is in advance, greatly in advance, of Greece and Rome, but it is the same in its ground-work. The material predominates over the spiritual. Men labor six days for this world and at most but one for the world to come. The great strife is for temporal goods, fame, or pleasure. God, the soul, heaven, and eternity, are thrown into the background, and almost entirely disappear in the distance. Right yields to expediency, and duty is measured by utility. The real character of Protestantism, the result to which it must come, wherever it can have its full development, may be best seen in France, at the close of the last century. The church was converted into the pantheon, and made a resting place for the bodies of the great and renowned of earth; God was converted into a symbol of the human reason, and man into the man-machine; spiritualism fell, and the revolution marked the complete triumph of materialism.

Chapter V.—Reaction of Spiritualism

What I have said of the Protestant world cannot be applied to the present century without some important qualifications. Properly speaking, Protestantism finished its work and expired in the French revolution at the close of the last century. Since then there has been a reaction in favor of spiritualism. . . .

Protestantism, since the commencement of the present century, in what it has peculiar to itself, has ceased to gain ground. Rationalism in Germany retreats before the Evangelical party; the Genevan church makes few proselytes; English and American Unitarianism, on the plan of Priestley and Belsham,[3] avowedly material, and being, as it were, the jumping-off place from the church to absolute infidelity, is evidently on the decline. There is probably not a man in this country, however much and justly he may esteem Priestley and Belsham, as bold and untiring advocates of reason and of humanity, who would be willing to assume the defence of all their opinions. On the other hand Catholicism has revived, offered some able apologies for itself, made some eminent proselytes, and alarmed many Protestants, even among ourselves.

Indeed everywhere is seen a decided tendency to spiritualism. The age has become weary of uncertainty. It sighs for repose. Controversy is nearly ended, and a sentiment is extensively prevailing, that it is a matter of very little consequence what a man believes, or what formulas of worship he adopts, if he only have a right spirit. Men, who a few years ago were staunch rationalists, now talk of Spiritual Communion; and many, who could with difficulty be made to admit the inspiration of the Bible, are now ready to admit the inspiration of the sacred books of all nations; and instead of stumbling at the idea of God's speaking to a few individuals, they see no reason why he should not speak to everybody. Some are becoming so spiritual that they see no necessity of matter; others so refine matter that it can offer no resistance to the will, making it indeed move as the spirit listeth; others still believe that all wisdom was in the keeping of the priests of ancient India, Egypt, and Persia, and fancy the world has been deteriorating for four thousand years, instead of advancing. Men go out from our midst to Europe, and come back half Catholics, sighing to introduce the architecture, the superstition, the rites, and the sacred symbols of the middle ages.

A universal cry is raised against the frigid utilitarianism of the last century. Money-getting, desire for worldly wealth and renown, are spoken of with contempt, and men are evidently leaving the outward for the inward, and craving something more fervent, living, and soul-kindling. All this proves that we have changed from what we were; that, though materialism yet predominates and appears to have lost none of its influence, it is becoming a tradition; and that there is a new force collecting to expel it. Protestantism passes into the condition of a reminiscence. Protestant America cannot be aroused against the Catholics. A mob may burn a convent from momentary excitement, but the most protestant of the Protestants among us will petition the legislature to indemnify the owners. Indeed, Protestantism died in the French revolution, and we are beginning to become disgusted with its dead body. The East has reappeared, and spiritualism revives; will it again become supreme? Impossible.

Chapter VI.—Mission of the Present

We of the present century must either dispense with all religious instructions, reproduce spiritualism or materialism, or we must build a new church, organize a new institution free from the imperfections of those which have been.

The first is out of the question. Men cannot live in a perpetual anarchy. They must and will embody their ideas of the true, the beautiful, and the good—the holy, in some institution. They must answer in some way the questions, What is the holy? What is the true destination of man?

To reproduce spiritualism or materialism, were an anomaly in the development of humanity. Humanity does not traverse an eternal circle; it advances; it does not come round to its starting-point, but goes onward in one endless career of progress towards the infinite, the perfect.

Besides, it is impossible. Were it desirable, neither spiritualism nor materialism can to any considerable extent, or for any great length of time, become predominant. We cannot bring about that state of society which is the indispensable condition of the exclusive dominion of either.

Spiritualism just now revives; its friends may anticipate a victory; but they will be disappointed. Spiritualism, as an exclusive system, reigns only when men have no faith in material interests; and in order to have no faith in material interests, we must virtually destroy them; we must have absolute despotism, a sacerdotal caste, or we must have another decline and fall like that of the Roman empire, and a new irruption like that of the Goths, Vandals, and Huns.

None of these things are possible. . . .

Nor can materialism become sovereign again. It contains the elements of its own defeat. The very dicipline, which materialism demands to support itself, in the end neutralizes its dominion. As soon as men find themselves well off in a worldly point of view, they discover that they have wants which the world does not and cannot satisfy. The training demanded to insure success in commerce, industrial enterprises, or politics, strengthens faculties which crave something superior to commerce, to mere industry, or to politics. The merchant would not be always estimating the hazards of speculation; he dreams of his retirement from business, his splendid mansion, his refined hospitality, a library, and studious ease; the mechanic looks forward to a time when he shall have leisure to care for something besides merely animal wants; and the politician to his release from the cares and perplexities of a public life, to a quiet retreat, to a dignified old age, spent in plans of benevolence, in aiding the cause of education, religion, or philosophy. This low business world, upon which the moralist and the divine look down with so much sorrow, is not quite so low after all, as they think it. It is doing a vast deal to develop the intellect. It is full of high and expanded brows. . . .

We cannot then go back either to exclusive spiritualism, or to exclusive materialism. Both these systems have received so full a development, have acquired so much strength, that neither can be subdued. Both have their foundation in our nature, and both will exist and exert their influence. Shall they exist as antagonist principles? Shall the spirit forever lust against the flesh, and the flesh against the spirit? Is the bosom of humanity to be eternally torn by these two contending factions? No. It cannot be. The war must end. Peace must be made.

This discloses our Mission. We are to reconcile spirit and matter; that is, we must realize the atonement. Nothing else remains for us to do. Stand still we cannot. To go back is equally impossible. We must go forward, but we can take not a step forward, but on the condition of uniting these two hitherto hostile principles. Progress is our law and our first step is Union.

The union of spirit and matter was the result contemplated by the mission of Jesus. The church attempted it, but only partially succeeded, and has therefore died. The time had not come for the complete union. Jesus saw this. He knew that the age in which he lived would not be able to realize his conception. He therefore spoke of his "second coming." The church has always had a vague presentiment of its own death, and the birth of a new era when Christ should really reign on earth. For a long time the hierophants have fixed upon ours as the epoch of the commencement of the new order of things. Some have gone even so far as to name this very year, 1836, as the beginning of what they call the millennium.

The particular shape which has been assigned to this new order, this "latter day glory," the name by which it has been designated, amounts to nothing. That some have anticipated a personal appearance of Jesus, and a resurrection of the saints, should not induce us to treat with disrespect the almost unanimous belief of Christendom in a fuller manifestation of Christian truth, and in a more special reign of Christ in a future epoch of the world. All the presentiments of humanity are to be respected. Humanity has a prophetic power.—"Coming events cast their shadows before."

The "second coming" of Christ will be when the idea which he represents, that is, the idea of atonement, shall be fully realized. That idea will be realized by a combination, a union, of the two terms which have received thus far from the church only a separate development. This union the church has always had a presentiment of; it has looked forward to it, prayed for it; and we are still praying for it, for we still say, "Let thy kingdom come." Nobody believes that the Gospel has completed its work. The church universal and eternal is not yet erected. The corner stone is laid; the materials are prepared. Let then the workmen come forth with joy, and bid the Temple rise. Let them embody the true idea of the God-Man, and Christ will then have come a second time; he will have come in power and great glory, and he will reign, and the whole earth will be glad. . . .[4]

Chapter IX.—The Atonement

The great doctrine, which is to realize the atonement and which the symbol of the God-Man now teaches us, is that all things are essentially holy, that every thing is cleansed, and that we must call nothing common or unclean.

"And God saw every thing that he had made, and behold it was very good."[5] And what else could it have been? God is wise, powerful and good; and how can a wise, powerful and good being create evil? God is the great Fountain from which flows every thing that is; how then can there be any thing but good in existence?

Neither spiritualism nor materialism was aware of this truth. Spiritualism saw good only in pure spirit. God was pure spirit and therefore good; but all which could be distinguished from him was evil, and only evil, and that continually. Our good consisted in resemblance to God, that is, in being as like pure spirit as possible. Our duty was to get rid of matter. All the interests of the material order were sinful. St. Augustine declared the flesh, that is the body, to be sin; perfection then could be obtained only by neglecting and, as far as possible, annihilating it. Materialism, on the other hand, had no recognition of spirit. It considered all time and thought and labor bestowed on that which transcends this world as worse than thrown away. It had no conception of inward communion with God. It counted fears of punishment or hopes of reward in a world to come mere idle fancies, fit only to amuse or control the vulgar. It laughed at spiritual joys and griefs, and treated as serious affairs only the pleasures and pains of sense.

But the new doctrine of the atonement reconciles these two warring systems. This doctrine teaches us that spirit is real and holy, that matter is real and holy, that God is holy and that man is holy, that spiritual joys and griefs, and the pleasures and pains of sense, are alike real joys and griefs, real pleasures and pains, and in their places are alike sacred. Spirit and matter, then, are saved. One is not required to be sacrificed to the other; both may and should coexist as separate elements of the same grand and harmonious whole.

The influence of this doctrine cannot fail to be very great. It will correct our estimate of man, of the world, of religion, and of God, and remodel all our institutions. It must in fact create a new civilization as much in advance of ours as ours is in advance of that which obtained in the Roman empire in the time of Jesus.

Hitherto we have considered man as the antithesis of all good. We have loaded him with reproachful epithets and made it a sin in him even to be born. We have uniformly deemed it necessary to degrade him in order to exalt his Creator. But this will end. The slave will become a son. Man is hereafter to stand erect before God as a child before its father. Human nature, at which we have pointed our wit and vented our spleen, will be clothed with a high and commanding worth. It will be seen to be a lofty and deathless nature. It will be felt to be divine, and infinite will be found traced in living characters on all its faculties.

We shall not treat one another then as we do now. Man will be sacred in the eyes of man. To wrong him will be more than crime, it will be sin. To labor to degrade him will seem like laboring to degrade the Divinity. Man will reverence man.

Slavery will cease. Man will shudder at the bare idea of enslaving so noble a being as man. It will seem to him hardly less daring than to presume to task the motions of the Deity and to compel him to come and go at our bidding. When man learns the true value of man, the chains of the captive must be unloosed and the fetters of the slave fall off.

Wars will fail. The sword will be beaten into the ploughshare and the spear into the pruning hook. Man will not dare to mar and mangle the shrine of the Divinity. The God looking out from human eyes will disarm the soldier and make him kneel to him he had risen up to slay. The war-horse will cease to bathe his fetlocks in human gore. He will snuff the breeze in the wild freedom of his native plains, or quietly submit to be harnessed to the plough. The hero's occupation will be gone, and heroism will be found only in saving and blessing human life.

Education will destroy the empire of ignorance. The human mind, allied as it is to the divine, is too valuable to lie waste or to be left to breed only briars and thorns. Those children, ragged and incrusted with filth, which throng our streets, and for whom we must one day build prisons, forge bolts and bars, or erect gibbets, are not only our children, our brother's children, but they are children of God, they have in themselves the elements of the Divinity and powers which when put forth will raise them above what the tallest archangel now is. And when this is seen and felt, will those children be left to fester in ignorance or to grow up in vice and crime? The whole energy of man's being cries out against such folly, such gross injustice.

Civil freedom will become universal. It will be everywhere felt that one man has no right over another which that other has not over him. All will be seen to be brothers and equals in the sight of their common Father. All will love one another too much to desire to play the tyrant. Human nature will be reverenced too much not to be allowed to have free scope for the full and harmonious development of all its faculties. Governments will become sacred; and while on the one hand they are respected and obeyed, on the other it will be felt to be a religious right and a religious duty, to labor to make them as perfect as they can be.

Religion will not stop with the command to obey the laws, but it will bid us make just laws, such laws as befit a being divinely endowed like man. The church will be on the side of progress, and spiritualism and materialism will combine to make man's earthly condition as near like the lost Eden of the eastern poets, as is compatible with the growth and perfection of his nature.

Industry will be holy. The cultivation of the earth will be the worship of God. Workingmen will be priests, and as priests they will be reverenced, and as priests they will reverence themselves and feel that they must maintain themselves undefiled. He that ministers at the altar must be pure, will be said of the mechanic, the agriculturist, the common laborer, as well as of him who is technically called a priest.

The earth itself and the animals which inhabit it will be counted sacred. We shall study in them the manifestation of God's goodness, wisdom, and power, and be careful that we make of them none but a holy use.

Man's body will be deemed holy. It will be called the temple of the living God. As a temple it must not be desecrated. Men will beware of defiling it by sin, by any excessive or improper indulgence, as they would of defiling the temple or the altar consecrated to the service of God. Man will reverence himself too much, he will see too much of the holy in his nature ever to pervert it from the right line of truth and duty.

"In that day shall there be on the bells of the horses, *Holiness unto the Lord;* and the pots in the Lord's house shall be as the bowls before the altar. Yea, every pot in Jerusalem and in Judah shall be Holiness unto the Lord of hosts."[6] The words of the prophet will be fulfilled. All things proceed from God and are therefore holy. Every duty, every act necessary to be done, every implement of industry, or thing contributing to human use or convenience, will be treated as holy. We shall recall even the reverence of the Indian for his bow and arrow, and by enlightening it with a divine philosophy preserve it.

"Pure religion, and undefiled before God and the Father is this, To visit the fatherless and the widows in their affliction, and to keep one's self unspotted from the world."[7] Religious worship will not be the mere service of the sanctuary. The universe will be God's temple, and its service will be the doing of good to mankind, relieving suffering and promoting joy, virtue, and well-being. By this, religion and morality will be united, and the service of God and the service of man become the same. Our faith in God will show itself by our good works to man. Our love to the Father, whom we have not seen, will be evinced by our love for our brother whom we have seen.

Church and state will become one. The state will be holy, and the church will be holy. Both will aim at the same thing, and the existence of one as separate from the other will not be needed. The church will not be then an outward visible power, coexisting with the state, sometimes controlling it and at other times controlled by it; but it will be within, a true spiritual—not spiritualistic—church, regulating the heart, conscience, and the life.

And when this all takes place the glory of the Lord will be manifested unto the ends of the earth, and all flesh will see it and rejoice together. The time is yet distant before this will be fully realized. We are now realizing it in our theory. We assert the holiness of all things. This assertion becomes an idea, and ideas, if they are true, are omnipotent. As soon as humanity fully possesses this idea, it will lose no time in reducing it to practice. Men will conform their practice to it. They will become personally holy. Holiness will be written on all their thoughts, emotions and actions, on their whole lives. And then will Christ really be formed within, the hope of glory. He will be truly incarnated in universal humanity, and God and man will be one.

Chapter X.—Progress

The actual existence of evil, the effects of which are everywhere so visible, and apparently so deplorable, may seem to be a serious objection to the great doctrine of the atonement, that all things are essentially good and holy; but it will present little difficulty, if we consider that God designed us to be progressive beings, and that we can be progressive beings only on the condition that we be made less perfect than we may become, that we have our point of departure at a distance from our point of destination. We must begin in weakness and ignorance; and if we begin in weakness and ignorance we cannot fail to miss our way, or frequently to want strength to pursue it. To err in judgment or to come short in action will be our unavoidable lot, until we are instructed by experience and strengthened by exertion.

But this is no ground of complaint. We gain more than we lose by it. Had we without any agency of our own been made all that by a proper cultivation of our faculties we may become, we should have been much inferior to what we now are. We could have had no want, no desire, no good to seek, no end to gain, no destiny to achieve—no employment, and no motive to action. Our existence would have been aimless, silent, and unvaried, given apparently for no purpose but to be dreamed away in an eternal and unbroken repose. Who could desire such an existence? Who would prefer it to the existence we now have, liable to error, sin, and misery as it may be?

Constituted as we are, the way is more than the end, the acquisition more than the possession; but had we been made at once all that is promised us by our nature, these would have been nothing; we should indeed have had the end, the possession, but that would have been all. We should have been men without having first been children. Our earlier life, its trials and temptations, its failures and its successes, would never have existed. Would we willingly forego that earlier life? Dear to all men is the memory of childhood and youth; dear too is the recollection of their difficulties and dangers, their struggles with the world or with their own passions. We may regret, do regret, suffer remorse, that we did not put ourselves forth with more energy, that the enemy with which we had to contend was not more manfully met; but who of us is the craven to wish those difficulties and dangers had been less, or that the enemy's forces had been fewer and weaker?

God gave his richest gift when he gave the capacity for progress. This capacity is the chief glory of our nature, the brightest signature of its divine origin and the pledge of its immortality. The being which can make no further progress, which has finished its work, achieved its destiny, attained its end, must die. Why should it live? How could it live? What would be its life? But man never attains his end; he never achieves his destiny; he never finishes his work; he has always something to do, some new acquisition to make, some new height of excellence to ascend, and therefore is he immortal. He cannot die, for his hour never comes. He is never ready. Who would then be deprived of his capacity for progress?

This capacity, though it be the occasion of error and sin, is that which makes us moral beings. Without it we could not be virtuous. A being that does not make himself, his own character, but is made, and made all he is or can be, has no free will, no liberty. He is a thing, not a person, and as incapable of merit or demerit as the sun or moon, earthquakes or volcanoes. As much superior as is a moral to a fatal action, a perfection wrought out in and by one's self to a perfection merely received, as much superior as is a person to a thing, albeit a glorious thing, so much do we gain by being made for progress, by having a capacity for virtue, notwithstanding it be also a capacity for sin, so much superior are we to what we should have been, had we been created full grown men, with all our faculties perfected.

But moral evil, by the superintending care of Providence and the free will of man, is often if not always a means of aiding progress itself. The sinner is not so far from God as the merely innocent. He who has failed is further onward than he who has not been tried. The consequences of error open our eyes to the truth; the consequences of transgression make us regret our departure from duty and try to return; the effort to return gives us the power to return. Thus does moral evil ever work its own destruction. Rightly viewed, it were seen to be no entity, no positive existence, but merely the absence of good, the void around and within us, and which by the enlargement of our being, we are continually filling up. It is not then a person, a thing, a being, and consequently can make nothing against the doctrine, which asserts the essential holiness of all things.

But men formerly supposed evil to be a substantial existence, as much of an entity as goodness. But then came the difficulty, whence could evil originate? It could not come from a good source, for good will not and cannot produce evil. But evil exists. Then all things do not come from the same source. One good and holy God has not made whatever is. There must be more gods than one. There must be an evil god to create evil, as well as a good God to create good. Hence the notion of two gods, or two classes of gods, one good and the other bad, which runs through all antiquity, and under the terms God and the devil, is reproduced even in the Christian church.

But this notion is easily shown to be unfounded. If one of the two gods depend on the other, then the other must be its cause, its creator. In this case, nothing would be gained. How could a good God create a bad one, or a bad god create a good one? If one does not depend on the other, then both are independent, each is sufficient for itself. A being that is sufficient for itself, that has the grounds of its existence within itself, must be absolute, almighty. There are then two absolutes, two almighties; but this is an absurdity, a contradiction in terms. This notion then must be abandoned. It was abandoned, and the evil was transferred to matter. But matter is either created or it is not. If it be created, then it is dependent, and that on which it is dependent is answerable for its properties. How could a good God have given it evil properties? If it be not created, then it is sufficient for itself; it has the grounds of its own existence within itself; it is then absolute, almighty, and the absurdity of two absolutes, of two almighties, is reproduced.

Still we need not wonder that men, who saw good and evil thickly strown together up and down the earth, the tares every where choking the wheat, should have inferred the existence of two opposite and antagonist principles, as the cause of what they saw. Nor is it at all strange that men, who felt themselves restrained, hemmed in, by the material world, who carried about with them a material body for ever importuning them with its wants and subjecting them to a thousand ills, should have looked upon matter as the cause of all the evil they saw, felt, and endured. As things presented themselves to their observation they judged rightly. We may, by the aid of a revelation, which shines further into the darkness and spreads a clearer light around us and over the universe than any they had received, be able to correct their errors, and to perceive that the antagonism, in which they believed, has no existence in the world of reality; but we must beware how we censure them for the views they took. They saw what they could see with their light and from their position, and we can do no more. Future generations will have more favorable positions and a stronger and clearer light than we have, and they will be to us what we are to the generations which went before us. As we would escape the condemnation of our children, so should we refrain from condemning our fathers. They did their duty, let us do ours,—serve our own generation without defaming that to which we owe our existence and all that we are. All things are holy, and all doctrines are sacred. All the productions of the ever-teeming brain of man, however fantastic or unsubstantial their forms, are but so many manifestations of humanity, and humanity is a manifestation of the Divinity. The Son of Man is the incarnate God. He who blasphemes the spirit with which he works and fulfils his mission in the flesh, blasphemes the Holy Ghost. Silent then be the tongue that would lisp, palsied the hand that would write the smallest censure upon humanity for any of the opinions it has expressed, however defective, however far from embracing the whole truth, future or more favored inquirers may find them. Humanity is holy, let the proudest kneel in reverence.

This doctrine of progress, not only accounts for the origin of evil and explains its difficulties, but it points out to us our duty. The duty of every being is to follow its destiny, to seek its end. Man's destiny is illimitable progress; his end is everlasting growth, enlargement of his being. Progress is the end for which he was made. To this end, then, it is his duty to direct all his inquiries, all his systems of religion and philosophy, all his institutions of politics and society, all the productions of genius and taste, in one word all the modes of his activity.

This is his duty. Hitherto he has performed it, but blindly, without knowing and without admitting it. Humanity has but to-day, as it were, risen to self-consciousness, to a perception of its own capacity, to a glimpse of its inconceivably grand and holy destiny. Heretofore it has failed to recognize clearly its duty. It has advanced, but not designedly, not with foresight; it has done it instinctively, by the aid of the invisible but safe-guiding hand of its Father. Without knowing what it did, it has condemned progress, while it was progressing. It has stoned the prophets and reformers, even while it was itself reforming and uttering glorious prophecies of its future condition. But the time has now come for humanity to understand itself, to accept the law imposed upon it for its own good, to foresee its end and march with intention steadily towards it. Its future religion is the religion of progress. The true priests are those who can quicken in mankind a desire for progress, and urge them forward in the direction of the true, the good, the perfect. . . .

Notes: New Views

1. Gregory VII was pope from 1073 to 1085.
2. Leo X was pope from 1513 to 1521.
3. Joseph Priestley (1733–1804), scientist and theologian, was a founder of the Unitarian movement in England and had an influence on its development in the United States. Thomas Belsham (1750–1829) accepted Priestley's Unitarian pulpit at Hackney, England, when Priestley moved to the United States. He wrote frequently in defense of Unitarianism.
4. Chapters seven, "Christian Sects," and eight, "Indications of the Atonement," have been deleted here. Brownson argues in chapter seven that the present Christian sects overlook the important truth of the Atonement as a synthesis of matter and spirit. "Spiritualism and materialism are the two most comprehensive sectarian doc-

trines." Chapter eight maintains that at present there is a reappearance of a synthesis of spiritualism and materialism. This is evident in a new meeting of Eastern and Western values, the philosophy of eclecticism advocated by Cousin and in a new inspiration in the people. The current popularity of various associations also shows the movement of the age toward union. William Ellery Channing is the one man of the age who stands as a type of the new synthesis that is required in the nineteenth century.

5. Gn 1:31.
6. Zec 14:20–21.
7. Jas 1:27.

13. MR. EMERSON'S ADDRESS

SOURCE: *Boston Quarterly Review* 1 (October 1838): 500–514.

The following is Brownson's review of Ralph Waldo Emerson's An Address Delivered Before the Senior Class in Divinity College, Cambridge, Sunday Evening, 15 July 1838 *(Boston: James Munroe & Company, 1838). Although Brownson had an affection for Emerson, he was critical of the philosophical and theological grounds of Emerson's essay. Brownson finds in Emerson's essay no objective grounds for moral obligation, a failure to appreciate understanding, an unwarranted identification of the religious with the moral sentiment, an identification of God with the laws of the soul's perfection, and a failure to perceive the supernatural origin and development of Christianity. By concentrating so much upon the individual subject, Emerson has failed to present the objective grounds for the individual's progress and development in the life of the spirit. Religion, for Brownson, has an objective as well as a subjective referent.*

This is in some respects a remarkable address,—remarkable for its own character and for the place where and the occasion on which it was delivered. It is not often, we fancy, that such an address is delivered by a clergyman in a Divinity College to a class of young men just ready to go forth into the churches as preachers of the Gospel of Jesus Christ. Indeed it is not often that a discourse teaching doctrines like the leading doctrines of this, is delivered by a professedly religious man, anywhere or on any occasion.

We are not surprised that this address should have produced some excitement and called forth some severe censures upon its author; for

we have long known that there are comparatively few who can hear
with calmness the utterance of opinions to which they do not sub-
scribe. Yet we regret to see the abuse which has been heaped upon Mr.
Emerson. We ought to learn to tolerate all opinions, to respect every
man's right to form and to utter his own opinions whatever they may
be. If we regard the opinions as unsound, false, or dangerous, we
should meet them calmly, refute them if we can; but be careful to
respect, and to treat with all Christian meekness and love, him who
entertains them.

There are many things in this address we heartily approve; there is
much that we admire and thank the author for having uttered. We like
its life and freshness, its freedom and independence, its richness and
beauty. But we cannot help regarding its tone as somewhat arrogant,
its spirit is quite too censorious and desponding, its philosophy as
indigested, and its reasoning as inconclusive. We do not like its misti-
ness, its vagueness, and its perpetual use of old words in new senses. Its
meaning too often escapes us; and we find it next to impossible to seize
its dominant doctrine and determine what it is or what it is not.
Moreover, it does not appear to us to be all of the same piece. It is
made up of parts borrowed from different and hostile systems, which
"baulk and baffle" the author's power to form into a consistent and
harmonious whole.

In a moral point of view the leading doctrine of this address, if we
have seized it, is not a little objectionable. It is not easy to say what that
moral doctrine is; but so far as we can collect it, it is, that the soul
possesses certain laws or instincts, obedience to which constitutes its
perfection. "The sentiment of virtue is a reverence and delight in the
presence of certain divine laws." "The intuition of the moral sentiment is an insight of the perfection of the laws of the soul." These
"divine laws" are the "laws of the soul." The moral sentiment results
from the perception of these laws, and moral character results from
conformity to them. Now this is not, we apprehend, psychologically
true. If any man will analyze the moral sentiment as a fact of consciousness, he will find it something more than "an insight of the
perfection of the laws of the soul." He will find that it is a sense of
obligation. Man feels himself under obligation to obey a law; not the
law of his own soul, a law emanating from his soul as lawgiver; but a
law above his soul, imposed upon him by a supreme lawgiver, who has
a right to command his obedience. He does never feel that he is moral
in obeying merely the laws of his own nature, but in obeying the
command of a power out of him, above him, and independent on him.

By the laws of the soul, we presume, Mr. Emerson means our

instincts. In his Phi Beta Kappa Address, reviewed in this journal for January,[1] he speaks much of the instincts, and bids us "plant ourselves on our instincts, and the huge world will come round to us." The ethical rule he lays down is then, "follow thy instincts," or as he expresses it in the address before us, "obey thyself." Now if we render this rule into the language it will assume in practice, we must say, obey thyself,—follow thy instincts,—follow thy inclinations,—live as thou listest. Strike out the idea of something above man to which he is accountable, make him accountable only to himself, and why shall he not live as he listeth? We see not what restraint can legitimately be imposed upon any of his instincts or propensities. There may then be some doubts whether the command, "obey thyself," be an improvement on the Christian command, "deny thyself."

We presume that when Mr. Emerson tells us to obey ourselves, to obey the laws of our soul, to follow our instincts, he means that we shall be true to our higher nature, that we are to obey our higher instincts, and not our baser propensities. He is himself a pure minded man, and would by no means encourage sensuality. But how shall we determine which are our higher instincts and which are our lower instincts? We do not perceive that he gives us any instructions on this point. Men like him may take the higher instincts to be those which lead us to seek truth and beauty; but men in whom the sensual nature overlays the spiritual, may think differently; and what rule has he for determining which is in the right? He commands us to be ourselves, and sneers at the idea of having "models." We must take none of the wise or good, not even Jesus Christ as a model of what we should be. We are to act out ourselves. Now why is not the sensualist as moral as the spiritualist, providing he acts out himself? Mr. Emerson is a great admirer of Carlyle;[2] and according to Carlyle, the moral man, the true man, is he who acts out himself. A Mirabeau, or a Danton is, under a moral point of view, the equal of a Howard[3] or a Washington, because equally true to himself. Does not this rule confound all moral distinctions, and render moral judgments a "formula," all wise men must "swallow and make away with"?

But suppose we get over this difficulty and determine which are the higher instincts of our nature, those which we must follow in order to perfect our souls, and become,—as Mr. Emerson has it,—God; still we ask, why are we under obligation to obey these instincts? Because obedience to them will perfect our souls? But why are we bound to perfect our souls? Where there is no sense of obligation, there is no moral sense. We are moral only on the condition that we feel there is something which we *ought* to do. Why ought we to labor for our own perfection? Because it will promote our happiness? But why are we morally bound to seek our own happiness? It may be very desirable to promote our happiness, but it does not follow from that we are morally bound to do it, and we know there are occasions when we should not do it.

Put the rule, Mr. Emerson lays down, in the best light possible, it proposes nothing higher than our own individual good as the end to be sought. He would tell us to reduce all the jarring elements of our nature to harmony, and produce and maintain perfect order in the soul. Now is this the highest good the reason can conceive? Are all things in the universe to be held subordinate to the individual soul? Shall a man take himself as the centre of the universe, and say all things are for his use, and count them of value only as they contribute something to his growth or well-being? This were a deification of the soul with a vengeance. It were nothing but a system of transcendental selfishness. It were pure egotism. According to this, I am everything; all else is nothing, at least nothing except what it derives from the fact that it is something to me.

Now this system of pure egotism, seems to us to run through all Mr. Emerson's writings. We meet it everywhere in his masters, Carlyle and Goethe. He and they may not be quite so grossly selfish as were some of the old sensualist philosophers; they may admit a higher good than the mere gratification of the senses, than mere wealth or fame; but the highest good they recognise is an individual good, the realization of order in their own individual souls. Everything by them is estimated according to its power to contribute to this end. If they mingle with men it is to use them; if they are generous and humane, if they labor to do good to others, it is always as a means, never as an end. Always is the *doing,* whatever it be, to terminate in self. Self, the higher self, it is true, is always the centre of gravitation. Now is the man who adopts this moral rule, really a moral man? Does not morality always propose to us an end separate from our own, above our own, and to which our own good is subordinate?

No doubt it is desirable to perfect the individual soul, to realize order in the individual; but the reason, the moment it is developed, discloses a good altogether superior to this. Above the good of the individual, and paramount to it, is the good of the universe, the realization of the good of creation, absolute good. No man can deny that the realization of the good of all beings is something superior to the realization of the good of the individual. Morality always requires us to labor for the highest good we can conceive. The moral law then requires us to seek another good than that of our own souls. The individual lives not for himself alone. His good is but an element, a fragment of the universal good, and is to be sought never as an end, but always as a means of realizing absolute good, or universal order. This rule requires the man to forget himself, to go out of himself, and under certain circumstances to deny himself, to sacrifice himself, for a good which does not centre in himself. He who forgets himself, who is disinterested and heroic, who sacrifices himself for others, is in the eyes of reason, infinitely superior to the man who merely uses others as the means of promoting his own intellectual and spiritual growth. Mr. Emerson's rule then is defective, inasmuch as it proposes the subordinate as the paramount, and places obligation where we feel it is not. For the present, then, instead of adopting his formula, "obey thyself," or Carlyle's formula, "act out thyself," we must continue to approve the Christian formula, "deny thyself, and love thy neighbor as thyself."

But passing over this, we cannot understand how it is possible for a man to become virtuous by yielding to his instincts. Virtue is voluntary obedience to a moral law, felt to be obligatory. We are aware of the existence of the law, and we act in reference to it, and intend to obey it. We of course are not passive, but active in the case of virtue. Virtue is always personal. It is our own act. We are in the strictest sense of the word the cause or creator of it. Therefore it is, that we judge ourselves worthy of praise when we are virtuous, and of condemnation when we are not virtuous. But in following instinct, we are not active but passive. The causative force at work in our instincts, is not our personality, our wills, but an impersonal force, a force *we* are not. Now in yielding to our instincts, as Mr. Emerson advises us, we abdicate our own personality, and from persons become things, as incapable of virtue as the trees of the forest or the stones of the field.

Mr. Emerson, moreover, seems to us to mutilate man, and in his zeal for the instincts to entirely overlook reflection. The instincts are all very well. They give us the force of character we need, but they do not make up the whole man. We have understanding as well as instinct, reflection as well as spontaneity. Now to be true to our nature, to the whole man, the understanding should have its appropriate exercise. Does Mr. Emerson give it this exercise? Does he not rather hold the understanding in light esteem, and labor almost entirely to fix our minds on the fact of primitive intuition as all-sufficient of itself? We do not ask him to reject the instincts, but we ask him to compel them to give an account of themselves. We are willing to follow them; but we must do it designedly, intentionally, after we have proved our moral right to do it, not before. Here is an error in Mr. Emerson's system of no small magnitude. He does not account for the instincts nor legitimate them. He does not prove them to be divine forces or safe guides. In practice, therefore, he is merely reviving the old sentimental systems of morality, systems which may do for the young, the dreamy, or the passionate, but never for a sturdy race of men and women who demand a reason for all they do, for what they approve or disapprove.

Nor are we better satisfied with the theology of this discourse. We cannot agree with Mr. Emerson in his account of the religious sentiment. He confounds the religious sentiment with the moral; but the two sentiments are psychologically distinct. The religious sentiment is a craving to adore, resulting from the soul's intuition of the Holy; the moral sentiment is a sense of obligation resulting from the soul's intuition of a moral law. The moral sentiment leads us up merely to universal order; the religious sentiment leads us up to God, the Father of universal order. Religious ideas always carry us into a region far above that of moral ideas. Religion gives the law to ethics, not ethics to religion. Religion is the communion of the soul with God, morality is merely the *cultus exterior,* the outward worship of God, the expression of the life of God in the soul; as James has it, "pure religion,—external worship, for so should we understand the original,—and undefiled before God and the Father is this, To visit the fatherless and widows in their affliction, and to keep himself unspotted from the world."[4]

But even admitting the two sentiments are not two but one, identical, we are still dissatisfied with Mr. Emerson's account of the matter. The religious sentiment, according to him, grows out of the soul's insight of the perfection of its own laws. These laws are in fact the soul itself. They are not something distinct from the soul, but its essence. In neglecting them the soul is not itself, in finding them it finds itself, and in living them it is God. This is his doctrine. The soul then in case of the religious sentiment has merely an intuition of itself. Its craving to adore is not a craving to adore something superior to itself. In worshipping then, the soul does not worship God, a being above man and independent on him, but it worships itself. We must not then speak of worshipping God, but merely of worshipping the soul. Now is this a correct account of the religious sentiment? The religious sentiment is in the bottom of the soul, and it is always a craving of the soul to go out of itself, and fasten itself on an object above itself, free from its own weakness, mutability, and impurity, on a being all-sufficient, all-sufficing, omnipotent, immutable, and all-holy. It results from the fact that we are conscious of not being sufficient for ourselves, that the ground of our being is not in ourselves, and from the need we feel of an Almighty arm on which to lean, a strength foreign to our own, from which we may derive support. Let us be God, let us feel that we need go out of ourselves for nothing, and we are no longer in the condition to be religious; the religious sentiment can no longer find a place in our souls, and we can no more feel a craving to adore than God himself. Nothing is more evident to us, than that the religious sentiment springs, on the one hand, solely from a sense of dependence, and on the other hand, from an intuition of an invisible Power, Father, God, on whom we may depend, to whom we may go in our weakness, to whom we may appeal when oppressed, and who is able and willing to succor us. Take away the idea of such a God, declare the soul sufficient for itself, forbid it ever to go out of itself, to look up to a power above it, and religion is out of the question.

If we rightly comprehend Mr. Emerson's views of God, he admits no God but the laws of the soul's perfection. God is in man, not out of him. He is in the soul as the oak is in the acorn. When man fully developes the laws of his nature, realizes the ideal of his nature, he is not, as the Christian would say, god-like, but he is God. The ideal of man's nature is not merely similar in all men, but identical. When all men realize the ideal of their nature, that is, attain to the highest perfection admitted by the laws of their being, then do they all become swallowed up in the One Man. There will then no longer be men; all diversity will be lost in unity, and there will be only One Man, and that one man will be God. But what and where is God now? Before all men have realized the ideal of their nature, and become swallowed up in the One Man, is there really and actually a God? Is there any God but the God Osiris, torn into pieces and scattered up and down through all the earth, which pieces, scattered parts, the weeping Isis must go forth seeking everywhere, and find not without labor and difficulty? Can we be said to have at present anything more than the disjected members of a God, the mere embryo fragments of a God, one day to come forth into the light, to be gathered up that nothing be lost, and finally moulded into one complete and rounded God? So it seems to us, and we confess, therefore, that we can affix no definite meaning to the religious language which Mr. Emerson uses so freely.

Furthermore, we cannot join Mr. Emerson in his worship to the soul. We are disposed to go far in our estimate of the soul's divine capacities; we believe it was created in the image of God, and may bear his moral likeness; but we cannot so exalt it as to call it God. Nor can we take its ideal of its own perfection as God. The soul's conception of God is not God, and if there be no God out of the soul, out of the me, to answer to the soul's conception, then is there no God. God as we conceive him is independent on us, and is in no sense affected by our conceptions of him. He is in us, but not us. He dwells in the hearts of the humble and contrite ones, and yet the heaven of heavens cannot contain him. He is the same yesterday, to-day, and forever. He is above all, the cause and sustainer of all that is, in whom we live and move and have our being. Him we worship, and only him. We dare not worship merely our own soul. Alas, we know our weakness; we feel our sinfulness; we are oppressed with a sense of our unworthiness, and we cannot so sport with the solemnities of religious worship, as to direct them to ourselves, or to anything which does not transcend our own being.

Yet this worship of the soul is part and parcel of the transcendental egotism of which we spoke in commenting on Mr. Emerson's moral doctrines. He and his masters, Carlyle and Goethe, make the individual soul everything, the centre of the universe, for whom all exists that does exist; and why then should it not be the supreme object of their affections? Soul-worship, which is only another name for self-worship, or the worship of self, is the necessary consequence of their system, a system well described by Pope in his Essay on Man:

> "Ask for what end the heavenly bodies shine,
> Earth for whose use? Pride answers, ''Tis for mine:
> For me, kind nature wakes her genial power,
> Suckles each herb, and spreads out every flower;
> Annual for me, the grape, the rose, renew
> The juice nectareous, and the balmy dew;
> For me, the mine a thousand treasures brings;
> For me, health gushes from a thousand springs;
> Seas roll to waft me, suns to light me rise;
> My footstool earth, my canopy the skies.' "

To which we may add,

> "While man exclaims, 'See all things for my use!'
> 'See man for mine!' replies a pampered goose:
> And just as short of reason he must fall
> Who thinks all made for one, not one for all."

Mr. Emerson has much to say against preaching a traditional Christ, against preaching what he calls historical Christianity. So far as his object in this is to draw men's minds off from an exclusive attention to the "letter," and to fix them on the "spirit," to prevent them from relying for the matter and evidence of their faith on merely historical documents, and to induce them to reproduce the gospel histories in their own souls, he is not only not censurable but praiseworthy. He is doing a service to the Christian cause. Christianity may be found in the human soul, and reproduced in human experience now, as well as in the days of Jesus. It is in the soul too that we must find the key to the meaning of the Gospels, and in the soul's experience that we must seek the principal evidences of their truth.

But if Mr. Emerson means to sever us from the past, and to intimate that the Christianity of the past has ceased to have any interest for the present generation, and that the knowledge and belief of it are no longer needed for the soul's growth, for its redemption and union with God, we must own we cannot go with him. Christianity results from the development of the laws of the human soul, but from a supernatural, not a natural, development; that is, by the aid of a power above the soul. God has been to the human race both a father and an educator. By a supernatural,—not an unnatural—influence, he has, as it has seemed proper to him, called forth our powers, and enabled us to see and comprehend the truths essential to our moral progress. The records of the aid he has at different ages furnished us, and of the truths seen and comprehended at the period when the faculties of the soul were supernaturally exalted, cannot in our judgment be unessential, far less improper, to be dwelt upon by the Christian preacher.

Then again, we cannot dispense with Jesus Christ. As much as some may wish to get rid of him, or to change or improve his character, the world needs him, and needs him in precisely the character in which the Gospels present him. His is the only name whereby men can be saved. He is the father of the modern world, and his is the life we now live, so far as we live any life at all. Shall we then crowd him away with the old bards and seers, and regard him and them merely as we do the authors of some old ballads which charmed our forefathers, but which may not be sung in a modern drawing-room? Has his example lost its power, his life its quickening influence, his doctrine its truth? Have we outgrown him as a teacher?

In the Gospels we find the solution of the great problem of man's destiny; and, what is more to our purpose, we find there the middle term by which the creature is connected with the Creator. Man is at an infinite distance from God; and he cannot by his own strength approach God, and become one with him. We cannot see God; we cannot know him; no man hath seen the Father at any time, and no man knoweth the Father, save the Son, and he to whom the Son reveals him. We approach God only through a mediator; we see and know only the Word, which is the mediator between God and men.

Does Mr. Emerson mean that the record we have of this Word in the Bible, of this Word, which was made flesh, incarnated in the man Jesus, and dwelt among men and disclosed the grace and truth with which it overflowed, is of no use now in the church, nay, that it is a let and a hindrance? We want that record, which is to us as the testimony of the race, to corroborate the witness within us. One witness is not enough. We have one witness within us, an important witness, too seldom examined; but as important as he is, he is not alone sufficient. We must back up his individual testimony with that of the race. In the Gospel records we have the testimony borne by the race to the great truths it most concerns us to know. That testimony, the testimony of history, in conjunction with our own individual experience, gives us all the certainty we ask, and furnishes us a solid ground for an unwavering and active faith. As in philosophy, we demand history as well as psychology, so in theology we ask the historical Christ as well as the psychological Christ. The church in general has erred by giving us only the historical Christ; but let us not now err, by preaching only a psychological Christ.

In dismissing this address, we can only say that we have spoken of it freely, but with no improper feeling to its author. We love bold speculation; we are pleased to find a man who dares tell us what and precisely what he thinks, however unpopular his views may be. We have no disposition to check his utterance, by giving his views a bad name, although we deem them unsound. We love progress, and progress cannot be effected without freedom. Still we wish to see a certain sobriety, a certain reserve in all speculations, something like timidity about rushing off into an unknown universe, and some little regret in departing from the faith of our fathers.

Nevertheless, let not the tenor of our remarks be mistaken. Mr. Emerson is the last man in the world we should suspect of conscious hostility to religion and morality. No one can know him or read his productions without feeling a profound respect for the singular purity and uprightness of his character and motives. The great object he is laboring to accomplish is one in which he should receive the hearty cooperation of every American scholar, of every friend of truth, freedom, piety, and virtue. Whatever may be the character of his speculations, whatever may be the moral, philosophical, or theological system which forms the basis of his speculations, his real object is not the inculcation of any new theory on man, nature, or God; but to induce men to think for themselves on all subjects, and to speak from their own full hearts and earnest convictions. His object is to make men scorn to be slaves to routine, to custom, to established creeds, to public opinion, to the great names of this age, of this country, or of any other. He cannot bear the idea that a man comes into the world to-day with the field of truth monopolized and foreclosed. To every man lies open the whole field of truth, in morals, in politics, in science, in theology, in philosophy. The labors of past ages, the revelations of prophets and bards, the discoveries of the scientific and the philosophic, are not to be regarded as superseding our own exertions and inquiries, as impediments to the free action of our own minds, but merely as helps, as provocations to the freest and fullest spiritual action of which God has made us capable.

This is the real end he has in view, and it is a good end. To call forth the free spirit, to produce the conviction here implied, to provoke men to be men, self-moving, self-subsisting men, not mere puppets, moving but as moved by the reigning mode, the reigning dogma, the reigning school, is a grand and praise-worthy work, and we should reverence and aid, not abuse and hinder him who gives himself up soul and body to its accomplishment. So far as the author of the address before us is true to this object, earnest in executing this work, he has our hearty sympathy, and all the aid we, in our humble sphere, can give him. In laboring for this object, he proves himself worthy of his age and his country, true to religion and to morals. In calling, as he does, upon the literary men of our community, in the silver tones of his rich and eloquent voice, and above all by the quickening influence of his example, to assert and maintain their independence throughout the whole domain of thought, against every species of tyranny that would encroach upon it, he is doing his duty; he is doing a work the effects of which will be felt for good far and wide, long after men shall have forgotten the puerility of his conceits, the affectations of his style, and the unphilosophical character of his speculations. The doctrines he puts forth, the positive instructions, for which he is now censured, will soon be classed where they belong: but the influence of his free spirit, and free utterance, the literature of this country will long feel and hold in grateful remembrance.

Notes: Mr. Emerson's Address

1. "Emerson's Phi Beta Kappa Oration," *Boston Quarterly Review* 1 (January 1838): 106–20.
2. Thomas Carlyle (1795–1801) was a Scottish historian, essayist and moral teacher who opposed all materialistic philosophies.

3. Comte de Mirabeau (Honoré Gabriel Victor Rigueti, 1749–91) was a politician in the forefront of the French Revolution. Georges Jacques Danton (1759–94) was also a leader of the French Revolution. John Howard (1752–1827) was an American Revolutionary soldier, statesman and politician.
4. Jas 1:27.

VII.

LIFE BY COMMUNION:
1842–44

14. THE MEDIATORIAL LIFE OF JESUS:
A LETTER TO WILLIAM ELLERY CHANNING, D.D.

SOURCE: Boston: Charles C. Little and James Brown, 1842. See also
Works 4, pp. 143–72.

*The Mediatorial Life is Brownson's formal announcement of his
departure from Channing's liberal pietism. It is also Brownson's attempt to construct a theology of Christian life based upon Jesus' mediatorship. Christian life is more than the subjective religious experience
of the divinity within humanity. It is more than a natural religious
sentiment. It is a communion with the divine through the tradition
initiated by the God-Man Jesus. Here Brownson tries to demonstrate
the philosophical reasonableness of the Christian doctrine of Providence (that is, God's free intervention in history), sin and its transmission, and the salvation of the world through Jesus' mediation. Brownson is trying to provide some rational objective grounds for Christian
piety—for the experiences of prayer and forgiveness. Here, too, he
challenges those who have tended to exclude the supernatural from
nature and history. There is, he argues, a supernatural basis for the
Christian life. It is not just natural life developed to its highest potential.*

. . . I have sir, finally attained to a view of the plan of a world's
salvation through a Mediator, which I think reconciles all conflicting
theories, discloses new wisdom in that plan, and enables us to take, in

its most obvious and literal sense, without any subtlety or refinement, what the scriptures say of Jesus, and of salvation through his life. The Gospel becomes to me now a reality, and the teachings of the New Testament throughout realities, having their corresponding facts in the positive world. The views to which I have attained appear to me to be new, grand, and of the greatest importance. If I am not deceived they enable us to demonstrate with as much certainty as we have for our own existence several great and leading doctrines of the church universal, which have heretofore been asserted as great and holy mysteries, but unproved and unexplained. I think I can show that no small portion of the Bible, which is generally taken figuratively, is susceptible of literal interpretation, and that certain views of the Mediator, and his Life, from which, our Unitarian friends have shrunk, are nevertheless true, and susceptible of a philosophical demonstration. I think sir, I am able to show that the doctrine that human nature became depraved through the sin of Adam, and that it is redeemed only through the obedience of Christ; that the doctrine which teaches us that the Mediator is truly and indissolubly God-man, and saves the world by giving literally his life to the world, are the great "central truths" of Christianity, and philosophically demonstrable.

This, if it can be done, you will admit is important, and must involve a theological revolution. My purpose in writing you this letter, is to call your attention to the method by which it can be done, and to ask your judgment on that method. If I am right, I know you will rejoice with me, for the result will prove to be that *higher manifestation* of religious truth which you and so many others have been looking for, and asserting, must come.

Before I proceed to lay before you the important views themselves, I must be allowed to say a word as to the means by which I have attained to them; I do this that I may not arrogate to myself what does not belong to me. I have little other merit in attaining to these views, than that of following out to their legitimate conclusions, certain philosophical principles, which I have been assisted by others to obtain. The great principle which underlies the whole, I became master of about one year ago. I saw, at once its immense reach in the region of metaphysics; but did not see at the time very clearly its importance in the social world, or the religious world. Leroux,[1] in his work on *L'Humanité,* discovered to me its social applications. In endeavoring to point out, in a sermon a few Sundays since, this social application, which seemed to me to give new significance to the Communion, I perceived suddenly the theological application, of the principle in question, and the flood of light it throws on long-controverted dogmas.

This theological application, which I am about to point out, is all that I claim as original with myself, and all that I claim as novel in the views of which I speak. . . .

In the doctrines I am about to present, I claim no originality. I merely claim originality for the process by which I demonstrate their philosophical truth. The doctrines have been taught ever since the time of Jesus; they have never, before this attempt of mine, so far as my knowledge extends, been demonstrated. What I have to offer on the main subject of this Letter, I shall take the liberty to arrange under three general heads.

First.—Whence comes the Mediator? *Second.*—What is his work? *Third.*—What is the method by which he performs it?

These three inquiries will cover the whole ground that I wish at present to occupy, or that is necessary to enable me to bring out all the peculiar views I am anxious to set forth concerning Jesus as the Mediator and Saviour of the world.

First.—Whence comes the Mediator? I should not detain you a moment with this inquiry, were it not that there is a tendency in some minds among us, to rank Jesus in the category of ordinary men. I do not say that any among us question his vast superiority over all other men of whom history retains any record, but in this superiority they see nothing supernatural, no special interposition of Providence. Jesus was a man of greater natural endowments, and of more devout piety, truer and deeper philanthropy than other men. He has exerted a great and beneficial influence on the world, will perhaps continue to exert a beneficial influence for some time to come; but he is divine, it is said, in no sense in which all men are not divine, in no sense in which nature is not divine. He had a larger nature, and was truer to it, than other men, and this is all wherein he was distinguished from other men, or had any special divinity.

Persons who entertain this view, speak of him in very respectful, I may almost say, in very flattering terms. Their praise is high, warm, and no doubt sincere. But they do not seem to regard him as having been, in the strict sense of the term, a "providential man." He is providential only in that vague and unsatisfactory sense in which all nature, all men, and all events are providential. They do not look upon him as having been, in the plain, ordinary sense of the terms, sent from God to be the Redeemer and Saviour of the world. They give a very loose explanation of the text, "God so loved the world that he gave his only begotten Son to die, that whosoever should believe on him might not perish, but have everlasting life."[2] Jesus was the "Son of God" as all men are sons of God, and in no other sense, and "was given" as all men are given, and not otherwise. This is a conclusion, you are aware, to which some among us have come.

The same tendency which leads thus far, leads even further. It not only reduces Jesus to the category of ordinary men, but, as might be expected, it does the same by Moses and the prophets, by the apostles, and, indeed, by all who have generally been regarded as having been specially sent from God for the instruction and improvement of mankind. These men have not spoken to us from God, words given them by a higher power, and in the Name above all names, but out of their own hearts, from their own deep but natural experience. Their utterances are, no doubt, worthy of our respect. We may be refreshed by reading them, as by all genuine utterances, in which men are true to their great natures. The Bible, of course, ceases to be a book divinely inspired, a book authoritative, fit to be appealed to as decisive on matters lying beyond human experience; though it remains a very good book, containing many striking passages, much genuine poetry, some fine myths, some touching narratives, even some philosophy, and worthy to stand on the scholar's shelf with Homer, Shakespeare, Thomas Brown, and Emanuel Swedenborg.[3]

This tendency might go further still. The state of mind and heart which leads us to wish to exclude all special providence or interposition of the Deity from the person of Jesus, and the Bible and its authors, would, if followed to its legitimate result, lead us to exclude God from the moral world altogether. When excluded from the moral world, he of course will not be retained in the natural world, and then is God wholly excluded from the universe. We are then without God, and God, if he be at all, is only an Epicurean God, who reposes at an infinite distance from the universe, disturbing himself with its concerns not at all.

It seem to me, sir, that this tendency, which neither you nor I have wholly escaped, is a tendency to resolve God into the laws of nature, —the laws of the moral world, and those of the natural world. Now what is this but a tendency to sink God in nature, to lose him entirely, that is, to become atheists? I do not mean to say that you or I have been affected by this tendency to any very great extent, but you know that it has manifested itself in our midst. We have found it in our friends; we have met with it in our parochial visits; we have seen it in the doctrines put forth by men who profess to have outgrown the past; and indeed it has been the decided tendency of the literature and science of Christendom for the last century and a half. Men have deified nature, boasted the perfection and harmony of her laws, forgetful that there are such things as volcanoes, earthquakes, noxious damps and poisonous effluvia, blight and mildew. They shrink from admitting the doctrine of Providence. In reading ancient history they seek to resolve all that is marvellous or prodigious into natural laws, and some entire religious sects are so afraid of the interposition of God, that they say men are rewarded and punished according to the "natural laws." They see no longer the hand of God, but great Nature.

But I need hardly say to you that this whole tendency is anti-religious, and productive, in every heart that indulges it, of decided irreligion. The scriptures everywhere represent the agents and ministries of our instruction and improvement as sent by a heavenly Father. Noah, Abraham, Moses, David, Isaiah, Peter, James, John, and Paul, are always called of God, and sent. They come to us not of their own accord; they speak to us not in their own name, but as ambassadors for God. God gives to each a special mission, and sends him on an errand of love and mercy to his tribe, nation, or race. This is the only view compatible with religion.

When we resolve God into the laws of nature, whether as called the laws of the moral world or of the natural world, we have nothing remaining but nature. Nature, when there is no God seen behind it, to control it, to do with it as he will, in fact, that wills to overrule its seeming evil for real good, is a mere fate, an inexorable destiny, a dark, inscrutable, resistless necessity. It has no freedom, no justice. It sweeps on regardless of what it crushes or carries away before it; now with its lightnings striking down the old man in his sins, and now the infant in its innocence. Where is the ground for religious emotion—religious exercise? All is fixed, irrevocable. What shall we do? or wherefore attempt to do any thing? We may fear and tremble at the darkness before and behind us, but wherefore love, or be grateful? We may be anxious about the future, but wherefore pray? We may wish to be forgiven our sins, but who can forgive them? What is the ground of penitence and pardon?

Prayer, many amongst us have felt, is quite useless, if not improper, saving as a sort of æsthetic exercise, saving its spiritual effect on the one who prays. Forgiveness of sins men have seemed, to a very great extent, to consider as altogether out of the question. They either seek on the one hand a scape-goat, a substitute, some one to suffer for their sins, in their place, or they say God leaves us to the *natural* consequences of our deeds. There is no God, who of his own free grace, pardons the sinner, and receives and embraces the returning prodigal.

In fact, sir, not a few among us, though they admit, in words, that there is a God, do virtually deny his existence, by failing to believe in his freedom. You have contended for human freedom, and declared that man is annihilated just in proportion as his freedom is abridged. You may say as much of God. Freedom and sovereignty are one and the same. It has been felt that God has hedged himself in by natural laws, laws of his own establishing, so that he is no longer free to hear and answer prayer, or to comfort and forgive the penitent. God acts undoubtedly in accordance with invariable and eternal laws, but these laws are not the *natural* laws, not laws which he has enacted, but the laws of his own being; that is to say, he acts ever in conformity with himself, according to his own immutable will. The laws which he is not free to violate are not laws out of himself, but which he himself is. That is to say again, God is not free to be other than himself, and in this fact he is proved to be absolutely free.

This tendency to resolve God into nature, is unscriptural and fatal to religion. Either we must give up all pretensions to religion or follow an opposite tendency. Either we must give up all ground for piety, or suffer Providence to intervene in the affairs of the world, and of the human race. We must also guard with great care against all disposition to revolt at this intervention. The true religious theory requires us to regard the authors of the Bible as supernaturally endowed, as sent specially by our Father on special missions, and the Bible therefore as a supernatural book, belonging to a different category from that of all other books.

According to this view, we must regard Jesus, not as *coming,* but as *sent,* not as raising himself up to be the Mediator, but as having been raised up by the Father in heaven. He is from God, who commends his love to us by him. It is God's grace, not human effort or human genius, that provides the Mediator. It is impossible then to press Jesus into the category of ordinary men. He stands out alone, distinct, peculiar. This much, I must be permitted to assume in regard to Jesus, if I am to concern myself with Christianity at all. In answer then to the question, Whence comes the Mediator? I reply, from God, "who so loved the world that he gave his only begotten Son to die, that whosoever should believe on him might not perish, but have everlasting life."

Second.—But, assuming that God sent the Mediator, what did he send him to do? What was the work to be done for human redemption and sanctification? In other words, what is the condition in which the Gospel assumes the human race to be *without Christ,* and from which God, through the mediation of Christ, is represented as saving it? A great question this, and one on which I feel that I cannot so fully sympathize with your views as I once did. You say, in the sermon to which I have already alluded, that "In ourselves are the elements of the

Divinity. God, then, does not sustain a figurative resemblance to man. It is the resemblance of a parent to a child, the likeness of a kindred nature."[4] I am not sure that I catch your precise meaning in these sentences, but from these and from your writings generally, I infer that you hold man to be created with a *nature* akin to that of the Divinity. In other words, man is created with a divine nature, and therefore the human and divine must be at bottom identical. This is the doctrine I have been accustomed to draw from your writings, and which is termed, amongst your admirers, the doctrine of the divinity of humanity.

This doctrine, which you have set forth on so many occasions, with all the power of your rich and fervid eloquence, I must needs believe is the real parent of that deification and worship of the human soul, which has within a few years past manifested itself among our transcendentalists. Men more ardent but less discriminating than yourself, have seized upon this expression, "in ourselves are the elements of the Divinity," and have inferred that God is nothing but the possibility of man. In your mind, I presume the expression only means that it is in ourselves that we find the germs, not of God, but of the idea of God. Others, however, have interpreted you differently, and have gone so far as to say that God is merely the complement of humanity; and some whom we have been loath to call insane, have not illogically though absurdly proceeded to say of themselves, "*I* am God;" "I and my Father are one,"—thus interpreting of the human soul, all that is said in the Bible of Jesus, of the Logos, and therefore by implication all that is said of the infinite God.

You will not understand me to intimate that you have had any sympathy with this extravagant, not to say blasphemous conclusion, which not a few of our friends have drawn from what they have supposed to be your premises. I know well that while you have wished to defend the freedom of those who have drawn it, and to do justice to the moral purity of their characters, you have shrunk from the conclusion itself. Yet, you must allow me to say that I feel that you have in some measure warranted this deification and worship of the human soul. Assuming the divinity of human nature as the starting point, as you do, I see not well how a logical mind, not restrained by an abundant stock of good sense, can avoid coming to this conclusion. I must confess that I cannot see how one can avoid it, save at the expense of his consistency.

I certainly shall not deny that there is something divine in man; but I do deny that what is divine in man is original in his nature, save as all nature is divine, inasmuch as it is the work of God, and made at bottom,—if one may so speak, and mean any thing,—out of divine substance. But neither you nor I have ever intended to favor pantheism. We do not therefore confound nature with God, any more than we do God with nature. I see not, then, how it is possible for man in any intelligible or legitimate sense of the word, to be *naturally* divine. The two terms seem to me to involve a direct contradiction. There is something divine in the life of man, I am willing to own; but this divinity which you find there, I think has been communicated to man, superinduced upon his nature, if I may so speak, by the grace of God through our Lord Jesus Christ. The error which I seem to myself to find in your view of man is, that you assume his *natural* likeness to God, that he contains, as essential elements of his nature, the elements of the Divinity. I am unable to reconcile with this fact of possessing a divine nature, my own experience, or the recorded experience of the race. Man, if so lofty, so divine, having in himself the elements of God, and therefore of infinity, should not be so foolish, so weak, and so wicked as we know him to have been in all past ages, and as we find him to be even in ourselves. It does well enough now and then for declamation to talk of man's likeness to God, but alas! few there are who have not been obliged, by painful experience, to exclaim with the Hebrew prophet, "it is not in man that walketh to direct his steps."[5]

Allow me to say, that I think it is an error to assume that Christianity takes the divinity of humanity as its point of departure. Christianity seems to me to assume throughout as its point of departure, man's sinfulness, depravity, alienation from God and heaven. It treats man everywhere as a sinner, as morally diseased, morally dead, and its work is always to restore him to moral life and health; not to a consciousness of the greatness and divinity of his soul, but to righteousness, to a spiritual communion and union with God. And after all, is not this view the true one? Is not man a sinner? Who is there of us, however exalted or however low our estate, cultivated or uncultivated our minds, however pure and blameless may be our lives, that does not bear on his heart the damning stain of sin? Who has not exclaimed, nay, who does not perpetually exclaim, "I am a sinner; the good I would I do not, and the evil that I would not that I do. O wretched man that I am, who shall deliver me from the body of this death?"[6] The universal conscience of the race bears witness to the fact that all men sin, and come short of the glory of God. All religions are so many additional witnesses to this fact, for they are all so many methods dictated to man, or devised by him, for getting rid of sin, and placing himself at one with God.

This much you, I know, will admit, however it may or may not be reconcilable with what you say of man's divinity. But I think Christianity goes further than this. It assumes not only that all men are actual sinners, but also that human nature itself has been corrupted, is depraved, so that men by nature are prone to do evil. This is the doctrine which I know you have opposed; but I think I can present it in a light in which you will not refuse to accept it; because I see how I can accept it, and find also a place for the doctrine which you yourself have so much at heart.

This doctrine of the depravity of human nature is, you will admit, a doctrine of universal tradition. With me tradition is always good evidence when its subject-matter is not intrinsically improbable. This is, I am aware, a broad principle, but I am able to demonstrate its soundness. The pure reason is always incompetent to decide on questions which go out of the department of mathematics. In what concerns the race, tradition is the criterion of certainty, only we must not forget that the individual man must be free to sit in judgment on the question, what is or is not tradition. The doctrine of human depravity is admitted on all hands to be a doctrine of universal tradition. If men were not universally conscious of its truth, of its conformity to what they know of themselves, how could they universally believe it? If it were false, it would be right in the face and eyes of what each one knows of himself, and we should naturally expect to find it universally rejected. Men cannot even by your rich and kindling eloquence, which is seldom surpassed, be made to believe, to any great extent, in your doctrine of the divinity of humanity. Even those of us the most anxious to embrace it, find ourselves unable to do so. We are too conscious of our own weakness and unworthiness. If the opposite doctrine were not more true to our experience, we should find equal difficulty in believing that.

Moreover, the Scriptures seem to me to teach very clearly, that the actual sins of mankind, are not all the difficulties in the way of our salvation, that are to be overcome. I will say nothing now of Genesis; I confine myself to the New Testament. Paul teaches, beyond all question, that all men died in Adam, that through Adam sin entered into the world, and by sin a corruption of human nature. It was through the disobedience of one man that many, the many, that is, all men, were made sinners. Thus John, when he points to Jesus, says, "Behold the Lamb of God which taketh away the *sin* of the world."[7] He does not say *sins,* but *sin,* that is, the original depravity of human nature.

Experience also, I think, indicates at least that there is in all men, even now, an under-current of depravity, by virtue of which men, if left to themselves, delight in sin rather than in holiness. Children are not always the sweet innocents we sometimes pretend. The little rogues not unfrequently show animation, spirit, intelligence, only when doing some mischief. Moreover, if human nature were not depraved, if it were what you represent it, and if there were no sin but actual sin, how could there be even actual sin? How comes it to pass that men, pure by nature, and possessing in themselves the very elements of God, do no sooner begin to develop their pure and godlike nature than they sin? What is it that works in us, and manifests itself in our acts? Is it not human nature? Since then the workings of this nature are unquestionably sinful, must not the nature itself be depraved?

I am willing to admit that the doctrine of human depravity, has assumed a form which is somewhat objectionable. Not indeed because it has been said to be total, that is, extending to and over all the faculties of the human soul. For the human soul is not many, but one, and acts ever as a unity. It would be grossly absurd then to assume that one phasis of it could remain undepraved while another was depraved. Sin also blunts the intellect as well as corrupts the heart. They who have pleasure in unrighteousness are easily deluded. They are the pure in heart who see God. But the error has been in assuming perfection as the point of departure for man and nature, and therefore in considering the imperfection we now see in man and nature to be the result of a fall from a perfect state. A fall from such a state is inconceivable. But man being originally created imperfect, as he must have been, naturally, if not inevitably, sinned, and this sin necessarily corrupted human nature.

I say *necessarily*. Grant me what you will not deny, that the first man, whether called Adam or not, sinned, and the doctrine of the inherent, hereditary depravity of human nature follows inevitably, necessarily. This may seem to be a strong statement, but I can justify it.

The old doctrine on this subject, is that God made a covenant with Adam, by virtue of which Adam became the federal head of humanity, so that all his posterity should be implicated in his transgression. I do not like the term *covenant*. Say that God so created man, and subjected him to such a law of life, that the first man could not sin without involving all his posterity in his sin, and you will say what I believe to be the strict truth. But how can this be? Shall the innocent be involved in the fate of the guilty? They are so in nature, and in this life, to some extent, in providence. This world does not realize our conceptions of justice. Hence the promise and the hope of another. But this is not the point.

Philosophy has succeeded in demonstrating,—what everybody has always believed without perceiving its full significance,—that we are dependent beings, and are in no case and in no sense able to live by and in ourselves alone. Man can no more *live* by himself alone, than he can *exist* alone. Cut him off from all communion with nature, and could he live? Cut him off from all communication with other men, with his race, would he not die? Does not man die in solitude? In perfect solitude could he ever be said to live, that is to live a human life? Could any of his affections, moral, religious, social, or domestic, be ever developed? Certainly not. Here then is a fact of immense importance.

Let us begin by distinguishing *life* from *being*. To be is not necessarily to live. Inorganic matter *is,* but we can hardly say that it *lives.* To live is to manifest. But no being except God the self-existent, and the self-living being, is able to manifest itself by itself alone. There is no act, no function that man can perform in a state of perfect isolation. He cannot think without thinking himself as the subject of the thought, and thinking something not himself as its object. He has the capacity to love, but he cannot manifest it, that is live it, without loving; and he cannot love without loving something, some object. This which I say of love I may say of all of man's capacities, whether physical, intellectual, sentient, or sentimental. To deny this, and to assume that man can in any case be his own object, were to assume that man is capable of living in himself alone; which would imply that he, like the infinite God is self-existent and self-living.

If to live is to manifest ourselves, and if we cannot manifest ourselves without communion with an object which we are not, it follows that our life is at once subjective and objective. A man's life is not all in himself. It is in himself and in his object—the object by means of which he lives. This, if we say man is a dependent being, insufficient for himself, is what we necessarily affirm.

Now man's object, by communion with which he lives, is other men, God, and nature. With God and nature he communes only indirectly. His direct, immediate object is other men. His life, then, is in himself and in other men. All men are brought by this into the indissoluble unity of one and the same life. All become members of one and the same body, and members one of another. The object of each man is all other men. Thus do the race live *in solido,* if I may use a legal term, the objective portion of each man's life being indissolubly in all other men, and, therefore, that of all men in each man.

It follows necessarily from this oneness of the life of all men, that no one member can be affected for good or evil, but the whole body, all humanity in space, time, and eternity must actually or virtually be affected with it.

Assume now, that the first man sinned, and it is a fair presumption that he did sin, to say the least. This man must have been the object by virtue of communion with which his children were enabled to live. They could not live without an object, and he must be that object. Life is indissolubly subjective and objective. He must furnish the objective portion of their life. This portion of their life must partake of his moral character. He had polluted himself by sin. This pollution is necessarily transmitted by virtue of the fact that he is their object, to them, who corrupted in the objective portion of their life, must needs be corrupted in the subjective portion.

Adam's sin must necessarily have been transmitted to his children, not solely by natural generation, as some have contended, but by moral generation. Nor could it stop there. His children must have been the object of their children, and thus have transmitted it to them. These again must have transmitted it to a later generation; and thus, since the preceding generation furnishes always the objective portion of the life of the succeeding generation, it must necessarily be transmitted from generation to generation forever, or till the race should cease to exist; unless the current were arrested and rolled back by a foreign power.

Bearing in mind this law of life, which philosophy has succeeded in demonstrating without once suspecting its application, and I think you will agree with me in accepting the doctrine in question, in believing that Paul meant what he said, that all die in Adam, and that through the disobedience of one man all were made sinners, and that, therefore, death hath passed upon all men. I think, also, that you will agree that the church generally, with which we have both warred on this point, has been right in asserting original sin, and the innate, hereditary depravity of human nature. The church seems to me to have erred only in considering this depravity, hereditary by virtue of a covenant or imputation, on the one hand, or by natural generation on the other. It is hereditary by virtue of the fact stated, that the preceding generation always furnishes the objective portion of the life of the succeeding generation, and without the objective portion the subjective portion would be as if it were not.

This principle of life which I have set forth is one of an immense reach. It shows at a glance the terrible nature of sin. In sin this principle is reversed, but is not destroyed. It operates for evil as, when in its normal condition, it does for good. By virtue of this principle, sin, whatever its degree, however great or however slight, by whomsoever committed, necessarily propagates itself, and must continue to propagate itself eternally, if not arrested by the sovereign grace of God. Humanity has originally in itself no more inherent power to overcome it than a body once set in motion has to arrest itself. How little then do they know of the true philosophy of life, who treat sin as if it were a light affair!

I am now prepared to answer the question, what is the work to be done? It is to redeem human nature from its inherent depravity, communicate to it a new and divine life, through which individuals may be saved from actual transgression, and raised to fellowship with the Father, by which they shall become really sons of God, and joint-heirs of a heavenly inheritance.

Third.—Having now determined the work there was for a Mediator to perform, I pass in the third and last place to consider the method by which he performs it; and I think I shall succeed in demonstrating the truth of the four following positions which are held by the church generally.

1. Man naturally does not and cannot commune directly with God, and therefore can come into fellowship with him only through a Mediator.

2. This Mediator must be at once and indissolubly, in the plain literal sense of the terms, very God of very God, and very man of very man; and so being very God of very God, and very man of very man, he can literally and truly mediate between God and men.

3. Jesus saves man, redeems him from sin, and enables him to have fellowship, as John says, with the Father, by giving his life literally not only for him but to him.

4. Men have eternal life, that is, live a true normal life, only so far forth as they live the identical life of Jesus. "He that hath the Son hath life;" "he that hath not the Son hath not life;" "except ye eat the flesh and drink the blood of the Son of Man ye have no life in you."[8]

These are strong positions, and such as we Unitarians have not generally embraced in a very literal sense; but I think I can show them to be not only tenable, but positions that we may accept without giving up any thing we now have, that we really value. They may require us to enlarge our faith, but not to alter or abandon it. Nay, they are virtually implied in what we are every day preaching.

Jesus says, in answer to a question put to him by Thomas, "I am the way, the truth, and the life."[9] These words have a profound significance, and a literal truth, which I confess I for one have been but slow to comprehend. I confess, sir, that I have honestly believed, that we might have a very sufficient Christianity without including the historical person we call Jesus; not indeed that I have ever failed, in my own view of Christianity, to include him. But I have taught from the pulpit, and from the press, that Christianity did not necessarily and could not be made to stand or fall with the fact whether there ever was or was not such a person as Jesus. This I now see was a grave error. Christ, the literal person we call Christ, *is* Christianity. All begins and ends with him. To reject him historically is to reject Christianity. This is the truth which they have had who have accused some of us of advocating the "latest form of infidelity," though under other aspects we who have been so accused, have been much further from infidelity than our accusers.[10]

The fact is, sir, that the language, in which the catholic or universal church clothes the doctrines I have set forth in the propositions enumerated, has prevented a large number of us from seeing the realities concerned. Many of us have even believed that there were no realities there, that the doctrines of the church do not concern realities at all, but mere covenants, bargains, imputations, legal fictions, etc. Finding no reality under the symbols of the church, we have concluded them to be empty forms, with which it were useless for us to attempt to satisfy the wants of either our minds or our hearts. We consequently rejected them, and sought to find what we needed in the everlasting truth and nature of things. All well enough up to a certain point; but we sought it unfortunately in the *abstract* truth and nature of things, not in *real life.* Consequently Jesus became to us a law, an abstract principle according to which man was made. This has been the case with myself in nearly all that I have written. In my *New Views,* Jesus has for me a high *representative* value. But having once attained to the principle represented, to the everlasting truth signified, I felt that the representative became as unnecessary as the scaffolding after the temple is erected.

On the other hand were our Unitarian friends of what has been called the old school. These with great truth hung on to the person and life of Jesus, and accused us who sought to resolve Jesus into an abstract law of the moral world, of rejecting Christianity altogether. But they did not help our difficulties. True they retained a personal Jesus, but they did not seem to us to retain any great matter for him to do; and when they talked of the importance of his life they failed to show us that importance. With the best intentions in the world, we could not see how, except in words, they made out that Jesus was any thing more than a very exemplary sort of a man, a very zealous and able reformer, whom we should do well to respect and to remember along with Plato, Alfred, Luther, and Swedenborg. We felt that there must be a deeper, a more permanent Christ than this, and we sought him, as I have intimated, in abstract philosophy.

You, sir, I know have said much of the life of Christ, and have spoken of its intimate relation to Christianity; but I confess that I do not find its importance according to your views, save as an example, and as well fitted to give force and efficacy to his instructions. You seem to me to make Jesus the way, and the truth, an example for man to imitate, and a teacher, through his life as well as through his words, of the truth; although I find, in what you say of him, I admit, almost a presentiment of the fact that he is the Life. Now, I apprehend that Christendom feels very deeply that Jesus was something more to humanity than a picture hung up on the cross for the world to gaze at, and something more, too, than a teacher of truth; for as a mere teacher, I apprehend he has slight claims to originality. I have been unable to find a single doctrine, a single precept, absolutely peculiar to the New Testament. It will hardly do to stop with Jesus as an eminent teacher and true model man. We have all felt, nay, we all feel, that something more was necessary. As a model man, he serves us very little purpose, because we see him in but a very few of the relations of life, and because his perfections are above, altogether above the reach of us human beings. If none could be Christians but those who can be in all respects what he was, we should have no Christians. Taken as a mere teacher, the Gospel histories become to us almost a farce. The little that is brought forth in this way hardly justifies the prodigies recorded.

Allow me to say again, that I think there is a significance in what Jesus says, when he says, "I am the way, the truth and the life," which those of us who have asserted the abstract Christ, and those of us who have reduced Jesus to the capacity of an exemplar and teacher of truth and righteousness, have not attained unto,—a significance which once attained unto, will save the one class of us from our alleged coldness, and the other from our abstractions, and give to us all what we and the world need—LIFE.

I begin by assuming that the finite cannot commune directly with the infinite. Like does not and cannot commune with unlike. Moreover, the finite when regarded as depraved, all will agree, cannot commune, hold fellowship with infinite holiness. Man then could not commune directly with God; both because finite and because sinful. Then he must remain ever alienated from God, or a medium of communion, that is, a Mediator, must be provided. And this Mediator must of course be provided by the infinite, and not by the finite. It would be absurd to say that man, unable to commune with God, can nevertheless provide a medium of communion with him. God must provide it. That is, he must condescend, come down to the finite, down to man, and by so doing, take man up to himself.

The Mediator, or medium of communion must needs be both human and divine. For if it do not touch man on the one hand, and God on the other, it cannot bring the two together, and make them one. Moreover, it must be really, literally, and indissolubly human and divine, God-man; not figuratively, symbolically, or mythically, for the Gospel deals only with realities. Types and shadows disappeared with the Mosaic dispensation.

Now, if you will recall what I have said of life, and the law of life, you will see at once how truly, and how literally Jesus was this Mediator between God and men. To live is to manifest one's self, and no being, except the self-living being, God, can manifest itself save by communion with some object. Life, then, in all beings, but the Unbegotten, is at once subjective and objective. This is the principle of life, which philosophy has demonstrated beyond the possibility of cavil.

Jesus, you admit, to say the least, was an extraordinary personage. I have already shown in this letter that he does not belong to the category of ordinary men. He is special, distinct, peculiar. Say now that God takes humanity, in the being we term Jesus, into immediate communion with himself, so that he is the direct object by means of which Jesus manifests himself. The result would be LIFE; that life, like all derivative life, at once subjective and objective, must necessarily be, in the strictest sense of the terms, human and divine, the life of God and the life of man, made indissolubly one. For God being the object, would be the objective portion, and man being the subject would be the subjective portion, which united is God-man. Here is the Mediator at once God-man, and that in no figurative sense, in no over-strained, refined sense, but all simply and literally, as the most simple-minded must understand the terms.

According to this view, it is the life that mediates; that is, the Mediator is the living Jesus, not Jesus the latent, the unmanifested, and, therefore, to all practical purposes the same as no Jesus at all. The living Jesus, the life, is the Christ, and the Christ is then, what Paul and the church have always asserted, *God manifest in the flesh.* How true, now, is what Jesus said, "I am the way, the truth, and the Life!" All those passages which speak of Jesus Christ as the Son of God, the only begotten of the Father, become now literally true. Christ is literally the Son of God, begotten of the Father by spiritual generation, and being born from the immediate communion of the human and divine, is in the strictest sense in which you can use the terms, very God of very

God, and very man of very man; and as God, distinguishable, as the church has always contended, from God the Father only as the begotten must needs be distinguishable from the unbegotten.

If I am right in this, Jesus lived not as we do, merely by virtue of communion with other men and nature, but by virtue of immediate and unrestrained communion with God. The Scriptures nowhere represent Jesus as living an independent, and underived life. He is begotten of the Father; he is the Son; and he says expressly that he lives *by* the Father. I need on this point make no quotations. He never professes to live without the Father, but professes to live always by the Father and in the Father.

Now Jesus being at once God and man in his life, answers precisely the condition of a Mediator between God and men. God and man are nothing to us save so far as they are living. They exist for us only so far forth as they live. Jesus is all to us in his life. The Jesus men saw and communed with was the life of Jesus, the living Jesus, that is to say, the Christ. Being human he was within the reach of human beings, and being at the same time indissolubly God, by communing with him they necessarily communed with God. Whoso touched him, laid his hand on God. "Have I been so long with thee, and yet hast thou not known me, Philip? He that hath seen me, hath seen the Father."[11]

It is the life that mediates. Jesus, I have said, so has said the church, saves the world by communicating to it his life, not as a life for them to look at, to contemplate as an example, and to seek to copy, to imitate, but for them literally to live, to be *their* life. This is now quite explicable. Jesus was placed in the world in the midst of men. Men communed with him while he was in the flesh. Then by the very principle of life already stated, he must have become the objective portion of their life. Then his life literally enters into and becomes an inseparable portion of the life of those human beings, say his disciples, who lived in and by communion with him. He was the object to his disciples; then, the objective portion of their life, by virtue of which their subjective life was developed.

But the human race lives, as we have seen, *in solido;* all are members of one and the same body, and members one of another. There is a oneness of life which runs through them all, making them so strictly one, that the whole must feel whatever affects any one. The slightest vibrations in the heart of the least significant member are felt through the mighty heart of the whole. Consequently, the very moment that this new life of Jesus was communicated to the disciples, it was communicated virtually to the race. The disciples became objects with which others communed, and by means of their communion with others, necessarily imparted this life to others, by virtue of that very principle of life by which they had received it, and by virtue of which, when reversed, we have seen the sin of Adam necessarily extended to all his posterity. By the fact that one generation overlaps another, and thus becomes its objective life, the generation in which Christ appeared must necessarily transmit it to its successor, and that successor to its successor, and thus generation carry it on to generation, so long as the succession of generations should last.

This doctrine of the transmission of the Life from generation to generation, is denied by no sect, to my knowledge, except the Baptists, who seem to me to mistake more fundamentally the real character of Christianity, than any other sect to which the Protestant reformation has given birth. In all other churches it is borne witness to by the doctrine of infant baptism. Children are baptized because it is felt that there is a sense in which the children of elect or believing parents are born into the kingdom. Infant baptism, then, has an important meaning. It is the symbol of a vital doctrine of Christianity, which is, to my understanding, rejected by all those who admit only baptism of adults, on voluntary profession of faith. The same doctrine of the transmission of the life from man to man in time and space, by what I have termed spiritual generation, is borne witness to by what is termed apostolic succession. Without meaning to accept this last doctrine, in its episcopal sense, I must say that I see a great truth which it covers. This divine life was communicated to the world through the apostles, and mainly through those who succeeded them in the ministry. A virtue evidently, according to the principle of life, must have been communicated by the apostles to their successors. They who have not received this virtue cannot be true ministers of Jesus. For how can I communicate to others the divine life of Jesus, if I have not myself received that life? The doctrine of apostolic succession teaches us simply that the church has held that this divine life is communicable from man to man by spiritual generation. Hence with singular propriety has she called her clergy, *spiritual fathers.* Every true clergyman is the father of his flock, and verily begets in them a true life. The error of the church has been in supposing that this life could be communicated by laying on of the hands of the presbytery. Probably, however, at bottom, nothing more has ever been meant by this, than that the communion between us who are to minister at the altar and the apostles, and through them with Jesus, must be real and unbroken. And if the view I have taken be true, this communion depends on no arbitrary ceremony; it is real, and the very principle of life itself prevents it from being interrupted in any case whatever. Perhaps also, if we were really filled with this divine life, as we should be, we might impart somewhat of it, merely by the laying on of hands.

We see, now, how Jesus can be literally the Mediator between God and men, and how by the fact that he lived in communion with men, he must communicate his life to the world, to human nature, so that it must become henceforth the life of humanity, a new life, by virtue of which the human race comes under a new dispensation, and is able, so to speak, to commence a new series. Assume what we have assumed, that this life is at once human and divine, we can readily perceive that its introduction into the life of humanity would redeem humanity from the corruption which was by Adam, so that what Paul says must be literally true, "As in Adam all die, even so in Christ shall all be made alive."[12] And this discloses the necessity of regarding the life of Jesus as supernatural, superhuman. The life of any man would pass into the life of all men as I have shown must have passed the life of Jesus; but unless that life was a life above that of humanity, it could not redeem humanity, and raise it to a higher life. The merit of the life of Jesus, and the reality of the redemption by him, must be then in exact proportion to his divinity. To deny his divinity would be the denial of all in Christianity worth affirming.

Happily this divinity is easily demonstrated; at least, we can easily demonstrate the supernatural, the superhuman character of the life of Jesus. It is historically demonstrable that the life of Jesus was altogether superior to the age in which he lived. He must then have lived in communion with an object which that age, and therefore nature, could not furnish; that is to say, in communion with an object above the world, above nature, superhuman. Here then is his supernatural character established at once. Then the introduction of his life into humanity, was a redemption of humanity. He becomes then our Redeemer, the Father of a new age.

Nor is this all. By virtue of the fact that the life of Jesus has passed into the life of humanity, humanity is able to commune with God. Through Jesus who is our life, we have access to the Father, may come into communion, as John says, into *fellowship,* with him. Then we may live in communion with God, and consequently be every moment deriving new life and strength from him. Thus the life of Jesus does not grow fainter and fainter as echoed by generation after generation, but stronger and stronger, as the path of the just grows brighter and brighter into the perfect day. Hence his life becomes more powerful unto life than the sin of Adam was unto death, and so through Jesus we shall be more than conquerors. This is what Paul means when he says, "not as the offense so is the free gift; for if by one man's offense death reigned by one, *much more* they which receive abundance of grace shall reign through one Jesus Christ." "But where sin, abounded grace did *much more* abound."[13] Life is stronger than death, and must be ultimately victorious, especially since by virtue of the indwelling Christ, which is our life, we have access to the Father and can renew our life at the Fountain of Life itself day by day.

I intended to adduce a large number of passages of Scripture in support of these views, but I have not room, nor is it necessary. These passages will readily occur to all who are familiar with the writings of John and Paul. They always speak of Christ and Christianity as the Life. "That," says John, in his first Epistle, "that which was from the beginning which we have heard, which we have seen with our eyes, which we have looked upon, and our hands have handled, of the Word of Life; (for the Life was manifested, and we have seen it, and bear witness, and show unto you, that eternal Life, which was with the Father, and was manifested unto us;) that which we have seen and heard, declare we unto you, *that ye may have fellowship with us; and truly our fellowship is with the Father and with his son Jesus Christ.*"[14] This is quite to my purpose. But here is a passage more so still. Jesus says, "As the living Father hath sent me, and as I live by the Father, even so he that eateth me shall live by me."[15] *As the living Father has sent me.* The Father hath life in himself, and needeth not others in order to be able to live. This self-living Life hath sent me. *As I live by the Father.* Here is the assertion of the fact that Jesus lives by communion with the Father, and therefore of the fact that his life is indissolubly God-man. *Even so he that eateth me shall live by me.* Eating is merely a figurative expression for partaking, receiving. It is not the literal flesh, for the flesh profiteth nothing, that we are to receive and assimilate, but the spirit, the very life of Jesus. To those who thus receive him, he is the object with whom they commune, and they live by him precisely as he lives by the Father; and as he by living by the Father lives the life of God immediately, so they by living by him do live the life of God mediately.

This view gives new meaning to the doctrine of brotherhood. You have done much to make us all feel that whatever our condition in life, or position in society, we are all brothers, members of one and the same great family. But the doctrine I am bringing out goes even further, and shows us that the relation subsisting between men is actually more intimate than that which we ordinarily express by the term brotherhood. All men are not only members of one family, but they are all members one of another. The life of each man is indissolubly in himself and in all other men. The injury done to the life of one man is an injury done to the life of all men: the least significant member, however incrusted with filth or polluted with sin, cannot suffer but the whole body must suffer with him. Regard for our own welfare and disinterested regard for others may combine then to ameliorate the moral, intellectual, and physical condition of mankind. Here is the doctrine that shall give power to the preacher, the philanthropist, the genuine reformer, whether moral or social.

This intimate relation of all men in the unity of one and the same life, explains the Eucharist or Communion. That rite of the church is not merely commemorative of the last supper of Jesus with his disciples. All Christianity clusters around it, centres in it; for all Christianity is in this one word *communion.* Jesus was the living bread which came down from heaven to give life to the world. This Life, the new Life, Eternal Life, the Life by living which we are redeemed from sin and united to God, could be communicated to the world, only by virtue of a communion between Jesus and his disciples, and to the rest of mankind in time and space only by communion with them. The great fact here affirmed is that the life of Jesus is communicated to the world, and spread from man to man according to the very principle of human life itself. It becomes human life, and men become one with Jesus, and one with God, just in proportion as it is lived. Then in order to enable all men to live this life, we must seek to facilitate the means of communion for all men in both time and space. This translated into practical life will be the organization of all our domestic and social institutions in obedience to the strictest order and most unrestrained freedom compatible with order. Nay, our domestic and social order, instead of being a check on freedom, should be so organized as to be the support of freedom, or of man's uninterrupted communion with man, according to the normal wants of his nature and his life.

We may now understand and accept what is said of the dignity of human nature. Taken as we find it to-day, in the bosom of Christian civilization, it unquestionably has a recuperative energy, even, if you will, a divine worth. My objection to what you have alleged of human nature, is that you affirm it of human nature originally and universally. You and the church in some respects agree. Both speak of human nature to-day, without intimating that the mission of Christ has in the least affected it. If human nature were always what you say, I cannot conceive what need there was of a Redeemer; if it be now what the church generally affirms, that is, inherently and totally depraved, I am equally unable to conceive what the Redeemer has done. If there be any truth in the doctrine of life as I have set it forth; if there be any truth in the alleged fact that the Life of Jesus was a new life, a life *above the human life of the age in which he came;* then assuredly has the coming of Jesus redeemed human nature, and communicated to it higher and diviner elements. Human nature is not to-day what it was before the coming of Jesus. In speaking of human nature, meaning thereby the powers and capacities of man, we must have regard to chronology. It is false, what we say, that human nature is the same in all ages. The law of human life is the same in all ages; but that life is never the same for two successive generations, or else where were the idea of progress, without which the whole plan of Providence would be inexplicable? To assert that human nature is the same to-day that it was before the coming of Christ, is to "deny the Lord that bought us"; because it either denies that Jesus has come at all, or that he has come to any effect.

The coming of Jesus has communicated a new life to the race, which by means of *communion* of man with man shall extend to all individuals. This new life has not as yet, we all know, wholly overcome and effaced the death which was by Adam; but it is in the heart of humanity, an incorruptible seed, I had almost said, a seminal principle of divinity. The humanity of to-day has in its life, which is the indwelling Christ, the Christ that was to be with us unto the end of the world, a redeeming power, a recuperative energy, by virtue of which it is able to come into fellowship with the Father, and thus work out its own salvation. The possession of this principle, this energy, this life, literally, as I have endeavored to prove, the Christ, is that wherein human nature differs now from what it was before Jesus came. Then it had in its life no redeeming principle, now it has. This divinity is not *it,* but Christ formed within it, the hope of glory. Human nature in some sense then I own possesses to-day the divine worth you claim for it; not by virtue of its own inherent right, but by virtue of its union through the law of life to Christ, who is our head, and who is one with God. This union virtually complete, is actually incomplete. To complete it, and therefore to make all men one in Christ, and through him one with the Father, thus fulfilling his prayer, as recorded in the seventeenth chapter of John's Gospel, is the work to be done, towards which Christian civilization is tending, and to which all true Christians direct all their efforts, individual and social. We may be even far from this glorious result as yet, and we may even be in ourselves weak and inefficient; but the Life is in the world; Christ has entered into the life of humanity; the Word has become Flesh, and dwells among us; and as individuals and as a race we may do all things through Christ strengthening us. We can effect this, because God works in us both to will and to do. By communion with Jesus, we derive life, as I have said, from God himself; we are led by the Spirit of God, are sons of God; clothed upon with a life, majesty, and power, before which the empire of darkness and sin must be as chaff before the wind. We are placed at one with God. All things then are for us. The winds are our messengers, and flames of fire our ministers. Even the spirits shall obey us. Who can set bounds to our power, since our strength is not ours, but God's; since our life is hid in God, in whom we dwell, and who through his Son dwells in us. O, sir, I believe it will prove to be literally true, what Jesus said, "he that believeth on me, greater works than these shall he do."[16] We know little of the power, of the moral force with which to overcome the world, true fellowship of man with man in the life and spirit of Jesus will give us. God is for us, who can be against us? Here, sir, is my hope. The world lieth in wickedness; man preys upon man; discordant sounds of wrongs, outrages and grief and death strike my ear on every hand; but I despair not; Christ is our life, because he lives we shall live also; Christ is our life, a true life, and I fear not but life will finally swallow up death in victory, and the new heavens and the new earth, wherein dwelleth righteousness, become a glorious reality, an everlasting inheritance for the generations of men.

Longer I would detain you; I would endeavor to show that by virtue of the law of life which binds in one indissoluble whole all the individuals of the race in space, time, and eternity, the mission of Jesus must therefore necessarily be retroactive, extending back to the first born man as well as forward to the latest born; thus giving a meaning to what is said of his preaching to the spirits in prison, to the inhabitants of the world before the flood, and also a meaning to the practice of baptizing for the dead, of which Paul speaks. But this would carry me too far for my present purpose. I can only say, that this law of life appears to me to be a key to most of the mysteries connected with our faith. It throws a flood of light on many, very many points, which have hitherto been dark and perplexing. It gives to the whole Gospel an air of reality; nay, makes it a living reality. We get rid of all types and shadows, symbols and myths, representative, symbolical, or mythical interpretations. We are able now to take the Gospel as it is, with docile minds, and in simplicity of heart, in its plain obvious sense, without any mystical refinement or philological subtlety.

For myself, sir, I value the view I have presented, because it removes all doubts with regard to the origin of the Bible. Here is a doctrine of Life contained in the New Testament, which has been asserted, preached, believed, denied, controverted, for eighteen hundred years, unproved, unexplained, and pronounced by all the world to be inexplicable, and held to be a mystery by its most devout and enlightened believers. The latest discoveries of philosophy furnish us a key to this mystery, and instantly it is plain, simple, demonstrable. Now, am I to believe that man could have found out and written, what it has taken the race eighteen hundred years of close study to be able to begin to see the reasonableness of? Believe so who can; I cannot. In this simple fact alone, I see that in writing the New Testament there was employed a superhuman mind, and a mind which after eighteen hundred years of growth none of us can equal. For I see there depths which philosophy is yet in no condition to sound. But when every discovery in philosophy but tends to make more apparent and certain the truth of the Book, can I for a moment hesitate to believe that these depths, when sounded, will be found to contain the richest treasures of divine love and wisdom? The Bible is therefore removed at once out of the category of ordinary books, and I can clasp it to my heart as the Word of God, in which is recorded the truths I am to believe, and contained ample authority for asserting them. Though I have come slowly to this conclusion, do not believe that I have come so slowly as my writings would seem to indicate, as they who know me best can readily testify. I have seemed to the world to have altogether less faith in the Bible than I have really had, because, as you well know, I have for these last ten years been laboring to bring under religious influences, a class of minds to whom the Bible is an offense rather than an authority. All I say now is that the view I have presented, shows so much wisdom and beauty in the New Testament, so much and so profound truth, altogether beyond the age in which the book was written, that I feel more deeply than ever its supernatural character; and am more and more willing to yield to it as an authority. I can take it now all simply, and do not feel called upon to refine away any portion of it.

I have now, I feel, a doctrine to preach. I can preach now, not merely make discursions on ethics and metaphysics. The Gospel contains now to me not a cold abstract system of doctrine, a collection of moral apothegms, and striking examples of piety and virtue. It points me to Life itself. Metaphysical studies have indeed brought me, through the blessing of God, to the understanding of the doctrine, but having come to it, it suffices for itself. I now need to know nothing but Jesus and him crucified. I can shut up all books but the Bible and the human heart, and go forth and preach Christ crucified, to the Jew a stumbling-block, and to the Greek foolishness no doubt, but to them that are called, Christ the power of God, and the wisdom of God. I have something besides abstract speculations and dry moral precepts, or mysterious jargon to offer. I have the doctrine of Life, the Word of Life to proclaim. I have an end to gain; it is to bring men into communion with each other, so that the Word of Life may have free course among them, and be glorified in binding them together in that love wherewith God hath loved us.

I feel too, that I can now go and utter the very word this age demands. That word is COMMUNION. The age is waiting for it. It is sick of divisions, sick of mere forms, wearied and disgusted with mere cant; no better pleased with mere metaphysical speculations; impatient of dry disquisitions, and of cold, naked abstractions. It demands Life and Reality. Away with your formulas; away with your seeming and make-believe Life and Reality; give us Life and Reality! Life and Reality we can give, for such the Gospel now proves itself to be. The doctrine that man lives by communion with man, and through the life derived from Jesus with God, will bring us together on one platform, in the unity of life itself, and the church will become one in Christ, "from whom the whole body fitly joined together, and compacted by that which every joint supplieth, according to the effectual working in the measure of every part, maketh increase of the body unto the edifying of itself in love;"[17] the church shall in very deed become one and universal, and be the living body of our Lord, and the race will speak with one tongue, have one faith, one Lord, one baptism. The great doctrine of Life may now be preached, and whoso preaches that will bring the world to the Life, and through the Life save it from death and raise it to God.

Nor is this all. With this doctrine of life, I feel that I may go forth in a higher name than my own. I was wrong some time since, as I was understood, in saying that man should not presume to speak to man authoritatively in the name of God, although I was right in my own thought. What I wished to protest against was, an artificial priesthood, the members of which by virtue of their membership, should deem themselves authorized to speak to us, nay, to command us in the name of God. My protest was against man-made priests, priests after the order of Aaron, whose authority is in their gown and band. These were the priests I said we must destroy, and for saying which my wise countrymen abused me from one end of the Union to the other. But priests in this sense, I say now, away with. They are dumb dogs that will not bark. They are foolish builders that daub with untempered mortar; blind leaders of the blind; spoilers not feeders of the flock. Yes, away with them, if such there be. Let us have priests after the order of Melchisedec; priests anointed with an unction from the Holy One, whose tongues are touched with a live coal from off God's altar; whose authority is engraved by the great head of the church on their very hearts. These are the priests that we want, and the only ones we want,—priests of God's calling, not man's. Nevertheless no man should attempt to preach unless he may speak in a higher name than his own. Man is a poor, frail worm of the dust, and what is his authority worth? Let me speak in my own name, who will hear, nay, who ought to hear? I feel, and so does every man feel, when he rises to preach, that is, if he have any humility, that he is insufficient and altogether unworthy. How can I speak? These are older, wiser, more learned, nay, it may be, better than I. Have I the presumption to stand up to instruct, to warn, admonish, rebuke, exhort? Nay, I cannot. I cannot preach; I can only reason, discuss, or dispute; I must not speak from the height of the Christian pulpit, as one having authority, but from the level of the multitude I address. Every minister, worthy of the name, has felt this. For years I felt it, and never pretended to preach. I addressed the people who came to hear me. I discoursed to them as well as I could, but did not preach. I could not preach. I had no authority to preach; except the laying on of the hands of the presbytery, and that I felt was not sufficient. But now I feel that I have authority, because now I can say "the doctrine is not mine." I have God's truth to preach, and I go to preach it not in my own name, nor in the name of any man, nor any set of men, but on the authority of God's Word. So far as I am true to the doctrine, so far as I am faithful to the Life, I know God will speak through me, and give efficacy to the word.

More I would say, but enough. I have addressed you with freedom, but I trust not with disrespect. I have spoken freely of myself, for I have wished to make certain explanations to the public concerning my faith. I have spoken earnestly, for the view which I have presented of the mediatorial Life of Jesus has deeply affected me. I have been verging toward it for years; some of my friends tell me they had obtained it some time ago from my public communications; but I myself have not seen it clearly until within a few weeks. Had I seen it earlier, the obscurities and seeming inconsistencies with which I have been charged, I think would never have occurred. I have found it a view which clears up for me my own past, and enables me to preserve the continuity between the past of humanity, its present, and its future. More than all this; it has touched my heart, and made me feel an interest in the Gospel, in my fellow men, and in the upbuilding of God's kingdom on the earth, deep as my interest has long been in these subjects, which I have never known before. What before was mere thought has now become love; what was abstraction has become life;

what was merely speculation has become downright, living earnestness. God is to me my Father; Jesus my life; mankind my brethren. I see mankind practically divided, worrying and devouring each other, and my heart bleeds at the wrong they do each other; and I have no thought, no wish but to bring them back to unity and fraternity in Christ Jesus; so that we may all be one. My early profession I therefore resume, with a love for it I never felt before. I resume it because my heart is full, and would burst could it not overflow. I must preach the Gospel. Necessity is laid upon me, and woe is me if I do not.

Forgive the liberty I have taken, and believe me, as ever.

Yours, with sincere respect,

O. A. BROWNSON

Notes: The Mediatorial Life of Jesus

1. Pierre Leroux (1797–1871) was a humanitarian communist who has been credited with coining the term *socialism*.
2. Jn 3:16.
3. Thomas Brown (1778–1820) was a Scottish philosopher; he revived David Hume's argument on causality, demonstrating that it need not lead to theological skepticism. He criticized and modified the reigning Scottish Common Sense Realism. Emmanuel Swedenborg (1608–1772) was a Swedish scientist, mystical thinker and author of *Divine Love and Wisdom* (1763) and *The True Christian Religion* (1771). He had a significant influence upon some of the transcendentalists.
4. William Ellery Channing's *Likeness to God* (1828), reprinted in David Robinson, *William Ellery Channing: Selected Writings* in *Sources of American Spirituality* (New York: Paulist Press, 1985), p. 150.
5. Jer 10:23.
6. Rom 7:14, 19, 24.
7. Jn 1:29.
8. 1 Jn 5:12; Jn 6:53.
9. Jn 14:6.
10. Reference is to Andrews Norton's *A Discourse on the Latest Form of Infidelity* (Cambridge, MA, 1839), an attack upon Emerson's and George Ripley's denial of "the miracles attesting to the divine mission of Christ."
11. Jn 14:9.
12. 1 Cor 15:22.

13. Rom 5:15, 20.
14. 1 Jn 1:1–3.
15. Jn 6:57.
16. Jn 14:12.
17. Eph 4:16.

VIII.

A CATHOLIC: 1845–76

15. THE FATHERS OF THE DESERT

SOURCE: *Brownson's Quarterly Review* 10 (July 1853): 385–96. A review of Rev. Dr. Challoner's *The Lives of the Fathers of the Eastern Desert* (New York: D. & J. Sadlier & Co., 1852).

Although Brownson half-consents "to the non-Catholic horror of Catholic i.e., monastic asceticism," he mourns the loss of the sense of the supernatural in his own world and advocates Christian practices of mortification and self-denial that will restore a sense of the supremacy of the spiritual to the material life. Catholic immigrants and native Americans need to be reminded that the world lives under a supernatural destiny. Restoring the doctrine of God's Providence will encourage Christian prayer and renew hope because that doctrine makes Christians conscious of God's freedom and his responsiveness to the cries of his people.

. . . The work before us is not a work to be reviewed either favorably or unfavorably. It is a work to be read, not for its style or its literary graces, but for the edification the pious soul cannot fail to derive from communing with the saints whose lives it records. To our age, however, these Oriental saints, with their contemplations, their austerities, their mortifications, their fasts, and their macerations of the body for the sake of the soul, appear any thing but attractive, and even many comparatively good Catholics are disposed to speak of their conduct as a sublime folly. It is not and never was a doctrine of the Catholic

Church, that all they did or suffered is necessary in the case of every one for salvation. Nor is every one recommended to aspire to imitate their austerities. All are not called to such things, although for all mortification in some degree is necessary. They are only for those who are enabled to endure them by the special grace of God. Yet though not, to the extent carried by these Oriental anchorets and Fathers, necessary for salvation in the case of all men, they are well pleasing to God, and are never wholly wanting in those who aspire to the highest degree of merit, and make it the business of their lives to live and labor only for Christian perfection. To inherit eternal life we have only to keep the commandments, but if we would be perfect we must sell what we have, and give to the poor, and follow Christ, and follow him, too, in the way of the cross, and share with him his passion.

Simple nature, no doubt, recoils from these austerities, for nature is unequal to them, save as elevated and assisted by grace, and can see in them only her own crucifixion. They cannot be performed unless inspired by the Holy Ghost, by a supernatural love; and they are supernatural in their principle and character. No man can endure them unless sustained by a supernatural strength, or safely attempt them without a supernatural sympathy with the passion of our Lord, and a supernatural longing to bear with him his cross. This is wherefore the men and women of the world are unequal to them, wherefore they have no ability to appreciate them, and wherefore they are repelled and even disgusted by them. They have no vocation to them. They love their own ease, the ease of the body, the gratification of their tastes, the satisfaction of their appetites. In them the flesh predominates, and they deem its mortification a calamity, as something to be avoided and guarded against. Their minds are worldly and their hearts are set on vanities and lies. To them these old Fathers, these glorious old saints,—who lived only for heaven, and were ambitious only to immolate themselves with Christ, their dear Lord and Master, on his cross,—seem to have missed the purpose of life, and to have thrown away their lives. They almost regard them as criminal, as guilty of a sort of moral suicide, in refusing to enjoy the good things of this world, and in seeking to mortify all their senses. At least they esteem them to be fools, ignorant of the liberality and indulgence of our good Father, and ungrateful in turning their backs upon the riches with which he has filled the earth, and the profusion of beauty with which he has adorned it. See how the bird carols, the flower blooms, the butterfly expands its golden wings, and all nature decks herself in beautiful apparel, and steps forth blithesome and glad, as if enjoying one perennial holiday. Why not imitate her, and enjoy, with a glad heart, the

good things a bountiful Father with a liberal hand provides us? Can he
envy us our happiness? Can he send us joy, and be angry with us if we
indulge it?

So think and so reason the men and women of this world, all in
the dark as to the hidden joy of the saints amid their greatest austerities, and the secret fulness of their souls when suffering the greatest
hunger and thirst. They know not, cannot conceive, that the life of
these great servants of God is as happy a life as it is possible for us to
live this side of heaven, away from our home. What were the sufferings
of St. Mary of Egypt, during her long years of solitude and penance,
compared with those she endured as the miserable daughter of pleasure, or what was the pleasure of her gay and sensual life compared
with the serene peace and pure joy she experienced in her sweet communion with her heavenly Spouse in the desert? But let us not speak of
sinful pleasures. Take what is called an honest secular life, a life which
brings with it no pain of neglected duties, no memory of wrongs done,
no bitter remorse of conscience, but a life that consists in collecting
and enjoying, in moderation, if you will, the good things of this world,
and it is far enough from being a happy life. Our Lord said, that
whoever forsakes all for him shall receive a hundred-fold in this world,
and everlasting life in the world to come; and his words are true. There
is nothing solid, nothing durable, even in innocent sensual enjoyment,
and do our best we can only stifle, never satisfy, the deep spiritual
wants of our souls with sensible goods, in whatever abundance we
possess them, or with whatever prudence, moderation, or taste we may
partake of them. They always leave us empty and unsatisfied. The
people whom we generally regard as favored, and as leading a very
happy and enviable life, are, for the most part, deserving of our com-
miseration. On the simple score of happiness or real enjoyment, there
can be no doubt that the religious life is far preferable, and that the
most austere and mortified monk or anchoret enjoys a hundred-fold
more than the least unhappy of seculars, living a strictly secular life.

This, no doubt, sounds to our age like folly or enthusiasm, but the
reason is, that we have to a great extent lost the sense of the supernatural, and have come to live as if a natural life, natural goods, and a
natural beatitude were all that Christianity proposes, requires, or
counsels. The tendency of our age, perhaps, in a greater or less degree,
of every age, is to exclude God, and to fall back on nature. Man and
nature take the place of God and heaven. The strength of man comes
from himself, and the end of man is to produce, accumulate, and
enjoy the good things of this world. We conceive of, we relish, none
but sensible good. All labor *not* for the meat that perisheth is regarded

as so much labor thrown away. We have given ourselves up, heart and soul, to this world. We have become immensely active, terribly energetic; we cover the ocean with our ships, we bring to light the treasures hid in the bowels of the earth; we make the winds our servants and the lightnings our messengers, and annihilate time and distance by our inventions. The whole world is laid under contribution, and the sea and the land, the air and the light, are forced to own man for their master, and to wear his livery. The hammer of industry rings from morning till night, till far into the night. Every nerve is strung, every sinew is stretched, every wit is racked, to invent, to produce, to multiply and bring to our doors the arts and appliances of a worldly and luxurious life; and we boast of this as the evidence of the marvellous progressiveness of our race, in these our days. In the more advanced nations, at least those who call themselves the more advanced, like Great Britain and the United States, poverty is regarded, not as a blessing, not as endearing us to Him who for our sakes became poor, but as a crime, and is actually punished as such. Your Union Workhouses and your poor-houses are veritable prisons, where you punish men and women for the heinous crime of being poor, and in need of help from others to keep their soul and body together. Wealth is respectability, is virtue, and, if combined with polished manners, kind feelings, and good taste, is heroic sanctity. Christianity is effete, the Church is a rickety old building, which encumbers the site wanted for a cotton-mill, a woollen-factory, a warehouse, a ship-yard, a canal-basin, or a railroad-station, and if now and then propped up and preserved, it is only as affording a respectable shelter for gentlemen's younger sons, or such as lack the talent and energy to get on in the world; the Christian virtues are out of date,—are not compatible with the spirit of the age; hell is laughed at as are the bugbears with which our nurses frightened us in our infancy; the Devil is a philanthropic old gentleman, who has the real interests of mankind at heart, and has been greatly belied and traduced for his love to man, and his disinterested efforts to emancipate him from the spiritual bondage in which he is held by the priesthood, and to teach him to rely on himself, to be independent, a free man, abounding in lofty, manly virtue; heaven is the refuge of disappointed love, or of silly old women who take to piety instead of tea and gossip, and is worthy of the thought or aspiration of a wise man only as it comes in this world in the shape of a ball or a rout, an abundant crop of corn, cotton, or tobacco, a heavy freight, a rich cargo, a rapid sale at a high advance, or a fat dividend. . . .

There is nothing strange in all this. If they have called the master of the house Beelzebub, how much more those of his household? What was the grand objection of the old carnal Jews to our Lord, and why did they reject him? They had become carnal, and understood the promise of a Messiah in a carnal sense. They expected a temporal prince, who would bring with him temporal prosperity; in other words, they held the kingdom he was to set up would be a worldly kingdom, and secure for its subjects all conceivable worldly greatness, prosperity, and felicity. When, then, our Lord came, not in the pomp of an earth-born grandeur, not as a temporal prince, using his supernatural power to establish a universal temporal kingdom, and to secure to his subjects an abundance of all conceivable sensible goods, and enable them to enjoy them in peace, each sitting under his own vine and fig-tree, with none to molest or to make him afraid, but as the poor carpenter's son, in the form of a servant, pronouncing a woe upon the rich and a blessing upon the poor, denouncing pride and commanding humility, enjoining a life of self-denial, of detachment from the world, trampling upon all earthly greatness, and teaching men to live and labor, not for the temporal and the sensible, but for the eternal and the spiritual, to wean their affections from all that perisheth, and to aspire only to gain, through tribulation and sorrow, a heaven after death,—a reward glorious indeed, but distant and invisible,—they saw in him no beauty or comeliness that they should desire him, and they rejected him in their wrath, and in their fury cried out, "Crucify him! Crucify him!" So is it now. The men and women of the world ask for a temporal religion, a religion that gives them worldly respectability, that fills their coffers, that saves them from poverty and want, multiplies for them sensible goods, renders labor superfluous, and gives to every one a complete satisfaction for all his natural appetites and passions; in one word, that secures a sensible or material heaven on earth for all worldly and sensual men. Such a religion all the world knows the Catholic religion is not. She is spiritual, and esteems only spiritual goods. She pampers no appetite. She is complacent to no natural passion; and affords no encouragement to those who crave only a life of sensual enjoyment. She is true to the letter and the spirit of her heavenly Spouse, and bids us treat as matters unworthy of serious thought all those things after which the heathen seek. The poor are her jewels, and white-robed virgins, who have renounced the world and its pomps, her diadem. She enjoins what the world hates. She denounces what the world loves. She feels a thrill of maternal joy through her whole heart when her children give themselves up to the great work of laying up for themselves treasures in heaven, but looks sad and sorrowful when she sees them wedded to the world, and devoted to the accumulation of mere earthly treasures, or simple material goods, which distract the mind, withdraw the heart from God and heaven, and are as empty and as desolating for the soul as the east wind. She is intent on the well-being and final salvation of the soul, and does not worship thrift as a god, or honor it as the first of virtues. Therefore carnal men and women cannot endure her; therefore they condemn her as a superstition, denounce her as unfriendly to the industry, prosperity, and wealth of nations, and seek with the fierce old carnal Jews to destroy her from the face of the earth.

This carnal Judaism which breaks out upon us in all the sects, and in all classes of modern reformers and philanthropists, is not without some influence even upon Catholics. Amongst ourselves there are not a few who dream of a heaven on earth, and think the kingdom of Christ ought to be, if it is not, a temporal kingdom set up for the temporal prosperity and enjoyment of mankind. These follow Christ for the loaves and fishes, and have very little sympathy with Oriental asceticism. They can see no use in the contemplative life, and are inclined to regard the contemplative orders as a nuisance. They think it was very wrong for Mary to sit at the feet of Jesus and feast her soul on the gracious words which fell from his lips, while she left to Martha all the cares of the household. She ought to have foregone that pleasure, and performed her share of the household duties. The only religious orders they can tolerate are the active orders. Martha, not Mary, is supposed to have chosen the better part. The Sisters of Charity they can endure, for these, in part at least, devote themselves to the corporal works of mercy; but the orders whose duty it is to pray, to give themselves up to contemplation, to intimate communion with God, they regard at best as only so many lazy drones, who contribute nothing to the general well-being of society, and are simply a burden upon its industry. We ourselves are more or less affected by the spirit of the age, and in our hearts, if not in our words, half consent to the non-Catholic horror of Catholic asceticism.

All this comes from forgetfulness of the fact that our destiny is supernatural, and our heaven is neither from this world nor in this world, and also from a forgetfulness of the fact that we live, not under the natural, but the supernatural providence of God. We are apt to imagine, not only that our good lies in the natural order, but that it is attainable, when attainable at all, by the exertion of our own unassisted natural forces,—two capital mistakes. . . .

In all the reasoning of our politicians and economists, we may remark, no account is made of God's gracious providence. States and empires have arisen, have become wealthy and powerful without

Christianity, but they have all fallen; not one of the great civilized states and empires that flourished when our Lord tabernacled in the flesh is now standing, and the world knows them now only from the massive ruins they have left behind them, the page of the chronicler, or the song of the bard. Wherefore have they fell? Simply because they forgot God, and put their trust in their own wisdom and strength. It is idle to attempt to explain, with Volney[1] the rise and fall of empires on natural principles alone. The wicked flourisheth like a green bay-tree, for a time, but he passes away, and his place is not to be found. Yet you can assign no strictly natural reason which alone explains why he flourished for so long a time, or why he ceased to flourish at the moment he did. There are times when a nation is invincible, and times when, although its natural resources are greater, its armies more numerous and better disciplined, nothing can save it. All experience proves that the race is not always to the swift, nor the battle to the strong. "There is a Divinity that shapes our ends, rough-hew them how we will." There is, therefore, no greater mistake conceivable, than to make, in our philosophizing on the temporal as well as spiritual well-being of nations or of individuals, no account of the action of Divine Providence, and to seek to explain all by simple natural causes. God raises up whom he will, and whom he will he casts down. What *natural* relation of cause and effect was there between the prayers, the fasting, and the penance in sackcloth and ashes of the Ninevites, and their deliverance from the awful judgments denounced against them by the prophet Jonas? Yet they were its condition. Could they have been its condition if God, as a free providence, that is, as a supernatural providence, did not interfere in the affairs of men and nations? "Elias was a man passible like unto us; and with prayer he prayed that it might not rain upon the earth; and it rained not for three years and six months. And he prayed again, and heaven gave rain, and the earth yielded her fruit."[2] Surely, then, God intervenes supernaturally even in temporals, and that, too, which is directly to our purpose, in answer to prayer; and in vain, then, would we explain the ruin or the prosperity of nations without taking into the account his supernatural providence, and the prayers of the saints which ascend as sweet incense before his throne.

He, then, who prays is no idle drone in the state, and may be regarded as contributing more to its prosperity and defence than he who ploughs or he who fights. If, then, we consider the contemplative orders in their relation with the gracious providence of God, we shall find that, so far from weakening the state, from lessening its resources, and consuming the fruits of its industry in idleness and sloth, they constitute its main support, and are the best pledge we can have of its strength and prosperity. God governs the world in reference to his saints, whom he loves and delights to honor,—his saints whom he has redeemed, and who are members, through his sacred flesh, taken from the womb of the Virgin, of his body, and intimately united with him, their Head, by a living union. Remember Sodom, and the intercession of Abraham for its preservation. If there had been ten just persons found among her inhabitants, for the sake of them she had been spared. We despise the contemplative orders, and count all lost not engaged in active industry, because we forget that God counts for something in human affairs; because we forget that he loves and honors his saints, and that he is flexible to their prayers. A cold and stern fatalism, or a lax and enervating Epicureanism, has taken possession of our minds. Many use the word Providence only as a respectable name for fate, and fancy that God, because immutable, is not free; that he is so bound by the laws of nature that he cannot interpose in human affairs, except through and in virtue of those laws,—the real fatalism of the old Stoics. Others, again, run away with the notion, that God has created the world, launched it into space, and left it to go ahead on its own hook, taking no further care of it,—the foolish imagination of the old Epicureans. There is nothing new under the sun, and error, in all her endless variety, does but repeat herself. God holds the reins of empire in his own hands, and is as free to interpose for a creature as he was to create him from nothing, according to the type he saw in his own mind. He has never abandoned any thing he has made. He loveth all the things he hath created, and his tender mercies are over all the works of his hand. Even when we sinned, transgressed his law, forsook him to follow the devices of our own hearts, he did not forsake us, nor leave us to perish of our own folly. He sent his Son to redeem us. His care extendeth over all. Not a sparrow falls to the ground without his notice, and the very hairs of our head are numbered. In vain, then, would we pretend either that he cannot or will not interpose in our affairs, or that we depend on nature and not on his free gracious providence for whatever good we do or can receive.

With this view of the subject, these old saints who retired to the deserts to pray, to fast, and to spend their lives in penitential works, did not abandon their country, or fail to perform their duty to their brethren. Even in view of this world, the contemplative orders should rank as the very best public servants, and perhaps we should regard it as one of the heaviest calamities of our times that they find, now-a-days, so little encouragement, and that so few have vocations to enter them. Nothing better evinces the healthy state of Christianity in a community than the number of religious vocations, and the most discouraging thing we discover in our own country is the comparatively small number of vocations, not only to a religious life, but even to the priesthood. Catholicity owes its principal increase here to the immense emigration, for the last few years, from foreign countries, chiefly from Ireland and Germany. The emigrants mostly leave home for the sake of bettering their temporal condition, and come here rather to provide a home for themselves and children than to diffuse or to enjoy their faith. Religion is not the moving cause of their emigration, and it is perfectly natural that, on entering this New World, the temporal rather than the spiritual should have the ascendency in their thoughts. The spirit of the country is also worldly, unspiritual, material, if we may so speak, and the inducements to worldly enterprise are, in general, too strong and too advantageous to be withstood. Hence the world gains too great an empire over the great mass of our Catholics, and our children grow up with their minds and hearts bent on distinction in secular life, which is a grave obstacle to the operations of Divine grace. The laity emigrate without their clergy, and it is impossible for our bishops to provide for all their spiritual wants, and hence, again, many become cold and indifferent, and almost forget their religion. Many neglect the practice of their religion, and some few apostatize, while large numbers of the children grow up without any religion. These are discouragements, for when the time has come for the conversion of a people, and God visits them to reconcile them to himself, we may always count on numerous vocations to the priesthood, and also to the monastic life. The fields here are white already to the harvest, but the laborers are few, and we must pray that the Lord will multiply their numbers. If we were less worldly, if we had more of the spirit which led St. Anthony into the desert of Thebais, we should thus pray, and our prayers would be answered. . . .

Notes: The Fathers of the Desert

1. Constantin Volney (1757–1820) was a French philosopher, deist and historian, who wrote *Les Ruines, ou Méditations sur les révolutions* (1791). This book, conceived in Benjamin Franklin's Paris study, promoted deism. Brownson quoted from the English translation in his spiritual diary, Sunday afternoon 6 April 1823 (pp. 45–54).
2. Jas 5:17.

16. THE CONVERT; OR, LEAVES
FROM MY EXPERIENCE

SOURCE: New York: Dunigan & Brother, 1857. See also *Works* 5, pp. 132–40.

The Convert *demonstrates, among other things, how Pierre Leroux's doctrine of life by communion led Brownson into Catholicism. In the chapter immediately preceding the following selection, Brownson shows how this doctrine opened up for him an entire new world of the supernatural. That doctrine made it intellectually possible for him to accept a world that was flexible, not fixed, that is, open to God's supernatural intervention, not closed by the inexorable laws of nature. In the following selection Brownson recalls how after he had been led to an acceptance of the supernatural he was, through Leroux's doctrine, eventually led to a Catholic conception of grace.*

Chapter XV.—Providential Men

Pierre Leroux was not, like myself, wholly ignorant of Catholic theology, and he was able to give me some glimpses of what is called by my Puseyite friends, "the sacramental system." He knew the Catholic doctrine of grace, and made use of it in explaining his doctrine of progress. His aim was to find a philosophical equivalent for the infused habits of grace, asserted by the church, but rejected by all classes of Protestants, and which I had not at that time even so much as heard of; but in his effort to do this, and to show that what Catholics mean by infused habits, is attainable by the natural communion of man with man, or of the individual with the race, he enabled me to see that grace might be infused, in accordance with the law of life, and without the slightest violence to nature or reason.

According to the law of all dependent life, man lives not by himself alone, but by communion with an object not himself; and his actual life partakes alike of the object and the subject, of which it is the joint product. In the fact of life, the object is not passive, but active, as active, to say the least, as the subject; for, if purely passive, it would offer no counteraction to the subject, and be practically no object at all. The object acts on the subject no less than the subject on the object. They mutually act and react on each other, and in their mutual action and reaction the fact of life is generated. The object by its action flows into the subject, and becomes a real element of the life of the subject. If, then, we suppose the object supernaturally elevated, the life of the subject will be elevated also, and his progress secured. Now, as I held that the divine, though distinguishable in reality from the human, could flow into us only through the human, I saw that, by a providential elevation of individuals by the Creator to an extraordinary or supernatural communion with himself, they would live a divine life, and we by communion with them would also be elevated, and live a higher and more advanced life. Thus the elevation and progress of the race would be provided for in accordance with the law of life, by the aid of these individuals providentially elevated, and called by Leroux, "Providential Men."

In this, though I had by no means reached the Catholic thought, I was enabled to conceive the natural and the supernatural as corresponding one to the other; and that it is possible for God to afford us supernatural aid without violence to our natures, and without suspending, superseding, or impairing the laws of our natural life. This, to one who had been accustomed to hold that nature and grace, reason and revelation, can be asserted only as mutually repugnant one to the other, that the one cannot be asserted, as Calvinism, indeed all Evangelicalism, had taught me, without denying the other, was no slight advance. Moreover, it placed me in harmony with the universal belief of the race, for the human race has universally attributed all its elevation and progress to God through inspired prophets, apostles, Messiahs,—in a word, providential men, or men raised up and extraordinarily endowed by the Creator, to aid his creature man in his ceaseless march through the ages.[1]

I was far enough from being free from grievous errors, and as yet had not once thought of seeking the old church; but it is clear that I had made some progress, and had embraced, without ceasing to exercise my reason freely, or failing in my pledge to myself of being faithful to my own rational nature, the great principles and facts which placed me on the route to the Catholic Church. I found I could reasonably accept the ideas of providence, special as well as general, supernatural inspiration, supernatural revelation, and Christianity as an authoritative religion, and must do so, or be false alike to history and my hopes of progress. I felt, as I had felt from my boyhood, that I had need of an authoritative religion; and that a religion which does not and cannot speak with divine authority, is simply no religion at all.

I did not, indeed, conclude from the possibility of the providential men I asserted, that they have actually been raised up and sent; I did not, from the fact that God can give us the needed supernatural aid through them, without violence to nature and reason, and in accordance with the great law of all life, conclude that therefore he actually does so give it. I never yet was so poor a logician as to do that. I was always ready and anxious to believe, providing I could see my way clear to do so without violence to reason, or the abnegation of my own manhood. I never wanted reasons for believing: what I wanted was, to have the real or imaginary obstacles to believing removed. More than this I never needed, never sought; and therefore, precisely as were removed my reasons against believing, I believed.

Most people, born and reared in Christian countries, who reject Christianity, are very much in the condition I was. They reject Christianity, not because they see no good reasons for believing, but because they see, or think they see, many and stronger reasons against believing. They refuse to believe, because they do not understand how supernatural assistance can be rendered without violence to nature; or an authoritative revelation, or a revelation that is to be regarded as authority for reason, can be accepted and submitted to without an abandonment of reason. Such had been the case with me, and consequently, as this obstacle to believing was removed, I believed without seeking any further reason for believing.

This was not wholly irrational or unphilosophical. To believe is normal, to disbelieve is abnormal. When the mind is in its normal state, nothing more is ever needed for belief than the removal of the obstacles interposed to believing; for, if we consider it, the mind was created for truth. Truth is its object, and it seeks and accepts it instinctively, as the new-born child seeks the mother's breast, from which it draws its nourishment. Place the mind and truth face to face, with nothing interposed between them, and the truth evidences itself to the mind, and the mind accepts it, without seeking or needing any further reason. The assent termed knowledge follows immediately from the joint forces of the intelligible object and the intelligent subject. So in belief. Practically, it is never a reason for believing, but the removal of reasons against believing, that is demanded. Hence, we always believe what a man tells us, when we have no reason for not believing him: and the business of life could not go on were it otherwise. For belief reason never requires any thing but the mutual presence, with nothing interposed between them, of the credible object and the creditive subject.

I held then, as I hold now, that the office of proof or even demonstration, is negative rather than affirmative. Neither ever goes further than to remove the *prohibentia,* or obstacles to assent. Demonstration, the most rigid and the most conclusive, only shows the object without envelope or disguise, and motives assent only by removing every reason for not assenting. The assent itself is always immediate and intuitive. Truth needs no voucher, and, when immediately presented to the mind, evidences or affirms itself. The will may be perverse, and withdraw the intellect from the contemplation of truth; prejudice or passion may darken the understanding, so that it does not for the moment see or recognize the object; but, whenever the truth is immediately present, and reason looks it full in the face, it knows that it is truth without further evidence, without any thing extrinsic to prove that it is truth. To deny this would be to deny to the soul the faculty of intelligence, the faculty of knowing at all. To know a thing is to know that it is true, for nothing but truth is or can be an object of knowledge. To say that you know a thing, and yet do not know whether it be true or not, is only saying that you do not know the thing at all. No man does or can know falsehood, for falsehood is nothing, is a nullity, a mere negation, and therefore no intelligible object. Falsehood is intelligible only in the truth it denies, and is known only in knowing that truth. In so far as any proposition is false, it is unintelligible, and never known. In all errors we know only the element of truth which they contain; and the part of error is simply the part of our ignorance, the part in which nothing is known. To know something, and to know it to be true, is one and the same thing; and this is what is meant when we say truth is the object of the intellect. Hence, no logical process is ever needed to prove to the mind that the object it immediately apprehends is truth, or is true. That it is true or truth is included in the fact that the mind apprehends it as its object, or knows it. To suppose the contrary, to suppose that a logical process is needed to demonstrate that the object in immediate relation to the mind is true, would be absurd; for it would demand an infinite series of logical processes to every single act of knowledge or mental assent. There is no reasoning except from premises or principles, and no valid reasoning from either false or unknown principles. How are these premises or principles to be obtained? Not by reasoning, not by a logical process, for, without them, no reasoning, no logical process is possible, and no such thing as proof or demonstration conceivable. They must, then, precede reasoning, be intuitive, that is, evident of themselves. Then, nothing is necessary, in the last analysis, to knowledge, but the immediate presence to each other of the intelligible object and the intelligent subject. So is it in the case of knowledge or science in the natural order, where the object is immediately intelligible to reason.

The principle must hold true, as far as applicable, in the supernatural order, and in regard to faith as well as in regard to science. Faith or belief is assent to propositions not immediately known, on the authority affirming them; that is, it is assent on testimony. The understanding does not assent to them because it sees immediately their truth, as in case of science or knowledge, but because it sees the sufficiency of the authority or testimony affirming them. The immediate object of belief is the veracity of the witness, or the fact that the authority in the case can neither deceive nor be deceived; and here the assent is immediate as soon as the obstacles are removed, because to believe is normal. If the supernatural and the natural correspond one to the other, as it is here assumed that they do, the same holds true of belief in the supernatural order. We cannot believe the supernatural things revealed without what are called motives of credibility; but these motives do not, so to speak, motive the assent of the mind to the veracity or sufficiency of the authority affirming them. They only show that the authority is credible; that is, remove all the reason we may have, or imagine we have, for regarding it as incredible or untrustworthy. The assent to its veracity or sufficiency when these reasons are removed, is immediate, by the joint forces of the credible object and creditive subject as in the natural order. My conduct, then, in believing in the supernatural order the moment my reasons against believing in it were removed and I saw its accordance with nature and reason, was not rash or precipitate, but truly reasonable and philosophical, in accordance with the principle of all belief, and, indeed, of all science. I asked, and I needed nothing more.

My doing so was justified, also, by the view which I then took, and still take, of the inspiration of the human race. I held that the race lives by immediate communion with God, therefore inspired by him, and hence in its normal state aspires to him. Man lives by immediate communion with God as his object, and therefore the objective element of his life is divine, and through this objective element his life is the life of God. Man thus in his natural life even partakes of God, and this partaking of God I called inspiration. I did not mean by this that the race is supernaturally inspired; I only meant what the Scriptures say, that "there is a spirit in men, and the inspiration of the Almighty giveth understanding;"[2] or, in other words, that man is intelligent, is a rational existence, only by virtue of the immediate presence of God, simultaneously the creator, the object, and the light of his reason. This is the doctrine I now hold, and which I am supposed to have borrowed from Gioberti,[3] but which I held before Gioberti had published it, and long before I had seen his writings or heard his name. Cousin and Leroux had held something like it, but made it, in their explanation of it, a pantheistic doctrine. They did not distinguish with sufficient care between the human reason and the reason of God; and while they made the immediate presence of God in the soul the condition of our intelligence, they did not regard that presence as creating our reason, or faculty of intelligence, and becoming immediately, in the act of creating it, its object and its light; but left it to be inferred that it is God himself who knows and loves in us: which is virtually pantheism. I distinguished where they did not, and held that it is not God who knows and loves in us, but God in us who creates in us our power to know and to love. The divine reason is not our reason, but, so to speak, the reason of our reason. It creates our reason, and is its immediate light and object. This doctrine is well known to the theologians under the names of the presence of God in all his works, and the divine concurrence in all the acts of his creatures. All theologians teach that it is in God we live, and move, and are, and that his reason is the light of our reason. Hence St. John, speaking of the Word or Logos, one with God, says, he was "the true light which enlighteneth every man coming into this world."[4]

Saying with Eliu in the book of Job, "There is a spirit in men, and the inspiration of the Almighty giveth understanding,"[5] I concluded the human race is inspired. God gives understanding, not only in the sense that he creates the faculty, but also in the sense that he is its object. In being the object of the intellect, he is also that of the will, and affirms himself both as the true and the good, as alike the object of knowledge and of love. Hence it is we understand and love, know and aspire. This affirming himself as the true and the good in natural reason is natural inspiration, and the cause of the universal aspiration of the race to God as the infinitely true and the supremely good. In this inspiration and this aspiration of the race, I detect the dignity and authority of the race. In it I find the worth and legitimacy of reason, and vindicate my right to take the reason of the race as a legitimate ground of belief. The reason of the race may be safely followed, because it is the inspiration of the Almighty, who can neither deceive nor be deceived. The race has always recognized, in some form, supernatural communion with God, and held that it is only by virtue of this supernatural communion, that is, a communion in a higher sense than that by which we are rendered capable of knowing and loving in the natural order, that the race is elevated and set forward in its career of progress. Then, to believe in the reality of this communion, in the fact of this supernatural aid or assistance, is not an irrational belief, or a belief on an inadequate authority. The race has always believed that men are elevated and set forward by supernatural assistance, obtained through the agency of specially inspired individuals, or what I call providential men. Wherever you find man, you find him with some sort of religion; and all religions, the lowest and most corrupt, as well as the highest and purest, recognize a supernatural element in human life, and claim, each for itself, the assent of mankind, on the ground of being the channel or medium through which it is attained, or flows into the natural, and supernaturalizes human action. This is the essential, the vital principle of all the religions which are or ever have been. Take this away, and you leave nothing to which the common-sense of mankind does or can give the name of religion. As this supernatural element may flow in without violence or injury to the natural, what reason have you to assert that this common belief of mankind is false or unreasonable? For you, who concede an authoritative religion, propounded and interpreted by an authoritative church, what higher authority is or can there be for believing any thing, than the reason of the race? It is your highest reason after the immediate and express word of God; and not to believe it without a higher reason for discrediting it, is not to follow reason, but to reject reason.

My conduct, then, was not unreasonable, but reasonable; and the joy I felt at finding myself believing in the supernatural providence of God, was no silly joy, but such as I might well indulge, for it proceeded from the recognition by the soul, though as yet but partially and dimly, of the object to which I had always aspired. I had made the greatest step I had yet made, in this recognition of the fact that the human race is advanced by the aid of providential men. In it I seemed to assert my own freedom, and what is more, the freedom of God. No matter how I had reasoned or talked, I had regarded God as a *Fatum,* or an invincible necessity, creating from the necessity of his own being, and hedged in and bound by the invariable and inflexible laws of nature. This is more generally the case with our modern philosophers, and so-called free-thinkers, than is commonly supposed. The real obstacle in many minds to the acceptance of Christian faith, is the want of belief in the freedom of God. Read the works of all your non-Catholic philosophers, and you will find that they nowhere admit providence, or the free intervention of God in the affairs of the universe he has himself created. What they call the providential is always the fixed, the invariable, the inexorable, the fatal. They reject miracles, the supernatural, or voluntary interpositions on the part of the Creator, because they are assumed to be marks of change, of variability, and forbidden by the laws of nature. I had, in asserting providential men, risen above this difficulty, and become able to understand that, while God binds nature, nature cannot bind him; that being in himself sufficient for himself, no necessity compels him to operate externally, or to create a world; and therefore creation itself must be, on his part, a free, voluntary act, and much more so his intervention in the government of what he has created. This threw a heavy burden from my shoulders, and in freeing God from his assumed bondage to nature, unshackled my own limbs, and made me feel that in God's freedom I had a sure pledge of my own. God could, if he chose, be gracious to me; he could hear my prayers, respond to my entreaties, interpose to protect me, to assist me, to teach me, and to bless me. He was free to love me as his child, and to do me all the good his infinite love should prompt. I was no longer chained, like Prometheus, to the Caucasian rock, with my vulture passions devouring my heart; I was no longer fatherless, an orphan left to the tender mercies of inexorable general laws, and my heart bounded with joy, and I leaped to embrace the neck of my Father, and to rest my head on his bosom. I shall never forget the ecstasy of that moment, when I first realized to myself that God is free. . . .

Notes: The Convert

1. See "Reform and Conservativism," *Boston Quarterly Review* 5 (January 1842): 60–84. See also *Works* 4, pp. 79–99, especially pp. 91–96.
2. Jb 32:8.
3. Vincenzo Gioberti (1801–52) was an Italian priest, politician and religious philosopher who is known in the history of ideas primarily for his ontologism; that is, the doctrine that the human mind directly perceived the absolute necessary Being, God, the creative cause of all existences and the immediate source of human knowledge. On Gioberti, see Gerald McCool, S.J., *Catholic Theology in the Nineteenth Century: The Quest for a Unitary Method* (New York: The Seabury Press, 1977), pp. 113–82.
4. Jn 1:9. This was one of Brownson's favorite biblical passages, one that he frequently quoted since his early Universalist days.
5. Jb 32:8.

17. REVIVALS AND RETREATS

SOURCE: *Brownson's Quarterly Review* 15 (July 1858): 289–93, 303–8, 310–22.

In the midst of the Protestant revivals of 1858 and the increase in Catholic retreats and parish missions, Brownson delineated in the following his ideas on the value of using "religious excitement." By *using "sensible devotion," which Brownson defines here, retreats and parish missions try to awaken souls from their religious lethargy and to induce them to a lively consciousness and experience of God and moral duty.*

The past few years have been marked in the Catholic community of the United States by the unusual number and the great success of the Retreats or missions which have been given by the members of several Religious Congregations, in almost every ecclesiastical province and diocese; both in our overflowing city churches, and also in the country parishes both large and small. These missions have thus excited the attention not only of Catholics, to a great part of whom they were something altogether new and strange, but also of the Protestant community, the preachers and editors particularly, who have been astonished to find such an engine at work in the Catholic Church, and have usually styled it a new masterpiece of Roman policy, a fresh proof of the superhuman cunning of the Man of Sin. The newspapers of the day have also chronicled within the past year an unusual series of religious Excitements or Revivals within several Protestant denominations. It is a singular fact that these Protestant Revivals have, to some extent, followed in the wake of the Catholic missions which have been given within the last six months; and have sprung out of efforts inspired by a spirit of rivalry which has been excited by the crowded congregations and the general enthusiasm witnessed in Catholic churches on these occasions. To superficial observers, there appears to be a close resemblance between these religious movements in the Catholic and Protestant churches, and although we shall prove satisfactorily enough, in the course of this article, that this is a great mistake, yet there is doubtless a certain grotesque likeness in this as well as in other features of Protestantism to that grand Catholic system of which the former is only a poor imitation. As there is doctrine held in common with the Catholic Church by certain sects, episcopal regimen and a liturgy borrowed from her in others, so there is something in a series of special services and sermons continued for days and weeks in succession, in which the matters relating to the salvation of the soul and eternity are commended with especial earnestness to the attention of all, as practised in certain other sects, which is akin to the spiritual exercises of Catholic Retreats and missions. It seems not improper, then, to treat of both in the same connection, and in the remarks which follow on Protestant Revivals and Catholic missions, we shall endeavor to take up the question of religious excitement, its legitimate use, and its abuse, the points of resemblance, and the points of contrast, between the Protestant and the Catholic methods of handling this powerful instrument for working on the religious susceptibilities of the community. . . .

These revivals, and the general question of the propriety of employing excitement in religion, have been much discussed by the Protestant clergy. The High Church and the Latitudinarian sections have condemned them as fanatical. The more sober, grave, and dignified portion of the clergy have always been averse to the boisterous and extravagant forms of revivalism. Those who have been the most consistent and severe in condemning the use of excitement in religion and deprecating all popular outbursts of religious enthusiasm, have been the High Church clergy of the Episcopal Church. They love quietness and decorum in religion, grave and solemn liturgical services, churches dark and still, the ancient chant, chastened and finished discourses, tranquil meditation, and reading prayers by yourself out of a book composed by an old Church-of-England divine. This spirit is no doubt derived from the Catholic Church, and in itself we are not disposed to quarrel with it. It is, however, too one-sided, narrow, and exclusive. It leaves out of view the necessity of change and variety in religious exercises, and the necessity of more popular means for acting on the people, and for exciting those who have lived for a long time asleep in a state of profound religious lethargy, or buried in vice. And even some of the highest churchmen of the Episcopal Church have of late felt and acknowledged this to be the case. They have detected a great defect in their system; which, however, they are unable to supply. It cannot be denied that the Congregationalists, Methodists, and other sects have had in this respect an advantage over the Episcopalians, and have had in their hands an instrument for working on the people, which they have used with energy and effect. Hence, many intelligent Protestants have held the opinion expressed by one of the most eminent literary men of the country, a regular attendant at the Episcopal Church, that "the Episcopal Church is the best for the educated class, and the Methodist Church for the mass of the people."

The principle of excitement is and must be made use of in all great movements in which men are interested. For example, this is the case in politics. What is eloquence but a powerful means of producing an intellectual, moral, and sensible excitement, as seen in the senate, in the courtroom, at the hustings, and in the popular assembly. Even those who deprecate excitement in religion, really employ it in another form. For what is the effect of grand architecture, solemn music, fine statuary and paintings, impressive ceremonies, beautiful poetry, devotional prayers and reading, but an *excitement,* more subtle and refined, but not less powerful, than that of stirring sermons, and popular devotions, and exercises of piety. The whole class of these influences and impressions belong to *sensible devotion.* The essence of devotion consists merely in a supernatural faith in the truth revealed, joined with an alacrity of the will to do those things which belong to the service of God. But this, taken by itself alone, is something so purely spiritual and sublime, and when existing by itself so extremely difficult, and it involves such a perfect crucifixion of human nature, that it is far above the reach of any except the most perfect and heroic souls. Sensible devotion, although in itself of little worth, very much open to delusion, and liable to great abuse, is nevertheless, as a general rule, a most necessary and useful auxiliary of solid devotion. Man is not a pure spirit, and is not entirely swayed by his reason. His nature is mixed and compound; he has a body, passions, and senses. The number of those whose reason is highly cultivated, and whose will is thoroughly disciplined, is small. Hence, the sensible element must enter more or less into the religion of man. It must exist in a certain degree in the religion of the most intellectual, the most spiritual, and the most perfect. And in proportion as these qualities are less highly educated, the sensible element must predominate more. Religion must appeal to the heart, rouse the passions, strike on the senses, affect the sensibilities. It must awaken enthusiasm, strike the chords that vibrate through the popular mind, take hold strongly on masses of men, and be able to master and sway the wills, not only of the educated, but of the ignorant, the gross, the debased, and vicious even. It appears, then, that we cannot condemn the revival movements of Protestant sects, on the mere ground that they employ excitement as a means of producing religious impressions. On the contrary, by so doing, Protestant preachers are only acting in accordance with human nature, and doing just what all other men do, who wish to interest masses of men in any kind of enterprise or undertaking, and to gain influence over them. The only question there can be relates to the manner in which they make use of this excitement, and their ability to turn it toward its true and legitimate end in a successful manner. The different means by which a strong tide of popular enthusiasm in relation to religious subjects can be evoked, may be skilfully and prudently used, or they may be abused by extravagance and excess. The legitimate end for which such means ought to be employed—that is, to induce men to do those things by which they will be reconciled to God and secure their salvation—may be attained, or it may fail of being attained, and all this religious enthusiasm may be wasted and misdirected, through the incompetence of those who guide its movements.[1] . . .

We have already laid down the principle that a moderate and judicious use of religious excitement is not to be condemned, and may have good and salutary results. This principle is sanctioned and acted on by the Catholic Church, as is particularly seen in the Retreats and missions which are given by her clergymen of different orders, both secular and regular, with her full approbation. A certain superficial resemblance between a Catholic mission, when conducted with enthusiasm in a large and crowded congregation (especially of our ardent and demonstrative Irish Catholics), and a Revival, has sometimes been the cause that both Protestants and ill-informed Catholics have thrown on missions the aspersion of being imitations of the "Protracted Meetings," and revival operations of the Methodists and other sects. A momentary glance at their history will show, however, that in their origin and in their spirit they are purely Catholic. They are among the inventions of saintly and apostolic men in the Catholic Church, who had in view the renovation of piety and reformation of morals in those Catholic communities where in the lapse of time they had fallen into decay. We find them as far back as the foundation of the Dominican and Franciscan Orders, in the 13th century; and one of the most celebrated of these early missionaries was St. Anthony of Padua,[2] around whose place of preaching and confessing immense crowds, both of the nobles and the common people, used to encamp and pass the whole night, in order to hear him preach the word of God, and to receive the Sacraments at his hands. Sometimes, as many as thirty thousand received communion on one of his missions. St. Vincent Ferrer,[3] in the 14th century, was even more famous and successful than St. Anthony. Rohrbacher[4] relates, that he was called to this mode of life in a supernatural manner, while living at the court of Peter de Luna at Avignon;[5] and he devoted the rest of his life to these "sacred expeditions," as they have been called by Pope Pius IX.,[6] traversing Spain, Portugal, France, Italy, and even England, where he went by the special invitation of King Henry IV.[7] St. Vincent usually devoted himself entirely to preaching and giving spiritual advice and instruction; but he was accompanied by a large number of secular priests, sometimes as many as thirty, who heard the confessions of the people. In more recent times, it is needless to enlarge on the well-known labors of this sort, performed by Blessed Leonard of Port Maurice, F. Segneri, St. Vincent de Paul, St. Alphonsus Liguori, Father Brydayne, Father Bernard, and a host of others in every country of Europe, and in the United States.[8] In modern times, especially since the time of the great master in the spiritual life and consummate artist in the "*ars artium regimen animarum,*" St. Ignatius,[9] the whole work of Retreats and missions has been systematized. The celebrated "Spiritual Exercises" of the great contemplative of Manresa form the basis of Retreats, and in a more popular form of the course of Sermons for a mission. These exercises have been approved repeatedly by several Sovereign Pontiffs, and have received the united suffrage of the Catholic world. Missions also have received the sanction of the Church. Some of the most distinguished missionaries, as St. Vincent Ferrer, B. Leonard, St. Francis Regis, St. James de la Marche, St. Jerome of Naples, and St. Alphonsus have been canonized, and the Missionary Institutes founded for the express purpose of giving missions, as the Congregation of the Mission, of the Most Holy Redeemer, of the Passion, of the Oblates of Mary, etc., have received the approbation of the Holy See.[10] Among the Catholic practices condemned by the Jansenistic Synod of Pistoia,[11] are missions and the popular devotion connected with them, and this judgment of that petty little conciliabulum has been specifically condemned by Pope Pius VI., in the Bull "*Auctorem fidei.*"[12] The present Pope has in various ways manifested his warm interest in missions, and done every thing in his power to uphold and encourage them. The Catholic Bishops of every country have shown themselves most anxious to foster and promote missions in their dioceses. And we cannot refrain here from citing the opinion of one of the most illustrious members of the hierarchy, Cardinal Wiseman.[13]

In one of the articles contained in his collection of Essays on various subjects, His Eminence writes: "We utter not only our individual convictions, but the expressed opinion of many, more experienced in the missionary life, and the judgment of long attention to results attained, when we say, that no greater blessing could be granted us than a body of priests devoted to the task of going from town to town, relieving the local overworked clergy of part of their labors, by giving well-prepared and systematic courses of instruction, and arousing the slumbering energies of congregations, in which stronger excitement is required than the voice of ordinary admonition. By this means, we have no doubt that many stray sheep would be brought back to the true fold, and 'that odious Protestantism,' which 'sticks in people's gizzards,' [words of Mr. Froude,] be thence salubriously extracted. In France, the saintly American Bishop Flaget,[14] has been visiting several dioceses to preach in favor of the Œuvre de la Propagation; and, though his tour has been limited, we have it on authority that it will have had the effect of raising the funds of that beautiful institution from seven hundred thousand to upwards of a million of francs. We have also reason to know that he is bent upon having such a system as we have suggested, of movable missionaries, established in America, as the only means of propagating the Catholic religion on a great scale. In fact, it is the true *Apostolic* method, first taught by our Lord, when he sent his seventy-two before his face during his own lifetime, and afterwards deputed the twelve to the nations of the earth; and subsequently practised by all those who, imitating their example, and copying their virtues, have gone forth to those that sit in darkness. It was the plan pursued in our regard, not only to rescue our Saxon fathers from paganism, but what is still more in point, for undeceiving the earlier Christians as to the errors of Pelagianism. Difficulties—some suggested by timidity, others by prudence—may, we are aware, be raised against this proposal. Some will fear fanaticism, or excessive zeal; but this will be easily prevented by wholesome regulation, authoritative control, and still more, by a system of training and preparation that shall act on the feelings and mind, as well as on the outward forms to be observed. Others will say, where are the instruments and the means for such an undertaking?—the individuals who will dedicate themselves to the laborious, self-denying duties it will impose, and the funds requisite for conducting it? We answer, let but the word be given, by the authority under whose guidance it must be ever carried on—let an accordant plan be concerted, giving to all the benefit of such an institution, and we will engage that no difficulties will be incurred on any of these grounds. There is abundance of zeal and activity in the Catholic body, and especially among its clergy, to insure success to any plan based upon experience and approved methods, for propagating truth and combating error."[15] Nothing can be more evident than that missions, in their spirit and their methods, are completely Catholic. Those who call them imitations of protracted meetings, revivals, and other similar doings of Protestant sects, betray their own profound ignorance. If there is any borrowing in the matter, the sects must have imitated the Catholic Church. And whatever resemblance there may appear to be, it reflects no dishonor on the Church, if the things themselves are good.

Revivals are attended with excitement, and so are missions. In this they are alike. But this is no objection against missions, unless it be proved that revivals are to be condemned, precisely because of the excitement they produce, and that all use of excitement in religious doings is noxious. This, we think, cannot be done. We believe, with Cardinal Wiseman, that sometimes, for the purpose of "arousing the slumbering energies of congregations," "*stronger excitement is required* than the voice of ordinary admonition." We admit that a mission is likely to produce, and is intended to produce, this stronger excitement in a congregation where one is given. But we maintain that in the Catholic Church this excitement is judiciously directed and moderated, and made subservient to a good end, that end being the preparation of the soul for the supernatural gifts of divine grace. In the natural world perpetual calm and quiet are noxious. A thunderstorm, or a brisk shower of rain, is very useful for clearing the atmosphere and refreshing the earth. So it is in religion. Too great and long-continued quiet subsides into stupor and death. An occasional excitement is like a little mental electricity. The ordinary character of the services of the Church is calm and quiet. But in Lent and Advent of each year, she seeks to make them more solemn and arousing in their character, and bids her priests excite the people to penance and prayer in a special manner. By her missions she arouses them more powerfully still. But these are occasional. In stationary and well-ordered congregations, it is only about once in from five to seven years that a mission can be given with salutary effect. Thus, the Church is careful not to overdo the matter, knowing that too frequent an administration of tonics and stimulants, is as hurtful in the spiritual as in the natural order. But, in their proper place, she is not afraid to use them. Excitement is necessary for a large class, who are so far gone in spiritual lethargy, that nothing short of a powerful stimulant will have any effect upon them. The missionaries of the Catholic Church intend and expect to get hold of the worst, the most negligent, and the most vicious part of the population. Souls stupefied by drunkenness, or obdurate through long impenitence, and sunk in sensuality, must be brought to reflect seriously, to do penance, and to renounce their evil courses. How is it possible to make the smallest impression on them, without something startling, interesting, exciting, which shall act as a counter-stimulant to the influence of vice and passion. Numbers, everywhere, have ceased to receive the Sacrament, to attend Church, to say their prayers even; are profoundly ignorant of their religion, and completely indifferent to it, and are bringing up their families without any religion, except a remembrance that they have been baptized and call themselves Catholic. How are such people to be drawn to the Church, instructed, and made good and attentive Christians, unless there is some powerful attraction to stimulate their curiosity, to work on their senses and feelings, and thus to prepare them to receive truth and to be brought to their duty? For such, missions are the necessary and almost the only means of salvation. And even for the well-instructed and exemplary portion of a congregation, it is very salutary to listen to a series of sermons on the eternal truths, and a complete course of instructions, and to pass a few days in extraordinary exercises of devotion. For a small class habituated to meditation, no doubt, a calm, quiet retreat spent in solitude and silence, is more agreeable and more salutary. But these are few; the majority, even of the higher and more educated class, can only take part in, and be benefited by, what are called *popular devotions,* and the only way of giving them the benefit of the spiritual exercises is by means of a mission. . . .

. . . Catholic preachers are far more skilful in varying their subjects and discourses, giving them a regular order, appealing to different passions and emotions, and thus avoiding the error of wearying their hearers and exhausting their power of attention and feeling, by monotonous harping on one string. Then again, together with the more exciting sermons, plain, didactic, practical instructions are interspersed, addressed to the understanding, and thus advantage is taken of the appetite awakened, to feed the mind with solid information and wholesome doctrine on matters relating to morality and practical piety. In the sermons also on the eternal truths, the imagination and the feelings are aroused, only that through them the reason and the will may be reached, and the deeper, more spiritual affections of the soul be excited. In this way, a morbid and excessive excitement of the sensibilities, which is necessarily transient and succeeded by disgust, is avoided.

We do not mean to say that there are no instances of ill-managed or mismanaged missions, and that there are no indiscreet, incompetent, unskilful men among Catholic preachers and missionaries. In the Catholic Church, there is a wide margin left for individuality, and there is great necessity for prudence, a careful training, and the direction of wise superiors, in order that missions, retreats, and similar works may be successfully conducted. The best things may degenerate and become mischievous in bad hands. But this only shows the necessity of confiding the work of missions, and the preparation and direction of those who are called to this peculiar department of the priesthood, to those who understand it thoroughly, and who are acquainted with the country, with the people, and with the circumstances amid which the providence of God has placed them.

The beautiful and attractive ceremonies of Catholic missions are admirably calculated both to increase the enthusiasm of the people, to draw crowds to the church, to make deeper and more permanent the impression of the sermons, and at the same time to allay undue or morbid excitement, and relieve the mind, by directing it from its own subjective moods to something out of itself. These external ceremonies have the same effect that walking out on a fine day in a beautiful country, or looking at the moonlit, starry heavens, has upon an anxious, sorrowful, or depressed mind that has been too much shut up within itself. Yet, they do not weaken, they strengthen, the impressions of religion in the soul. How touching it is to see, in the early part of a mission, the children of the congregation, sometimes to the number of five or seven hundred, dressed in white, full of earnestness and yet full of childlike joy, at an early morning hour, gathered together in the church to receive communion, their parents looking on with tearful eyes, and one of the fathers kneeling among them, reciting in a subdued and solemn voice the prayers and aspirations appropriate to the holy occasion, while the priest at the altar is proceeding with the Mass. What a spectacle for angels to contemplate with delight, and fitted to touch the heart of the coldest skeptic, the haughtiest philosopher, when they approach, rank after rank, and kneeling down at the communion rail, receive the bread of life, then returning to their places, join in the concluding prayers of thanksgiving, and are then dismissed, and scatter away in happy groups, their hearts filled with hallowing and sanctifying influences, while the gayety of their youthful spirits is undiminished, and their cheerful, open brows are unshadowed by the least tinge of sadness or constraint.

Station yourself at early dawn in a remote gallery of some spacious and magnificent church while early Mass is going on, until the first rays of the rising sun begin to illumine the stained windows and throw variegated light on the altar and on the mass of people kneeling in the nave, as the lights are extinguished, and the obscure, dark mass of worshippers come gradually out into the distinct light of day. Look at the Masses which are going on at different altars, the robed priests, the surpliced boys moving about the altars; listen to the little tinkling bell, and see the long lines of communicants pressing up to receive communion. Notice the varied and picturesque groups, gray-headed men, gentle maidens, children, grotesque old women in every comical fashion of hood and gown, making the stations, telling the beads, reading the prayer-book, crowding around the confessionals. . . .

Enter one of our largest and most imposing cathedrals on the night of the Dedication to the Blessed Virgin Mary, or the Renovation of the Baptismal Vows. There you see the statue of the Queen of Heaven on a lofty throne, crowned with the most costly jewels, surrounded with lights and with a profusion of the most exquisite flowers. The baptismal font towers up at the side of the altar, decorated with the expressive symbols of baptismal grace; the altar is adorned and illuminated; the bishop with his clergy in their most splendid vestments, with a troop of surpliced boys, and a hundred little girls in white, with wreaths on their heads and tapers in their hands, fill the sanctuary. As the missionary in the pulpit, having finished the discourse, kneels down to recite the prayer of consecration, eight thousand human beings, by one simultaneous movement, bend the knee and bow the head in veneration of Mary. The baptismal vows are renewed, and the roar of human voices ascends, repeating the promises made in that sacrament. Eight thousand tongues at once, renounce the devil and swear allegiance to Jesus Christ; and then all falling on their knees, the priest raises his crucifix and gives them the Papal Benediction. The swelling chant of Magnificat or Te Deum, ascends to Heaven, clouds of incense fill the sanctuary, the Benediction of the Blessed Sacrament closes the solemn scene, and as the priests retire from the sanctuary, the crowd linger, they continue to gaze with riveted eyes on the brilliant altar, or the font, as if Heaven itself were open to their view, and they are loath to depart. They would gladly die where they are rather than return to the wicked world. Intelligent and highly educated Protestants have repeatedly declared, after witnessing such a scene, that it was the most sublime spectacle they had ever witnessed in their lives.

The Confessional is another most powerful means of influence which the Catholic priest possesses, and which is in full operation in a mission. One of the princes of the royal house of Prussia, we have been told, attended the exercises of a mission while a student. He was greatly astonished at the remarkable effects he saw produced, and desirous of accounting for the fact that Catholic priests were able to produce these effects, while Protestant ministers were not able to do the same, unless on a small scale. It cannot be, said he, the learning, eloquence, or zeal of the preacher, for we can equal them in these respects; it must be, then, the power of the Confessional. There was much truth in the remark of the prince. In the Confessional, that vast crowd which fills the church passes slowly, one by one, through the hands of the priest, and those truths and admonitions which are given in general terms in the pulpit are applied here to the individual conscience. Here, also, to the believing Catholic, there is a specific and certain way of relieving his burdened conscience, and bringing tranquillity to his bosom. Thus, while the Confessional deepens and renders permanent the impressions of religious truth, it quiets that excitement which would soon prove hurtful, or wear itself out; it changes the current of the feelings, gives hope the ascendency over fear, and diffuses through the soul a calm serenity. Hence, while in a Protestant Revival the people become haggard, worn, and exhausted as it proceeds, in a Catholic mission they become more serene and tranquil as it approaches its close. The change is manifest even in their countenances, and although the interest in the exercises increases, yet the whole assumes a more joyous character. The reason of all this is, that the disturbed and alarmed conscience has found a precise and satisfactory means of regaining peace.

The effect of the daily and frequent celebration of the Sacrifice of the Mass and the communion of the people is another thing peculiar to Catholic missions. The early morning hour, and the quiet, solemn, liturgical service, have something in them refreshing, invigorating, and soothing to the spirit. Then, in the Communion, the soul is strengthened by spiritual food. There is something objective, real, sensible. It is according to sound medical principles, and to sound common sense, that when a keen appetite has been created by a tonic or by fresh air and exercise, a generous and abundant diet must be supplied. The fire must have fuel to feed on. So also the soul, stimulated by powerful spiritual appliances, and hungry after some supernatural good, cannot feed on excitement, or be sustained by its own subjective acts, but requires sustenance from without. In the Holy Communion it finds this; and thus the Sacraments are the proper complement of the sermons. The Sacraments have in themselves all that grace which the soul needs. When the soul is healthy, she wants nothing more. But when the soul is sick and languid, she needs to be purified and stimulated, that she may be prepared to receive her proper food with appetite, and to assimilate it in a due manner. . . .

We may reduce all that we have been saying in our foregoing remarks to this statement. . . . In Catholic Retreats and missions, excitement[16] is wisely managed, and made simply a means. So far, for the mere philosophy of the matter. But, for the theology of it, we must resort to the principles of the Catholic Faith. . . . Retreats and missions must be approved, because they are a vehicle of the supernatural graces and gifts of God. The Holy Ghost is in the Catholic Church; the grace of God is with the preaching of the Divine Word, the administration of the Sacraments, and all other acts of the ministry. The Catholic Priest preaches with authority from Heaven; he proclaims a certain and divine faith; he can reconcile the sinner to God in the sacrament of penance, give him the body of Jesus Christ in the Sacrament of the altar, and, if empowered to do so by the Pope, a plenary indulgence for his sins. He tells the sinner, who wishes to be reconciled with God, and to live in such a way as to be sure of pleasing him, and meriting heaven, what he has to do; and he tells him with authority and unerring certainty, as the minister of an Infallible Church. Retreats and missions have an extraordinary grace attached to them, because they were devised by saints; and have the sanction and blessing of the Vicar of Jesus Christ. For this reason it is, that they produce such wonderful and lasting results. It is by these results that they must be judged; by the moral and spiritual benefit which they impart to the individual soul and to a community. . . . Feelings of sensible devotion do not constitute the essence of piety. Sometimes they proceed from nature, sometimes from the devil, and sometimes from God. When they proceed from God, they are not to be rested in, as an end, but to be accepted and used as an auxiliary means for the attainment of solid virtue. When, therefore, a Catholic missionary has drawn a crowded congregation to church,—when he sees them attentive to the truths of the Divine Word, serious, moved in conscience, perhaps weeping, and showing other signs of strong emotion, he does not rest there, and he is not at all satisfied with what he has gained. Each one of that multitude has to be brought, alone, to kneel at his feet, and disclose the wounds and diseases of his soul. There, he will not be let off with expressing a "trust in the merits of Christ," or "indulging a hope," or professing to have "passed from death unto life," or even professing to be resolved to "love God with all his heart, and act always from the pure love of God." It may be that he is already in the grace of God, as hundreds and thousands are, who come to the Confessional. If so, there is no question of reconciling him to God now, and his confession, though a source of sanctifying grace to him, is a short and simple affair. But we wish to speak of the sinner; for it is for such, chiefly, that missions are given. Perhaps this sinner is a drunkard; if so, he has to renounce his drunkenness, and take the means of avoiding the occasions of it in future. Perhaps he keeps a vile haunt of drunkenness; if so, he must renounce his infamous business. He may be unlawfully married; and if so, unless his case comes within the reach of the Church's power, he must break these ties. Or he may be impure; and he must break off every unlawful connection, and renounce every such sin, even in thought or desire. He has calumniated some person, or is at enmity; he must go and make reparation, and be reconciled. He has committed an injustice; he must make restitution, even though it be of thousands of dollars. Thus, every one has to examine his conscience and life, to place the result before a spiritual judge and physician, and specifically to detect and renounce every mortal sin which he has committed. The Catholic missionary is not, however, satisfied with reconciling to God for the present moment all who are in the state of sin. He seeks to produce a permanent change in them. And he bends all his efforts to instruct them, to place in their hands means of perseverance, and to bring them to commence a holy and virtuous life, and to persevere in it until death. What the actual results of Catholic Missions are, could only be known by collecting the testimony of the pastors, in whose congregations they have been given, and of the people themselves. The immediate, practical results are manifest to all. The conversion of the most impious, the most negligent, the most vicious, and most completely abandoned, is obvious. The sudden and almost total cessation of drunkenness, and every species of disorder and immorality, is equally so. Great numbers of adults, even of those advanced in years, receive for the first time the Sacraments; and young people, particularly those living in the country and neglected by their parents, in great numbers, are instructed and prepared for their first Communion. Restitutions are made in great numbers, and sometimes to a large amount. Occasionally, an instance which becomes necessarily public, finds its way into the papers. But the greater number of cases remain forever unknown. With few exceptions, the mass of the Catholic people who are reached by the mission, receive the Sacraments with every appearance of sincerity and goodwill. It is impossible to doubt that the majority of them are really, for the time being, sincerely penitent, and in a state of reconciliation with God. This alone, by itself, is an immense good done. Jesus Christ died on the cross to give the grace of God even to those who by their own fault abuse and forfeit it. The Catholic priest should be animated by the same spirit, and be satisfied to destroy mortal sin, and communicate the grace and mercy of God to sinners, to the greatest extent possible, without considering how many of the souls benefited by his labors, will be finally saved or lost. When a thousand, or five thousand souls receive the Sacraments, the question, how many of these will persevere, and be finally saved, is one that God alone can answer. The Catholic Church does not believe in irresistible or inamissible grace. She gives no one a warrant of his final salvation, on the ground that he has "experienced a change," or "been converted." She gives no security even to one of her own baptized children, who at present has a moral certainty that he is in a state of grace, that he will persevere. The kingdom of heaven must be merited by good works, and conquered by a long, hard, and victorious combat. When we inquire, therefore, for the permanent and final results of a successful mission, we are met by great difficulties. It is made an objection by some to missions, that their effects disappear, that the good produced is temporary, and that a large portion relapse into mortal sin. We concede, in part, the truth of the assertion. But the very same objection may be made against the sacraments of Penance, Confirmation, and Communion; against the Paschal Season, against the ordinary ministration of the Divine Word and Sacraments, against the sacrament of Baptism, against the Church, against the Cross of Jesus

Christ, against the grace and mercy of God himself. The effects of all these are, apparently, to a great extent nullified by sin, and swallowed up by the world. . . . The Catholics of the United States, generally, have a great eagerness to hear the Word of God, and a great devotion to the Sacraments, when they are invited to receive them, and special facilities are furnished them. And much as we may see of sin and vice to deplore among them, yet it is undeniable that the impression of a mission upon them produces a great and general renovation of the spirit of faith and piety. It prepares the way for their pastors to labor with more fruit and effect among them. An enthusiastic and successful mission gives the pastor a fulcrum, on which he can work with great power, and to great advantage; and it increases and extends, immensely, his influence over his flock. It lightens, also, the load of his labors, in a great variety of ways. It is for this that missions are intended. Missionaries are for the aid and assistance of the local clergy, and missions are an adjunct to the ordinary and regular ministrations of the Church. That a mission does actually produce a very great improvement in a congregation, could easily be proved by the testimony of pastors. Some have testified, that for a year after a mission, there was no drunkenness in the parish, where before it had been the prevailing vice; others, that the number of monthly communicants had been doubled. What proportion of those who have been reclaimed from a vicious life persevere afterwards, can never be ascertained. Every experienced missionary, however, and every parish priest, in a situation to know the facts, has personal knowledge of numbers of the worst and most wicked characters, who are permanently reformed, and who persevere in a Christian life. That a certain proportion do actually continue in the grace of God, which they have gained during the mission, and finally persevere, is beyond a doubt. And of those who relapse, very few fall back to the point where they were before. Though they relapse into sin, they do not become such careless and habitual sinners as they were before. Faith, conscience, and piety, are quickened in them; they have taken up the habit of prayer, they attend Mass, great numbers make their Easter Duty, and others come, at least occasionally, to confession.

The mission is for them a *terminus a quo,* and the probability is much greater, that at the hour of death they will receive the last Sacraments with good dispositions and save their souls. Look at the condition of the masses of the poor in our cities. Reflect on the state in which canallers, river-men, sailors, railroad operatives, and factory girls; the wives and children of drunken fathers and husbands; and many other classes of human beings to whom God has given the faith and baptism in the Catholic Church, are placed in relation to virtue, piety, and final salvation! Protestantism disowns, scorns, and neglects such souls, for the most part, and can do nothing with them, if she tries her best. But the Catholic Church embraces them, and seeks to save them. The wonder is that she does so much, not that she does so little. And whoever will consider their condition, and the amount of good-will they show, in spite of all their misery and weakness, must believe that God will treat them with great mercy and indulgence. How many will eventually be saved, is a matter we do not wish to enter into. There is a great difference among theologians on this point. Some consider the number of the elect as small, relatively to the whole number of the adult faithful. Others regard it as very large. It is enough for us, that Catholic Missions, in conjunction with the labors of zealous parish priests, are among the most powerful means for saving souls that God has given to his Church. The conversion of Protestants is also a frequent effect of missions, not lightly to be passed over. There is nothing so well calculated to arrest the attention of the Protestant community, and to make a favorable impression upon it; and this, experience has already abundantly proved, and we may hope will prove still more abundantly in the future. The conversion of Protestants is a frequent occurrence in missions. Within seven years, several hundreds, at least, among whom are many of the first grade of intelligence and social position, have been received into the Catholic Church on Missions. . . . In addressing Catholics, a Catholic preacher exhorts them to nothing which they are not already firmly convinced they ought to do, and the only object of his efforts is, to bring them to obey the dictates of their reason, their faith, and their conscience. In the case of a non-Catholic, he is not hurried into an unreasonable and imprudent act, on the spur of blind excitement, but he is carefully instructed and examined on the grounds of faith, and is received into the Church only on a calm and intelligent conviction of the truth, a firm and a reasonable faith in the Catholic doctrine.

Another objection against missions made by some is, that they cause people to become cracked or crazy. Very few such cases ever occur. When they do happen, the individuals are usually predisposed to it, and of that morbid temperament that the least unusual excitement sets them astray, the fault in such cases lies with the parties themselves or their injudicious friends who allow them to attend the exercises of the mission. Every prudent priest would forbid them to do so. If a missionary happens to meet such a person, he does his utmost to soothe his mind, and to induce him to stay at home and keep quiet.

Business, politics, study, and every other human pursuit may be followed to excess, and occasion derangement, and so may religion. In a vast institution like the Catholic Church, there must be some weak-minded and foolish people, and some mismanagers. And through the imprudence of individuals these incidental evils may and must sometimes occur. But they are not to be laid at the door of the Catholic Religion, or its institutions. On the contrary, for the scrupulous, the timid, and those who are unduly depressed in spirits, and too much troubled about their spiritual condition, there is no remedy like the Confessional for calming, tranquillizing, and invigorating the soul.

The Catholic Church is the perfection of wisdom in a human and in a supernatural view. She is a masterpiece, unquestionably, as heretics and infidels are wont reluctantly to confess. But she is the workmanship of God, and her excellence is from him. The different sects, devised by men, and carried on by merely human skill, may have each something which is admirable and appears to give them a likeness to her. One may have a beautiful and impressive liturgy, a quiet and orderly discipline, and a method of administering the Church, pleasing to the educated and refined. Another may have more popular ways, and a more working zeal. Another may have tenacity of doctrine, and a fourth a merciful and indulgent spirit. But the Catholic Church is able to combine every thing into a perfect and majestic whole. The splendor of a princely hierarchy and the poverty of an austere monasticism, stationary bodies of parochial clergy, and movable corps of Missionaries, the sublimity of the highest philosophy and theology and the most popular forms of teaching and preaching, the calm majesty of liturgical worship, the routine of regular sermons and services, and the more exciting spiritual exercises of a mission; all these she is able to unite in one harmonious system, and by these and a thousand similar means, she is able to accomplish every species of good, to reach every class and every individual, to adapt her methods to every age and every nation, and thus to accomplish her divine task of sanctifying and saving the world.

Notes: Revivals and Retreats

1. I deleted from this text most of Brownson's polemic against Protestant revivalism and have selected only those passages that relate to his evaluation of Catholic retreats and parish missions.
2. St. Anthony of Padua (1195–1231) was a Franciscan friar renowned for his theological knowledge and his eloquent preaching

against usury and avarice in the vicinity of Padua, Italy. Catholic piety has regarded him as a patron saint of the poor. Catholics also ask him to intercede to help them recover lost property.

3. St. Vincent Ferrer (1350–1419) was a Dominican itinerant preacher in Spain, southern France and Lombardy. He tried to heal the Great Western Schism (1378–1415) with his preaching skills.

4. René François Rohrbacher (1789–1856) was a French priest and ecclesiastical historian who glorified the role of the papacy in his 28 volume ultramontane *Histoire universelle de l'Eglise catholique* (1842–49).

5. Cardinal Peter de Luna (1328–1423) was a canon lawyer who during the Great Western Schism followed the anti-pope Clement VII in Avignon and later succeeded to Avignon as anti-pope Benedict XIII (1394–1417).

6. Pius IX (1792–1878) was pope (1846–78) during most of Brownson's life as a Catholic.

7. Henry IV (1553–1610) was king of France (1589–1610) and a convert to Catholicism in 1593.

8. St. Leonard of Port Maurice (1676–1751) was a Franciscan ascetic and famous preacher of popular missions, retreats and lenten sermons. Catholic piety considers him the patron saint of missionaries. Paolo Segneri (1624–94) was a Jesuit priest reckoned the greatest pulpit orator of Italy after St. Bernardino of Sienna and Savonarola. St. Vincent de Paul (1580–1660) was founder of the Vincentians, also called Lazarists (the Congregation of the Missions), who were formed to give missions and train clergy. He also founded the Sisters of Mercy to care for the sick and the poor. St. Alphonsus Liguori (1697–1787) was a moral theologian, spiritual writer and founder of the Redemptorists (Congregation of the Most Holy Redeemer), who were formed for pastoral work among the poor. I could not identify Brownson's references to Fathers Brydayne and Bernard.

9. St. Ignatius Loyola (1491?–1556) was founder of the Jesuits (the Society of Jesus) and author of *The Spiritual Exercises,* a classic of spiritual life in post-Tridentine Catholicism.

10. St. John Francis Regis (1597–1640) was a Jesuit missionary to the French Huguenots during the Counter-Reformation. St. James de la Marche (1393–1476) was an early leader of the Franciscan Observants; he was known for his missionary work in Italian towns around Naples. I could not identify Brownson's reference to St. Jerome of Naples. Perhaps he is referring to St. Jerome

Emiliani (1481–1537), who founded the Order of Somascha, whose principal work was to care for orphans, the poor and the sick.

11. The Synod of Pistoia (1786) was a local Italian diocesan synod under the presidency of Bishop Scipio de Ricci. The synod attempted to reform the church along lines pursued by some French Jansenists and Gallicans. It declared, among other things, that "the spirit of compuncion and fervour cannot be bound down to a fixed number of Stations (of the Cross), or to arbitrary regulations that are often false, more often capricious, and always full of pitfalls." Passage quoted in Charles A. Bolton, *Church Reform in 18th Century Italy (The Synod of Pistoia 1786)* (The Hague: Nijhoff, 1966), p. 103.

12. Pistoia had denigrated the external activities that accompanied parish missions and pious devotions because they produced nothing other than the transient emotions of nature. Eighty-five articles from the Pistoian canons were condemned by Pius VI's papal decree *Auctorum fidei* (1794). On the condemnation Brownson is referring to here, see Henricus Denzinger, ed., *Enchiridion Symbolorum* (Rome: Herder, 1967), no. 2665.

13. Nicholas Patrick Stephen Cardinal Wiseman (1802–65) was the first Catholic Archbishop of Westminster (1850–65) after the restoration of the Catholic hierarchy in England in 1850. He supported the ultramontane revival of devotions in England.

14. Benedict Joseph Flaget (1763–1850) was bishop of Bardstown and Louisville, Kentucky (1808–50).

15. Nicholas Wiseman's "Froude's Remains" was originally published in the *Dublin Review* for May of 1839. Brownson is using the reprint here. See Wiseman's *Essays on Various Subjects,* vol. 2 (Baltimore: John Murphy & Co., 1853), pp. 94–96.

16. *excitement* for "it" in original.

18. SANCTITY SEEKS OBSCURITY

SOURCE: *Ave Maria* 3 (March 2, 1867): 132–34.

Brownson here articulates his world-denying spirituality. Sanctity has its origins in divine grace and the person who is sanctified is one who has a firm consciousness that the Kingdom of God, the true end of human life, is not found in fleeting fame and fortune. In fact, sanctity appears frequently in the unpretentious.

"My kingdom is not of this world." [St. John, xviii, 36.]

When our Lord says His kingdom is not of this world, He does not mean that His kingdom or His Church is not established in this world; or that it has nothing to do with the affairs or the government of this world, for it was set up on the earth, and its design is to make the kingdoms of this world the kingdoms of God and of His Christ. He simply means that His kingdom does not hold from the kingdoms of this world, is not founded on the principles of this world, and is not sustained and advanced by the means and methods approved and adopted by earthly kingdoms. "If My kingdom were of this world, My servants would strive [struggle or fight] that I should not be delivered into the hands of the Jews."

The authority of our Lord was unlimited. He held all power in heaven and on earth. He held it by an original, underived title as God, by inheritance as the only begotten Son of God, and by the gift of the Father. "All power is given to Me in heaven and on earth." He could ask His Father, who would send Him twelve legions of angels to defend or to deliver Him from His enemies; He could with a word or a look strike to the ground any forces sent to arrest Him, and walk away in perfect freedom. Yet, He offers no resistance: suffers His servants to attempt no rescue: bids Peter put up his sword; as a lamb before the shearer He was dumb: He opened not His mouth in His own defence, or to proclaim His innocence: and suffered Himself to be led as a sheep to the slaughter. He was a King, greater than any earthly king, and yet He acted in a way which was by no means that of earthly kings. They require their subjects to fight for them, and even to lay down their lives for them; He, on the contrary, lays down His own life for His subjects, and dies on the cross that they may live.

The kings of this world place their glory in their success, and their success in slaying or triumphing over their enemies; He, in being slain or crucified as a malefactor for His, and in looking for victory, glory and honor from defeat and disgrace. We may well say, then, that His kingdom is not of this world, and is neither founded on the principles, or advanced by the means that earthly kings adopt. Indeed, He reverses all the maxims of this world, or at least gives them a sense the world does not give them, and does not and can not understand. The world says: blessed are the rich, and cursed are the poor; our Lord founds His kingdom on the maxim: Blessed are the poor in spirit, for theirs is the Kingdom of heaven. The world blesses those who are high spirited, quick to resent injuries, and to vindicate what they call their honor; He says: Blessed are the meek for they shall inherit the earth. The world blesses those who are prosperous, joyous, and know no sorrow; He says: Blessed are they who mourn, for they shall be comforted. The world blesses those who seek successfully after riches, honors, and place; He says: Blessed are they who hunger and thirst after righteousness, for they shall be filled. The world has no respect for peacemakers, and blesses those who stir up strife, and are powerful in war; but He says: Blessed are the peacemakers, for they shall be called the children of God. The world turns its back on those who are unpopular, and in disgrace; but He says: Blessed are they that suffer persecution for justice' sake, for theirs is the Kingdom of heaven. Blessed are ye when men shall revile you, and persecute you, and shall say all manner of evil against you falsely, for My sake.

The world worships success, and turns away with contempt from those who suffer defeat. It makes success the test of merit, and failure a proof of demerit. The cause that succeeds on earth, is for it the just cause. It cries: all hail to the victor, and woe to the vanquished. It holds all causes lost on earth as bad causes, and causes that ought to have been lost. Had Austria, in the recent struggle, succeeded against Prussia and Italy, she would have been in the right; but Prussia and Italy having succeeded, they are right; and the world does homage to Von Bismark and Victor Emmanuel.[1] The Holy Father having failed to preserve against the powers of this world his temporal possessions unmutilated, and being deserted and betrayed by the princes of the earth, is manifestly in the wrong, and the judgment of the world is against him: only the weak, the superstitious, or the craven can desire his blessing. The world counts all causes lost on earth as bad causes, and all causes that succeed on earth as just causes, visibly approved by Heaven. It knows not that causes may be lost on earth to be found in heaven.

The world is always heathen. The heathen worshiped success, counted the successful the favorites of the gods, and held the unsuccessful, the unfortunate, to be under the divine wrath, and regarded it as flying in the face of the gods to pity them, or to seek to relieve them. So holy Job's friends, when they saw his worldly possessions gone, himself reduced to poverty, and covered over with boils, held that he was a great sinner, or he could not suffer such things, and called upon him to confess his sin. Though unable to convict of any sin, they still insisted that a great sinner he must be, and charged him with adding to his other sins the sin of hypocrisy. Yet the righteous, they who are just before God, are rarely, in a worldly sense, the most prosperous, and seldom fail to prove that whom the Lord loveth He chasteneth, and scourgeth every son that He receiveth. The unsuccessful on earth may be successful in the world to come.

The saints are rarely the popular men of their age, and they almost invariably incur the opposition, often the real persecution of those whom their age and country count the greatest, wisest, and best, and most delight to honor. Mordechai sits in the king's gate unheeded, while Haman is grand vizier to the king.[2] The lives of the saints all bear witness to the fact that if the world is ready to build the tomb and garnish the sepulcher of the saint when he has passed to his reward, and the Church has canonized him, it has little power to detect his sanctity, and seldom fails to treat him with dishonor and contempt while he lives in its midst. Good men, learned men, Priests, Bishops, and even Popes not unfrequently fail to discern the saint when he appears, and treat him as half insane, as wild, and extravagant, or as an impostor, moved by an unholy rather than by a holy spirit. St. Teresa's spiritual directors for a long time were doubtful whether she was under satanic delusions or really inspired by the Holy Ghost.[3] The order dismissing St. Francis Regis from the Society of Jesus, was made out, and would have been issued if he had not died before it could be done.[4] The holy founders of religious orders and congregations have always had to labor long in obscurity with their supernatural virtues unrecognized, to encounter opposition, often downright persecution, not from the worldly and profane alone, but from good men, earnest men, devoted to the interests of religion and humanity.

Why is this so? It is because the principles and methods of the Kingdom of God are not those of this world; because as the Son of God, when He came to redeem mankind, veiled His Divinity under the form of a man, and when He gives Himself as food for the sustenance of the faithful, He veils both His Divinity and His Humanity under the forms of bread and wine, so does sanctity always veil itself under humble forms, and we recognize it not. We may say of the saint when he appears, as of our Lord Himself: there is no beauty, or comeliness in him, that we should desire him; his look is, as it were, hidden and despised, and we esteem him not. Sanctity seeks concealment, for it shrinks from the praise of men. The saint would not, nay, does not know his own sanctity; he would be known of God alone. God is the Beloved, the Spouse of his soul, and he would be to Him and with Him alone. He fears the praise of men—glory from the world, as coming between him and his Love, and painfully distracting his thoughts from his God. He not only conceals his sanctity from others, but even from himself. It is not strange, then, that the world should mistake him, and that his life in the world should be lowly and obscure. It is humility which makes him count himself nothing, and God everything, and which is the root of every Christian virtue, that deceives the wisdom of this world. He is humble after the example of our Lord, and has that mind which was in Christ Jesus, who, being in the form of a man, thought it no robbery Himself to be equal with God, but made Himself nothing: taking the form of a servant, being made in the likeness of man, and in shape formed as a man, He humbled Himself; becoming obedient unto death, even the death of the cross. The Blessed Virgin, the holy Mother of God, was the humblest, and, therefore, the most blessed of women. Before men, before the world, she was nobody; she was only the poor carpenter's spouse; but she was full of grace, the Mother of Her Creator, Queen of Saints, Queen of Angels, Queen of Heaven.

Well might our Lord say, "My kingdom is not of this world." It surely is not, and because it is not, because its subjects seek not their own glory, and look only to the glory hereafter to be revealed, is it able to overcome the world, and maintain faith, truth, justice and love on the earth. Its subjects are powerful, precisely because they assert not themselves, but live the life, and rely on the power of Him who is all-powerful; and glory follows them even among men, because they seek it not, studiously avoid it, and seek only the glory of God. Fit type is Mary of sanctity, nay, of the Church herself.

Notes: Sanctity Seeks Obscurity

1. Otto von Bismarck (1815–98) was primarily responsible for the unification of Germany and the formation of the German Empire under Prussia toward the end of the nineteenth century. He initiated the *kulturkampf* against Catholicism, but was ultimately unsuccessful in destroying Catholic influence. Victor Emmanuel II (1820–78), king of Piedmont-Sardinia (1849–78) and first king of Italy (1861–78), was involved in the unification of Italy during the second half of the nineteenth century.
2. Mordechai was Queen Esther's uncle (see Esther 2:5ff) and a Jewish advisor to King Assuerus of Persia (486–65 B.C.). He uncovered a plot against the king's life. Haman was King Assuerus's prime minister. He hated the Jews and convinced the king to massacre all Jews in the Persian kingdom, but his plan was thwarted by Esther, and he was himself hanged (see Esther 3:6–15; 6:14–7, 10).
3. St. Teresa of Avila (1515–82) was a mystic and spiritual writer best known for her reforms of the Carmelites and her *Interior Castle,* a

classic book on prayer. In 1970 she was proclaimed a Doctor of the Church.
4. See, p. 266, n.10, on Francis Regis.

19. OUR LADY OF LOURDES

SOURCE: *Brownson's Quarterly Review* 24 (July 1875): 381–86, 388, 391, 395–401. Review of Mgr. de Ségur's *The Wonders of Lourdes,* trans. Anna T. Sadlier (New York: D. & J. Sadlier & Co., 1875).

After becoming a Catholic in 1844, Brownson frequently wrote on the cult of the saints and devotion to Mary. His doctrine of communion provided the theological foundation for these Catholic devotions. In the following, Brownson again reminds his readers that because God is free, he can intervene in the world at any time to perform a miracle or create a saint. The Christian who believes in God's freedom can have no a priori *against such a possibility.*

There is to the Christian mind, or to the mind that believes in God, the Creator of heaven and earth and all things therein, no a-priori difficulty in believing any duly attested miracle, or presumption against it, for God, as Creator, must be distinct from his works, independent of, and supreme over them, their sovereign Lord and Proprietor. They, then, can interpose no obstacle to his working a miracle, if he chooses or judges it proper. To pretend, as some do, that God is tied up by the so-called laws of nature, or is bound in his free action by them, is to mistake entirely the relation of Creator and creature. God, if at all, is supercosmic, and cosmic laws are dependent on him, and subject to his will. They are, therefore, incapable of binding him, or impeding his free action. Creation itself is a miracle, and our personal existence is a standing miracle, for we exist at any moment only by virtue of the continuous creative act of God. God, being free in all his acts *ad extra,* can perform any act he pleases, not intrinsically impossible, or that does not imply a contradiction.

The Christian order, though it supposes nature and completes it, is itself supernatural, and a manifestation of the supernatural power and action of the Creator. Miracles, which are the direct and immediate acts of the Creator, are in some sense in the Christian order. Man and the universe are perfected, or fulfil their destiny, only in the supernatural, that is, in the Christian, order. This order being supernatural and the expression of the supernatural providence of God, miracles have in them nothing anomalous, nothing illogical, or not concordant with it, and hence are as credible as any other class of facts. They serve the purpose or end of the Christian order, and therefore tend to perfect or fulfil the design of God in creation. Being supernatural as to their cause, they express the supernatural order; but being in the natural and even sensible order as to their effects, they are as provable, as facts, by ordinary testimony, as if they were natural facts as to their cause. They prove of themselves their supernatural origin and character.

Our Lord promised that miracles should always remain in the Church, and they always have remained. It is of faith that miracles continue with the faithful; and whoever has paid any attention to the subject is well aware that nothing is or can be better authenticated or more conclusively proved than the fact that miracles have never ceased in the Christian Church. Yet we are slow in crediting any particular alleged miraculous fact. Every alleged miracle stands, so to speak, on its own bottom, and is to be received or rejected according to the direct proofs in the case. If I am asked to believe the reality of this or that alleged miracle, I must have proofs which conclusively establish it, and leave no room for a reasonable doubt. We find amongst good people, whose faith is lively and strong, hundreds of things passing as miracles, which, while we by no means deny them to be miraculous, we do not accept as miracles, because we do not find them to be proved as such. The Christian temper inclines neither to incredulity nor to credulity.

The alleged appearance to the shepherds of our Lady of la Salette we have never seen proved to our satisfaction, yet it may have been a real appearance; for we know no reason why our Lady should not appear to mortals, if such is the pleasure of her divine Son.[1] That she has so appeared at different times cannot be doubted, unless we doubt all historical testimony. We know no reason why she should not so appear, if such appearance enters the divine economy, for nothing hides her or any of the saints from us but a mimetic veil, which nothing hinders our Lord from withdrawing as he did in his own case and that of Moses and Elias, in his transfiguration on the mount in presence of Peter, James, and John.[2]

The Blessed Virgin, the saints, and the angels are not separated from us by space, or hidden from our view by physical distance, as with our false views of space and time we are apt to imagine. The state of the blessed is changed, but not their place, for they dwell in the bosom of God, are made one with him: and he is everywhere present, dwells not in space, but in immensity, and inhabits not time, but eternity. We are apt to forget that space and time are nothing in themselves. Ideal space has been well defined to be the power of God to externize his act, or to create *ad extra;* and ideal time, his power to externize his act successively or progressively. We should never think of God as physically remote from us; or of the Blessed Virgin, the saints, and the angels, as separated from us by distance, unless it be, unhappily, by a moral distance. In all other respects, they are present with us, as is our Lord himself. If we see them not, it is not because they are distant, but because the mimetic veil is before our eyes. Yet we must remember, as Dr. Watts sings, heretic as he was, that

> The saints above, and the saints below
> Do but one communion make.

We all profess in the Creed to believe in "the communion of saints." They who are separated do not commune. We think of God as here, and of him and the saints and angels as ever present with us. Our God is nigh unto every one of us, if haply we seek after him. The natural order is not separated from the supernatural, but is, so to speak, immersed in it, and forming only one complete whole with it. The natural proceeds from the supernatural, lives in it, is sustained by it, and completed only by returning to it, and becoming one with it, as the Creator and the creature become one in the Incarnate Word.

There is nothing incredible in the supposition that, from time to time, the blessed show themselves to the living in furtherance of the gracious designs of God to individuals or nations. We do not reject modern spiritism, falsely called *Spiritualism,* because we doubt that the souls of the departed are still really living, or because we hold it impossible for them to appear by divine permission to persons in the flesh; but because we have no proofs that the spirits that appear are the spirits of the dead, and not evil spirits, fallen angels, who personate them. The literal facts alleged by the spiritists, or facts of the same order, we do not dispute, though there is connected with them much fraud, and no little jugglery. The proofs of miracles are not more conclusive than are the proofs of the satanic prodigies, that is, as simple facts; and in either case they are sufficient, if we accept historical testimony at all. What we deny in regard to spiritism is, not the facts as alleged, but the induction from them, that the spirits are really the spirits of the departed.[3]

Nothing is more certain than that Satan imitates, as far as in his power, genuine miracles, and seeks to deceive by his prodigies. We must never assume that the superhuman, or what surpasses the power of man, is supernatural and divine. Satan, though a creature, has a superhuman power, and is able to work, not miracles, but prodigies, which imitate miracles, and which the unwary may mistake for them. But Satan, being a creature, has no creative, and, therefore, no supernatural power. He can operate only within the cosmos, and can never exhibit any real supercosmic power; whereas every real miracle is a manifestation of supercosmic, and, therefore, of creative power. There are certain diseases that Satan can heal,—diseases which demand for their cure only the vitality of the diseased; but those which demand more, or a *vis* the system has lost, he cannot heal. Hence he cannot raise the dead, or restore a dead person to life, for that demands a creative power, as much as the production of an existence from nothing. In all cases where there is an exhibition of creative power, we must see the finger of God, not a satanic prodigy; a real miracle, not a lying wonder.

Many of the alleged cures related of persons visiting holy shrines do not surpass the power of Satan; and corresponding cures are recorded as having been effected in the temples of Æsculapius and other heathen shrines.[4] They cannot, therefore, be taken as conclusive proofs, in themselves, of the divine interposition. They are such proofs only when effected under such circumstances as exclude the supposition of their being effected by satanic influence.

We reject the induction of the spiritists, that the spirits they profess communicate with them, because their communications are not truthful, and they prove themselves lying spirits. They teach what we know to be false, and hurtful to the soul. They deviate from the apostolic doctrine, and lead to separation from the apostolic communion. Everything about them indicates that they are lying spirits, are trying to pass for what they are not, and are practising a gross imposition upon their dupes. In fact, spiritism is only a revived demonism, or the renewed effort of Satan to get himself worshipped as God. Saints and angels, when they appear, come as the messengers of the living God, show themselves to be engaged in his work, in promoting his worship, and leading souls to union with him: the supernatural end for which they are created. Their mission is to enlighten, to elevate, and perfect, or to help man to fulfil his destiny. They calm, they soothe, and they give peace to the troubled soul. They exert a directly contrary influence from that exerted by the lying spirits followed by the spiritists.

Though, as we have said, we are slow to believe this or that alleged miracle, we cannot help believing this of our Lady of Lourdes. The evidence in the case seems to us absolutely conclusive that she actually appeared to the poor girl Bernadette, and that she honors the shrine consecrated to her. We cannot doubt the perfect truthfulness of M. Henri Laserre's book, or that of Mgr. de Ségur, so beautifully translated by our young friend, Anna T. Sadlier, now before us;[5] and which we have read with a renewal of our love and devotion to our Blessed Mother, conceived without original stain, who is all fair, without spot or blemish. We cannot doubt the reality of the appearance, or the fact of the many marvellous cures related,—cures often instantaneous and complete; and which are undeniably beyond the greatest medical science or skill, and also beyond any known natural therapeutic agent. We cannot deny them as facts, and are utterly unable to account for them without the supposition of a supernatural intervention.

Yet, as we have already intimated, not all these alleged cures are to us conclusive proofs of miraculous intervention. We had a near relative who for six months had been rendered utterly helpless by inflammatory rheumatism. She was unable to move herself in bed, or even to raise her hand. A Mormon Elder asked her husband for a night's lodging, which was refused on the ground of the illness of his wife. The Elder replied that that was no reason for refusing his request, for, if he would let him see his wife, he doubted not he could cure her. He was led to her bedside, where he kneeled down and made a short prayer; at the end of the prayer she was completely cured—as well as ever she was in her life. We do not believe that God wrought a miracle at the prayer of the Mormon Elder, nor are we willing to suppose an intervention of the Evil One. There are moral or non-physical causes whose operation we but imperfectly understand, and which produce effects on the physical system that seem to us little less than miraculous. Till we know the extent of these causes, or the moral *vis medicatrix* of nature, we cannot take these sudden and inexplicable cures as conclusive proofs of a supernatural intervention.

But there is a class of facts and cures that are to us conclusive. None but God can work a real miracle, because in every real miracle there is an exhibition of creative power, or the production of something from nothing, or where nothing was before: and God alone has creative power. Now, in the wonders related of Lourdes, we find facts which seem to us to involve the act of creation. When Moses smote the rock and the water gushed forth it was a miracle, for there was no water in the rock; and it was as purely an act of creation to cause the water to flow from the rock where previously there was none, as if there had been no water in existence. So to us, the opening, by Bernadette of the fountain which continues to flow, in the rocks of Massabielle, or Massavielle, seems a miracle of the same kind, and impresses us much more forcibly than most of the cures related. . . .

Taking, as we do, the fact as related, there is here all that is necessary to constitute a real miracle, and, therefore, full proof of the actual apparition of the Blessed Virgin, the Immaculate Conception, as she named herself, to the poor child. The continuousness of the fountain, and its copious flow of water still, is a standing proof of the reality of the miracle, or what seems to us an unmistakable miracle, though we are forbidden, if we mistake not, to pronounce it positively a miracle till declared to be such by the judgment of the Holy See, which, so far as we are aware, has not been rendered in this case, though we are told that it has sanctioned the devotion to our Lady of Lourdes.

When our Lord raised the widow's son to life, or restored Lazarus to his weeping sisters, after he had lain four days in the grave, it was a miracle, and as much an act of creative power as the original production of life itself, for it was the production of life where there was no life. No power but that which can give life can restore the dead to life. Now, we find a case in these wonders of Lourdes that is marvellously the restoration of the dead to life. . . .

Supposing the facts in the case to be as narrated, this is virtually a restoration of the dead to life, and therefore a real miracle. It must not, however, be supposed because we single out this case, that we recognize no supernatural intervention in the numerous other cures related, and, no doubt, truthfully related, but that this and the opening of the fountain are to our own mind decisive. The fountain was supernaturally opened through the instrumentality of the Blessed Virgin; and as the water of the fountain possesses in itself no medicinal properties, the cures effected by its use must be ascribed to the same instrumentality, and therefore be held to be effected by supernatural intervention. They are to be considered as parts of one whole, or integral elements of one and the same supernatural manifestation or event. The fact of the reality of the apparition of our Lady to the child Bernadette, and the opening of the miraculous fountain under her auspices, removes the whole question from the order of facts adduced by the spiritists, places it in the order of divine and supernatural facts, and justifies the faith of those who use the water, or resort to it in their physical maladies. There is no superstition in resorting to it, for, springing from a supernatural cause, and, therefore, an omnipotent cause, the effects sought are from an adequate, not an inadequate, cause.

Why our Lady should seek a special shrine at Massabielle, or why she should favor one spot, or grant her favors at one spot more than at another, or why certain pictures and images of her should receive greater marks of her favor than others, we do not know, and by no means attempt to explain. Perhaps, in reality, she does not confine her favors to them, but is equally ready to show favor to her clients anywhere, wherever they invoke her patronage with equal love and devotion to her divine Son, with equal concentration of faith and fervor. These sacred shrines, perhaps, serve chiefly to fix the attention, to intensify faith, kindle fervor, inflame devotion, and prepare the heart for the reception of supernatural favors. . . .

We wish Mgr. de Ségur had judged it advisable to hint, at least, to his readers that the Blessed Virgin, however powerful as the Mother of God with her divine Son, has of herself no miracle-working power. She is, though exalted above all below the Ineffable Trinity, still a creature, and as destitute of creative power as any other creature. Not she, but our Lord, wrought the miracle of Cana of Galilee. She has power with her divine Son to obtain from him a miracle by her prayers, for she can ask nothing not in strict accordance with his will, or not inspired by him. Moreover, the relation of mother and son subsists, and ever must subsist, between them. But though she may, by her prayers, obtain favors, and even miracles, for us, it is God who works the miracles and bestows the favors. Every Catholic knows this, and Mgr. de Ségur has probably neglected to state it, because assured that it is a point on which no Catholic can fall into a mistake. But, as it is a point on which non-Catholics suppose or pretend that we do fall into a mistake, and a most grievous mistake, too, that of giving to the creature the glory that belongs to the Creator, we think the author should have expressly guarded, not against our falling into the mistake, but against others supposing it possible for us to do so.

We do not, we may remark by the way, ask the Blessed Virgin to pray for us because we cannot pray directly to God for ourselves, or because we feel that she loves us better than does her Son, and is more ready to favor us, or, as far as depends on her, to hear and grant our petitions. He is as near us as she is, and no less tender and merciful to us, since he loved us well enough to die for us on the cross. It is not because we can more easily approach them, because they have a greater, a tenderer, sympathy with us, or are more ready to help us, that we pray to Mary and the saints, and ask them to intercede with our Lord for us, or to bear for us our petitions to the throne of grace, for our Lord is perfect man as well as perfect God, and God himself is the fountain of all love, mercy, tenderness, and compassion to which we appeal in them. The reason is, the mediatorial character of the kingdom of God, as we have so often done our best to explain. The principle of the order founded by the Incarnation of the Word is the deification of the creature, to make the creature one with the Creator, so that the creature may participate in the divine life, which is love, and in the divine blessedness, the eternal and infinite blessedness of the Holy and Ineffable Trinity, the one ever-living God. Creation itself has no other purpose or end; and the Incarnation of the Word, and the whole Christian order, are designed by the divine economy simply as the means to this end, which is indeed realized or consummated in Christ the Lord, at once perfect God and perfect man, indissolubly united in one divine person.

The design of the Christian order is, through regeneration by the Holy Ghost, to unite every individual man to Christ, and to make all believers one with one another, and one with him, as he and the Father are one. All who are thus regenerated and united are united to God, made one with him, live in his life, and participate in his infinite, eternal, and ineffable bliss or blessedness. Herein we see the super-abounding goodness of the Creator. God is infinite, perfect, in all respects sufficient for himself, and therefore is and must be infinitely happy in himself. He could, therefore, have been moved to create only by his infinite goodness, in order to diffuse his own life, which is the light of men, love, and happiness, *ad extra,* as say the schoolmen. Creation is a manifestation of the love and goodness of the Creator; and as the purpose of God in creating was to give to creatures a share in his own infinite life and blessedness, he must be infinitely more loving, tender, compassionate than any creature, however exalted or glorified. It is from him that the glorified saints and angels draw whatever of love, tenderness, or compassion we appeal to in them.

But the goodness of God does not stop here. He not only permits the glorified creature to participate in his own life, love, and happiness, or beatitude, but he also permits his creatures to be co-workers with him in his work, and to participate in the glory of its accomplishment. He makes, in some sense, the creature a medium of effecting its perfection; that is to say, he uses created agents and ministers in effecting his purpose, and in gaining the end for which he creates them, and thus enables them to gain the signal honor of sharing in the glory of the Creator's and the Redeemer's work, that is, in the glory of the kingdom of God. Hence it is that the true followers of Christ enter into glory with him, or participate in the glory of his kingdom; which they could not do, if they had done nothing towards founding and advancing it. It is not that he needs them for himself; but because, in his super-abounding goodness, he would bestow on them the honor and blessedness of sharing in his work, and of being, so to speak, employed in his service, and meriting his approbation and reward. It is his love to his Blessed Mother that makes her the channel of his grace; his love to his saints, his friends, that leads him to employ them in his service, that gives them the high honor of being intercessors for us. This is not only a high honor to them, but a great joy and blessedness, for they are filled with his love, and, like him, overflow with love and goodness to all his creatures. The Cultus Sanctorum flows naturally, so to speak, from the principle of the Incarnation, the deification of man or the creature; and in it we not only honor the saints, but show forth our faith in the superabounding love and goodness of God, which permits them to work with him for the fulfilment of his design in creation, and to participate in its glory.

The fact, that God does employ the saints and angels as agents and ministers in carrying on his mediatorial work, is indisputable. If anything is clear and certain from the Holy Scriptures, it is this. It is implied in the very fact of the Incarnation, which makes the creature one with the Creator. It is only the universal extension of the sacerdotal principle which underlies all religion, and cannot be denied without denying the very principle of the Christian order. . . .

Indeed, the whole system of creation is a system of means to ends, and, in fact, could not be otherwise, since its prototype is in the ever-blessed Trinity, which it copies, or faintly expresses *ad extra,* as the three Divine Persons express the divine essence *ad intra.* In the Holy Trinity, the Holy Triad, we have principle, medium, and end. The Father is principle, the Son is medium, and the Holy Ghost is end— the consummator. As the *idea exemplaris,* or type of creation, is in the eternal essence of God, it must, through the free act of the Creator, express in a faint degree, *ad extra,* the Triad which expresses that eternal essence *ad intra,* or which, if we may so speak, constitutes that essence. Then everything in creation must express, in some degree, principle, medium, and end; and the end is unattainable without the medium or means, as we see all through even the natural world. We are promised seed-time and harvest, but we must cultivate the soil, and sow the seed, or no crop will be obtained. In no case is the end gained but by the proper use of the divinely-appointed means.

Now, in the Christian world, founded by the Incarnation, the appointed means to the end is prayer. God grants his favors only to those who ask for them, perhaps because only those who ask have the internal disposition to profit by them. We can, of course, ask him directly for whatever we think we have need of; but when we ask also the saints to ask him for us, we act in accordance with his love for them, and unite with him in honoring them, by engaging them in working out his designs. We also give them the opportunity of serving him in us, and showing forth their love both for him and us. We honor God in honoring with our love and confidence those whom he delights to love and honor; and, in invoking their prayers, we use the appointed means of gaining the blessings we crave, and we enlist, in aid of our own prayers, the prayers of those whose sanctity renders them dear to our Lord and God.

If we have made ourselves understood, we have shown why it is we, in the old sense of the word, worship Mary and the saints, and why it is that God himself, in fulfilling his design in creation, especially the "new creation," or teleological order, uses the ministry of saints and angels, and chiefly, as their Queen, his Blessed Mother, from whose chaste womb he took his human nature. . . .

The Blessed Virgin is the Queen of saints and angels, and, as the Mother of God, is exalted above every other creature, and is only below the Ineffable Trinity. Whom, then, should God more delight to honor, or more delight to have honored by us? She is the Spouse of the Holy Ghost, she is his Mother; and nothing seems more in accordance with his love and goodness, and the very design, the very idea, if we may use the term, of his mediatorial kingdom, as revealed in the Gospel, than that he should do her the honor of making her his chief agent in his work of love and mercy,—the medium through which he dispenses his favors to mortals. There is joy in heaven among the angels of God, we are told, over one sinner that repenteth. The saints and angels, filled with the spirit of God, and in perfect concord with the divine purpose in creation, and with the Word in becoming incarnate, are full of love to all the creatures of God, and join with him into whose glory they have entered, in seeking the blessedness of those he has redeemed by his own precious blood. They take an interest in the salvation of souls, the repentance of sinners, and the growth and perfection of the regenerated, and consequently love their mission, and perform their task with their own good-will, and with joy and alacrity. This love, this interest, this good-will, must be greatest in their Queen, the ever-blessed Virgin. As she is exalted above every other creature, only God himself can surpass her in his love for his creatures.

We understand, then, why Mary holds so distinguished a place in Christian worship, and performs so important a mission in furtherance of the mediatorial work of her divine Son. Her love is greater, for she is full of grace, greater than that of any other creature. She is more intimately connected with the Holy Trinity, and holds a relation to God which is held and can be held by no other creature. In some sense, as the Mother of the Incarnate Word, she is the medium through which is effected the deification of man,—the end of the supernatural

order. She cannot be separated from that end. We can easily understand, then, why God should assign her a part assigned to no other
creature. Her love is only less than his, and her heart is always in
perfect unison with the Sacred Heart of her Son, and Mother and Son
are strictly united and inseparable. Equally easy is it now to understand why the Christian heart overflows with love and gratitude to
Mary; why Christians recur to her with so much confidence in the
efficacy of her prayers, the success of her intercession; and why Catholics offer her the highest worship below the supreme worship offered in
the Holy Sacrifice, but never offered except to God alone.

We have not given, or attempted to give, a complete discussion of
the great subject we have opened, or rather which the appearance of
our Lady of Lourdes has opened. We have only aimed to throw out a
few thoughts and suggestions, which, if followed up, will show that
such appearances, that miracles, that the love and veneration of the
blessed Mary, and the Cultus Sanctorum, as practised by Catholics, are
not anomalous, but grow out of the very principles of the supernatural
or Christian order, the mediatorial kingdom of God's dear Son; and
are in strict accordance with the design or purpose of the ever-blessed
Trinity, and tend to further and realize it as appropriate means to an
end. . . .

We repeat, all in Christianity proceeds from, depends on, and
clusters around, the Incarnation, in which the design of God in creation, the deification of the creature, is consummated. The devotion to
Mary, the veneration of the saints, grow out of the Incarnation, as does
the Church herself, and tend to keep alive faith in that crowning act of
the Creator. We need, then, place no restraint on our love to Mary, or
our love and veneration for the glorified saints of God. In loving,
venerating, and invoking them, we are acting in accordance with the
design of the Holy Trinity.

Notes: Our Lady of Lourdes

1. Our Lady of La Salette refers to an apparition of Mary to two
   children at La Salette in the French diocese of Grenoble on September 19, 1846.
2. Brownson frequently contrasted mimesis with methexis. "Methexis
   means literally having with, that is participation, and is used to
   express the relation of genera and species to their ideas or types in
   the divine mind. Mimesis means imitation, copy or sensible representation. In Christian philosophy the mimesis is the explication of
   the methexis by genera and species and the explication of genera

and species by individuals, and is partly intelligible and partly sensible." The mimetic viel, therefore, is real and not merely phenomenal or sensible because it always participates in the methexis; but limited human beings do not always possess the ideal reality that is mirrored through the individual mimetic viel. See *Works* 8, pp. 51–52.

3. Brownson repeatedly wrote against spiritism, which he saw as evidence of demonic possession in contemporary life. On this, see *The Spirit-Rapper, An Autobiography* (Boston: Little Brown & Co., 1854); *Works* 9, pp. 1–234; "Spiritism and Spiritists," *Catholic World* 9 (June 1864): 289–302; "Spiritualism and Materialism," *Catholic World* 9 (August 1861): 619–34; "Owen on Spiritism," *Catholic World* 14 (March 1872): 803–12.

4. Aesculapius, son of Apollo, was the god of medicine and healing in Roman mythology.

5. St. Bernadette of Lourdes (1844–79) experienced numerous apparitions of Mary at Massabielle Rock near Lourdes, France, where Mary revealed herself in 1858 as "the Immaculate Conception."

20. NATURE AND GRACE

SOURCE: *Catholic World* 6 (January 1868): 509–27.

In the following, Brownson argues that although a moral antagonism exist between the flesh and the spirit, no antagonism exist between nature and grace. The natural, that is, the created or initial order of existence, and the supernatural, that is, the teleological order, are really two distinct parts or phases of one dialectical whole. God's creative act, which established the natural order, and his redemptive act in the Incarnation, which provided means toward the teleological order, are both supernatural acts. Man's return to God, initiated by the Incarnation, is a free, not necessary fulfillment and perfection of God's creative act. The perfection and completion of the natural order in the teleological order is accomplished without violence to the created order. Grace perfects or fulfills nature; it does not destroy, annihilate, or absorb it. Nature in its origin as in its destiny is supernatural, but it cannot reach its destiny without the medium of the Incarnate Word.

In the article on *Rome and the World* in the Magazine for November last, it was shown that there is an irrepressible conflict between the spirit which dominates in the world and that which reigns in the church, or the antagonism which there is and must be between Christ and Satan, the law of life and the law of death;[1] and every one who has attempted to live in strict obedience to the law of God has found that he has to sustain an unceasing warfare between the spirit and the flesh, between the law of the mind and the law in the members. We see the right, we approve it, we resolve to do it, and do it not. We are drawn away from it by the seductions of the flesh, our appetites, passions, and carnal affections, so that the good we would do, we do not, and the evil we would not, that we do. This, which is really a struggle in our own bosom between the higher nature and the lower, is sometimes regarded as a struggle between nature and grace, and taken as a proof that our nature is evil, and that between it and grace there is an inherent antagonism which can be removed only by the destruction either of nature by grace, or of grace by nature.

Antagonism there certainly is between the spirit of Christ and the spirit of the world, and in the bosom of the individual between the spirit and the flesh. This antagonism must last as long as this life lasts, for the carnal mind is not subject to the law of God, neither indeed can be; but this implies no antagonism between the law of grace and the law of nature; for there is, as St. Paul assures us, "no condemnation to them who are in Christ Jesus, who walk not according to the flesh." (Rom. viii. I.) Nor does this struggle imply that our nature is evil or has been corrupted by the fall; for the Council of Trent has defined that the flesh indeed inclines to sin, but is not itself sin. It remains even after baptism, and renders the combat necessary through life; but they who resist it and walk after the spirit are not sinners, because they retain it, feel its motions, and are exposed to its seductions. All evil originates in the abuse of good, for God has never made anything evil. We have suffered and suffer from original sin; we have lost innocence, the original righteousness in which we were constituted, the gifts originally added thereto, or the integrity of our nature—as immunity from disease and death, the subjection of the body to the soul, the inferior soul to the higher—and fallen into a disordered or abnormal state; but our nature has undergone no entitative or physical change or corruption, and it is essentially now what it was before the fall. It retains all its original faculties, and these all retain their original nature. The understanding lacks the supernatural light that illumined it in the state of innocence; but it is still understanding, and still operates and can operate only *ad veritatem;* free-will, as the Council of Trent defines, has been enfeebled, attenuated, either positively in itself by being despoiled of its integrity and of its supernatural endowment, or negatively by the greater obstacles in the appetites and passions it has to overcome; but it is free-will still, and operates and can operate only *propter bonitatem.* We can will only good, or things only in the respect that they are good, and only for the reason they are good. We do not and cannot will evil as evil, or for the sake of evil. The object and only object of the intellect is truth, the object and only object of the will is good, as it was before the prevarication of Adam or original sin.

Even our lower nature, *concupiscentia,* in which is the *fomes peccati,* is still entitatively good, and the due satisfaction of all its tendencies is useful and necessary in the economy of human life.[2] Food and drink are necessary to supply the waste of the body and to maintain its health and strength. Every natural affection, passion, appetite, or tendency points to a good of some sort, which cannot be neglected without greater or less injury; nor is the sensible pleasure that accompanies the gratification of our nature in itself evil, or without a good and necessary end. Where, then, is the evil, and in what consists the damage done to our nature by original sin? The damage, aside from the *culpa,* or sin and consequent loss of communion with God, is in the disorder introduced, the abnormal development of the flesh or the appetites and passions consequent on their escape from the control of reason, their fall under Satanic influence, and the ignoble slavery, when they became dominant, to which they reduce reason and free-will as ministers of their pleasure. All the tendencies of our nature have each its special end, which each seeks without respect for the special ends of the others; and hence, if not restrained by reason within the bounds of moderation and sobriety, they run athwart one another, and introduce into the bosom of the individual disorder and anarchy, whence proceed the disorder and anarchy, the tyranny and oppression, the wars and fightings in society. The appetites and passions are all despotic and destitute of reason, each seeking blindly and with all its force its special gratification; and the evil is in the struggle of each for the mastery of the others, and in their tendency to make reason and free-will their servants, or to bring the superior soul into bondage to the inferior, as is said, when we say of a man, "He is the slave of his appetites," or "the slave of his passions," so that we are led to prefer a present and temporary good, though smaller, to a distant future and eternal beatitude, though infinitely greater. Hence, under their control we not only are afflicted with internal disorder and anarchy, but we come to regard the pleasure that accompanies the gratification of our sensitive appetites and passions as the real and true end of life. We eat and drink, not in order to live, but we live in order to eat and drink. We make sensual pleasure our end, the motive of our activity and the measure of our progress. Hence we are carnal men, sold under sin, follow the carnal mind, which is antagonistic to the spiritual mind, or to reason and will, which, though they do in the carnal man the bidding of the flesh, never approve it, nor mistake what the flesh craves for the true end of man.

The antagonism here is antagonism between the spirit and the flesh, not an antagonism between nature and grace—certainly not between the law of nature and the law of grace. The law of nature is something very different from the natural laws of the physicists, which are simply physical laws. Transcendentalists, humanitarians, and naturalists confound these physical laws with what theologians call the natural law as distinguished from the revealed law, and take as their rule of morals the maxim, "Follow nature," that is, follow one's own inclinations and tendencies. They recognize no real difference between the law of obedience and the law of gravitation, and allow no distinction between physical laws and moral law. Hence for them there is a physical, but no moral order. The law of nature, as recognized by theologians and moralists, is a moral law, not a physical law, a law which is addressed to reason and free-will, and demands motives, not simply a mover. It is called natural because it is promulgated by the Supreme Lawgiver through natural reason, instead of supernatural revelation, and is, at least in a measure, known to all men; for all men have reason, and a natural sense of right and wrong, and, therefore, a conscience.

Natural reason is able to attain to the full knowledge of the natural law, but, as St. Thomas maintains, only in the *élite* of the race. For the bulk of mankind a revelation is necessary to give them an adequate knowledge even of the precepts of the natural law; but as in some men it can be known by reason alone, it is within the reach of our natural faculties, and therefore properly called natural. Not that nature is the source from which it derives its legal character, but the medium of its promulgation.

The law of grace or the revealed law presupposes the natural law—*gratia supponit naturam*—and however much or little it contains that surpasses it, it contains nothing that contradicts, abrogates, or overrides it. The natural law itself requires that all our natural appetites, passions, and tendencies be restrained within the bounds of moderation, and subordinated to a moral end or the true end of man, the great purpose of his existence; and even Epicurus, who makes pleasure the end of our existence, our supreme good, requires, at least theoretically, the lower nature to be indulged only with sobriety and moderation. His error is not so much in the indulgence he allowed to the sensual or carnal nature, which he was as well aware as others, needs the restraints of reason and will, as in placing the supreme good in the pleasure that accompanies the gratification of nature, and in giving as the reason or motive of the restraint, not the will of God, but the greater amount and security of natural pleasure. The natural law not only commands the restraint, but forbids us to make the pleasure the supreme good, or the motive of the restraint. It places the supreme good in the fulfilment of the real purpose of our existence, makes the proper motive justice or right, not pleasure, and commands us to subordinate inclination to duty as determined by reason or the law itself. It requires the lower nature to move in subordination to the higher, and the higher to act always in reference to the ultimate end of man, which, we know even from reason itself, is God, the final as well as the first cause of all things. The revealed law and the natural law here perfectly coincide, and there is no discrepancy between them. If, then, we understand by nature the law of nature, natural justice and equity, or what we know or may know naturally is reasonable and just, there is no contrariety between nature and grace, for grace demands only what nature herself demands. The supposed war of grace against nature is only the war of reason and free-will against appetite, passion, and inclination, which can be safely followed only when restrained within proper bounds. The crucifixion or annihilation of nature, which Christian asceticism enjoins, is a moral, not a physical crucifixion or annihilation; the destruction of pleasure as our motive or end. No physical destruction of anything natural, nor physical change in anything natural, is demanded by grace or Christian perfection. The law of grace neither forbids nor diminishes the pleasure that accompanies the satisfaction of nature; it only forbids our making it our good, an end to be lived for. When the saints mortify the flesh, chastise the body, or sprinkle with ashes their mess of bitter herbs, it is to maintain inward freedom, to prevent pleasure from gaining a mastery over them, and becoming a motive of action, or perhaps oftener from a love of sacrifice, and the desire to share with Christ in his sufferings to redeem the world. We all of us, if we have any sympathies, feel an invincible repugnance to feasting and making merry when our friends, those we tenderly love, are suffering near us, and the saints see always the suffering Redeemer, Christ in his agony in the garden and on the cross, before their eyes, him whom they love deeply, tenderly, with the whole heart and soul.

But though the law of nature and the law of grace really coincide, we have so suffered from original sin, that we cannot, by our unassisted natural strength, perfectly keep even the law of nature. The law of nature requires us to love God with our whole heart and with our whole soul, and with all our strength and with all our mind, and our neighbor as ourselves. This law, though not above our powers in integral nature, is above them in our fallen or abnormal state. Grace is the supernatural assistance given us through Jesus Christ to deliver us from the bondage of Satan and the flesh, and to enable us to fulfil this great law. This is what is sometimes called medicinal grace; and however antagonistic it may be to the moral disorder introduced by original sin and aggravated by actual sin, it is no more antagonistic to nature itself than is the medicine administered by the physician to the body to enable it to throw off a disease too strong for it, and to recover its health. What assists nature, aids it to keep the law and attain to freedom and normal development, cannot be opposed to nature or in any manner hurtful to it.

Moreover, grace is not merely medicinal, nor simply restricted to repairing the damage done by original sin. Where sin abounded, grace superabounds. Whether, if man had not sinned, God would have become incarnate or not is a question which we need not raise here, any more than the question whether God could or could not, congruously with his known attributes, have created man in what the theologians call the state of pure nature, as he is now born, *seclusa ratione culpæ et pœnæ,*[3] and therefore for a natural beatitude; for it is agreed on all hands that he did not so create him, and that the incarnation is not restricted in its intention or effect to the simple redemption of man from sin, original or actual, and his restoration to the integrity of his nature, lost by the prevarication of Adam. All schools teach that as a matter of fact the incarnation looks higher and farther, and is intended to elevate man to a supernatural order of spiritual life, and to secure him a supernatural beatitude, a life and beatitude to which his nature alone is not adequate.

Man regarded in the present decree of God has not only his origin in the supernatural, but also his last end or final cause. He proceeds from God as first cause, and returns to him as final cause. The oriental religions, the Egyptian, Hindu, Chinese, and the Buddhist, etc., all say as much, but fall into the error of making him proceed from God by way of emanation, generation, formation, or development, and his return to him as final cause, absorption in him, as the stream in the fountain, or the total loss of individuality, which, instead of being perfect beatitude in God, is absolute personal annihilation. But these religions have originated in a truth which they misapprehend, pervert, or travesty. Man, both Christian faith and sound philosophy teach us, proceeds from God as first cause by way of creation proper, and returns to him as final cause without absorption in him or loss of individuality. God creates man, not indeed an independent, but a substantive existence, capable of acting from his own centre as a second cause; and however intimate may be his relation with God, he is always distinguishable from him, and can no more be confounded with him as his final cause than he can be confounded with him as his first cause. Not only the race but the individual man returns to God, and finds in him his supreme good, and individually united to him, through the Word made flesh, enjoys personally in him an infinite beatitude.

God alike as first cause and as final cause is supernatural. And man therefore can neither exist nor find his beatitude without the intervention of the supernatural. He can no more rise to a supernatural beatitude or beatitude in God without the supernatural act of God, than he could begin to exist without that act. The natural is created and finite, and can be no medium of the infinite or supernatural. Man, as he is in the present decree of God, cannot obtain his end, rise to his supreme good or beatitude, without a supernatural medium. This medium in relation to the end, or in the teleological order, is the Word made flesh, God incarnate, Jesus Christ, the only mediator between God and men. Jesus Christ is not only the medium of our redemption from sin and the consequences of the fall, but of our elevation to the plane of a supernatural destiny, and perfect beatitude in the intimate and eternal possession of God, who is both our good and the Good in itself. This is a higher, an infinitely greater good than man could ever have attained to by his natural powers even in a state of integral nature, or if he had not sinned, and had had no need of a Redeemer; and hence the apostle tells us where sin abounded grace superabounded, and the church sings on Holy Saturday, *O felix culpa.*[4] The incarnate Word is the medium of this superabounding good, as the Father is its principle and the Holy Ghost its consummator.

Whether grace is something created, as St. Thomas maintains, and as would seem to follow from the doctrine of infused virtues asserted by the Council of Trent, or the direct action of the Holy Ghost within us, as was held by Petrus Lombardus,[5] the Master of Sentences, it is certain that the medium of all grace given to enable us to attain to beatitude is the Incarnation, and hence is termed by theologians *gratia Christi,* and distinguishable from the simple *gratia Dei,* which is bestowed on man in the initial order, or order of genesis, commonly the natural order, because its explication is by natural generation, and not as the teleological order, by the election of grace. The grace of Christ by which our nature is elevated to the plane of the supernatural, and enabled to attain to a supernatural end or beatitude, cannot be opposed to nature, or in any sense antagonistic to nature. Nature is not denied or injured because its author prepares for it a greater, an infinitely greater than a natural or created good, to which no created nature by its own powers, however exalted, could ever attain. Men may doubt if such a good remains for those who love our Lord Jesus Christ and by his grace follow him in the regeneration, but nobody can pretend that the proffer of such good, and the gift of the means to attain it, can be any injury or slight to nature.

There is no doubt that in the flesh which resists grace, because grace would subordinate it to reason and free-will, but this, though the practical difficulty, is not the real dialectic difficulty which men feel in the way of accepting the Christian doctrine of grace. Men object to it on the ground that it substitutes grace for nature, and renders nature good for nothing in the Christian or teleological order—the order of return to God as our last end or final cause. We have anticipated and refuted this objection in condemning the pantheistic doctrine of the orientals, and by maintaining that the return to God is without absorption in him, or loss of our individuality or distinct personality.

The beatitude which the regenerate soul attains to in God by the grace of our Lord Jesus Christ is the beatitude of that very individual soul that proceeds, by way of creation, from God. The saints by being blest in God are not lost in him, but retain in glory their original human nature and their identical personal existence. This the church plainly teaches in her *cultus sanctorum*. She invokes the saints in heaven, and honors them as individuals distinct from God, and as distinct personalities; and hence, she teaches us that the saints are sons of God only by adoption, and, though living by and in the Incarnate Word, are not themselves Christ, or the Word made flesh. In the Incarnation, the human personality was absorbed or superseded by the divine personality, so that the human nature assumed had a divine but no human personality. The Word assumed human nature, not a human person. Hence the error of the Nestorians and Adoptionists,[6] and also of those who in our own times are willing to call Mary the mother of Christ, but shrink from calling her Θεοτόκος, or the Mother of God. But in the saints, who are not hypostatically united to the Word, human nature not only remains unchanged, but retains its human personality; and the saints are as really men, as really human persons in glory, as they were while in the flesh, and are the same human persons that they were before either regeneration or glorification. The church, by her *cultus sanctorum,* teaches us to regard the glorified saints as still human persons, and to honor them as human persons, who by the aid of grace have merited the honor we give them. We undoubtedly honor God in his saints as well as in all his works of nature or of grace; but this honor of God in his works is that of *latria,* and is not that which is rendered to the saints.[7] In the *cultus sanctorum,* we not only honor him in his works, but we also honor the saints themselves for their own personal worth, acquired not, indeed, without grace, but still acquired by them, and is as much theirs as if it had been acquired by their unassisted natural powers; for our natural powers are from God as first cause, no less than grace itself, only grace is from him through the Incarnation. You say, it is objected, that grace supposes nature, *gratia supponit naturam,* yet St. Paul calls the regeneration a new creation, and the regenerated soul a new creature. Very true; yet he says this not because the nature given in generation is destroyed or superseded in regeneration, but because regeneration no more than generation can be initiated or sustained without the divine creative act; because generation can never become of itself regeneration, or make the first motion toward it. Without the divine regenerative act we cannot enter upon our teleological or spiritual life, but must remain for ever in the order of generation, and infinitely below our destiny, as is the case with the reprobate or those who die unregenerate. But it is the person born of Adam that is regenerated, that is translated into the kingdom of God's dear Son, and that is the recipient of regenerating, persevering, and glorifying grace. This is the point we insist on; for, if so, the objection that grace destroys or supersedes nature is refuted. The whole of Catholic theology teaches that grace assists nature, but does not create or substitute a new nature, as is evident from the fact that it teaches that in regeneration even we must concur with grace, that we can resist it, and after regeneration lose all that grace confers, apostatize from the faith, and fall even below the condition of the unregenerate. This would be impossible, if we did not retain our nature as active in and after regeneration. In this life it is certain that regeneration is a moral, a spiritual, not a physical change, and that our reason and will are emancipated from the bondage of sin, and are simply enabled to act from a higher plane and gain a higher end than it could unassisted; but it is the natural person that is enabled and that acts in gaining the higher end. Grace, then, does not in this life destroy or supersede nature, and the authorized *cultus* of the saints proves that it does not in the glorified saint or life to come.

The same conclusion follows from the fact that regeneration only fulfils generation. "I am not come," said our Lord, "to destroy, but to fulfil." The creative act, completed, as to the order of procession of existences from God, in the Incarnation or hypostatic union, which closes the initial order and institutes the teleological, includes both the procession of existences from God and their return to him. It is completed, fulfilled, and consummated only in regeneration and glorification. If the nature that proceeds from God is changed or superseded by grace, the creative act is not fulfilled, for that which proceeds from God does not return to him. The initial man must himself return, or with regard to him the creative act remains initial and incomplete. In the first order, man is only initial or inchoate, and is a complete, a perfect man only when he has returned to God as his final cause. To maintain that it is not this initial man that returns, but, if the supposition be possible, another than he, or something substituted for him, and that has not by way of creation proceeded from God, would deny the very purpose and end of the Incarnation, and the very idea of redemption, regeneration, and glorification, the grace of Christ, and leave man without any means of redemption or deliverance from sin, or of fulfilling his destiny—the doom of the damned in hell. The destruction or change of man's nature is the destruction of man himself, the destruction of his identity, his human personality; yet St. Paul teaches, Rom. viii. 30, that the persons called are they who are redeemed and glorified: "Whom he predestinated, them also he called; and whom he called, them also he justified; and whom he justified, them also he glorified."

We can, indeed, do nothing in relation to our end without the grace of Christ; but, with that grace freely given and strengthening us, it is equally certain that we can work, and work even meritoriously, or else how could heaven be promised us as a reward? Yet it is so promised: "He that cometh to God must believe that he is, and is the rewarder of them that seek him." (Heb. xi. 6.) Moses "looked to the reward"; David had respect to the divine "retributions"; and all Christians, as nearly all heathen, believe in a future state of rewards and punishments. We are exhorted to flee to Christ and obey him that we may escape hell and gain heaven. The grace by which we are born again and are enabled to merit is unquestionably gratuitous, for grace is always gratuitous, *omnino gratis,* as say the theologians, and we can do nothing to merit it, no more than we could do something to merit our creation from nothing; but though gratuitous, a free gift of God, grace is bestowed on or infused into a subject already existing in the order of generation or natural order, and we can act by it, and can and do, if faithful to it, merit heaven or eternal life. Hence says the apostle, "Work out your salvation with fear and trembling; for it is God that worketh in you both to will and to do, or to accomplish." (Philip. ii. 12.) But this no more implies that the willing and doing in the order of regeneration are not ours than that our acting in the order of nature is not ours because we can even in that order act, whether for good or for evil, only by the divine concurrence.

The heterodox confound the gift of grace by which we are able to merit the reward with the reward itself; hence they maintain, because we can merit nothing without grace, that we can merit nothing even with it, and that we are justified by faith alone, which is the free gift of God, conferred on whom he wills, and that grace is irresistible, and once in grace we are always in grace. But St. James tells us that we are "justified by our works, and not by faith only, for faith without works is dead." (St. James ii. 14–25.) Are we who work by grace and merit the reward the same *we* tha⁺ prior to regeneration sinned and were under wrath? Is it we who by the aid of grace merit the reward, or is it the grace in us? If the grace itself, how can it be said that *we* are rewarded? If the reward is given not to us who sinned, but to the new person or new nature into which grace is said to change us, how can it be said that *we* either merit or are rewarded? Man has his specific nature, and if you destroy or change that specific nature, you annihilate him as man, instead of aiding his return to God as his final cause. The theologians treat grace not as a new nature or a new faculty bestowed on nature, but as a *habitus,* or habit, an infused habit indeed, not an acquired habit, but none the less a habit on that account, which changes not, transforms not nature, but gives it, as do all habits, a power or facility of doing what without it would exceed its strength. The subject of the habit is the human soul, and that which acts by, under, or with the habit is also the human soul, not the habit. The soul, as before receiving it, is the actor, but it acts with an increased strength, and does what before it could not; yet its nature is simply strengthened, not changed. The general idea of *habit* must be preserved throughout. The personality is not in the habit, but in the rational nature of him into whom the habit is infused by the Holy Ghost. In our Lord there are the two natures; but in him the divine personality assumes the human nature, and is always the subject acting, whether acting in the human nature or in the divine. In the regenerated there are also the human and the divine; but the human, if I may so speak, assumes the divine, and retains from first to last its own personality, as is implied in the return to God without absorption in him or loss of personal individuality, and in the fact that, though without grace, we cannot concur with grace, yet by the aid of grace we can and must concur with it the moment we come to the use of reason, or it is not effectual. The sacraments are, indeed, efficacious *ex opere operato,* not by the faith or virtue of the recipient, but only in case the will, as in infants, opposes no obstacle to the grace they signify. Yet even in infants the concurrence of the will is required when they come to the use of reason, and the refusal to elicit the act loses the habit infused by baptism. The baptized infant must concur with grace as soon as capable of a rational act.

The heterodox who are exclusive supernaturalists, because we cannot without grace concur with grace, deny that the concurrence is needed, and assert that grace is irresistible and overcomes all resistance, and, as *gratia victrix,*[8] subjects the will. Hence they hold that, in faith, regeneration, justification, sanctification, nature does nothing, and all that is done is done by sovereign grace even in spite of nature; but the fact on which they rely is not sufficient to sustain their theory. The schoolmen, for the convenience of teaching, divide and subdivide grace till we are in danger of losing sight of its essential unity. They tell us of prevenient grace, or the grace that goes before and excites the will; of assisting grace, the grace that aids the will when excited to elect to concur with grace; and efficacious grace, the grace that renders the act of concurrence effectual. But these three graces are really one and the same grace, and the *gratia præveniens,* when not resisted, becomes immediately *gratia adjuvans,* and aids the will to concur with grace, and, if concurred with, it becomes, *ipso facto* and immediately, *gratia efficax.* It needs no grace to resist grace, and none, it would seem to follow from the freedom of the will, *not* to resist it. Freedom of the will, according to the decision of the church in the case of the *gratia victrix* of the Jansenists, implies the power to will the contrary, and, if free to resist it, why not free not to resist? There is, it seems to us, a real distinction between not willing to resist and willing to concur. Nothing in nature compels or forces the will to resist, for its natural operation is to the good, as that of the intellect is to the true. The grace excites it to action, and, if it do not will to resist, the grace is present to assist it to elect to comply. If this be tenable, and we see not why it is not, both the aid of grace and the freedom and activity of the will are asserted, are saved, are harmonized, and the soul is elevated into the order of regeneration without any derogation either from nature or from grace, or lesion to either.

We are well aware of the old question debated in Catholic schools, whether grace is to be regarded as *auxilium quod* or as *auxilium quo;*[9] but it is not necessary either to inquire what was the precise sense of the question debated, or to enter into any discussion of its merits, for both schools held the Catholic faith, which asserts the freedom of the will, and both held that grace is *auxilium,* and therefore an aid given to nature, not its destruction, nor its change into something else. The word *auxilium,* or aid, says of itself all that we are contending for. St. Paul says, indeed, when reluctantly comparing his labors with those of the other apostles, that he had labored more abundantly than they all, but adds, "Yet not I, but the grace of God with me." But he recognizes himself, for he says, "grace with *me*"; and his sense is easily explained by what he says in a passage already quoted, namely, "Work out your own salvation; for it is God that worketh in you to will and to do," or to accomplish, and also by what he says in the text itself. (I Cor. xv. I,) "By the grace of God, I am what I am";[10] which has primary reference to his calling to be an apostle. God by his grace works in us to will and to do, and we can will or do nothing in relation to our final end, as has been explained, without his grace; but, nevertheless, it is *we* who will and do. Hence St. Paul could say to St. Timothy, "I have fought a good fight, I have finished my course, I have kept the faith. For the rest, there is laid up for me a crown of justice, which the Lord, the just Judge, will render to me at that day: and not to me only, but to them also who love his coming." (2 Tim. iv. 7, 8.) Here St. Paul speaks of himself as the actor and as the recipient of the crown. St. Augustine says that God, in crowning the saints, "crowns his own gifts," but evidently means that he crowns them for what they have become by his gifts; and, as it is only by virtue of his gifts that they have become worthy of crowns, their glory redounds primarily to him, and only in a subordinate sense to themselves. There is, in exclusive supernaturalists and exaggerated ascetics, an unsuspected pantheism, no less sophistical and uncatholic than the pantheism of our pseudo-ontologists. The characteristic mark of pantheism is not simply the denial of creation, but the denial of the creation of substances capable of acting as second causes. In the order of regeneration as in the order of generation we are not indeed primary, but are really secondary causes; and the denial of this fact, and the assertion of God as the direct and immediate actor from first to last, is pure pantheism. This is as true in the order of regeneration as in the order of generation, though in the order of grace it is thought to be a proof of piety, when, in fact, it denies the very subject that can be pious. Count de Maistre[11] somewhere says, "The worst error against grace is that of asserting too much grace." We must exist, and exist as second causes, to be the recipients of grace, or to be able even with grace to be pious toward God, or the subject of any other virtue. In the regeneration we *do* by the aid of grace, but we are, nevertheless, the doers, whence it follows that regeneration no more than generation is wholly supernatural. Regeneration supposes generation, takes it up to itself and completes it, otherwise the first Adam would have no relation to the second Adam, and man would find no place in the order of regeneration, which would be the more surprising since the order itself originates in the Incarnation, in the God-Man, who is its Alpha and Omega, its beginning and end.

Many people are, perhaps, misled on this subject by the habit of restricting the word *natural* exclusively to the procession of existences from God and what pertains to the initial order of creation, and the word *supernatural* to the return of existences to God as their last end, and the means by which they return or attain that end and complete the cycle of existence or the creative act. The procession is initial, the return is teleological. The initial is called natural, because it is developed and carried on by natural generation; the telological is called supernatural, because it is developed and carried on by grace, and the election by grace takes the place of hereditary descent. This is well enough, except when we have to deal with persons who insist on separating—not simply distinguishing, but separating, the natural and the supernatural, and on denying either the one or the other. But, in reality, what we ordinarily call the natural is not wholly natural, nor what we call the supernatural is wholly supernatural. Strictly speaking, the supernatural is God himself and what he does with no other medium than his own eternal Word, that is, without any created medium or agency of second causes; the natural is that which is created and what God does through the medium of second causes or created agencies, called by physicists natural laws. Thus, creation is a supernatural fact, because effected immediately by God himself; generation is a natural fact, because effected by God mediately by natural laws or second causes; the hypostatic union, or the assumption of flesh by the Word, which completes the creative act in the initial order and institutes the teleological or final order, is supernatural; all the operations of grace are supernatural, though operations in and with nature; the sacraments are supernatural, for they are effective *ex opere operato,* and the natural parts are only signs of the grace, not its natural medium. The water used in baptism is not a natural medium of the grace of regeneration; it is made by the divine will the sign, though an appropriate sign, of it; the grace itself is communicated by the direct action of the Holy Ghost, which is supernatural. Regeneration, as well as its complement, glorification, is supernatural, for it cannot be naturally developed from generation, and regeneration does not necessarily carry with it glorification; for it does not of itself, as St. Augustine teaches, insure the grace of perseverance, since grace is *omnino gratis,*[12] and only he that perseveres to the end will be glorified. Hence, even in the teleological order, the natural, that is, the human, reason and will have their share, and without their activity the end would not and could not be gained. Revelation demands the active reception of reason, or else it might as well be made to an ox or a horse as to a man; and the will that perseveres to the end is the human will, though the human will be regenerated by grace. Wherever you see the action of the creature as second cause you see the natural, and wherever you see the direct action of God, whether as sustaining the creature or immediately producing the effect, you see the supernatural.

The fact that God works in us to will and to do, or that we can do nothing in the order of regeneration without grace moving and assisting us, no more denies the presence and activity of nature than does the analogous fact that we can do nothing even in the order of generation without the supernatural presence and concurrence of the Creator. We are as apt to forget that God has any hand in the action of nature as we are to deny that where God acts nature can ever cooperate; we are apt to conclude that the action of the one excludes that of the other, and to run either into Pelagianism on the one hand, or into Calvinism or Jansenism on the other; and we find a difficulty in harmonizing in our minds the divine sovereignty of God and human liberty. We cannot, on this occasion, enter fully into the question of their conciliation. Catholic faith requires us to assert both, whether we can or cannot see how they can coexist. We think, however, that we can see a distinction between the divine government of a free active subject and of an inanimate and passive subject. God governs each subject according to the nature he has given it; and, if he has given man a free nature, his government, although absolute, must leave human freedom intact, and to man the capacity of exercising his own free activity, without running athwart the divine sovereignty. How this can be done, we do not undertake to say.

But be this as it may, there is no act even in the natural order that is or can be performed without the assistance of the supernatural; for we are absolutely dependent on the creative act of God in everything, in those very acts in which we act most freely. The grace of God is as necessary as the grace of Christ. God has not created a universe, and made it, when once created, capable of going alone as a self-moving machine. He creates substances, indeed, capable of acting as second causes; but these substances can do nothing, are nothing as separated from the creative act of God that produces them, upholds them, is present in them, and active in all their acts, even in the most free determinations of the will. Without this divine presence, always an efficient presence, and this divine activity in all created activities, there is and can be no natural activity or action, any more than, in relation to our last end, there can be the first motion toward grace without

grace. The principle of action in both orders is strictly analogous, and
our acting with grace or by the assistance of grace in the order of
regeneration is as natural as is our acting by the divine presence and
concurrence in the order of generation. The human activity in either
order is equally natural, and in neither is it possible or explicable
without the constant presence and activity of the supernatural. The
two orders, the initial and the teleological, then, are not antagonistical
to each other, are not based on two mutually destructive principles,
but are really two distinct parts, as we so often say, of one dialectic whole.

The Holy Scriptures, since God is *causa eminens,* the cause of
causes, the first cause operative in all second causes, speak of God as
doing this or that, without always taking special note of the fact that,
though he really does it, he does it through the agency of second causes
or the activity of creatures. This is frequently the case in the Scriptures
of the Old Testament, and sometimes, though less frequently, in the
New Testament, though never in either without something to indicate
whether it is the direct and immediate or the indirect and mediate
action of God that is meant. Paying no attention to this, many overlook the distinction altogether, and fall into a sort of pantheistic fatalism, and practically deny the freedom and activity of second causes, as
is the case with Calvin when he declares God to be the author of sin,
which on his own principles is absurd, for he makes the will of God the
criterion of right, and therefore whatever God does must be right, and
nothing that is right can be sin. On the other hand, men, fixing their
attention on the agency of second causes, overlook the constant presence and activity of the first cause, treat second causes as independent
causes, or as if they were themselves first cause, and fall into pure
naturalism, which is only another name for atheism. The universe is
not a clock or a watch, but even a clock or a watch generates not its
own motive power; the maker in either has only so constructed it as to
utilize for his purpose a motive power that exists and operates independently both of him and of his mechanism.

Men speak of nature as supernaturalized in regeneration, and
hence assume that grace transforms nature; but in this there must be
some misunderstanding or exaggeration. In regeneration we are born
into the order of the end, or started, so to speak, on our return to God
as our final cause. The principle of this new birth, which is grace, and
the end, which is God, are supernatural; but our nature is not changed
except as to its motives and the assistance it receives, though it receives
in baptism an indelible mark not easy to explain. This follows from the
Incarnation. In the Incarnation our nature is raised to be the nature of

God, and yet remains human nature, as is evident from the condemnation by the church of the monophysites and the monothelites.
Catholic faith requires us to hold that the two natures, the human and
the divine, remain for ever distinct in the one divine person of the
Word. Some prelates thought to save their orthodoxy by maintaining
that, after his resurrection, the two natures of our Lord became fused
or transformed into one theandric nature; but they did not succeed,
and were condemned and deposed. The monothelites asserted that
there was in Christ two natures indeed, but only one will, or that his
human will was absorbed in the divine. But they also were condemned
as heretics. Our Lord, addressing the Father, says, "Not my will, but
thine be done," thus plainly implying a human will distinct from,
though not contrary to, the divine will. Can we suppose that the grace
of regeneration or even of glorification works a greater change of
nature in us than the grace of union worked in our nature as assumed
by the Word? If human nature and human will remain in Christ after
the hypostatic union, so that to regard him after his resurrection as
having but one will or one theandric nature is a heresy, how can we
hold without heresy that grace, which flows from that union, either
destroys our nature or transforms it into a theandric or supernaturalized nature?

Let us understand, then, that grace neither annihilates nor supersedes or transforms our nature. It is our nature that is redeemed or
delivered from the bondage of sin, our nature that is translated from
the kingdom of darkness into the kingdom of light, our nature that is
reborn, that is justified, that by the help of grace perseveres to the end,
that is rewarded, that is glorified, and enters into the glory of our Lord.
It then persists in regeneration and glorification as one and the same
human nature, with its human reason, its human will, its human
personality, its human activity, only assisted by grace to act from a
supernatural principle to or for a supernatural end. The assistance is
supernatural, and so is the end; but that which receives the assistance,
profits by it, and attains the end, is human nature, the man that was
born of Adam as well as reborn of Christ, the second Adam.

We have dwelt long, perhaps to tediousness, upon this point,
because we have wished to efface entirely the fatal impression that
nature and grace are mutually antagonistic, and to make it appear that
the two orders, commonly called the natural and the supernatural, are
both mutually consistent parts of one whole; that grace simply completes nature; and that Christianity is no anomaly, no after-thought, or
succedaneum, in the original design of creation.

The heterodox, with their doctrine of total depravity, and the essential corruption or evil of nature, and their doctrine, growing out of this assumed depravity or corruption, of irresistible grace, and the inactivity or passivity of man in faith and justification, obscure this great fact, and make men regard nature as a failure, and that to save some God had to supplant and create a new nature in its place. A more immoral doctrine, or one more fatal to all human activity, is not conceivable, if it could be really and seriously believed and acted on prior to regeneration, which is impossible. The heterodox are better than their system. The system teaches that all our works before regeneration are sins; even our prayers are unacceptable, some say, an abomination to the Lord, and consequently, there is no use in striving to be virtuous. After regeneration there is no need of our activity, for grace is inamissible, and if really born again, sin as much as we will, our salvation is sure, for the sins of the regenerated are not reputed to them or counted as sins. There is no telling how many souls this exclusive and exaggerated supernaturalism (which we owe to the reformers of the sixteenth century) has destroyed, or how many persons it has deterred from returning to the Catholic Church by the common impression, that, since she asserts original sin and the necessity of grace, she holds and teaches the same frightful system. Men who are able to think, and accustomed to sober reflection, find themselves unable to embrace Calvinism, and, confounding Calvinism with Christianity, reject Christianity itself, and fall into a meagre rationism, a naked naturalism, or, worst of all, an unreasoning indifferentism; yet there is no greater mistake than to suppose that the church holds it or has the slightest sympathy with it. We have wished to mark clearly the difference between it and her teaching. Christian asceticism, when rightly understood, is not based on the assumption that nature is evil, and needs to be destroyed, repressed, or changed. It is based on two great ideas, liberty and sacrifice. It is directed not to the destruction of the flesh or the body, for in the creed we profess to believe in the "resurrection of the flesh." Our Lord assumed flesh in the womb of the Virgin; he had a real body, ascended into heaven with it, and in it sitteth at the right hand of the Father Almighty. He feeds and nourishes us with it in Holy Communion; and it is by eating his flesh and drinking his blood that our spiritual life is sustained and strengthened. Our own bodies shall rise again, and, spiritualized after the manner of Christ's glorious body, shall, reunited to the soul, live for ever. We show that this is our belief by the honor we pay to the relics of the saints. This sacred flesh, these sacred bones, which we cherish with so much tender piety, shall live again, and reenter the glorified body of the saint. Matter is not evil, as the Platonists teach, and as the false asceticism of the heathen assumes, and with which Christian asceticism has no affinity, though many who ought to know better pretend to the contrary. The Christian ascetic aims, indeed, at a moral victory over the flesh, labors by the help of grace to liberate the soul from its bondage, to gain the command of himself, to be at all times free to maintain the truth, and to keep the commandments of God; to bring his body into subjection to the soul, to reduce the appetites and passions under the control of his reason and will, but never to destroy them or in any manner to injure his material body. Far less does he seek to abnegate, destroy, or repress either will or reason, in order to give grace freer and fuller scope; he only labors to purify and strengthen both by grace. Nature is less abnormal, purer, stronger, more active, more energetic in the true ascetic than in those who take no pains to train and purify it under the influence of divine grace.

The principle of all sacrifice is love. It was because God so loved men that he gave his only-begotten Son to die for them that they might not perish, but have everlasting life. It was love that died on the cross for our redemption. Nothing is hard or difficult to love, and there is nothing love will not do or sacrifice for the object loved. The saint can never make for his Lord a sacrifice great enough to satisfy his love, and gives up for him the most precious things he has, not because they are evil or it would be sin in him to retain them; not because his Lord needs them, but because they are the most costly sacrifice he can make, and he in making the sacrifice can give some proof of his love. The chief basis of monastic life is sacrifice. The modern notion that monastic institutions were designed to be a sort of hospital for infirm souls is essentially false. As a rule, a virtue that cannot sustain itself in the world will hardly acquire firmness and strength in a monastery. The first monks did not retire from the world because unfit to live in it, but because the world restrained their liberty, and because it afforded them no adequate field for the heroic sacrifices to which they aspired. Their austerities, which we so little robust as Christians, accustomed to pamper our bodies, and to deny ourselves nothing, regard as sublime folly, if not with a shudder of horror, were heroic sacrifices to the Spouse of the soul, for whom they wished to give up everything but their love. They rejoiced in affliction for his sake, and they wished to share, as we have already said, with him in the passion and cross which he endured for our sake, so as to be as like him as possible. There are saints to-day in monasteries, and out of monasteries in the world, living in our midst, whom we know not or little heed, who understand the meaning of this word *sacrifice,* and make as great and as pure sacrifices, though perhaps in other forms, and as thoroughly forego their own pleasure, and as cheerfully give up what costs them the most to give up, as did the old Fathers of the Desert. But, if we know them not, God knows them and loves them.

Yet we pretend not to deny that many went into monasteries from other motives, from weakness, disappointed affection, disgust of the world, and some to hide their shame, and to expiate by a life of penance their sins; but, if the monastery often sheltered such as these, it was not for such that it was originally designed. In process of time, monastic institutions, when they became rich, were abused, as often the priesthood itself, and treated by the nobles as a provision for younger sons or portionless daughters. We may at times detect in ascetics an exaggeration of the supernatural element and an underrating if not a neglect of the natural, we may find, chiefly in modern times, a tendency amongst the pious and devout to overlook the fact that manliness, robustness, and energy of mind and character enter as an important element in the Christian life; but the tendency in this direction is not catholic, though observed to some extent among Catholics. It originates in the same causes that originated the Calvinistic or Jansenistic heresy, and has been strengthened by the exaggerated assertion of the human and natural elements caused by the reaction of the human mind against an exclusive and exaggerated supernaturalism. The rationalism and humanitarianism of the last century and the present are only the reaction of human nature against the exaggerated supernaturalism of the Reformers and their descendants, the Jansenists, who labored to demolish nature to make way for grace, and to annihilate man in order to assert God. Each has an element of truth, but, neither having the whole truth, each makes war on the other, and alternately gains a victory and undergoes a defeat. Unhappily, neither will listen to the church who accepts the truth and rejects the exclusiveness of each, and harmonizes and completes the truth of both in the unity and catholicity of the faith once delivered to the saints. The Catholic faith is the reconciler of all opposites. These alternate victories and defeats go on in the world outside of the church; but it would be strange if they did not have some echo among Catholics, living, as they do, in the midst of the combatants, and in constant literary and intellectual intercourse with them. They create some practical difficulties for Catholics which are not always properly appreciated. We cannot assert the natural, rational, and the human element of the church without helping, more or less, the exclusive rationalists or naturalists who deny the supernatural; and we can hardly oppose them with the necessary vigor and determination without

seeming at least to favor their opponents, the exclusive supernaturalists, who reject reason and deny the natural. It is this fact very likely
that has kept Catholics for the most part during the last century and
the present on the defensive; and as, during this period, the anti-
supernaturalists have been the most formidable enemy of the church,
it is no wonder if the mass of devout Catholics have shown some
tendency to exaggerate the supernatural, and been shy of asserting as
fully as faith warrants the importance of the rational and the natural,
or if they have paid less attention to the cultivation of the human side
of religion than is desirable.

Some allowance must be made for the new position in which
Catholics for a century or more have been placed, and it would be very
wrong to censure them with severity, even if we found them failing to
show themselves all at once equal to the new duties imposed upon
them. The breaking up of old governments and institutions, founded
by Catholic ancestors, the political, social, and industrial revolutions
that have been and still are going on, must have, to some extent,
displaced the Catholic mind, and required it, so to speak, to ease itself,
or to take a new and difficult observation, and determine its future
course. Catholics to-day stand between the old, which was theirs, and
which is passing away, and the new, which is rising, and which is not
yet theirs. They must needs be partially paralyzed, and at a momentary
loss to know what course to take. Naturally conservative, as all men
are who have something to lose or on which to rely, their sympathies
are with the past, they have not been able as yet to accept the new state
of things, and convert regrets into hopes. A certain hesitation marks
their conduct, as if in doubt whether to stand out against the new at all
hazards, and, if need be, fall martyrs to a lost cause, or to accept it and
do the best they can with it. In this country, where Catholicity is not
associated with any sort of political institutions, and Catholics have no
old civilization to retain or any new order to resist, we, unless educated
abroad, are hardly able to appreciate the doubts, hesitations, and discouragements of Catholics in the old world, and to make the proper
allowances if at times they seem to attach as Catholics undue importance to the political and social changes going on around them, to be
too despondent, and more disposed to cry out against the wickedness
of the age, to fold their hands, and wait for Providence to rearrange all
things for them without their coöperation, than to look the changes
events have produced full in the face, and to exert themselves, with the
help of grace, to bring order out of the new chaos, as their brave old
ancestors did out of the chaos that followed the irruption of the north-

ern barbarians, and the breaking up of the Græco-Roman civilization. It is no light thing to see the social and political world in which we have lived, and with which we have been accustomed to associate the interests of religion and society falling in ruins under our very eyes, and we must be pardoned if for a moment we feel that all is gone or going.

But Catholic energy can never be long paralyzed, and already the Catholics of Europe are arousing themselves from their apathy, recovering their courage, and beginning to feel aware that the church depends on nothing temporary, is identified with no political or social organization, and can survive all the mutations of the world around her. Leading Catholics in Europe, instead of wasting their strength in vain regrets for a past that is gone, or in vainer efforts to restore what can no longer be restored, are beginning to adjust themselves to the present, and to labor to command the future. They are leaving the dead to bury their dead, and preparing to follow their Lord in the new work to be done for the new and turbulent times in which their lot is cast. "All these things are against me," said the patriarch Jacob, and yet they proved to be all for him and his family. Who knows but the untoward events of the last century and the present will turn out for the interests of religion, and that another Joseph may be able to say to their authors, "Ye meant it for evil, but God meant it for good?"[13]

In all great political and social revolutions there must always be a moment when men may reasonably doubt whether duty calls them to labor to retain what is passing away, or whether they shall suffer it to be buried with honor, and betake themselves with faith and hope and courage to what has supplanted it. That moment has passed in the Old World, and nothing remains but to make the best of the present, and to labor to reconstruct the future in the best way possible. Happily for us, the church, though she may lose province after province, nation after nation, and be driven to take refuge in the catacombs cannot be broken up, or her divine strength and energy impaired. While she remains, we have God with us, and our case can never be desperate. The church has seen darker days than any she now experiences; civilization has been much nearer its ruin than it is now in Europe, and Catholics have now all the means to surmount present difficulties, which sufficed them once to conquer the world. There is no sense in despondency. Cannot the millions of Catholics do to-day what twelve fishermen of Galilee did? Is the successor of Peter to-day more helpless than was Peter himself, when he entered Rome with his staff to preach in the proud capitol of heathendom the crucified Redeemer? The same God that was with Peter, and gave efficacy to his preaching, is with his successor; and we who live to-day have, if we seek it, all the divine support, and more than all the human means, that those Catholics had who subdued the barbarians and laid the foundation of Christian Europe. What they did we may do, if, with confidence in God, we set earnestly about doing it. The world is not so bad now as it was in the first century or in the sixth century; and there is as strong faith, as ardent piety, in this age, as in any age that has gone before it. Never say, "We have fallen on evil times." All times are evil to the weak, the cowardly, the despondent; and all times are good to the strong, the brave, the hopeful, who dare use the means God puts into their hands, and are prepared to do first the duty that lies nearest them.

We see many movements that indicate that our European brethren are regaining their courage, and, counting the past, so glorious for Catholics, as beyond recovery, are endeavoring to do what they can in and for the present, quietly, calmly, without noise or ostentation; and they will not need to labor long before they will see the "truths crushed to the earth rise again," and a new order, Phœnix-like, rising from the ashes of the old, more resplendent in beauty and worth, more in harmony with the divine spirit of the church, and more favorable to the freedom and dignity of man. Truth dies never. "The eternal years of God are hers." The Omnipotent reigns, and thus far in the history of the church, what seemed her defeat, has proved for her a new and more brilliant victory. The church never grows old, and we can afford to be patient though earnest in her service. The spirit of God never ceases to hover over the chaos, and order, though disturbed for a time, is sure, soon or late, to reappear.

We feel that we have very inadequately discussed the great question of nature and grace, the adequate discussion of which is far beyond the reach of such feeble abilities and such limited theological attainments as ours; but we have aimed to set forth as clearly and as simply as we could what we have been taught by our Catholic masters on the relation of the natural to the supernatural; and if we have succeeded in showing that there is no antagonism between nature and grace, the natural and the supernatural, the divine sovereignty and human liberty, and that we can be at once pious and manly, energetic as men, and humble and devout as Christians, or if we have thrown out any suggestions that will aid others in showing it to the intelligence of our age, and if we have been able to speak a word of comfort and hope to our brethren who find themselves in a position in which it is difficult to determine how to act, our purpose will have been accomplished, and we shall have done no great but some slight service to the cause to which we feel that we are devoted heart and soul. We have aimed to avoid saying anything that could wound the susceptibilities of any Catholic school of theology, and to touch as lightly as possible on matters debated among Catholics. We hope we have succeeded; for these are times in which Catholics need to be united in action as well as in faith.

Notes: Nature and Grace

1. Brownson, "Rome and the World," *Catholic World* 6 (October 1867): 1–19.
2. *Fomes peccati* in literal Latin is "the tinder of sin." Reference here is to the source of sin, that is, the inborn concupiscence of the newborn child which will ultimately issue in sin.
3. Latin for "separated by reason of guilt and punishment."
4. Latin for "O Happy Fault," a reference to the Fall. According to St. Ambrose who first used the phrase the Fall was happy because it led to Christ's redemption of humanity.
5. Peter Lombard (1095–1160) was a theologian whose *Book of Sentences,* which presents without much speculation the whole of Christian doctrine in one brief volume, was widely used in the Middle Ages as a source book for Christian theology.
6. Nestorians are followers of the heresy of Nestorius, Bishop of Constantinople (d. 451). Nestorius held that in Christ there were two persons joined together. Mary, being human, could only be the mother of his humanity. She could not, therefore, be called Mother of God. Nestorius was condemned by the Council of Ephesus (451). Adoptionists were those who held that Christ as man is only the adopted son of God.
7. *Latria* is the homage or religious worship that is due to God alone. It is distinguished from *dulia,* which is reverence or homage that is due to the saints on account of their supernatural excellence and union with God, and from *hyperdulia,* which is special homage paid to Mary on account of her dignity as Mother of God.
8. Latin for "victorious grace."
9. *Auxilium quod* is literally "the help which." *Auxilium quo* is literally "the help by which" and usually refers to irresistible grace or the divine assistance, which inevitably brings about a result.
10. 1 Cor 15:10.
11. Joseph Marie de Maistre (1754–1821) was a French politician and philosophical writer who opposed the *philosophes* throughout his

life. He was leader of the anti-revolutionary movement in France and a prominent proponent of traditionalism. His masterpiece, *Du Pape* (1819), supported his doctrine of papal supremacy and became the charter of nineteenth-century ultramontanism.

12. Latin for "entirely gratuitous."

13. Gn 50:20.

A SELECTED BIBLIOGRAPHY

The best bibliography on Brownson, although it is by no means exhaustive, is in Thomas R. Ryan, C.PP.S., *Orestes A. Brownson: A Definitive Biography.* (Huntington, IN: Our Sunday Visitor, Inc., 1975), pp. 851–64.

WORKS BY BROWNSON

Boston Quarterly Review (1838–42).
Brownson's Quarterly Review (1844–64; 1873–75).
Henry F. Brownson, ed. *The Works of Orestes A. Brownson.* 20 vols. Detroit: Thorndike Nourse, 1882–87.
Alvan S. Ryan, ed. *The Brownson Reader.* New York: P. J. Kenedy and Sons, 1955.

WORKS ON BROWNSON

Brownson, Henry F. *The Early Life of Orestes A. Brownson, 1803–1844.* Detroit: Henry F. Brownson, 1898.
———. *The Middle Life of Orestes A. Brownson, 1845–1855.* Detroit: Henry F. Brownson, 1899.
———. *The Latter Life of Orestes A. Brownson, 1856–1876.* Detroit: Henry F. Brownson, 1900.
Capognigri, A. Robert. "Brownson and Emerson: Nature and History," *New England Quarterly* 28 (1945): 368–90.

Farrell, Bertin. *Orestes Brownson's Approach to the Problem of God. A Critical Examination in the Light of the Principles of St. Thomas Aquinas.* Washington, D.C.: The Catholic University of America Press, 1950.

Gilhooley, Leonard, C.F.X. *Contradiction and Dilemma. Orestes Brownson and the American Idea.* New York: Fordham University Press, 1972.

———, ed. *No Divided Allegiance: Orestes A. Brownson.* New York: Fordham University Press, 1978.

Hutchison, William R. *The Transcendentalist Ministers: Church Reform in the New England Renaissance.* New Haven: Yale University Press, 1959.

Lapati, Americo D. *Orestes Brownson.* Twaynes's United States Author Series, No. 88. New Haven, CT: College and University Press, 1965.

Leliaert, Richard M. "Brownson's Approach to God: The Catholic Period." *The Thomist* 40 (1976): 574–607.

Lewis, R.W.B. *The American Adam: Innocence, Tragedy, and Tradition in the Nineteenth Century.* Chicago: University of Chicago Press, 1955.

Maynard, Theodore. *Orestes Brownson. Yankee, Radical, Catholic.* New York: Macmillan Co., 1943.

Raemers, Sidney A. *America's Foremost Philosopher.* Benedictine Historical Monographs 5. Washington, D.C.: St. Anselm's Priory, 1931.

Robinson, David. *The Unitarians and the Universalists.* Westport, CT: Greenwood Press, 1985.

Rose, Anne C. *Transcendentalism as a Movement.* New Haven: Yale University Press, 1983.

Ryan, Alvin S. "Orestes Brownson: The Critique of Transcendentalism." In *American Classics Reconsidered: A Christian Appraisal.* Ed. Harold C. Gardner. New York, 1958.

Ryan, Thomas R., C.PP.S. *The Sailor's Snug Harbor: Studies in Brownson's Thought.* Westminster, MD, 1952.

———, ed. *Orestes Brownson on Saint Worship, the Worship of Mary.* Paterson, NJ, 1963.

———. *Orestes A. Brownson: A Definitive Biography.* Huntington, IN: Our Sunday Visitor Press, 1975.

———. *The Pope's Champion in America.* Chicago: Franciscan Herald Press, 1978.

Schlesinger, Jr., Arthur M. *A Pilgrim's Progress. Orestes A. Brownson.* Boston: Little, Brown, and Co., 1939.

Sveino, Per. *Orestes A. Brownson's Road to Catholicism.* New York: Humanities Press, 1970.

Wellek, René. "The Minor Transcendentalists and German Philosophy," *New England Quarterly* 15 (1942): 652–80.

INDEX TO INTRODUCTION*

* General Introduction to the book.

311

INDEX TO TEXTS

315

God's freedom, 248–49;
renewed to preach, 228–30;
theological discovery, 206–07;
Universalist sermons, 83–86,
86–88, 88–90, 95–101,
102–04, 104–14.

Calvin, John, 298
Calvinism, 59, 62, 64, 102–03,
243, 297, 300, 302
Carlyle, Thomas, 195–97, 200
Catholicism, 107, 265;
disappearance of, 155; mission
of, 155; and the poor, 264;
and Protestantism, 180;
revival of, 182
Catholics: defensive, 303; and
preaching, 263; and temporal
kingdom, 238
Causality, secondary, 289, 295
Children, 100–01
Christ: abstract Christ, 219; as
Christianity, 218; as example,
111–12; psychological, 202;
Son of God, literally, 220;
teaching action over belief, 108
Christian character, 107, 113–14
Christianity: of Christ, 164; of
church, 164; doing over
believing, 132–33; Emerson
on historical, 200–01;
practical 110–14; spirit and
form of, 142; spirit of reform,
134, 136, 143; theory of
107–10
Church: Body of Christ, 167;
doctrines of, 218; first
Christian, 126; future of, 163;
infallibility of, 172; and Jesus,
166; and kingdom, 268;
mission of, 170; no salvation

out of, 172; and political and
civil liberty, 174; and reason,
173; and reform, 136, 187;
and righteousness, 128; as
sect, 127; and state, 188;
supremacy of, 172; symbols
of, 218
Cicero, 112
Classes in society, 141–42
Clergy, the, 125, 138, 222, 142
Closet Companion, 72, 91n46
Communion of the Saints, 274,
281–82
"Concern of Mind," 62
Concupiscence, 285
Concurrence of Creator, 247, 297
Confessional, 259–61, 265
Confucius, 112
Congregationalist, 107, 251
Consciousness, 143, 157
Constant, Benjamin, 150–63
Contemplation, 238
Contemplative orders, 240
Conversion experience, 63–64
Covenant, 214
Convert, The, 242
Cousin, Victor, 246
Creation: free divine act,
248–49; as miracle, 272;
originally imperfect, 214;
purpose of, 278–79
Creature: as medium of
perfection, 279
Creeds, 108, 123, 177;
Universalist, 114–17, 117–20
Cult of the Saints, 280–82, 290–
91

Damnation, 102, 118–19
Death, 60, 67, 73, 80, 102, 212,
216, 226

Other Volumes in This Series